THE EU AND ITS MEMBER STATES' JOINT PARTICIPATION IN INTERNATIONAL AGREEMENTS

EU law has developed a unique and complex system under which both the Union and its Member States can act under international law, separately, jointly or in parallel. International law was not set up to deal with such complex and hybrid arrangements, which raise questions under both international and EU law.

This book assesses how EU law has adapted to cope with the constraints of international law in situations in which the EU and its Member States act jointly in relations with other States and international organisations. In an innovative scholarly approach, reflecting this duality, each chapter is jointly written by a team of two authors. The various contributions offer new insights into the tension that continues to exist between EU and international law obligations in relation to the (joint) participation of the EU and its Member States in international agreements.

Volume 108 in the Series Modern Studies in European Law

Modern Studies in European Law

Recent titles in this series:

Constitutional Law of the EU's Common Foreign and Security Policy:
Competence and Institutions in External Relations
Graham Butler

The Juridification of Individual Sanctions and the Politics of EU Law
Eva Nanopoulos

Sixty Years of European Integration and Global Power Shifts:
Perceptions, Interactions and Lessons
Edited by Julien Chaisse

Fundamental Rights and Mutual Recognition in the Area of
Freedom, Security and Justice: A Role for Proportionality?
Ermioni Xanthopoulou

Law and Judicial Dialogue on the Return of Irregular
Migrants from the European Union
Edited by Madalina Moraru, Galina Cornelisse and Philippe De Bruycker

Framing Convergence with the Global Legal Order: The EU and the World
Edited by Elaine Fahey

EU Citizenship at the Edges of Freedom of Movement
Katarina Hyltén-Cavallius

The Internal Market 2.0
Edited by Sacha Garben and Inge Govaere

New Directions in European Private Law
Edited by Mateja Durovic and Takis Tridimas

Standing to Enforce European Union Law before National Courts
Hilde Ellingsen

The Relative Authority of Judicial and Extra-Judicial Review:
The EU Courts, the Boards of Appeal and the Ombudsman
Michal Krajewski

Responsive Human Rights: Vulnerability and the ECtHR
Corina Heri

The Architecture of Fundamental Rights in the European Union
Šejla Imamovic

The EU and its Member States' Joint Participation in International Agreements
Edited by Nicolas Levrat, Yuliya Kaspiarovich, Christine Kaddous and Ramses A Wessel

For the complete list of titles in this series, see
'Modern Studies in European Law' link at
www.bloomsburyprofessional.com/uk/series/modern-studies-in-european-law

The EU and its Member States' Joint Participation in International Agreements

Edited by
Nicolas Levrat
Yuliya Kaspiarovich
Christine Kaddous
and
Ramses A Wessel

•HART•
OXFORD • LONDON • NEW YORK • NEW DELHI • SYDNEY

HART PUBLISHING
Bloomsbury Publishing Plc
Kemp House, Chawley Park, Cumnor Hill, Oxford, OX2 9PH, UK
1385 Broadway, New York, NY 10018, USA
29 Earlsfort Terrace, Dublin 2, Ireland

HART PUBLISHING, the Hart/Stag logo, BLOOMSBURY and the Diana logo are trademarks of Bloomsbury Publishing Plc

First published in Great Britain 2022

A catalogue record for this book is available from the British Library.

Library of Congress Cataloging-in-Publication data

Names: Levrat, Nicolas, 1964- editor. | Kaspiarovich, Yuliya, editor. | Kaddous, Christine, editor. | Wessel, Ramses A, editor.

Title: The EU and its member states' joint participation in international agreements / edited by Nicolas Levrat, Yuliya Kaspiarovich, Christine Kaddous and Ramses A Wessel.

Other titles: European Union and its member states' joint participation in international agreements

Description: Oxford ; New York : Hart, 2022. | Series: Modern studies in European Law ; volume 108 | Includes bibliographical references and index.

Identifiers: LCCN 2021044686 (print) | LCCN 2021044687 (ebook) | ISBN 9781509945870 (hardback) | ISBN 9781509945917 (paperback) | ISBN 9781509945894 (pdf) | ISBN 9781509945887 (Epub)

Subjects: LCSH: Treaty-making power—European Union countries. | European Union countries—Foreign relations—Law and legislation.

Classification: LCC KJE5106 .E93 2022 (print) | LCC KJE5106 (ebook) | DDC 341.242/24—dc23/eng/20211013

LC record available at https://lccn.loc.gov/2021044686

LC ebook record available at https://lccn.loc.gov/2021044687

ISBN: HB: 978-1-50994-587-0
ePDF: 978-1-50994-589-4
ePub: 978-1-50994-588-7

Typeset by Compuscript Ltd, Shannon

FOREWORD

The external relations of the EU and its 27 Member States is a fascinating subject, which attracts ever more attention and debate among politicians, practitioners and scholars. Since the 1960s, the EU has been able to greatly expand its role as an international actor, without, however, completely overtaking the foreign policy space of its Member States.

In fact, as long as the Member States continue to be viewed as independent states in their own right, with national foreign policy agendas and stances not always in line with the positions or interests of the EU, the Union will be unable to assume a role as a global player similar to that of, say, the United States or China. That said, the combined force of the EU and its Member States does constitute a factor to reckon with in international relations, particularly in areas where the Union enjoys an exclusive competence, notably in the area of trade policy.

In other areas, such as the environment, human rights and sustainable development, it is a more mixed bag, with the activities of the Union and the Member States intertwined but sometimes also more or less separate from each other. In some other areas, notably in security and defence, the role of the Member States (particularly some of them) continues to be predominant. The great complexity of the institutional and other aspects of EU and Member States' external relations makes this subject a heaven for scholars of law and political science. At the same time, this complexity contributes to the formidable problems the EU is facing in trying to assert a role as a global player able to project its economic strength, standard-setting power and value agenda to the rest of the world.

These challenges continue to merit further academic research, whether or not the current institutional complexity and behavioural cacophony (which I have somewhat impolitely referred to as a 'gaggle of geese'[1]) will continue or whether, some day, institutional and constitutional reforms could enable the EU to match the other global players on an equal footing. As long as the present situation continues, it is to be hoped that scholars do not limit their focus to legal rules and official documents while turning a blind eye to the actual practice of Union and Member States' institutions and the 'reality on the ground'.[2]

This is not to say that there is no need for legal scholarship. On the contrary, an understanding of EU external relations requires an understanding of relevant legal

[1] Allan Rosas and Lorna Armati, *EU Constitutional Law: An Introduction*, 3rd edn (Oxford, Hart Publishing, 2018) 244.

[2] Allan Rosas, 'EU External Relations Law: Time for a Reality Check?' (2020) 27 *Maastricht Journal of European and Comparative Law* 277–83.

rules, their application in practice and case law from Union and national EU courts. Much has already been done. There is, in fact, an abundance of literature on EU external relations law, including the intricate question of mixed agreements, that is agreements concluded by the Union as well as its Member States.[3]

Does this mean that the subject is already exhausted? No, that is certainly not the case, as demonstrated by the present volume. There are two main reasons why this book has added value. First, the focus is on joint participation of the Union and Member States in international agreements, without limiting the analysis to mixed agreements in the strict sense. Second, the perspective is not that of Union law only but the book also aims to see the problems through the lens of public international law, international treaty law in particular. It is also welcome that some of the chapters focus on concrete cases or subject areas rather than a general discussion at abstract level. The approach of involving two authors for each chapter, generally one more senior and the other more junior researcher, is refreshing.

All in all, the editors and authors should be congratulated for having produced a volume which clearly enhances our understanding of the participation of the EU and its Member States in international affairs.

Allan Rosas

[3] My own contributions to the literature on mixed agreements include Allan Rosas, 'The European Union and Mixed Agreements' in A Dashwood and C Hillion (eds), *The General Law of E.C. External Relations* (London, Sweet & Maxwell, 2000) 200–20; Allan Rosas, 'The Future of Mixity' in C Hillion and P Koutrakos (eds), *Mixed Agreements Revisited: The EU and its Member States in the World* (Oxford, Hart Publishing, 2010) 367–74; Allan Rosas, 'Mixity Past, Present and Future: Some Observations' in M Chamon and I Govaere (eds), *EU External Relations Post-Lisbon: The Law and Practice of Facultative Mixity* (Leiden, Brill – Nijhoff, 2020), 8–18; Rosas (n 2 above).

CONTENTS

LIST OF CONTRIBUTORS

Chloé Brière is Associate Professor of EU Law at the Université libre de Bruxelles. Her notably addresses the EU's external relations in criminal matters. She holds a PhD in Law from the Université libre de Bruxelles and the University of Geneva and is an alumna of the Erasmus Mundus GEM PhD School 'Globalisation, the EU & Multilateralism'. After her PhD, she held positions at the Vrij Universiteit Brussel, Dublin City University and the United Nations Office on Drugs and Crime.

Julija Brsakoska Bazerkoska is Associate Professor at Saints Cyril and Methodius University, Law Faculty in Skopje, Republic of North Macedonia. She finished her PhD studies *magna cum laude* at Cologne University, Law Faculty in Germany. She was engaged as a researcher under the Curriculum Research Fellowship programme at the Central European University in Budapest, Hungary. During summer 2019 she was a visiting fellow at the Lauterpacht Centre for International Law at the University of Cambridge, UK. Moreover, she was part of several EU funded projects within the Albanian Ministry of European Integration, the Skopje office of the Italian Ministry for Environment, Land and Sea, as well as on several projects within the domestic NGO sector.

Merijn Chamon is Assistant Professor of EU Law at Maastricht University and Visiting Professor at the College of Europe, Bruges. His research interests encompass EU constitutional law, EU institutional law and EU external relations law.

Cristina Contartese is Lecturer in EU Law at the Hague University of Applied Sciences. Previously, she was Lecturer in EU and International Law at the European Law and Governance School/European Public Law Organization (Athens). She held positions as a Postdoctoral Researcher at the University of Bologna, where she taught International Law, and at the University of Luxembourg (Marie Curie fellow/FNR-Luxembourg), where she researched dispute settlement mechanisms from EU and international law perspectives. She was a visiting researcher at the Max Planck Institute–Luxembourg, and at the iCourts Centre (University of Copenhagen). Her main research interests include EU constitutional law, EU external relations, international dispute settlement, international water law, and the European Convention on Human Rights. She has published on these subjects in edited books and peer-reviewed journals, such as *Common Market Law Review*, *Rivista di Diritto Internazionale* and *Legal Working Papers of the European Central Bank*. She is an analyst for 'EU Law Live Blog', and a member of the editorial board of *International Journal of Human Rights and Constitutional Studies* (IJHRCS).

Marise Cremona is Professor Emeritus at the European University Institute, Florence. She was Professor of European Law and a co-Director of the Academy of European Law at the European University Institute (2006–17), Head of the Department of Law at the EUI (2009–12) and President *ad interim* of the EUI (2012–13). She is a member of the Editorial Board of the *Common Market Law Review*. Her research interests are in the external relations law of the European Union, in particular the constitutional basis for EU external relations law and the legal and institutional dimensions of EU foreign policy.

Manon Damestoy is PhD candidate in Political Science at the University of Nantes (Alliance Europa and DCS labs) and at the University of Saint-Louis Brussels (IEE and CReSPo labs). After a year and a half as Parliamentary Assistant at the European Parliament (2017–18), she began a PhD in European studies and focused her research on European democracy and the negotiations of the so-called 'new generation' free trade agreements (CETA/TTIP).

Andrés Delgado Casteleiro is Assistant Professor of Law at Chile's Autonomous University. Previously, he was a Senior Research Fellow at the Max Planck Institute for Procedural Law in Luxembourg and a Lecturer at Durham University (UK) where he also co-directed its European Law Institute. He has a PhD and a Master of Research in International, Comparative and European Law from the European University Institute (Florence), and a Law degree from Universidad Carlos III de Madrid. His main research interests are EU external relations law, international economic law, international investment law and international dispute settlement.

Elaine Fahey is Erasmus + Jean Monnet Chair of Law & Transatlantic Relations and Professor of Law at the Institute for the Study of European Law (ISEL), the City Law School, University of London. She has been co-convener of the Institute for the Study of European Law (ISEL), City Law School since 2016. Her research interests span the relationship between EU law and global governance, trade, transatlantic relations, the EU's Area of Freedom, Security and Justice and the study of law beyond the state.

Joni Heliskoski is Justice at the Supreme Administrative Court of Finland. From 2010 to 2019 he was Director of EU Litigation at the Ministry for Foreign Affairs and the Agent of the Government of Finland before the Court of Justice of the European Union. He holds a PhD in EU Law from the University of Cambridge, England, on mixed agreements. Dr Heliskoski is also Adjunct Professor of International Law at the University of Helsinki. He has published extensively on external relations law of the EU.

Christine Kaddous is Professor of European and International Law at the University of Geneva, Jean Monnet Chair *ad personam*, and Director of the Centre d'études juridiques européennes (CEJE), Jean Monnet Centre of Excellence at the same University. She is also Director of the Master of Advanced Studies in European and International Governance (MEIG Programme). She is also Visiting Professor at the University Paris II (Panthéon Assas) and has been Visiting Professor notably at the College of Europe (Bruges/Natolin). She studied law in Neuchâtel (Switzerland) and in Cambridge (LLM, Cantab) as well as in Brussels (MA in European Studies, ULB). She practised as a lawyer for many years in the field of commercial law in Switzerland. She is President of the Swiss Society for International Law. Her academic interests and activities cover many areas of European Union law and international law, including the external relations of the European Union, the internal market, judicial protection, Swiss-EU bilateral agreements. She is author and editor of many books. Among her recent publications are: 'Politique commerciale commune' (forthcoming 2021); 'Die Zusammenarbeit zwischen der EU und der Schweiz' (forthcoming 2021); 'Directive 2004/38' (2020); *Les accords mixtes* (2019); 'Switzerland and the EU: Current Issues and New Challenges under the Draft Institutional Framework Agreement' (2019); 'The External Dimension of the EU Policies: Horizontal Issues; Trade and Investment' (FIDE General Report, 2018); 'The Transformation of the EU Common Commercial Policy' (2016); The European Union in International Organisations and Global Governance' (2015).

Yuliya Kaspiarovich is Assistant Professor in European Law at the University of Groningen. Previously, she was a Postdoctoral Researcher at the Global Studies Institute of the University of Geneva and an Emile Noël fellow at the Jean Monnet Center for International and Regional Economic Law and Justice, New York University School of Law. She holds a PhD in Law from the University of Geneva. Yuliya's thesis questioned the rationale behind investment protection in the EU legal order in the light of the principle of mutual trust. Her broader research interests cover European institutional law, EU external relations law and Brexit.

Marcus Klamert is Professor of European Law at the University of Graz and Legal advisor at the Federal Chancellery of Austria. He has represented Austria before the European Court of Justice, has practised law with Freshfields Bruckhaus Deringer in Vienna, and has worked for the European Commission in Brussels. He is the author of *The Principle of Loyalty in EU Law* (OUP 2014) and of *Services Liberalization in the EU and WTO – Concepts, Standards and Regulatory Approaches* (CUP 2014), and the co-editor of *The EU Treaties and the Charter of Fundamental Rights – A Commentary* (OUP 2019).

Panos Koutrakos is Professor of European Union Law and Jean Monnet Professor of EU Law at City, University of London. He is the author of *EU International Relations Law* (2nd ed., 2015) and many other publications on the law of the external relations of the European Union, covering trade, economic and political relations as well as the Union's security and defence policy. He is the joint editor of *European Law Review*.

Gesa Kübek is Assistant Professor in European Law at the University of Groningen, The Netherlands. Previously, she was a Research Associate at Leuphana University, Lüneburg, Germany. She holds a PhD from the University of Passau, Germany, on mixed agreements. Her research interests include EU external relations and trade law.

Mirka Kuisma is Legal Secretary at the Supreme Administrative Court of Finland. Her doctoral dissertation, 'Confronting Realities with the Legal Rule: On Why and How the European Court of Justice Changes Its Mind' (University of Turku, Finland) explored doctrinal change in the case law of the European Court of Justice and observed the development of the *ERTA* case law as an example of the Court's interlocutors' failed attempt to induce doctrinal change.

Joris Larik is Assistant Professor at Leiden University. His work has been acknowledged with several awards, including NATO's Manfred Wörner Essay Award (2008) and the Mauro Cappelletti Prize for the Best Doctoral Thesis in Comparative Law (2014) from the European University Institute. He is the author of *Foreign Policy Objectives in European Constitutional Law* (OUP, 2016), co-author of *ASEAN's External Agreements: Law, Practice and the Quest for Collective Action* (CUP, 2015), and co-editor of *Just Security in an Undergoverned World* (OUP, 2018) and *EU External Relations Law: Text, Cases and Materials* (2nd edn, Hart Publishing, 2020).

Nicolas Levrat is Professor of European and International Law at the University of Geneva since 2001. He was the director of the European Institute of the University of Geneva (2007–13), the founder and first director of the Global Studies Institute of the University of Geneva, the director of the International Law Department at the Law Faculty (2016–19), and is now again the director of the GSI. He is also the cofounder of the Geneva Transformative Governance Lab. His publications mostly deal with the articulation of legal orders and institutional legitimacy beyond state structures.

Makane Moïse Mbengue is Professor of International Law at the Faculty of Law of the University of Geneva and Director of the Department of International Law and International Organisation. He is also an Affiliate Professor at Sciences Po Paris (School of Law). He is a Member of the Curatorium of The Hague Academy of International Law. He is the author of several publications in the field of international law.

Tamás Molnár is Legal Research Officer at the EU Agency for Fundamental Rights (FRA) in Vienna. He is also a Visiting Lecturer on international migration law at the Department of International Relations at Corvinus University of Budapest (where he has held multiple positions since October 2003). Before joining FRA, he worked for a decade in various ministries in Hungary on international and EU migration law. He was also a delegate in migration-related EU Council preparatory bodies and negotiated international agreements on migration. He read law in Budapest and Brussels (LLM in EU law) and holds a PhD in international law. He published widely in the fields of international and EU migration law and relationship of legal orders. His latest monograph is titled *The Interplay between the EU's Return Acquis and International Law* (Edward Elgar Publishing, 2021).

Stian Øby Johansen is Associate Professor at the Centre for European Law, University of Oslo. He is also secretary and board member of the Norwegian branch of the International Law Association, as well as secretary and board member of the Norwegian branch of Fédération Internationale pour le Droit Européen (FIDE). His latest book is entitled *The Human Rights Accountability Mechanisms of International Organizations* (CUP, 2020).

Jed Odermatt is Lecturer at City Law School, University of London. His research interests include public international law, the law of international organizations, and the law of EU external relations. He is the author of *International Law and the European Union* (CUP, 2021).

Marja-Liisa Öeberg is Senior Lecturer in European Union Law at Lund University, Sweden. She holds a PhD from the European University Institute. Her main research interests lie in the borderlands of EU integration in external and internal contexts, third country integration to the EU, EU external relations law and the interaction between EU law and public international law. She is the author of *The Boundaries of the EU Internal Market: Participation without Membership* (CUP, 2020).

Vassilis Pergantis is Assistant Professor at the Law Faculty, Aristotle University of Thessaloniki and academic coordinator of a Jean Monnet Project on 'EU Responsibility in the International System [EURIS]'. His fields of interest focus on general international law, specifically, theory of international law and sources doctrine, the law of international organisations and the law of international responsibility, as well as human rights. He has published extensively in English, French and Greek and he is the author of a monograph on *The Paradigm of State Consent in the Law of Treaties* (Elgar, 2017).

Allan Rosas has served as a Judge at the European Court of Justice from 2002 until 2019. Formerly, Allan Rosas has been Armfelt Professor of Law at the Åbo Akademi University and later Principal Legal Adviser and Deputy Director-General of the Legal Service of the European Commission

Sabrina Schaefer is Doctoral candidate and Fellow of the Research Training Group 'Dynamic Integration – Law between Harmonization and Pluralization in Europe' at Humboldt Universität Berlin. Her PhD thesis explores the impact of Brexit on the external relations of the EU and the UK. Previously, she worked as a research and teaching fellow at the chair of Professor Dr. Georg Nolte and from 2017 to 2019 as a desk officer in the international treaty section of the German Federal Foreign Office.

Bartosz Soloch is Counsel in the International and European Law Department of the General Counsel to the Republic of Poland tasked with representing Poland in ISDS proceedings and supporting the government agent before the CJEU. He is also a PhD student on the University of Łódź. His dissertation explores the interrelation between the principle of autonomy of EU law and the access of private entities to international dispute settlement mechanisms. His research focuses on interactions between various legal systems.

Viktorija Soneca is Lawyer at Sorainen Latvia, former director of the CJEU Department of the Ministry of Justice of the Republic of Latvia and represented the Republic of Latvia at the CJEU. She also represented the Ministry of Justice in the Parliament, the Cabinet of Ministers, and inter-ministry meetings. Viktorija is currently a PhD student at the Faculty of Law of the University of Latvia.

Habib Badjinri Touré is Doctoral student in international law at the Centre d'Études et de Recherches Internationales et Communautaires (CERIC) at the Faculty of Law of Aix-Marseille University. He holds a master's degree in public international law and since 2017, he has been preparing a thesis on the withdrawal of member states from international organisations.

Flore Vanackère is PhD candidate in EU law at the Faculty of Law of the University of Geneva. She currently teaches EU law at the Global Studies Institute of the University of Geneva. Flore holds a master's degree in European Public Law at the ULB (Brussels). She taught constitutional law, as well as administrative law and methodology of research in public national and European law. From 2016 to 2019, she studied at the Faculty of Law of the University of Roma Tre.

Ramses A Wessel is full Professor of European Law at the University of Groningen, the Netherlands. He has published widely on international and European law with a focus on the interface between the two legal orders and on EU external relations law. Ramses Wessel is vice-president of the European Society of International Law (ESIL) and co-founder of the Centre for the Law of EU External Relations (CLEER) in The Hague. He is an editor for a number of international journals, including the *International Organizations Law Review*, the *Netherlands Yearbook of International Law*, *European Papers*, and the *European Foreign Affairs Review*. Recent books include *EU External Relations Law* (Hart, 2020) and *Research Handbook on the European Union and International Organizations* (Edward Elgar, 2019). A new book, *EU External Relations Law: The Cases in Context* (Hart, 2022), is in preparation.

Bruno de Witte is Professor of European Union law at Maastricht University and co-director of the Maastricht Centre for European Law. He is also a part-time professor at the Robert Schuman Centre of the European University Institute in Florence.

Introduction: Torn between Two Lovers: The Application of both EU and International Law to the Participation of the EU and its Member States in International Agreements*

NICOLAS LEVRAT, YULIYA KASPIAROVICH, CHRISTINE KADDOUS AND RAMSES A WESSEL

> The European Union being a hybrid conglomerate situated somewhere between a State and an intergovernmental organization, it is only natural that its external relations in general and treaty practice in particular should not be straightforward. The phenomenon of mixed agreements … offers a telling illustration of the complex nature of the EU … as an international actor.

These were the words of Allan Rosas in 1998.[1] Almost a quarter of a century later, the situation seems no clearer or simpler. The nature of the complex hybrid actor that is the EU and its Member States has not been better defined in legal terms, and the articulation of the rights and duties of the EU and its Member States, towards third countries or between themselves, under EU law or under international law, offers a multidimensional puzzle that may keep legal scholars busy for another few years, if not a generation.

I. On the Content of the Book

If international law does not adapt to take into consideration the specific original nature of the composite actor that is the EU and its Member States, including the legal relationship with and between Member States when both are simultaneously parties to a same agreement, it is far from certain that the EU will be able to unilaterally impose the recognition of its genuinely original and unique nature on foreign partners, as well as the legal consequences deriving from it.

* The title was inspired by the 1976 song by Mary MacGregor; see www.youtube.com/watch?v=w1F5BLLFAeM.

[1] Allan Rosas, 'Mixed Union-Mixed Agreements', in M Koskenniemi (ed), *International Law Aspects of the European Union* (Kluwer Law International, 1998) 125. Prof Rosas also wrote the Foreword to this book.

A. Competence Allocation and Mixed Agreements

Interestingly, even though the CJEU seemed to have developed an approach of EU and Member States' respective competences in external relations based on a very binary conception of mutually exclusive competences,[2] the practice of mixed agreements, a specific and original form of joint implementation of respective EU and Member States' competences, emerged as early as 1961.[3] The issue of the EU and its Member States' simultaneous participation, together with foreign partners, in a single internationally based legal regime is not new at all.[4] There seems, however, to be a trend in the development of mixed agreements. The emergence of shared competences within the EU domestic institutional setting could be an explanatory factor of this evolution. This is an interesting hypothesis, since the original reason for concluding mixed agreements was not to be found in the exercise of shared competences between the EEC and its Member States, but actually in the necessary mobilisation of two sets of non-overlapping exclusive competences, one from the EEC, and another set of (non-transferred) competences from the Member States (exclusive Member States competences). Consequently, the issue of the impact of the type of competences allocated to the EU by Member States, through treaty modifications and in line with the principle of conferral, has been debated for some years. Legal scholars remain divided on the relevance of this evolution as regards the exercise of external competences by the EU.[5]

Let us recall that the concept of 'non-exclusive competences', more positively defined as 'shared competences'. They formally appeared with the Treaty of Maastricht (1 November 1993), alongside the principle of subsidiarity.[6] Non-exclusive competences were a novelty in EU law. The concept emerged during negotiations within the Intergovernmental Conference leading to the Treaty of Maastricht as a concession by the most progressive states to the conservative ones (the latter under the leadership of the UK during the Intergovernmental Conference). In exchange for a substantial widening of EEC competences and its transformation into the EC, most new competences

[2] In its extensively analysed *ERTA* ruling Case 22/70, *Commission v Council*, EU:C:1971:32, the CJEU declares: 'These Community powers exclude the possibility of concurrent powers on the part of Member States, since any steps taken outside the framework of the Community institutions would be incompatible with the unity of the Common Market and the uniform application of Community law', para 31.

[3] See Council Decision 61/106/EEC on the conclusion of the Agreement establishing an Association between the European Economic Community and Greece, [1963] OJ 26.

[4] Joni Heliskoski, *Mixed Agreements as a Technique for Organizing the International Relations of the European Community and Its Member States* (Kluwer Law International, 2001); D O'Keeffe and H G Schermers (eds), *Mixed Agreements* (Kluwer Law and Taxation Publishers, 1983); C Hillion and P Koutrakos (eds), *Mixed Agreements Revisited: The EU and Its Member States in the World* (Hart Publishing, 2010).

[5] Allan Rosas in 2014 on the issue: 'Exclusive, shared and national competence in the context of EU external relations: do such distinctions matter?' in I Govaere et al (eds), *The European Union in the World* (Brill Nijhoff, 2014) 17–43; see also Christine Kaddous, 'Les accords mixtes' in N Aloupi et al (eds), *Les accords internationaux de l'Union européenne (Commentaire J. Mégret)*, 3rd edn (Editions de l'Université de Bruxelles, 2019), 301–43.

[6] Art G(7) of the Maastricht Treaty, adding a new Art 3b in the EC Treaty, reads: 'In areas which do not fall within its exclusive competence, the Community shall take action, in accordance with the principle of subsidiarity, only if and in so far as the objectives of the proposed action cannot be sufficiently achieved by the Member States and can therefore, by reason of the scale or effects of the proposed action, be better achieved by the Community' [1992] OJ C 191.

transferred to the Community would not be exclusive, as was the case before Maastricht. These competences, non-exclusively allocated to the EU, could only be implemented by the latter after a 'test of subsidiarity' could be successfully passed at the time of the materialisation of shared competence through an act of the EU institutions. These initially marginal non-exclusive competences quickly grew up during the next decade to become, in the TFEU as modified by the Lisbon Treaty, 'a competence shared with the Member States in a specific area'.[7] Even more significantly, shared competences became the EU's default type of competences from 2009 onwards.[8]

The result is that the extension of EU competences was made possible by softening the distinction between EU and Member States competences. This allowed for a significant extension of competences of the EU as a whole, but at the expense of shrinking EU exclusive competences, thus fundamentally transforming the nature and the *modus operandi* of Community institutions in their relations to Member States.[9] The result is that in the exercise of their respective competences, the EU and its Member States, at least as regards internal policies, were not only 'in the process of creating an ever closer union among the peoples of Europe', but also in the process of creating an ever more entangled institutional system between the EU and its Member States. Does this original evolution of the internal institutional system of the EU also affect the EU and its Member States' exercise of their competences on the international stage, especially as regards entering into and implementing conventional obligations?

In its Opinion 2/15 rendered on 16 May 2017, the Court concluded, following a long and detailed examination, that the provisions on non-direct investments of the EU-Singapore FTA could not be approved by the EU alone:

> It is apparent from paragraphs 80 to 109 and 226 to 242 of this opinion that the commitments contained in Section A of Chapter 9 of the envisaged agreement fall within the common commercial policy of the European Union and, therefore, within the latter's exclusive competence pursuant to Article 3(1)(e) TFEU in so far as they concern foreign direct investment of Singapore nationals in the European Union and vice versa. On the other hand, those commitments fall within a competence shared between the European Union and the Member States pursuant to Article 4(1) and (2)(a) TFEU in so far as they concern other types of investment. *It follows that* Section A of Chapter 9 of *the envisaged agreement cannot be approved by the European Union alone.*[10]

The wording of this paragraph, in conjunction with the substantial developments on the issue of mixed agreements set out by Advocate General Sharpston in her conclusions in the same case,[11] reignited a fierce debate on the issue,[12] to the point that some authors

[7] See Art 2(2) TFEU.

[8] See Art 4(1) TFEU.

[9] See Nicolas Levrat, 'L'intégration européenne à la lumière de la subsidiarité. Ou pourquoi l'Union européenne ne devient pas les États-Unis d'Europe', in F Espoito and N Levrat (eds), *L'Europe: de l'intégration à la Fédération* (Bruylant-Academia, 2010) 33–69.

[10] Opinion 2/15, *Free Trade Agreement between the EU and Republic of Singapore*, EU:C:2017:376 paras 243–4 (emphasis added).

[11] Sharpston AG in Opinion 2/15, EU:C:2016:992.

[12] Marise Cremona, 'Shaping EU trade policy post-Lisbon: opinion 2/15 of 16 May 2017: ECJ, 16 May 2017, Opinion 2/15 Free Trade Agreement with Singapore' (2018) 14 *European Constitutional Law Review* 14 231–59.

wondered if a long-established EU exclusive competence, such as common commercial policy, could be challenged and that mixity should be considered for some new-generation FTAs.[13] In reaction to these developments, the European Commission proposed distancing the EU from the practice of mixed agreements, and envisaged concluding, for example for future new-generation comprehensive trade agreements, two parallel agreements. One agreement would be an EU-only agreement – which thanks to Article 216(2) TFEU would also bind Member States – and in parallel and at the same time, another agreement would be concluded in a mixed format. In its conclusions of 22 May 2018 'on the negotiation and conclusion of EU trade agreements', the Council took careful note of this proposal:

> The Council notes that in the future the Commission intends to recommend draft negotiating directives for FTAs covering exclusive EU competence on the one hand and separate mixed investment agreements on the other, with a view to strengthening the EU's position as a negotiating partner. It is for the Council to decide whether to open negotiations on this basis. It is equally for the Council to decide, on a case-by-case basis, on the splitting of trade agreements.[14]

The matter is obviously not settled, and legal as well as political considerations will have to be kept in a proper balance,[15] as careful reception of the Commission's proposal by the Council shows.

B. An Issue not Limited to Mixed Agreements

It also recently emerged that the legal debate on the respective roles and commitments of the EU and its Member States with respect to international agreements is not limited to mixed agreements. It thus appears that distinct but parallel participation of the EU and its Member States in a same international agreement may be no less problematic in legal terms. For example, as regards the accession of the EU to the ECHR as requested by Article 6(2) TEU, it became clear in the opinion of the CJEU that it also raises immense and serious legal difficulties. In the words of the CJEU:

> In so far as the ECHR would, in requiring the EU and the Member States to be considered Contracting Parties not only in their relations with Contracting Parties which are not Member States of the EU but also in their relations with each other, including where such relations are governed by EU law, require a Member State to check that another Member State has observed fundamental rights, even though EU law imposes an obligation of mutual trust between those Member States, accession is liable to upset the underlying balance of the EU and undermine the autonomy of EU law.[16]

[13] Opinion 2/15, *Free Trade Agreement between the EU and Republic of Singapore*, ECLI:EU:C:2017:376; Opinion 1/17, *CETA*, EU:C:2019:341.

[14] Press release: www.consilium.europa.eu/en/press/press-releases/2018/05/22/new-approach-on-negotiating-and-concluding-eu-trade-agreements-adopted-by-council/. The quote comes from the draft conclusions that were discussed on 8 May 2018 (Annex to Doc 8622/18 of 8 May 2018).

[15] On that issue, see in this volume the chapter by Manon Damestoy and Nicolas Levrat.

[16] Opinion 2/13, *EU's accession to the ECHR*, EU:C:2014:2454.

Thus, joint or parallel participation of the EU and its Member State in the same treaty may entail implementation difficulties.[17] This is why the CJEU had to conclude, despite the clear provision of Article 6(2) TEU enjoining the EU to accede to the ECHR, that it was impossible from the perspective of EU law. In the words of the CJEU:

> The approach adopted in the agreement envisaged, which is to treat the EU as a State and to give it a role identical in every respect to that of any other Contracting Party, *specifically disregards the intrinsic nature of the EU* and, in particular, fails to take into consideration the fact that the Member States have, by reason of their Membership of the EU, accepted that relations between them as regards the matters covered by the transfer of powers from the Member States to the EU are governed by EU law to the exclusion, if EU law so requires, of any other law.[18]

What this episode reveals (for a more detailed analysis of this specific case, see the contribution by Vassilis Pergantis and Stian Øby Johansen in this volume) is that the insertion of the EU (and its Member States) as a complex legal subject into the international legal order is far from easy.[19] Contributions to this volume aim to analyse this interplay between the EU legal system's specific requirements and its capacity to be a legally reliable actor in international relations, both from an international law and an EU law perspective.

C. The International Law Perspective

Both the EU and its 27 Member States are subjects of international law. As such, they can all conclude international agreements. This is indisputable for states, as Article 6 of the 1969 Vienna Convention on the Law of Treaties, codifying customary international law, states: 'Every State possesses capacity to conclude treaties'. It thus appears as an intrinsic characteristic of the international personality of states.

The EU also enjoys international personality,[20] and a derived capacity to enter international agreements, as practice also shows. For want of a better categorisation, the EU should still legally be considered under international law as an international organisation, even though the EU specific legal order and institutional scheme certainly make it a very peculiar kind of international organisation.[21] Nonetheless, the international

[17] See, inter alia, Christine Kaddous, 'De quelques défis liés à la conclusion des accords mixtes', in *Liber amicorum Antonio Tizzano, De la Cour CECA à la Cour de l'Union: le long parcours de la justice européenne* (G Giappichelli Editore, 2018) 448–60.

[18] Opinion 2/13, *EU's accession to the ECHR*, EU:C:2014:2454 para 193 (emphasis added).

[19] See for a general reflection on that issue, Nicolas Levrat, 'The Implications of Supranationality and Legitimacy. A legal perspective', chapter in A Weyembergh and M Telo (eds), *The Supranational Governance at stake* (Routledge, 2020) 26–44, which questions the ability of a supranational entity, such as the EU, to join a supranational regime, such as the one instituted by the ECHR.

[20] The issue of the legal personality of the EU has been a subject of doctrinal debates between 1993 and 2009, as the EU was co-existing with the European Communities, and the institutions were those of the EC, not of the EU. Since the entry into force of the Lisbon Treaty (1 December 2009), the issue is settled, according to Art 1(3) TEU, which states that 'The Union shall replace and succeed the European Community' and Art 47 TEU.

[21] Christina Eckes and Ramses A Wessel, 'The European Union: An International Perspective', in T Tridimas and R Schütze (eds), *Oxford Principles of European Union Law* Vol 1: The European Union Legal Order (Oxford University Press, 2018) 74–102.

community does not seem ready to acknowledge the singularly original nature of the EU as a complex and composite actor of international relations, as the failed attempt by the EU Member States to have this singular nature recognised by the UN General Assembly reveals.[22] Nonetheless, international organisations as such may also have the right to enter international agreements, as the ICJ recognised in its famous 1949 Advisory Opinion.[23] Following this, the UN International Law Commission (hereafter ILC) prepared an international multilateral convention 'on the Law of Treaties between States and International Organisations or between International Organisations', which was open for signature on 21 March 1986 in Vienna. Even though it is not yet in force,[24] it clearly shows that the issue of participation in international agreements by international organisations (IOs) is no longer a controversial issue under general international law.

It appears as a result of the work of the ILC that the current structure of international law, as codified by the ILC, makes a fundamental distinction between states and IOs, as two distinct categories of legal persons, whose relationships are regulated by international law. The EU and its Member States do not fit well into this alternative system, since the EU tries to assert itself as a full-fledged actor in international relations, with its Member States remaining full subjects of international law. There may thus be situations where both the EU (as an international legal person) and its Member States (also as international legal persons) are jointly bound by international treaty obligations. Such situations, according to the current structure of international law, should be dealt with separately in relation to each (Member) State's obligations and the EU's obligations (as an international organisation and taking into account 'the rules of the organisation'; see below). In this respect, the EU and its Member States represent a unique case study. The practice of concluding mixed agreements stands out as an exemplification of its complex composite legal personality under international law. Despite their genuinely original character, the conclusion of mixed agreements by the EU and its Member States has – perhaps pragmatically – been widely accepted by their international partners, despite the fact that it sits uneasy with international treaty law.

International agreements being, according to Article 38 of the statute of the International Court of Justice, the first 'source' of public international law, as well as one of the oldest fields of public international law, it is no surprise that the General Assembly of the UN, within the mandate conferred on it by Article 13 of the Charter to promote 'the progressive development of international law and its codification' gave

[22] The EU Member States, following the entry into force of the Lisbon Treaty and the reorganisation of its modalities of external representation, proposed that the UNGA should recognise a special observer status to the EU in front of the UNGA. The UN Member States adopted the UNGA Resolution 65/276 (2011), 'Participation of the European Union in the work of the United Nations', on 3 May 2011, in which the EU was classed as a 'regional organisation', of which there are many. No special status of the EU was acknowledged.

[23] ICJ, 11 April 1949, *Advisory Opinion on Reparation for Injuries Suffered in the Service of the United Nations*.

[24] According to its Art 85(1): 'The present Convention shall enter into force on the thirtieth day following the date of deposit of the thirty-fifth instrument of ratification or accession by States or by Namibia, represented by the United Nations Council for Namibia.' There are currently 31 states that have ratified the Convention (not including Namibia, but including the state of Palestine. On their side, 12 international organisations (not including the EU) have ratified this Convention.

the International Law Commission the task of codifying international treaty law in 1949. The First ILC Rapporteur on the issue (Sir Humphrey Waldock), submitted a first complete draft proposal for a Convention on the Law of Treaties addressing the ability of states, both as sovereign and independent states and as Member States of a federal union or an international organisation, to enter international agreements in 1961.[25] However, after lengthy debates in 1961 and 1962, considering the complexity of the issue, the ILC decided to focus its work on treaties between states, a choice that was approved by the sixth committee of UNGA. This choice led to the adoption of the 1969 Vienna Convention on the Law of Treaties between states (VCLT69). This was the point at which attention to specific complex situations, such as the EU and its Member States, was lost, both in the ILC working methods and in international law in general. This led to an alternative logic dominating international law as regards an international organisation and its Member States, impacting both their capacities to enter into international agreements (treaty law), as well as their respective duties for implementing such obligations (international responsibility).

While this way of codifying the law of treaties certainly made things easier for the ILC, it resulted in the disappearance – here again following substantial debates within the ILC – of the 'federal clause'. In 1962, the draft articles included a long article on the federal principle, which dealt with both the international commitments of federal states and the issue of the capacity to conclude international agreements for states that are 'Members of a Union of States'. The whole article was removed in favour of the very succinct Article 6 VCLT69.

When the International Law Commission pursued its codification mission on the law of treaties by extending its efforts to treaties between states and international organisations or between international organisations,[26] it did not resurrect a federal clause for international organisations and their Member States. The desire to closely align the provisions of this new Convention with those of the 1969 Convention led to a similarly concise formula: 'The capacity of an international organisation to conclude treaties is governed by the rules of that organisation'.[27] This formulation does not identify the specific case of mixed agreements where an international organisation *and* its Member States, on the one hand, and a third entity, on the other hand, bind themselves through

[25] This question of the capacity to conclude treaties had not been addressed by the first special rapporteur. The second Special Rapporteur, Sir Humphrey Waldock, proposed in a first report an Art 3 which dealt with the capacity of states to conclude treaties as independent states (Art 3(1)), as states members of a federation or a union of states (Art 3(2)), as dependent states whose conduct of international relations has been entrusted to another state, as well as the treaty practice of international organisations and institutions which have their own legal personality (Art 3(4)). See *CIDA* (1962) II 40–41; or this version of his proposal submitted to the General Assembly by the Commission: *CIDA* (1962) II 179.

[26] In 1969, the Vienna Convention on the Law of Treaties, which codified the already existing customary rules governing the law of treaties between states, was opened for signature within the UN. In 1986, a '(Vienna) Convention on the Law of Treaties between States and International Organisations or between International Organisations was opened for signature', but it still didn't enter into force. The texts and structure of these two Conventions are very similar; see O Corten and P Klein (eds), *The Vienna Conventions on the Law of Treaties: a Commentary* (Oxford University Press 2011).

[27] Art 6 of the Vienna Convention on the Law of Treaties between States and International Organizations or between International Organizations, 1986 (VCLT86). See the commentary on this article in the work of Olivier Corten and Pierre Klein (n 26) 183–93.

a single treaty.[28] Yet, it does not exclude such types of agreements either, provided they are allowed by the rules of the organisation.[29] While not forbidden, from the perspective of international law, it should nonetheless be emphasised that EU law in this context should be considered as 'domestic rules' in relation to the international legal regime. All the more so since the Court's case law of the early 1960s famously insisted on the autonomy of EC law, detaching it from international law. In this respect, Article 46(2) VCLT86 clearly states that 'an international organisation may not invoke the fact that its consent to be bound by a treaty has been expressed in violation of the rules of the organization regarding competence to conclude treaties as invalidating its consent unless that violation was manifest and concerned a rule of fundamental importance'. And if a treaty binding both the EU and its Member States under international law is in force, according to Article 27 VCLT86, it should be the international law obligations that prevail over the rules of the EU as far as the EU is concerned.[30] As regards the EU Member State, the principle of the relative effect of treaties, as codified by Article 34 VCLT69, prevents it from invoking EU law to disrespect its international obligations.[31] We shall see in what follows that from the perspective of EU law, the legal nature and the rules of implementation of EU mixed agreements diverge and are quite different from how they are regarded under international law. From the international law perspective, a mixed agreement between the EU and its Member States on one side, and a third State on the other side, should be regarded as a multilateral agreement.[32] In contrast, the EU law doctrine almost unanimously considers it as a bilateral agreement.[33] Why such a different view?

D. The EU Law Perspective

In the 1960s, the CJEU considered the legal regime of the relationship between the EEC and its Member States as constituting 'a new legal order of international law',[34] and even went further by asserting that 'the law stemming from the Treaty, an independent source of law' was of a 'special and original nature'.[35] Even if this was largely accepted by

[28] Rafael Leal-Arcas, 'The European Community and Mixed Agreements' (2001) 6 *European Foreign Affairs Review* 502.

[29] This reference to 'rules of the organisation' is quite broad and is clearly not limited to the constitutive act or formal texts, but also includes practices or implicit competences. For developments of this notion within the framework of Art 6 of the 1986 Vienna Convention on the Law of Treaties, see Nicolas Levrat, 'Commentary of the Art 6 of the 1986 Vienna Convention' in O Corten and P Klein (n 26) 121–23.

[30] Art 27(2) of the VCLT reads: 'An international organisation party to a treaty may not invoke the rules of the organisation as justification for its failure to perform the treaty.'

[31] Art 34 VCLT reads: 'A treaty does not create either obligations or rights for a third State without its consent'.

[32] See Marise Cremona, 'The withdrawal agreement and the EU's international agreements' (2020) 45 *European Law Review* 237–50.

[33] For a more nuanced reading see the chapters by Joni Heliskoski and Gesa Kübik, and by Christine Kaddous and Habib Badjinri Touré in this volume. See also on this issue Christine Kaddous, 'Les accords mixtes' (n 5).

[34] Case 26/62, *Van Gend & Loos v Netherlands*, EU:C:1963:1.

[35] Case 6/64, *Costa v ENEL*, EU:C:1964:66.

the EU Member States, such a claim comes close to a 'declaration of independence' of the EU legal order from the realm of international law.[36] According to the CJEU, a treaty provision, even similarly worded, may have different legal consequences depending on whether it is interpreted as a provision of international law, or as a provision of EU law.[37]

This raises, as the Court recognises, major difficulties as regards the implementation of international treaties by EU Member States, when they happen to be bound by such treaties both as EU Member States (that is under EU law) and as a party to a treaty under international law. As regards the implementation of treaties to which the EU is a party, EU law deals with the issue through Article 216(2) TFEU which states that 'agreements concluded by the Union are binding upon the institutions of the Union and on its Member States'. Therefore, from the perspective of EU law, the implementation of treaty provisions within the EU legal order is a matter strictly confined to EU law. And in that respect, the situation within EU law is the same, regardless of whether only the EU or the EU and its Member States are bound by an international agreement.[38] This provision, whose matrix is also often found in federal constitutions as regards the legal effects of international agreements upon Member States (be they *Länder*, Provinces, Cantons, etc),[39] turns international obligations into domestic obligations within the contracting party's jurisdiction. This may work fine for federal states in which Member States are not themselves subjects of international law and also underlies the assumption that Article 216(2) seems to allow the CJEU to make.[40] However, unlike the Member States of federations, it is undisputed that the EU Member States are themselves subjects of international law,[41] and therefore, if they are themselves party to a treaty under international law (even alongside the EU), they are also potentially bearers of an international responsibility.

When only the EU is party to an international agreement, potential tensions or even contradictions as regards the meaning and consequences of the EU international commitments may be addressed differently when viewed 'domestically' under EU law – including in its relations with the Member States – and under international law with third parties. In the worst-case scenario, the EU would see its international responsibility invoked – as could happen for a state – which usually entails very few legal consequences, unless an international dispute settlement mechanism is actioned to

[36] See the references above to *Vand Gend & Loos v Netherlands* (n 34) and *Costa v ENEL* (n 35); also Opinion 2/13 (n 18) para 193, and the consequences the CJEU derives from that autonomisation of the EC (nowadays the EU) law from international law.

[37] In the 1991 Opinion on the draft EEA Agreement, the CJEU went as far as stating that: 'The fact that the provisions of the agreement and the corresponding Community provisions are identically worded does not mean that they must necessarily be interpreted identically. An international treaty is to be interpreted not only on the basis of its wording, but also in the light of its objectives' Opinion 1/91, *creation of the EEA*, EU:C:1991:490 para 14.

[38] See for an apparently divergent opinion: Sharpston AG in Opinion 2/15, EU:C:2016:992 para 77.

[39] See for example Art 25 BGG as regards Germany, or Art 5(4) of the Swiss Federal Constitution.

[40] Based on Art 228(2) TEC (which has the same wording than Art 216(2) TFEU, see Case C-181/73, *Haegemann V Belgium*, EU:C:1974:41 paras 3–5; it is worth emphasising that the Court came to the conclusion that a mixed agreement is also part of EU law.

[41] See on the issue Nicolas Levrat and Yuliya Kaspiarovich 'Are EU Member States still States according to International Law?', GSI Working Paper Prof. PhDc LAW 2019/02.

invoke such responsibility.[42] However, whenever both the EU and its Member States are simultaneously, each as legal persons of international law, bound by the regime of international law (under an international treaty) as well as by the regime of EU law (including the provisions of the international treaty as provisions of EU law according to Article 216(2) TFEU), structural and practical difficulties make the situation, at least theoretically, unsustainable. The two regimes, while being of a different nature,[43] overlap, each determining the scope of the state's obligations according to its own rules of interpretation, with the risk of leading to diverging requirements for the state party (as an international law subject) and the Member State of the EU.[44] The risk of either discrepancies or strange loops within and/or between the legal systems becomes high[45] as the autonomy of the EU legal order may be at stake (as we have seen with the issue of the EU acceding to the ECHR as a party alongside its Member States).

Therefore, when internal constitutional requirements (consistency and coherence of the EU legal order) meet external international rules (in particular specific treaty provisions to be interpreted according to international treaty law), the EU and its Member States' joint participation in international agreements becomes problematic. This is all the more problematic as the treaties explicitly task the EU to strictly abide by international law: Article 3(5) TEU asserts that, 'in its relations with the wider world, the Union … shall contribute … to the strict observance and the development of international law'. There is therefore a consistency issue that the EU has to deal with, as regards the sometimes diverging demands from EU and international law.[46]

Many recent cases have underlined that such a tension still exists and is becoming even more apparent due to the Union's increasing external activities. And the difficulties, once again, are not confined to mixed agreements, as recent examples show, but include issues such as the representation of the EU and/or its Member States in international organisations,[47] cases on investment treaties[48] or cases related to questions of international responsibility. In many of these cases, EU Member States struggle to be both EU Member States and states as subjects of international law at the same time, with both legal statuses entailing different, and not always compatible, obligations.

[42] See the chapter by Andrés Delgado Casteleiro and Cristina Contartese in this volume.

[43] As the court famously said in its 1964 *Costa* decision (n 35): 'By contrast with ordinary international treaties, the EEC Treaty has created its own legal system […]'.

[44] Opinion 2/13 (n 18) paras 192–194.

[45] For the concept of strange loops and its applicability to different fields of human activity, see Douglas R Hofstadter, *Gödel, Escher & Bach* (Harvester Press, 1979). For more recent developments, see Julia Anten et al, 'An Adaptive Computational Network Model for Strange Loops in Political Evolution in Society' *International Conference on Computational Science* (Springer, 2020) 604–17.

[46] See for an example of this difficult articulation, the CJEU decisions in the '*Kadi* saga' especially joined Cases C-402/05 P and C-415/05 P, EU:C:2008:461, or Case C-104/16 P, *Front Polisario*, EU:C:2016:973.

[47] See for an example Case C-73/14, *ITLOS*, EU:C:2015:663, Case C-600/14, *Cotif*, EU:C:2017:935, Case C-399/12, *Vine and Wine*, EU:C:2014:2258, or joined Cases C-626/15 and C-659/16, *AMP Antartique*, EU:C:2018:925. Also, the contribution in this volume by Merijn Chamon and Marise Cremona. See also Christine Kaddous, 'The European Union in International Organisations: Functional Necessity or General Aspiration?', in *The European Union in International Organizations and Global Governance. Recent Developments* (Hart Publishing, 2015) 1–22.

[48] Opinion 2/15, *Free Trade Agreement between the EU and Republic of Singapore*, EU:C:2017:376; Opinion 1/17, *CETA*, EU:C:2019:341; Case C-284/16, *Achmea*, EU:C:2018:158.

This is why, in our view, the option of continuing to analyse joint participation of the EU and its Member States, in any form (mixed agreements, parallel participation, succession), without taking into account both the EU law and the international law perspective, is not sustainable; in particular concerning the position of the EU Member States, which have different identities.[49] Without pretending to be able to align the international and EU law horizons – as we are aware of and understand the reasons for the CJEU to stress the importance of the EU's autonomy from international law – the contributions collected in this volume point to the need of a converging approach between the two perspectives.[50]

II. On the Structure of the Book

In order to address this legal challenge, we propose to look at the EU and its Member States' joint participation in international agreements in a broad manner. Even if the case of EU mixed agreements seems to be of a particular importance, we consider that it is worth taking a step back and also to examine the EU and its Member States' joint international commitments under all their possible shapes and legal forms. From an EU law perspective, the EU Member States' participation in mixed agreements seems to leave them in the position of agents, in light of the division of competences combined with the principle of supremacy of EU law. From an international law perspective, Member States of the EU are still sovereign states and can enter international obligations on their own, especially when concluding international agreements as proper contracting parties. And, obviously, from an EU law perspective, the same states remain first and foremost Member States. This project thus covers a broader field than just mixed agreements. However, it remains deliberately restricted to issues related to international treaty participation and implementation, therefore not addressing the respective roles of the EU and its Member States in the whole spectrum of EU external relations law.

The central issue in that area concerns the law that is applicable to different kinds of relations: between the EU and its Member States (including, between Member States parties to the same treaty as the EU itself), between third parties and the EU and between third parties and EU Member States. Could a pluralist approach be envisaged to make sense of this complexity? If, alternatively, convergence between EU and international law is the aim, would it be possible to accomplish it without discarding the specificity and autonomy of EU law? Should international law be adapted to accept the unique nature of the 'EU and its Member States' as an original subject of international law? The purpose of this book is not to try and reach a definitive and univocal answer to these different possibilities. Depending on the case study and the methodology used by the

[49] Ige F Dekker and Ramses A Wessel, 'Identities of States in International Organizations' (2016) 12 *International Organizations Law Review* 293–318.

[50] See more generally on the unfortunate increasing separation between international and EU law also Ramses A Wessel, 'Studying International and European Law: Confronting Perspectives and Combining Interests', in S Garben and I Govaere (eds), *The Interface between International and EU Law* (Hart Publishing, 2019) 73–97.

authors, potential solutions may differentiate. This edited book is thus a contribution to an ongoing doctrinal, legal and political debate on the nature of 'the EU and its Member States' as a subject (or subjects) of international law.

The editors asked for each chapter of this volume to be written by a co-author team, more or less made up of a senior and a more junior scholar. This drafting method of chapters, co-signed by the joint authors with different academic status, thus also represents an original working method of 'joint participation', not commonly used in legal scholarship. Most 'junior' researchers were selected following a call for papers put out in November 2019 preceding a conference held online at the Global Studies Institute of the University of Geneva in November 2020. The more 'senior' researchers have all written extensively on the topic they are contributing to. Considering the final result, we are happy to be able to conclude that all the authors have enthusiastically met the challenge and produced chapters that illustrate specific and innovative aspects of the numerous possible legal situations. We are very thankful to all contributors for that.

The book is divided into four parts. Part I deals with mixed agreements from a 'constitutional EU law perspective'. Part II also examines mixed agreements, but from an international law perspective. Part III explores cases of parallel participation of the EU and its Member States in both the Council of Europe and in an UN Convention, and the difficulties in assessing compliance measures. The fourth and last part, entitled 'EU International Agreements in Uncertain Times', reflects and proposes a prospective dimension on the issues raised in previous chapters. Two chapters in this final part take advantage of the exceptional situation created by Brexit, which may shed a new light on the nature and robustness of this unique type of a complex, multi-level and multidimensional legal subject, by revealing – as in the case with the former argentic photographic process – the 'negative picture' of the 'EU and its Member States' joint participation.

Part I: Mixed Agreements from an EU Law Perspective

In chapter one, 'A Typology of EU Mixed Agreements Revisited', **Joni Heliskoski and Gesa Kübek** present a fresh look on different types of 'mixity'. Taking account of recent developments in case law and practice, this chapter revisits the classification of mixed agreements. It identifies two main criteria for a typology, namely the allocation of competence and the number of parties to an agreement and, on this basis, develops a conceptual and analytical framework for understanding mixed agreements. Through classifying mixed agreements into more general groups and categories, the chapter aims to help one to understand the complex and varying landscape of mixity for the purpose of gaining a more general understanding of the practice of mixed agreements.

In the next chapter, entitled 'The Continuing Contestation of ERTA: Conferral, Effectiveness, and the Member States' participation in Mixed Agreements', **Mirka Kuisma and Joris Larik** revisit the *ERTA* doctrine. More than 50 years after its emergence, it continues to be contested by the EU's Member States, reflecting their struggle to balance their three different 'hats': 'Masters of the Treaties', co-legislator, and international legal subjects at the same time. This doctrine, now imperfectly codified in the EU Treaties, implies that Member States are pre-empted from exercising their treaty-making powers on the international stage where this would affect common EU rules or alter their scope. This chapter analyses the Member States' disagreements with the Court in pre- and post-Lisbon case law. The crux of their opposition is that *ERTA*-based exclusivity is seen as limiting Member State participation in external action in a manner that is inconsistent with the principle of conferral. The authors argue that the Court is right to rebuff the Member States' attempts to roll back the *ERTA* effect through litigation – not despite the principle of conferral, but partly because of it. *ERTA* exclusivity can only arise as a result of the exercise of powers conferred upon the Union, in which the Member States play a crucial part through the Council. Ultimately, this limits their ability to additionally demand joint participation in international agreements concluded by the EU. If the Member States really wanted to reign in relation to the *ERTA* effect, they could either restrain themselves in producing more and more common rules, or, as Masters of the Treaties, choose much clearer language. They have thus far not chosen either of these routes.

In chapter three, **Marja-Liisa Öberg and Marcus Klamert** argue that the Member States' external action, including the conclusion of mixed agreements, is constrained not only by an obligation to conform to EU law as it is but also by an obligation to foresee or anticipate its future developments. The latter could concern either changes in legislation or policy, or the case law of the Court of Justice. Their chapter, entitled 'Foreseeability and Anticipation as Constraints on Member State Action under Mixed Agreements', discusses the relevance of both foreseeability and anticipation as concepts of EU law, generally and in the realm of EU external relations law particularly, with special regard to the conclusion of mixed agreements. Foreseeability demands anticipation or awareness of a future event or circumstance. Anticipation, on the other hand, suggests a prior action which takes into consideration a later action. The authors show that Union institutions must foresee certain future developments and events when taking action, both internally and externally, while elements of anticipation constrain Member States on the basis of the duty of sincere cooperation. They establish both the substantive and temporal scope of these duties imposed on the Member States and discuss their relevance with regard to the case law of the Court of Justice in the context of mixed agreements. Overall, the chapter intends to contribute to understanding the temporal, 'prospective' side of restrictions incumbent on the Member States' external action, especially in the context of mixed agreements.

Chapter four entitled 'The Mixed Nature of the EU–Canada FTA: Between Competences Distribution and Democratic Legitimacy', by **Manon Damestoy and Nicolas Levrat,** explores the procedural hazards inherent to the current procedure for concluding and ratifying mixed agreements, through the case study of CETA. Investigating the dramatic showdown between the Walloon parliament (blocking the signature of CETA by Belgium) and European institutions as well as the other EU Member States, they underline both the legal uncertainties and the democratic legitimacy issue raised in 2016 around the common commercial policy (CCP). Their chapter analyses the rationale and content of the 'Namur Declaration' and the responding 'Trading together Declaration', both drafted by academics to contextualise and conceptualise the issues of EU treaty-making power in the field of an extended CCP. The authors conclude that leaving a veto right on the outcome of such complex year-long negotiations to each national (or even subnational) parliament constitutes a 'Sword of Damocles', incompatible with the EU's wish to appear as a reliable commercial partner.

For this reason, they take inspiration from the early involvement of national parliaments as regards the respect of the subsidiarity principle, referring to the 'yellow and red card' procedures existing in Protocol no 2. Damestoy and Levrat suggest to associate national parliaments at an earlier stage of the negotiation process of new mixed agreements. They argue this would both diminish the uncertainty surrounding mixed agreements, and bring a renewed legitimacy to the EU CCP.

In Part I's closing chapter, 'The Representation of the EU and its Member States in Multilateral Fora: the *AMP Antarctique* Effect' **Merijn Chamon and Marise Cremona** discuss the implications of the Court's ruling in *AMP Antarctique* for the question of the EU and the Member States' representation in international fora established pursuant to mixed multilateral agreements. The chapter first outlines the legal framework governing the EU's and Member States' joint participation and representation in international fora and goes on to offer a critique of the reasoning of the Court in *AMP Antarctique.* The authors then consider the precedential value of *AMP Antarctique* and argue that although, in principle, the ruling could have significant repercussions, it also leaves enough flexibility for the Court to treat it as a special case and reduce its precedential value. As a result, an excellent opportunity to clarify the legal framework governing the joint representation of the EU and its Member States under mixed multilateral agreements has been missed. The question whether the Council has completely unfettered political discretion in deciding whether or not to exercise EU shared competence remains open. Finally, since the same principles govern both the issues of representation and participation, the question of the extent to which *AMP Antarctique* may shed light on the EU's and its Member States' participation in multilateral agreements is also addressed.

Part II: Mixed Agreements from an International Law Perspective

Chapter six, entitled 'EMU "Mixity": Overlap between EU and Member States Action in Economic Governance', examines some aspects of the economic governance of the EU, drawing a comparison between this hybrid field of EU governance and that of mixed agreements in the framework of the EU's and Member States' external relations. By doing so, **Flore Vanackère and Bruno de Witte** deal with the EU and its Member States' joint action within the framework of an internal policy that involves a special form of cooperation, based on a combination of EU law and international law. To that end, the chapter first examines the hybrid nature in terms of competences of the economic branch of the EMU, exemplified by the European Stability Mechanism. In a second section, the authors provide two concrete examples concerning such joint action of the EU and its Member States in the field of economic governance. First the establishment of the Single Resolution Fund in the context of the Banking Union, and second the negotiation and conclusion of memoranda of understanding in the context of the ESM. These raise a further question about the link between the unsettled distribution of competences and the political need for joint action. The chapter also underlines, as concluding remarks, the need to develop a better understanding of the allocation of responsibility between Member States and EU institutions involved in such hybrid systems as EMU governance or joint participation to proper international agreements.

In chapter seven entitled '*Nomen est Omen*? The Relevance of "EU Party" in International Law', **Sabrina Schaefer and Jed Odermatt** explore the notion of 'EU Party', as it has found its way into the text of a number of bilateral mixed agreements. Where used, it appears to underline the perception of the EU and its Member States as one party rather than as individual parties. Based on an extensive analysis of 36 trade agreements, this chapter explores patterns behind the use of the term 'EU Party' and the legal effects of such a designation under international law. The chapter argues that the term 'EU Party' does not denote a collective treaty party status. Instead, the EU and its Member States remain individual parties under international law, their consent covering all parts of the mixed agreements. The chapter shows, however, that it is precisely such 'full' conclusion that enables the specific use of 'EU Party': Instead of referring to the EU or its Member States individually, treaty provisions address the 'EU Party', accommodating internal shifts of competences. At the same time, the status of the EU and its Member States as 'full' individual parties places limits on the interpretation of the term 'EU Party'. Where international law requires action by all treaty parties, a reading of 'the EU Party' as the EU *and* its Member States remains mandatory.

The aim of chapter eight, 'Conformity of International Dispute Settlement Mechanisms with EU Law: Does the EU's Participation Really Matter?' by **Bartosz Soloch and Makane Moïse Mbengue,** is to examine whether and to what extent the European Union's participation in international agreements as opposed to the participation of EU Member States only, is determinative for the conformity of dispute settlement mechanisms contained therein with the principle of autonomy of EU law. Their chapter demonstrates that until the CJEU's *Opinion 2/13* concerning EU's accession to the ECHR, the possible challenges to the autonomy principle were intrinsically linked to the EU's participation in the agreements. In particular, *Opinion 2/13* evidenced that the structural problems connected to the coexistence between the ECHR and EU law were relevant for the principle of autonomy of EU law only in the context of the envisaged EU's accession, even if they already existed in the absence thereof. The CJEU's ISDS-related jurisprudence (*Achmea* judgment and *Opinion 1/17*) however, showed that this view cannot be sustained. First, in the *Achmea* judgment the CJEU made it clear that a dispute settlement mechanism may contradict the principle of autonomy of EU law even in the absence of the EU's accession. Further, in *Opinion 1/17*, the CJEU showed that, somewhat paradoxically, the EU's participation in ISDS mechanisms could have allowed for introducing solutions accommodating the autonomy-related concerns. Consequently, in the aftermath of the CJEU's ISDS-related judgments, it appears clearly that the EU's participation in a given dispute settlement mechanism is not, as such, determinative for its conformity with the principle of autonomy of EU law.

Andrés Delgado Casteleiro and Cristina Contartese assert that when speaking about a multilevel actor such as the EU, participation in an international agreement goes beyond formal participation. Their chapter, entitled 'International Responsibility of the EU and/or its Member States in International Agreements: From Joint Participation to "Participation"', approaches the question of participation from two angles: participation *stricto sensu*, or formal participation, and participation *lato sensu*, or 'participation'. Accordingly, the attribution of international responsibility to the EU and/or its Member States for breaches of an international agreement needs to be assessed in the context of the different forms of their participation in it. The analysis carried out by the authors shows that assessing whether the EU participates in international agreements alone or with its Member States is only the very first stage of the responsibility analysis. The degree of complexity of the relationship between the EU and its Member States requires extending the focus to other elements, from the division of competences to the notion of 'executive federalism'. It then appears that in mixed agreements as well as in EU-only agreements, the division of competences is only a part of the analysis, and in some circumstances, the doctrine of normative control will have to play an essential role as well.

Part III: The EU and its Member States' Parallel Participation in International Agreements

In the first chapter of this part, entitled 'The Future of the Istanbul Convention before the CJEU', **Panos Koutrakos and Viktorija Soņeca** argue that the accession to the Istanbul Convention has provided the backdrop for considerable tension in both the Member States and the Union. On the one hand, the participation of the former has been characterised by divergent approaches, tensions and controversies. On the other hand, there has been inter-institutional conflict about the signature and conclusion of the Istanbul Convention on behalf of the Union. The unfolding episode of the signature and conclusion of the Istanbul Convention, is, therefore, more than a dispute about this important human rights instrument. It provides a snapshot of the difficulties that the Union and Member States face in their effort to coexist within the framework of an international legal order organised within a manner that does not reflect the constitutional idiosyncrasies of the Union legal order.

Tamás Molnár and Chloé Brière study a particular example of an international agreement with joint participation of the EU and its Member States, from the oversight perspective. Chapter 11, entitled 'The New Review Mechanism of the UN Smuggling of Migrants Protocol: Challenges in Measuring the EU's and its Member States' Compliance', examines how the drafters of this Mechanism have addressed the specificities of 'mixity' stemming from both the EU's and its Member States' participation in the UN Smuggling of Migrants Protocol. The authors propose a clearer understanding of the challenges in measuring the EU's and its Member States' compliance under this new form of treaty monitoring. They also address the implications of such 'mixity' for future practice.

The contribution by **Vassilis Pergantis and Stian Øby Johansen** explores the effects of the principle of autonomy on the EU accession to the ECHR, focusing particularly on its interaction with the DAA (Draft Accession Agreement's) responsibility allocation provisions. Entitled 'The EU Accession to the ECHR and the Responsibility Question: Between a Rock and a Hard Place', chapter 12 first outlines the contours of the principle as applied by the CJEU to international dispute settlement mechanisms in treaties where the Union participates jointly with its Member States. Then, the rather convoluted provisions on attribution of conduct and shared responsibility as found in the 2013 DAA are untangled, and the reasons for the CJEU's finding that they represent a threat to the autonomy of the EU legal order are explained. The gist of the argument is that any allocation of responsibility by the ECtHR between the Union and its Member States will necessarily imply an assessment of competence allocation between them. Consequently, the only remaining option for the accession appears to be the further simplification of these rules, so that they can be applied more or less automatically, thus shifting any requisite regulation of the responsibility allocation question and the consequences of wrongfulness to EU internal rules. Yet, the authors' findings are that such an arrangement will not preserve the idea of the EU acceding to the Convention on equal footing, and therefore runs the risk of undermining the proper administration of justice. The DAA negotiators are thus stuck in no man's land, with no obvious way out. Ultimately, the authors conclude that the principle of autonomy hinders the joint participation of the Union and its Member States in treaties that confer rights on individuals and give them access to judicial dispute settlement mechanisms.

Part IV: EU International Agreements in Uncertain Times

Elaine Fahey and Julija Brsakoska Bazerkoska examine how much the EU Member States increasingly disrespect the duty of sincere cooperation within trade and at its margins, focusing upon its most complex international opponent and potential partner, China and its Belt and Road Initiative (BRI). The BRI is not an international organisation; yet its scale, span and ambitions increasingly impact upon understandings of international law, by regions and nation states vis-à-vis China. The BRI thrives upon soft law instruments and relies on processes outside of traditional frameworks for protection and promotion of investments. Chapter 13 entitled 'Social and Legal Relevance of Sincere Cooperation in EU External Relations Law in the Era of Expanding Trade: The Belt & Road Initiative in Context' focuses on the EU Member States' engagement with the Belt and Road Initiative of China, which is highly significant. It is an original and key study of joint participation, sincere cooperation and the ostensible irrelevance of EU action in such regime. The BRI engagements by the Member States are increasingly extraordinary and detrimental to the EU's own deepening relations with China. There is a distinctly law-light dimension to sincere cooperation where rules – if they may be so-called – often appear more visible in their breach. This chapter critically explores gaps in the reality of EU and Member States joint participation and its excessive formalism which, the authors argue, is mismatched with practice. It underlines that sincere cooperation is both chronically under- and over-enforced and creates unnecessary power imbalances, uncompensated by a minimalist case law which favours larger states.

The purpose of chapter 14 entitled 'The Status of the United Kingdom Regarding EU Mixed Agreements after Brexit' is to propose solutions in the event that an EU Member State activates the withdrawal clause of Article 50 TEU. To this end, **Christine Kaddous and Habib Badjinri Touré** analyse international and European Union law perspectives with regard to the recent practice relating to Brexit. As is well known, Article 50 TEU provides for the conditions and consequences of the withdrawal of a Member State from the EU. However, it is silent on the participation of the withdrawing state in mixed agreements. Firstly, EU-only treaties cease to apply on the date on which a Member State withdraws from the EU. Secondly, several mixed agreements contain a territorial application clause limited to the territories of EU Member States and corresponding third parties (neither of which correspond to the departing state). In these circumstances, although the UK may formally remain a party to such agreements under international law, such agreements would in practice cease to apply to it. As a matter of fact, the UK concluded new agreements with third countries. It replicated, as far as possible, the effects of the EU's trade arrangements with partner countries, as they were applied to the UK through mixed agreements prior to the end of the transition period.

According to **Yuliya Kaspiarovich and Ramses A Wessel**, having recourse to mixed agreements is a very 'convenient' way to evade difficult questions concerning the exact delimitation of competences between the EU and its Member States. After all, to the outside world, the EU and its Member States are often presented in these situations as one single party. Chapter 15, entitled 'Unmixing Mixed Agreements: Challenges and Solutions for Separating the EU and its Member States in Existing International Agreements', seeks to answer, from a new perspective, the classic but still complex question of how to differentiate between EU and Member States' competences and responsibilities under mixed agreements. The present chapter turns a classic problem in EU external relations law upside down by not looking at reasons for mixity, but for tools to 'unmix' existing international agreements concluded by the EU and its Member States. In order to do so, the authors first address possible reasons and situations that would require the ability to 'unmix' existing agreements. In a second section, they scrutinise legal tools that could be used to separate EU and Member States' commitments under a mixed agreement. Finally, they apply their findings to a concrete situation, by using CETA in the Brexit context as an example. It then appears that it is quite difficult to unscramble scrambled eggs, as 'mixity' is not just a legal exercise, and 'unmixing' may also be influenced by political considerations.

All in their own right, these various contributions offer new insights into the tension that continues to exist between the EU and international law obligations in relation to the (joint) participation of the EU and its Member States in international agreements. This tension is a logical consequence of two following developments. First, the posture of the EU as a separate international legal person which has (original as well as derived) external competences of its own, sits uneasy with an international system that is still largely 'state-based'. While international organisations are recognised as legal persons in international (treaty) law, different rules often still apply to states and international organisations. The European Union simply does not fit in as an entity that is not a state yet more than an international organisation. Secondly, their status as EU Members causes dilemmas for EU Member States that cannot easily be solved on the basis of traditional hierarchy of rules in international law. As we have seen, from an international law perspective, any argument derived from them being EU Member States are largely irrelevant and seen as belonging to the 'domestic' sphere. This is understandable as third states are by definition not parties to any of the EU Treaties and may rightfully, and in full conformity with customary rules of international law, find it difficult to accept EU law arguments from their treaty partners. For EU Member States, however, their international obligations do not, by definition, outrank their EU law obligations (and most probably they would, sometimes encouraged by CJEU rulings, list their EU law obligations on top). The EU itself, finally, has traditionally proclaimed its open attitude towards international law and considers itself bound not only by the international agreements to which it is a party, but also by other rules of international law. In fact, one of its objectives is to contribute to 'the strict observance and the development of international law' (Articles 3(5) and 21(1) TEU). At the same time, it would not have survived without the 'EU law first' rule, to ensure not only a harmonious application of the EU rules in all Member States, but also their exclusive interpretation by a single Court.

Indeed, the EU and its Member States seem 'torn between two lovers' and they cannot be asked to make a choice between EU law and international law; neither theoretically, nor in practice. If there is one thing that emerges from the various contributions to this book, it may be that it is time for international law (or the international legal system more generally) to get to grips with the very specific legal nature of the European Union as an integration organisation which has to some extend – but to some extent only, and this is where the difficulty lies – subsumed state competences.

PART I

Mixed Agreements from an EU Law Perspective

1

A Typology of EU Mixed Agreements Revisited

JONI HELISKOSKI AND GESA KÜBEK

I. Introduction

Mixed agreements have been aptly described as one of the 'defining characteristics'[1] of the European Union's constitutional structure and a 'hallmark'[2] of its external relations. They include among their contracting parties not only the Union but also all or some of the Member States and fall partly within the external competence of the Union and partly within that of the Member States.[3]

Mixity has always been topical. However, it became particularly contentious after the entry into force of the Lisbon Treaty, including before the Court of Justice. The Court's relevant case law has reduced the material fields *not* covered by the Union's exclusive external competence and, by inference, the scope for mixity.[4] Yet, the scope for mixity has certainly not disappeared. It is safe to conclude that mixity will remain of great practical significance for the EU's treaty-making, especially in view of the broad political discretion of the Council to resort to mixed agreements in areas of shared competence.[5]

Treaty-making practice shows that ideas of different types of mixed agreements have evolved over time, with several authors aiming at identifying a typology of mixed agreements.[6] In the light of the recent case law as well as developments in the actual

[1] C Hillion and and P Koutrakos, 'Introduction' in C Hillion and P Koutrakos (eds), *Mixed Agreements Revisited* (Oxford, Hart Publishing, 2010).

[2] P Eeckhout, *EU External Relations Law*, 2nd edn (Oxford, OUP, 2011) 212.

[3] J Heliskoski, *Mixed Agreements as a Technique for Organizing the External Relations of the European Community and its Member States* (The Hague, Kluwer Law International, 2001) 7.

[4] Case C-414/11, *Daiichi Sankyo*, EU:C:2013:520; Case C-137/12, *Commission v Council*, EU:C:2013:675; Opinion 3/15, *Marrakesh Treaty*, EU:C:2017:114; Opinion 2/15, *Free Trade Agreement between the EU and the Republic of Singapore*, EU:C:2017:376. For a recent analysis on the impact of the Court's case law on the scope of mixity, see J Heliskoski, 'Shaping the Future of Mixity' in M Chamon and I Govaere (eds), *EU External Relations Post-Lisbon. The Law and Practice of Facultative Mixity* (Leiden, Brill/Nijhoff, 2020) 396, 399–408, 423–24.

[5] Case C-600/14, *Germany v Council*, EU:C:2017:935. See further M Chamon and I Govaere (n 4). See also C Kaddous, 'Les accords mixtes' in N Aloupi, C Flaesch-Mougin, C Kaddous and C Rapoport, *Les accords internationaux de l'Union européenne* 3rd edn (Brussels, Commentaire J. Mégret, 2019) 301, 306–10.

[6] See HG Schermers, 'A Typology of Mixed Agreements' in D O'Keeffe and HG Schermers (eds), *Mixed Agreements* (Deventer, Kluwer, 1983) 23; M Dolmans, *Problems of Mixed Agreements* (The Hague, TMC Asser, 1985) 39–42;

practice, time now seems ripe for revisiting the classification of mixed agreements. The typology presented in this chapter aims to provide a conceptual and analytical framework for understanding the existing practice of the institutions, including the Court of Justice, with regard to mixed agreements. Certainly, treaty-making practice reflects the changes in the legal framework and in the political considerations concerning mixity, and should therefore be considered on its own merits.[7] A typology merely seeks to classify the vast and diverging practice of mixed agreements into more general groups or categories with a view to shedding light on the different facets of the phenomenon of mixity. It does not provide a detailed legal analysis of the mixed procedure or the problems associated with mixity. In our view, a typology of mixed agreements may nonetheless present an insightful overview or be a useful starting point for further analysis, especially as it is sometimes assumed that all mixed agreements are concluded for the same reasons and present the same challenges.[8] Specific problems of mixity are further discussed in the remaining chapters of this volume.

The present chapter is divided into two parts, based on two main criteria for a typology of mixed agreements: first, the distribution of competences and, secondly, the number of parties to an agreement. After a brief explanation on the rules and principles concerning the allocation of competence between the Union and the Member States, the first part explains the conceptual distinction between mandatory, facultative, and false mixed agreements. The second part of this chapter categorises mixed agreements based on the criterion of the number of parties – both on the side of the Union and on the side of the treaty partner(s) – and, accordingly, differentiates between complete and incomplete, as well as bilateral and multilateral mixed agreements. The conclusion illustrates our view of the purpose, limitations, and use of a typology of mixed agreements.

II. Distribution of Competence as a Criterion for a Typology

A. The Rules on the Distribution of Competence between the Union and the Member States

The legal justification or explanation for mixity boils down to the principle of conferral, defined in Article 5(2) TEU. Under that principle, the Union shall act only within

A Rosas, 'Mixed Union – Mixed Agreements' in M Koskenniemi (ed), *International Law Aspects of the European Union* (The Hague, Kluwer, 1998) 125, 128–33; A Rosas, 'European Union and Mixed Agreements' in A Dashwood and C Hillion (eds), *The General Law of E.C. External Relations* (London, Sweet & Maxwell, 2000) 200, 203–7; M Maresceau, 'A Typology of Bilateral Mixed Agreements' in C Hillion and P Koutrakos (eds), *Mixed Agreements Revisited* (Oxford, Hart Publishing, 2010) 11; E Neframi, *Les accords mixtes de la Communauté européenne: aspects communautaires et internationaux* (Brussels, Bruylant, 2007) 16–20; and AJ Kumin and P Bittner, 'Die "gemischten" Abkommen zwischen der Europäischen Union und ihren Mitgliedstaaten einerseits und dritten Völkerrechtssubjekten andererseits' in W Oberwexer (ed), *Die Europäische Union im Völkerrecht*, Zeitschrift Europarecht-Beiheft 2/2012 (Baden-Baden, Nomos, 2012) 75, 77–79.

[7] See Eeckhout (n 2) 214.

[8] See also A Rosas, 'Mixity Past, Present and Future: Some Observations' in Chamon and Govaere (n 4) 8, 12.

the limits of the competence conferred upon it by the Member States in the Treaties to attain the objectives set out therein. Competences not conferred upon the Union in the Treaties remain with the Member States. When the conclusion of an international agreement or convention falls in part within the competence of the Union and in part within that of the Member States, there is, in principle, either an obligation or a possibility to conclude that agreement or convention as a mixed agreement.

The more precise nature of a mixed agreement depends however on the way in which the competence to conclude international agreements is divided between the Union and the Member States in respect of a given agreement. That in turn depends on the general provisions of the Treaties governing the scope and nature of the Union's competence[9] as well as the power-conferring provisions (legal bases) authorising, either expressly or by implication, the Union to conclude international agreements in the various areas of its competence. While the concrete attribution of competence between the Union and the Member States under a given mixed agreement depends on the characteristics of that particular agreement, the provisions of the Treaties governing the division of competence between the Union and the Member States also enable us to classify mixed agreements for the purpose of establishing a typology of mixed agreements.[10] The purpose of the present section is to present such a typology based on the criterion concerning the distribution of competence.

Before presentation of the typology, there will be a brief look at the rules of the TFEU governing the scope and nature of the Union's external competence. The *scope* of that competence in respect of a given subject matter or area is determined by the relevant legal bases,[11] read in conjunction with Article 216(1) TFEU,[12] while the *nature* of that competence is determined by Title I of Part One TFEU governing the categories or areas of Union competence. Insofar as the nature of the Union's competence is concerned, there is a fundamental distinction between *exclusive* and *non-exclusive* Union competence.[13] Where the Union has an exclusive competence,[14] only it may legislate and adopt legally binding acts, the Member States being able to do so themselves only if so empowered by the Union or for the implementation of Union acts (Art 2(1) TFEU). In areas of non-exclusive Union competence, however, the

[9] See Title I TFEU and Art 216 TFEU.

[10] In the literature, the distribution of competence has been the central criterion for establishing typologies of mixed agreements. See, eg Schermers, (n 6) 23; Dolmans (n 6) 39–42; Rosas, 'Mixed Union – Mixed Agreements' (n 6) 128–33 and Rosas, 'European Union and Mixed Agreements' (n 6) 203–7 and; insofar as concerns bilateral mixed agreements, Maresceau (n 6) 14 et seq.

[11] See Art 2(6) TFEU.

[12] Under Art 216(1) TFEU, '[t]he Union may conclude an agreement with one or more third countries or international organisations where the Treaties so provide or where the conclusion of an agreement is necessary in order to achieve, within the framework of the Union's policies, one of the objectives referred to in the Treaties, or is provided for in a legally binding Union act or is likely to affect common rules or alter their scope.'

[13] See Case C-600/14, *Germany v Council*, EU:C:2017:935, para 46. On rationale of that distinction see esp. M Cremona, 'EU External Relations: Unity and Conferral of Powers' in L Azoulai (ed) *The Question of Competence in the European Union* (Cambridge, CUP, 2014) 33. On the outcome of the application of the principle of conferral more generally see I Govaere, 'To Give or to Grab: The Principle of Full, Crippled and Split Conferral of Powers Post-Lisbon' in M Cremona (ed) *Structural Principles in EU External Relations Law* (Oxford, Hart Publishing, 2018) 71.

[14] See Art 3 TFEU.

existence of that competence does not a priori preclude the Member States from exercising their competence. The notion of non-exclusive competence – which is not included in the Treaties – comprises the following categories of competence, in each of which the implications of the exercise of the Union's competence are different. In areas of shared competence,[15] Member States may exercise their competence to the extent that the Union has not exercised its competence (Art 2(2) TFEU).[16] In the areas where the Union has competence to carry out actions to support, coordinate or supplement the actions of the Member States,[17] the exercise of Union competence does not supersede the competence of the Member States (Art 2(5), first subpara, TFEU). The same is probably also true for the Union's competence to coordinate the economic and employment policies of the Member States (Art 2(3) TFEU),[18] and to define and implement a common foreign and security policy (Art 2(4) TFEU), even though the Treaty is silent on the implications of the exercise of the Union's competence in those areas. While the exercise of Union competence in the areas of shared competence may turn that competence into an exclusive one through the operation of the AETR principle[19] now codified in Article 3(2) TFEU[20] or, in any event, preclude the exercise of a corresponding Member State competence under Article 2(2) TFEU, the breadth of the above categories of non-exclusive competence, extending to the great majority of the policy areas of the Union (Arts 4 to 6 TFEU), shows that, in the attribution of competence upon the Union, non-exclusive competence is the rule and exclusive Union competence very much an exception. This aspect concerning the distribution of competence between the Union and its Member States provides the principal explanation for the wide-spread practice of concluding mixed agreements. Finally, insofar as *no* Union competence exists, there is, by definition, an exclusive competence of the Member States, in either a 'horizontal' or a 'vertical' sense. This distinction will be explained in detail further on.

Drawing on the above rules and principles governing the distribution of competence, one could present the general structure of a mixed agreement depicted in Figure 1.1, which could then be used as a 'matrix' for drawing up of a general typology (or typologies) of mixed agreements based on the criterion of distribution of competence:[21]

[15] See Art 4 TFEU.

[16] In the areas of research, technological development and space as well as those of development cooperation and humanitarian aid the exercise of Union competence shall not result in Member States being prevented from exercising theirs (Arts 4(3) and 4(4) TFEU, respectively).

[17] See Art 6 TFEU.

[18] See Art 5 TFEU.

[19] Case 22/70, *Commission v Council*, EU:C:1971:32, especially paras 17 and 22.

[20] Under Art 3(2) TFEU, '[t]he Union shall also have exclusive competence for the conclusion of an international agreement when its conclusion is provided for in a legislative act of the Union or is necessary to enable the Union to exercise its internal competence, or in so far as its conclusion may affect common rules or alter their scope.'

[21] This 'general structure of a mixed agreement' was originally presented in J Heliskoski, 'Mixed Agreements: the EU Law Fundamentals' in R Schütze and T Tridimas (eds), *Oxford Principles of European Union Law, Volume 1: The European Union Legal Order* (Oxford, Oxford University Press, 2018) 1174, 1183.

Figure 1.1 Structure of a mixed agreement

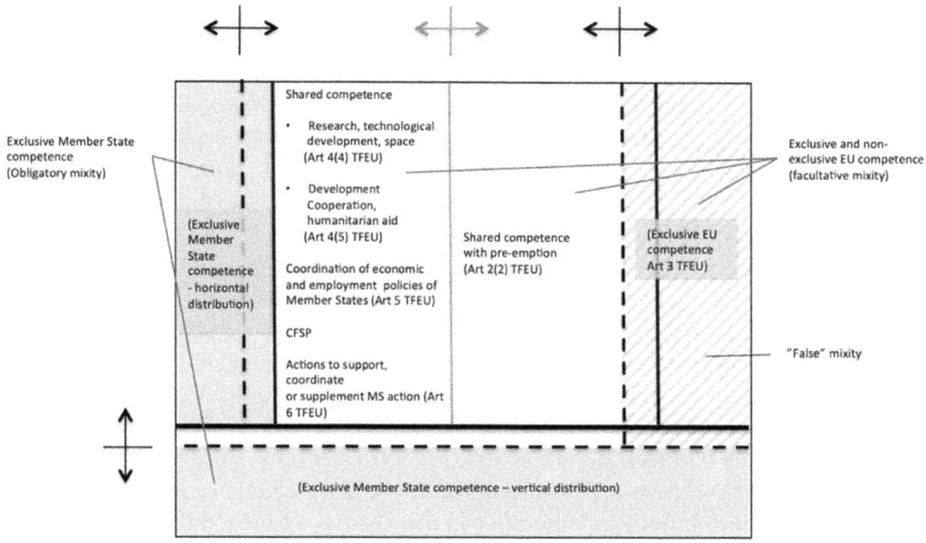

Such a typology (or typologies) would however easily risk becoming all too abstract and, as such, potentially incapable of describing the actual practice of mixity. Therefore, to us, a preferable option would be to use the above 'matrix' as a mere conceptual tool for understanding and assessing certain categories of mixed agreements that have originated from, and evolved in, the actual practice of the institutions, including the case law of the Court of Justice, and that now have a firm footing in the doctrine. In that regard, the most important distinction concerns the distinction between, on one hand, 'mandatory' mixed agreements (section II.B) and 'facultative' mixed agreements (section II.C). Reference is sometimes also made to so-called 'false' mixed agreements, that is, mixed agreements that could not legally have been concluded through the mixed procedure (section II.D). For the reasons of space, the present typology is limited to these principal categories and their variants.

B. Mandatory Mixed Agreements

The notion of mandatory mixed agreements refers to agreements for the conclusion of which there is *a legal obligation* to use the mixed procedure in light of the fact that the Union has no competence to act alone without the participation of its Member States. Otherwise, the principle of conferral would be infringed, the Union would act ultra vires under EU law, and would risk acting ultra vires under international law. The notion does not however refer to those cases where an international agreement itself requires its ratification by the Member States alongside with the Union,[22] or, for

[22] For such a 'subordination clause' see Art 52(3) of Customs Convention on the international transport of goods under cover of TIR carnets [1978] OJ L252/2. See further below, section III.D.

instance, where the participation of (some or all of) the Member States is required solely by the fact that the agreement requires them to amend (or possibly denounce) a prior international agreement to which they are parties.[23] The rationale of the notion of mandatory mixed agreement therefore has only to do with the idea of the Union as an entity based on a specific and limited authorisation – now embodied in the Treaty as the principle of conferral. If, along with the parts of the agreement falling within the exclusive competence of the Member States, there are also parts falling within the exclusive competence of the Union, the conclusion of the agreement as a mixed agreement becomes mandatory.[24]

Mixed agreements that are legally mandatory in the above sense are relatively rare in practice. Indeed, with the exception of the early Ruling 1/78, based on the Treaty establishing the European Atomic Energy Community,[25] there have been no cases where the Court of Justice would have regarded the use of a mixed agreement as legal *necessary* in the light of the Union not possessing the competence required for the conclusion of an agreement by the Union in its own right without its Member States.[26] In all other cases, the Court has only had to address the question as to whether a given agreement falls within the Union's exclusive competence and, as a corollary, whether a mixed agreement *may* be concluded or not – as opposed to whether there is a legal requirement to do so.

Nonetheless, the notion of mandatory mixed agreement is by no means a solely theoretical construction.[27] Perhaps the most obvious example of a multilateral convention for the conclusion of which by the Union alone there would be no authorisation in either the TEU or the TFEU is the United Nations Convention on the Law of the Sea (UNCLOS). Besides questions falling within the Union's exclusive competence, that agreement covers a whole range of matters falling within the corpus of international

[23] As the Court held in Opinion 1/76, *Draft Agreement establishing a European laying-up fund for inland waterway vessels*, EU:C:1977:63, paras 6–7. The same would apply to mixed agreements the territorial scope of application of which exceeds the territorial scope of application of the Treaties, which then justifies the participation of Member States in the agreement. See further below, section III.B. Corresponding to what we suggest in that section, one might classify instances where the rationale of the notion of mandatory mixed agreement does not follow from the criterion of distribution of competence but from criteria external to EU law (international law, territorial scope of application etc.) as 'special instances of mandatory mixity'.

[24] Rosas, 'European Union and Mixed Agreements' (n 6) 204–6, speaks of 'coexistent competences' in this respect. If, however, no part of an agreement falls within the Union's exclusive competence, the agreement could be concluded by the Member States without the participation of the Union.

[25] Ruling 1/78, *Draft Convention of the International Atomic Energy Agency on the Physical Protection of Nuclear Materials, Facilities and Transports*, EU:C:1978:202, para 36.

[26] It is true that, in Opinion 2/15, *Free Trade Agreement between the EU and the Republic of Singapore*, EU:C:2017:376, the Court held that 'Section A of Chapter 9 of the envisaged agreement [relating to investment protection] cannot be approved by the European Union alone' (para 244). However, by that conclusion, the Court had merely acknowledged the fact that there had been no possibility of obtaining the required majority within the Council for the Union to be able to exercise alone the external competence that it shares with the Member States in the area of non-direct foreign investment. See Case C-600/14, *Germany v Council*, EU:C:2017:935, para 68. See also Opinion 2/94, *Accession by the Community to the European Convention for the Protection of Human Rights and Fundamental Freedoms*, EU:C:1996:140, where the Court concluded that the Union had no competence to accede to the ECHR *even as a mixed agreement*.

[27] Prior to the entry into force of the Treaty of Lisbon, Art 133(6) EC even contained a specific provision rendering mandatory the conclusion of agreements relating to trade in cultural and audiovisual services, educational services, and social and human health services as mixed agreements. See Opinion 1/08, *Agreements modifying the Schedules of Specific Commitments under the General Agreement on Trade in Services (GATS)*, EU:C:2009:739, paras 134–5.

maritime law, as well as questions such as the exercise of jurisdiction over vessels, flagging and registration of vessels, and the enforcement of penal and administrative sanctions, conceived of as falling within the exclusive competence of the Member States.[28] Another example would be the Convention relating to Temporary Admission, certain provisions of which have been considered to fall outside the competence of the Union and, presumably, within the exclusive competence of the Member States in the field of taxation.[29] The UN Convention on the Rights of Persons with Disabilities (CRPD) may also be classified as a mandatory mixed agreement.[30] It governs rights that are exclusively guaranteed by national law[31] and rights that, albeit recognised in the EU Charter of Fundamental Rights, can only be guaranteed in accordance with the Member States' national laws governing the exercise of these rights.[32] While no exhaustive account of mandatory multilateral mixed agreements may be provided in the present context, it may be noted that a request by the European Parliament for an opinion under Article 218(11) TFEU concerning the Istanbul Convention on preventing and combating violence against women and domestic violence[33] is currently pending before the Court of Justice.[34] Should the Court find that the Convention contains provisions falling within the exclusive competence of the Member States and other provisions falling within the (exclusive) competence of the Union, that agreement would also become a mandatory mixed agreement.

Mixed agreements of a bilateral nature might contain provisions in respect of which no Union competence exists: reference could be made, for instance, to provisions regulating civil or administrative procedures of the Member States[35] or certain specific

[28] See the declaration concerning the competence of the European Community with regard to matters governed by the Convention ([1998] OJ L179/129).

[29] See the notification ([1993] OJ L130/75) made by the European Community pursuant to Art 24(6) of the Convention relating to Temporary Admission of 26 June 1990 providing that ' the Community … is competent for all the matters governed by the Convention, except: determination of the *duties, taxes, fees or other charges* referred to in Article 1 (b) of the Convention other than Community customs duties, charges having equivalent effect to Community customs duties, agricultural levies or other import charges provided for under the Community's agricultural policy, *notifications pursuant to Article 30 [Territorial extension]*' (emphasis added).

[30] See the declaration concerning the competence of the European Community with regard to matters governed by the Convention, [2010] OJ L23/55, and further M Chamon, 'Negotiation, ratification and implementation of the CRPD and its status in the EU legal order' in D Ferri and A Broderick (eds), *Research Handbook on EU Disability Law* (Cheltenham, Edward Elgar Publishing, 2020) 52, 55.

[31] Eg the right to acquire and change a nationality (Art 18(a) CRPD). The Court recognised that 'it is for each Member State, having due regard to Community law, to lay down the conditions for the acquisition and loss of nationality'. See eg Case C-135/08, *Rottmann*, EU:C:2010:104, para 39. The fact that due regard must be given to EU law in the exercise of a national competence does not alter the nature of that competence as such.

[32] Eg the right to marriage (Art 23(1)(a) CRPD). Further compare Art 9 of the EU Charter of Fundamental Rights.

[33] For the text, see www.coe.int/en/web/conventions/full-list/-/conventions/treaty/210.

[34] Opinion 1/19 (pending). The second question submitted to the Court is as follows: 'Is the conclusion by the European Union of the Istanbul Convention, in accordance with Article 218(6) TFEU, compatible with the Treaties in the absence of mutual agreement between all the Member States concerning their consent to be bound by that convention?'. That question is further discussed in section III.B, in the light of Advocate General Hogan's view (opinion of Hogan AG in Opinion 1/19, *Istanbul Convention*, ECLI:EU:C:2021:198). On mixity and the Istanbul Convention see also the chapter by Viktorija Soneca and Panos Koutrakos in this volume.

[35] See, eg, Arts 291 and 292 of the Trade Agreement between the EU and its Member States, of the one part, and Colombia and Peru, of the other part, [2012] OJ L354/3.

commitments that only the Member States may carry out.[36] Yet, the Court of Justice does not appear to consider that these provisions give rise to an independent external competence of the Member States.[37] As the parts of a bilateral mixed agreement that may be conceived as falling beyond scope of the Union's competence are usually excluded from the scope of provisional application of the agreement, the practice concerning provisional application of the EU's free trade, cooperation and association agreements[38] may also provide a useful illustration of the potential mandatory nature of certain mixed agreements. A more thorough analysis of those provisions would obviously exceed the limits of the present contribution.

It has been suggested that in respect of mandatory mixed agreements a distinction could be made between, on the one hand, a 'horizontal' and, on the other hand, a 'vertical' distribution of competence between the Union and the Member States.[39] The former would refer to the various substantive areas of cooperation (eg, in the case of UNCLOS, fisheries protection falling within the (exclusive) competence of the EU and questions concerning navigation and passage within that of the Member States) while the latter would highlight the exclusive competence of the Member States in the implementation and enforcement of those substantive provisions. It seems however that the Court of Justice is inclined to treat such vertical elements of an international agreement as subsidiary or ancillary provisions helping to achieve the primary objective of the agreement.[40] On the other hand, substantive provisions of an agreement falling within the exclusive competence of the Member States in the horizontal sense (eg, on navigation and passage, or taxation) – however marginal – should probably not be regarded as subsidiary or ancillary so as to remove the need for a mandatory mixed agreement. Otherwise, there would be a risk of the Union not only disregarding the principle of conferral but also acting ultra vires under EU law and, possibly, under international law.[41]

[36] See eg Art 17(3) of Agreement establishing an Association between the European Union and its Member States, on the one hand, and Central America on the other, [2012] OJ L346/3, providing that '[t]he Parties agree to cooperate to promote universal adherence to the Rome Statute [of the International Criminal Court] by: continuing to take steps to *implement the Rome Statute and to ratify and implement related instruments* (such as the Agreement on Privileges and Immunities of the International Criminal Court)' (emphasis added).

[37] In Opinion 2/15, the Council and some Member States submitted that individual provisions of the EU-Singapore Free Trade Agreement (EUSFTA) fall within the Member States' exclusive competence (eg provisions referring to administrative proceedings (Art 13.3 (EUSFTA), moral rights (Art 10.4 EUSFTA), certification schemes of timber and timber products (Art 12.7 EUSFTA) or diplomatic protection (now Art 3.23 EU-Singapore Investment Protection Agreement)). The Court however concluded that not a single provision of the EUSFTA falls within the Member States' exclusive competence. The Court stressed that the implementation of certain aspects of the EUSFTA by Member States has a direct impact on trade (see eg with regard to timber and timer products, para 160) and that the mere reference to international commitments of the Member States is not sufficient to determine the nature of the EU's external competence to conclude the EUSFTA (see, eg with regard to moral rights, para 129).

[38] See J Heliskoski, 'Provisional Application of EU Free Trade Agreements' in G Van der Loo and M Hahn (eds), *Law and Practice of the Common Commercial Policy: The first 10 years after the Treaty of Lisbon* (Boston, Brill, 2020) 586. On the law and practice of provisional application see generally A Quest Mertsch, *Provisionally Applied Treaties: Their Binding Force and Legal Nature* (Leiden, Brill, 2012).

[39] Rosas, 'European Union and Mixed Agreements' (n 6) 204–5, and Figure 1.1, above.

[40] See, eg, Case C-25/94, *Commission v Council*, EU:C:1996:114, para 47 (provisions concerning the imposition of possibly penal sanctions) and Case C-137/12, *Commission v Council*, EU:C:2013:675, para 70 (provisions concerning seizure and confiscation measures). Moreover, Art 2(1) TFEU foresees that the Member States may implement acts of the Union even in areas of the Union's exclusive competence.

[41] See M Chamon, 'Constitutional Limits to the Political Choice for Mixity' in E Neframi and M Gatti (eds), *Constitutional Issues of EU External Relations Law* (Baden-Baden, Nomos, 2018) 137, 142–47.

As regards the horizontal distribution of competence for those parts of a mandatory mixed agreement in respect of which a competence of the Union exists, the more precise nature of the agreement depends on the nature of Union competence (or competences) that is (are) exercised in a given case. Usually, there is a combination of exclusive and non-exclusive competence at work, as in the case of UNCLOS for instance (eg, conservation and management of sea fishing resources and maritime transport, respectively). As regards the areas of non-exclusive Union competence, a distinction should be made between, on the one hand, those areas in which the exercise of Union competence may either supersede the competence of the Member States pursuant to Article 2(2) TFEU or preclude the Member States from exercising their competence through the AETR effect (Art 3(2) TFEU) and, on the other hand, those areas in which no such pre-emption is possible – that is, areas where the Union has competence to carry out actions to support, coordinate or supplement the actions of the Member States (Art 2(5), first subpara, TFEU); research, technological development and space (Art 4(3) TFEU); development cooperation and humanitarian aid (Art 4(4) TFEU; and, possibly, coordination of the economic and employment policies of the Member States (Art 2(3) TFEU) as well as the CFSP (Art 2(4) TFEU). With the former category, one may speak of a 'concurrent' non-exclusive Union competence and, with the latter, of a 'parallel' non-exclusive Union competence.[42] Obviously, there may be mixed agreements with elements of both concurrent and parallel non-exclusive Union competence, alongside with elements of both exclusive Union competence and exclusive Member State competence. Such a hybrid distribution of competence is frequently present in many trade, cooperation or association agreements.

C. Facultative Mixed Agreements

Mixed agreements that are not mandatory in the sense explained above are usually described as facultative mixed agreements.[43] While in the case of a mandatory mixed agreement there is a legal obligation to have recourse to the mixed procedure, in the case of a facultative mixed agreement the use of that procedure is left to the Union's (political) choice. The latter scenario takes place where the conclusion of an international

[42] There are also sui generis cases that may be regarded as situations of a parallel competence that do not seem to be covered by any of the above Treaty provisions. One example is provided by matters where a 'self-contained' body of Union regulation is created by Union law that exist in parallel with the similar legal regulation of the Member States: see, eg, the Community trade mark created by Council Regulation (EC) No 40/94 of 20 December 1993 ([1994] OJ L11/1) that exists in parallel with the national marks. See Case C-53/96, *Hermès*, EU:C:1998:292, para 32. The Århus Convention on access to information, public participation in decision-making and access to justice in environmental matters ([2005] OJ L 124/4) could probably also be considered to involve elements of such parallel competence. See C-240/09, *Lesoochranárske zoskupenie*, EU:C:2011:125, para 42. The same would seem to be true with international human rights conventions laying down obligations directed at the same time to both the Union and its Member States. Therefore, should the EU one day accede to the European Convention on Human Rights and Fundamental Freedoms, that convention would also be likely to fall within this category.

[43] To our knowledge, the notion of 'facultative mixity' was first employed in the writings of Allan Rosas. See A Rosas, 'Mixed Union – Mixed Agreements' (n 6) 131–32 and A Rosas, 'European Union and Mixed Agreements' (n 6) 205–6. See also Chamon and Govaere (n 4).

agreement in its entirety would fall within the Union's competence but where that competence would not be exclusive for the whole of the agreement. In such cases, there would exist two possible ways to proceed: first, to conclude a 'pure' Union agreement between the Union and the other contracting party (or parties) or, secondly, to conclude a mixed agreement. The latter course of action would then result in a facultative mixed agreement. As a matter of fact, an overwhelming majority of mixed agreements fall within this category.

It has sometimes been argued that in areas falling within the shared competence of the Union and its Member States, the Union *cannot* exercise its competence externally if it has not first exercised its competence internally by adopting common rules in the sense of Article 3(2) TFEU.[44] It has also been suggested that, in the context of an international agreement falling in part within the Union's exclusive competence and in part within its non-exclusive competence, with no aspect of the agreement falling outside the scope of the Union's competence, the agreement should be concluded as a Union agreement instead of a mixed agreement. In other words, the Union's institutions, the latter argument says, would not be entitled to refrain from exercising the Union's non-exclusive competence where the Union would in any event exercise its exclusive competence.[45] However, it is clear that both of the above arguments are misconceived in the light of the case law of the Court.

The most recent and perhaps most unequivocal rejection of both the above arguments is contained in *Germany v Council (COTIF I)*.[46] In reaching that conclusion the Court followed a consistent line of opinions of Advocates General concerning the exercise of the Union's external competence, all of which had argued, albeit with certain nuances, that, in matters falling within the Union's non-exclusive competence, there is essentially *a political choice*, ultimately to be made by the Council, as to whether to exercise Union competence for the purpose of concluding an agreement as a Union agreement or, alternatively, to refrain from doing so, and thereby enabling the Member States to participate in the conclusion of a mixed agreement.[47] It is submitted that that finding is also entirely consistent with the Court's case law predating the entry into force of the Treaty of Lisbon. The Court had acknowledged that irrespective of whether Union competence for the conclusion of a given agreement existed, the Member States would nevertheless be entitled to participate in the conclusion thereof, if the Union's competence was not exclusive in respect of the agreement in its entirety.[48]

[44] See Case C-600/14, *Germany v Council*, EU:C:2017:935, paras 31–39.

[45] See P Eeckhout, *EU External Relations Law*, (Oxford, Oxford University Press, 2012) 265 and R Schütze, 'Federalism and Foreign Affairs: Mixity as a (Inter)national Phenomenon' in Hillion and Koutrakos (n 2) 83. See also Opinion of Kokott AG in Case C-13/07, *Commission v Council*, EU:C:2009:190, paras 83–84.

[46] See Case C-600/14, *Germany v Council*, EU:C:2017:935, para 68. See also opinion of Kokott AG in Joined Cases C-626/15 and C-659/16, *Commission v Council*, EU:C:2018:362, fn 71. According to her, it can be inferred from the COTIF judgment that 'the Union can decide in each individual case not to exercise its inherent powers in an area of shared competences fully, but only partially, thereby allowing scope for autonomous action by the Member States.'

[47] See the opinions of Sharpston AG in Opinion 2/15, EU:C:2016:992, paras 73–75; Wahl AG in Opinion 3/15, EU:C:2016:657, paras 119–21; and Szpunar AG in Case C-600/14, *Germany v Council*, EU:C:2017:935, para 84.

[48] See especially Opinion 2/91, *ILO Convention No 170*, EU:C:1993:106; Opinion 1/94, *WTO Agreement*, EU:C:1994:384; Opinion 2/92, *Third Revised Decision of the OECD on national treatment*, EU:C:1995:83; Opinion 2/00, *Cartagena Protocol on Biosafety*, EU:C:2001:664; and Case C-94/03, *Commission v Council*, EU:C:2006:2.

Of course, there are circumstances that may limit the discretion of the institutions in this respect, such as the principle of absorption of legal bases, the AETR principle as interpreted in the case law of the Court,[49] the principle of the duty of loyal cooperation, as well as international law.[50] Those circumstances do not however put into question the basic principle emerging from the case law.

Within the above basic definition of a facultative mixed agreement, there are, as in the case of mandatory mixed agreements, various different ways in which competence may be divided between the Union and its Member States. However, the elements of exclusive Member State competence (in both vertical and horizontal senses) are, by definition, lacking. This means that, over time, facultative mixed agreements with elements of (solely) concurrent non-exclusive Union competence might become covered, in their entirety, by an exclusive Union competence. In such a scenario, the participation of the Member States would no longer be legally justified. If, however, there were also elements of parallel non-exclusive competence, the Union would never be capable of entirely 'occupying the field' of the agreement. In the latter case, the agreement would always remain a genuinely facultative mixed agreement. Of course, as in the case mandatory mixed agreements, a facultative mixed agreement might involve elements of both concurrent and parallel non-exclusive EU competence.

D. False Mixed Agreements

In his early (1983) typology of mixed agreements,[51] *Schermers* introduced the notion of the 'false' mixed agreement to denote mixed agreements in respect of which the mixed procedure ought not to have been used at all given that they are covered entirely by the Union's exclusive competence.[52]

See also Case C-459/03, *Commission v Ireland*, EU:C:2006:345, para 96, where the Court refers to the need to establish '… whether and to what extent the Community, by becoming a party to the [United Nations Convention on the Law of the Sea], *elected to exercise* its external competence in matters of environmental protection.' (emphasis added).

[49] See esp Opinion 2/91, *Convention N° 170 of the International Labour Organization concerning safety in the use of chemicals at work*, EU:C:1993:106, para 25.

[50] See further, J Heliskoski, 'The Exercise of Non-Exclusive Competence of the EU and the Conclusion of International Agreements' in K Lenaerts et al (eds), *An Ever-Changing Union? Perspectives on the Future of EU Law in Honour of Allan Rosas* (Oxford, Hart Publishing, 2019) 293, 299–306. Insofar as concerns the impact of international law in this respect, see Joined Cases C-626/15 and C-659/16, *Commission v Council*, EU:C:2018:925, paras 127–33.

[51] Schermers (n 6) 27–28.

[52] See also PJ Kuijper et al (eds), *The Law of EU External Relations* (Oxford, OUP, 2013) 105, referring to agreements concluded as mixed agreements due to 'grounds that are manifestly untenable'. The notion of the false mixed agreement should however be distinguished from mixed agreements concluded in the mixed form as a result of what Rosas ('Mixed Union: – Mixed Agreements' (n 6) 147) has described as 'Member State manipulation with a view of making them mixed'. If, for instance, the Council (and the Member States) wish to include provisions falling beyond the Union's exclusive competence to an agreement to enable its conclusion as a mixed agreement, we should not be talking about a false mixed agreement. At the same time, one should remember that not any element, however marginal, falling outside the Union's exclusive competence can justify the conclusion of an agreement as mixed agreement. Such elements may well be considered as subsidiary or ancillary provisions that are 'absorbed' by the principal objective and content of the agreement.

In our submission, this is a rare as well as a rather contentious category. In practice, should an agreement have been concluded falsely as a mixed agreement, it only rarely retains its status as mixed agreement on a more permanent basis. The Commission would namely be likely to take the Council (or the Member States) to the Court of Justice, should Member States proceed to sign and ratify mixed agreements which, in the Commission's opinion, fall within the Union's exclusive competence. The European Convention on the legal protection of services based on, or consisting of, conditional access – which was first conceived by Member States a mixed agreement but which later became a pure Union agreement following a judgment of the Court – is one example of such an agreement.[53]

In the absence of a ruling by the Court, however, it is nearly always contentious as to whether a given agreement could legitimately have been concluded, or may remain in force, as a mixed agreement. Some might ask, for instance, whether the Member States are still entitled to remain contracting parties to the Agreement establishing the World Trade Organization, given the transfer of the Union's (entire) Common Commercial Policy to an exclusive competence by virtue of the Treaty of Lisbon (Art 207 TFEU) and the Court's case law laid down in *Daiichi Sankyo*[54] and in Opinion 2/15,[55] or whether that agreement has become a false mixed agreement. Therefore, until the Court has settled the issue in respect of a given agreement, the notion of false mixed agreement rather seems to be employed as a legal and (mainly) political device against the use of the mixed procedure on this or that occasion. Therefore, and given the fact that genuinely false mixed agreements only rarely tend to remain in place on a more permanent basis, one may ask whether the notion really is that useful in any typology of mixed agreements.

III. The Number of Parties as a Criterion for a Typology

Besides the division of competence, the type of mixity is determined by the number of parties to the agreement. Mixity is 'complete' when alongside the Union all of the Member States ratify the agreement in their own right (section 3.1). By inference, mixity is 'incomplete' when the agreement is concluded by one or more but not all of the Member States alongside the Union (section 3.2). Irrespective of whether mixity is 'complete' or 'incomplete', the number of participating third states may vary. Bilateral mixed agreements are concluded by the Union, the Member States, and a single third party or a single group of third parties (section 3.3.). Multilateral mixed agreements, by contrast, include the Union and the Member States as well as several third parties (section 3.4).

[53] See Case C-137/12, *Commission v Council*, EU:C:2013:675.

[54] Case C-414/11, *Daiichi Sankyo*, EU:C:2013:520. See further I Van Damme, 'Case C-411/11 Daiichi: The Impact of the Lisbon Treaty on the Competence of the European Union over the TRIPS Agreement' (2015) 4 *Cambridge International Law Journal* 73.

[55] Opinion 2/15, *Free Trade Agreement between the EU and the Republic of Singapore*, EU:C:2017:376.

A. Complete Mixed Agreements

Mixity is usually 'complete'.[56] The recourse to mixity is generally based on a collective decision by the Member States in the Council to exercise their retained treaty-making power for either legal or political reasons, implying that all Member States become contracting parties to the agreement in their own right. Incomplete mixity is rare in practice. As will be further explained below, this is especially the case for bilateral mixed agreements because they invariably require ratification by the Union and all the Member States as a criterion for entry into force. In practice, bilateral mixed agreements can therefore only become 'incomplete' in specific circumstances after they have entered into force.

Complete mixity ensures that the agreement applies to the territory of the Union in full. The Union and the Member States may commence treaty negotiations without pre-determining the more precise allocation of competences, so as to avoid competence battles within the Union.[57] In contrast to situations where mixity is 'incomplete', it is not necessary to consider in advance whether certain parts of the agreement do not apply to non-ratifying Member States. The attribution of responsibility can be determined at a later stage of the treaty-making process, if necessary.[58]

In the multilateral context, the Union and the Member States have to coordinate the deposition of their respective ratification instruments in order to ensure that a complete mixed agreement enters into force on the same day. It is a common practice for the Union to wait for the Member States' individual deposit of ratification instruments before depositing its own instrument. To that end, the Council, in its decision to conclude a mixed agreement, has at times called upon Member States to deposit their ratification instruments simultaneously with the Union and within a certain time frame.[59] Yet, ratification delays in one or more Member States can cause the Union to go ahead and submit its ratification instrument alone, which may temporarily make mixity 'incomplete'.[60]

B. Incomplete Mixed Agreements

If only some, but not all, of the Member States become parties to a mixed agreement, the question arises to what extent the agreement also applies to the non-ratifying Member States. Pursuant to Article 216(2) TFEU, international agreements concluded by the Union are binding on the Member States. The extent to which an incomplete mixed

[56] To our knowledge, the terms 'complete' and 'incomplete' mixity were introduced by Schermers (n 6) 26.

[57] See esp Heliskoski (n 3).

[58] On the international responsibility of the EU and the Member States in the context of mixed agreements see further M Cremona, 'External Relations of the EU and the Member States: Competence, Mixed Agreements, International Responsibility, and Effects of International Law' (2006) 22 *EUI Working Paper Law*, 15 et seq; and the chapter by Andres Delgado Casteleiro and Cristina Contartese in this volume.

[59] See eg Art 6(1) of the Council Decision (EU) 2015/1339 of 13 July 2015 ([2015] OJ L 207/1) or Art 3 of the Council Decision (EEC) 88/540 of 14 October 1988 ([1988] OJ L 297/8).

[60] See eg the case of the Paris Convention, discussed further below.

agreement applies to the territory of non-ratifying Member States by virtue of EU law depends on the extent to which the Union exercises treaty-making competence and assumes responsibility for that agreement. Especially for third states, the scope of application and responsibility for incomplete mixed agreements may be difficult to grasp.[61] A detailed declaration of competence could indicate the scope of Union's and the Member States' respective treaty-making power and responsibility.[62] Yet, as mentioned above, mixity is often purposefully chosen by the Union and the Member States to avoid a concrete attribution of competence. It is therefore unsurprising that EU declarations of competence tend to 'suffer from a lack of clarity and elegance'.[63] In the absence of a detailed declaration of competence, incomplete mixity may however become problematic, as the carve-out of some provisions from the scope of legal obligations assumed by the Union may be perceived as an unlawful reservation by third parties.[64]

Despite the complexities surrounding incomplete mixity, the Court of Justice recognised in *Opinion 1/76* that the joint conclusion of an agreement by the (then) Community and only some Member States can, in specific circumstances, be 'explain[ed] and justif[ied]'.[65] In *Opinion 1/76*, 'a special problem' arose, as the Inland Waterway Transport Agreement required six Member States to amend two agreements, namely the Mannheim Convention on the Navigation of the Rhine and the Luxembourg Convention on the Canalisation of the Moselle, to which they alone were parties.[66] The (then) Community legislature solved this problem by allowing these six Member States to become contracting parties in their own right to the Inland Waterway Transport Agreement, and the Court subsequently confirmed the legality of the participation of those six Member States 'for this particular undertaking'.[67] The geographical scope of application of the Mannheim and Luxembourg Convention explains why they were only concluded by some Member States and why only these Member States participated in the Inland Waterway Transport Agreement. Although, based on the number of parties, the Inland Waterway Transport Agreement qualified as an incomplete mixed agreement, it is a special instance of incomplete mixity because the decision of some Member States *not* to participate results from the geographical area to which the Mannheim and Luxembourg Convention as well as the Inland Waterway Transport Agreement applied.

Such a special instance of incomplete mixity was more recently considered by AG Kokott in her reasoning in *AMP Antarctique*.[68] Although the AG asserted that there

[61] See also J Czuczai, 'Mixity in Practice: Some Problems and Their (Real or Possible) Solution' in Hillion and Koutrakos (n 1) 229–48, 241 et seq. For third parties' perspective of on mixity, see Heliskoski (n 3) 121 et seq; PM Olson, 'Mixity from the Outside: The Perspective of a Treaty Partner' in Hillion and Koutrakos (n 1) 331; and J Odermatt, 'Facultative Mixity in the International Legal Order – Tolerating European Exceptionalism?' in Chamon and Govaere (n 4) 291.

[62] On EU declarations of competences see esp J Heliskoski, 'EU Declarations of Competence and International Responsibility' in M Evans and P Koutrakos (eds), *The International Responsibility of the European Union: European and International Perspectives* (Oxford, Hart Publishing, 2013) 189–214; and A Delgado Castelleiro, *The International Responsibility of the European Union: From Competence to Normative Control* (Cambridge, CUP, 2016) 110–29.

[63] Opinion of Maduro AG in Case C-459/03, *MOX Plant*, EU:C:2006:42, para 36.

[64] Rosas (n 8) 17.

[65] Opinion 1/76, *Inland Waterways*, EU:C:1977:63, para 7.

[66] Ibid, para 6.

[67] Ibid.

[68] Opinion of Kokott AG in Joined Cases C-626/15 and C-659/16, *AMP Antarctique*, EU:C:2018:362.

would not be scope for the voluntary participation of the Member States alongside the Union, she recognised that the territorial interests of individual Member States may justify incomplete mixity. As the contested decisions 'offered *all* Member States and not just *individual* Member States the possibility of participating … alongside the Union', they would however 'quite clearly go beyond what would be necessary to safeguard those territorial interests.'[69] The Court of Justice did not follow the AG's view and found that mixity was necessary for the adoption of the contested decisions as a matter of international law.[70] The Court's conclusion in *Opinion 1/76* that in certain situations the participation in EU external relations of only some, but not all, of the Member States is justifiable nevertheless remains good law. This is all the more so where incomplete mixity is an inevitable result of an agreement's geographical scope of application.

Over time, incomplete mixity arose not only as a result of the geographical scope of application of certain agreements but turned into a deliberate treaty-making technique. Incomplete mixity was used inter alia to speed up the ratification process on the side of the Union. The most prominent example is the Paris Agreement on Climate Change. The Union and all the Member States signed the Paris Agreement on 22 April 2016.[71] Pursuant to Article 21(1) Paris Agreement, it enters into force 'on the thirtieth day after the date on which at least 55 Parties to the Convention accounting in total for at least an estimated 55 per cent of the total global greenhouse gas emissions have deposited their instruments of ratification'. At the end of September 2016, approximately one month prior to the US elections, 61 countries had ratified the agreement, including the US and seven EU Member States; but they accounted for only 48% of global emissions. In order to 'spee[d] up the entry into force of the Paris Agreement',[72] the Council decided to deviate from its common practice to wait for the completion of the remaining Member States' internal ratification processes and concluded the agreement on behalf of the Union on 5 October 2016.[73] The ratification by the Union triggered the 55 per cent ratification threshold and the Paris Agreement entered into force on 4 November 2016 – four days prior to the US election.[74] Pursuant to Article 28 of the Paris Agreement, a party may only withdraw from the Paris Agreement three years after its entry into force. The newly elected President Trump was therefore unable to initiate US withdrawal from the Paris Agreement, despite signalling his wish to do so. By October 2017, all of the Member States had ratified the Paris Agreement also in their own right.

In other situations, incomplete mixity has not been a deliberate ratification technique but a consequence of a Member State's decision *not* to continue the ratification process of, or to withdraw from, a formerly (envisaged) complete mixed agreement. For example, all Member States were originally signatory parties to the 1994 Government

[69] Ibid, para 123, emphasis in original.

[70] Joined Cases C-626/15 and C-659/16, *AMP Antarctique*, EU:C:2018:925, para 133. See further the chapter by Merijn Chamon and Marise Cremona in this volume.

[71] See https://treaties.un.org/Pages/ViewDetails.aspx?src=TREATY&mtdsg_no=XXVII-7-d&chapter=27&clang=_en.

[72] Council of the European Union, press release, 'Climate change: Council speeds up process for EU ratification of Paris Agreement', 30.9.2016, 541/16.

[73] Council Decision (EU) 2016/1841 of 5 October 2016 ([2016], OJ L 282/1).

[74] United Nations, Reference: C.N.735.2016.TREATIES-XXVII.7.d, Depository Notification Paris Agreement, https://treaties.un.org/doc/Publication/CN/2016/CN.735.2016-Eng.pdf.

Procurement Agreement (GPA). In the end, however, the 1994 GPA was ratified by the (then) Community 'with regard to' its Member States. Some Member States nevertheless submitted individual ratification instruments on the same day as the (then) Community.[75] Technically, the 1994 GPA therefore qualified as an incomplete mixed agreement.[76] Another example is the Energy Charter Treaty (ECT), to which originally all the Member States and the EU were parties. In 2016, Italy however withdrew from the ECT, turning the ECT into an incomplete mixed agreement.[77]

In recent discussions, incomplete mixity has been suggested as a solution to the non-ratification of mixed agreements by individual Member States.[78] In its request for *Opinion 1/19*, the EP asked the Court of Justice to confirm the legality of that solution. The EP asked the Court of Justice inter alia if the conclusion of the Istanbul Convention by the Union is 'compatible with the Treaties in the absence of mutual agreement between all the Member States concerning their consent to be bound by that convention'.[79] The Istanbul Convention has been signed by the Union and all of the Member States.[80] Yet, some Member States, including in particular Bulgaria, whose highest court found the Istanbul Convention unconstitutional,[81] have since declared that they no longer wish to become contracting parties. Provided that the Council may decide by a QMV to conclude the agreement, incomplete mixity could provide a technique for the Union to become a party to the Istanbul Convention despite the opposition of individual Member States. The question which parts of the Convention would, in such a scenario, apply to the non-ratifying Member States would become particularly complex should the Court, as mentioned above,[82] find that the Istanbul Convention is a mandatory mixed agreement falling in part within the Union's (exclusive) competence and in in part within the exclusive competence of the Member States.[83] AG Hogan, in his opinion, held that the Council is obliged neither to await the common accord of the Member States nor to conclude a mixed agreement immediately after signing it.[84] The choice to opt for an incomplete mixed agreement is, in his view, fully at the discretion of the Council. The AG however noted that, in the case of the Istanbul Convention, incomplete mixity would raise problems under international law.[85] If the EU were to conclude

[75] WTO, *Status of WTO Legal Instruments* [2015] 124–25. See further esp R Kampf, '81. Verordnung (EG) Nr. 816/2006' in HG Krenzler, C Herrmann, and M Niestedt (eds), *EU-Außenwirtschafts- und Zollrecht*, Stand: Oktober 2019, 14. Erg.-Lfg. (Munich, C. H. Beck, 2019) para 31.

[76] The revised GPA was then concluded by the EU alone, irrespective of the individual ratification of the 1994 GPA by some Member States. See Council Decision (EU) 2014/115 of 2 December 2013 ([2014] OJ L 68/1).

[77] See www.energycharter.org/who-we-are/members-observers/countries/italy.

[78] See esp G van der Loo and RA Wessel, 'The non-ratification of mixed agreements: Legal Consequences and Solutions' (2017) 54 *CML Rev* 735.

[79] Request for Opinion 1/19 (n 34).

[80] See www.coe.int/en/web/conventions/full-list/-/conventions/treaty/210/signatures.

[81] See further V Radosveta, 'Bulgaria's Constitutional Troubles with the Istanbul Convention' (2018) *Verfassungsblog*, https://verfassungsblog.de/bulgarias-constitutional-troubles-with-the-istanbul-convention.

[82] See further section II.B.

[83] On the EU's treaty-making powers for, and problems with regard to, the ratification of the Istanbul Convention see esp. S Prechal, 'The European Union's Accession to the Istanbul Convention' in Lenaerts et al (n 50) 279.

[84] Opinion of Hogan AG in Opinion 1/19, Istanbul Convention, ECLI:EU:C:2021:198, para 223. For an analysis see M Chamon, 'Op-Ed: "AG Hogan's Opinion in Avis 1/19 regarding the Istanbul Convention"' (2021) *EU Law Live Analysis* https://eulawlive.com/op-ed-ag-hogans-opinion-in-avis-1-19-regarding-the-istanbul-convention-by-merijn-chamon/.

[85] Opinion of Hogan AG in Opinion 1/19, Istanbul Convention, ECLI:EU:C:2021:198, para 205 et seq.

the Convention without some of its Member States, it could be held liable, under international law, for actions of the non-participating Member States, even if the latter acted within the realm of their exclusive competence under EU law. While such problems may be solved by an EU declaration of competence functioning as a reservation, the Istanbul Convention does not permit reservations that could be used for that purpose.[86] Moreover, in contrast to other multilateral mixed agreements, the Istanbul Convention does not provide for a regional integration organisations (RIO) clause, requiring the EU to declare the scope of its competence in respect to matters governed by a specific agreement.[87] It remains to be seen whether the Court will address the legal specificities of the Istanbul Convention in the context of incomplete mixity and/or establish the legal limits of having to recourse to incomplete mixity.

C. Bilateral Mixed Agreements

Bilateral mixed agreements are concluded between the Union and the Member States, of the one part, and a single third party (eg Canada[88]) or a single group of third parties (eg the Andean states[89] or the EFTA states[90]), of the other part. Although they aim to establish contractual relations between two (groups of) parties, bilateral mixed agreements therefore have to be ratified by at least 29 parties in accordance with their respective national constitutional requirements.

Bilateral mixed agreements generally prescribe that all parties must complete their respective internal ratification requirements before they may enter into force.[91] Provided that all Member States are listed as contracting parties, the entry into force clause of bilateral mixed agreements hence precludes incomplete mixity *ab initio*. Bilateral mixed agreements may however become 'incomplete'.[92] That risk emerges in particular after the accession of new Member States to the Union. New Member States join the set of existing EU mixed agreements through so-called accession protocols.[93] If there is a gap in time between the date of accession and the entry into force of the accession

[86] Art 78 Istanbul Convention.

[87] Compare, for example, Art 44(1) second and third sentence of the UN Disability Convention (n 30): 'Such organizations shall declare, in their instruments of formal confirmation or accession, the extent of their competence in respect to matters governed by the present Convention. Subsequently, they shall inform the depositary of any substantial modification in the extent of their competence.'

[88] Comprehensive Economic and Trade Agreement (CETA) between Canada, of the one part, and the European Union and its Member States, of the other part [2017] OJ L 11/23.

[89] Trade Agreement between the European Union and its Member States, of the one part, and Colombia and Peru, of the other part [2012] OJ L 354/3; Protocol of Accession to the Trade Agreement between the European Union and its Member States, of the one part, and Colombia and Peru, of the other part, to take account of the accession of Ecuador [2016] OJ L 356/3.

[90] See eg Agreement on the European Economic Area [1994] OJ L 1/ 3. On the EEA's classification as a bilateral mixed agreement see esp. C Hillion, 'Brexit means BR(EEA)XIT: The UK Withdrawal from the EU and its Implications for the EEA' (2018) 55 *CML Rev* 135.

[91] eg Art 30.7(2) CETA.

[92] See further van der Loo and Wessel (n 78).

[93] These accession protocols are in themselves mixed agreements. Yet, the acts of accession provide for a simplified ratification procedure, empowering the Council to conclude the accession protocols on behalf of the Member States, which significantly reduces the gap in time between the new Member States' accession to the EU and the entry into force of the accession protocols. See further eg Czuczai (n 61) 240.

protocols, the EU's mixed agreements become temporarily 'incomplete'. Yet, the effects of incomplete mixity are, in that context, rarely tangible, as the acts of accession oblige new Member States to apply the provisions of EU mixed agreements 'as from the date of accession, and pending the entry into force of the necessary protocols'.[94]

Certain categories of bilateral agreements were usually concluded under the mixed procedure, including association agreements, cooperation agreements, and, until recently, free trade agreements (FTAs).[95] However, the Court found, in *Opinion 2/15*, that all aspects of contemporary FTAs fall within exclusive Union competences, except for investments other than direct investments (or portfolio investments) and investor-state-dispute settlement (ISDS).[96] In practice, a 'new architecture' involving a splitting of FTAs into 'EU-only' FTAs and 'mixed' investment protection agreements (IPAs) has emerged.[97] In this way, *Opinion 2/15* has therefore considerably narrowed the scope for mixity. Bilateral mixity will nevertheless remain relevant, especially for association agreements,[98] IPAs, and comprehensive trade and investment agreements, such as the Comprehensive Economic and Trade Agreement (CETA) with Canada.[99]

D. Multilateral Mixed Agreements

A majority of the Union's multilateral relations are governed by mixed agreements.[100] The continuing trend towards mixity for multilateral agreements is certainly facilitated by the Member States' strong political preference to remain visible sovereign actors on the international stage in general, and within international organisations in particular.[101] Historically, mixity also evolved because numerous multilateral agreements entered into force prior to the founding of the EEC in 1957, and/or originally did not allow for international organisations to become contracting parties. The EEC Member States were, for example, already parties to the 1947 General Agreement on Tariffs and Trade (GATT), and

[94] See eg Art 6(4) of the Act concerning the conditions of accession of the Republic of Bulgaria and Romania and the adjustments to the Treaties on which the European Union is founded ([2005] OJ L 157/203) or Art 6(3) of the Act concerning the conditions of accession of the Republic of Croatia and the adjustments to the Treaty on European Union, the Treaty on the Functioning of the European Union and the Treaty establishing the European Atomic Energy Community ([2012] OJ L 112).

[95] On the different categories of bilateral mixed agreements see esp. M Maresceau (n 6) 11–29.

[96] Opinion 2/15, *Free Trade Agreement between the EU and the Republic of Singapore*, EU:C:2017:376, operative part. See further M Cremona, 'Shaping the EU Trade Policy post-Lisbon: Opinion 2/15 of 16 May 2017'(2018) 14 *European Constitutional Law Review* 231.

[97] On the new architecture see G Kübek and I Van Damme, 'Facultative Mixity and the European Union's Trade and Investment Agreements' in Chamon and Govaere (n 4) 137, 158 et seq.

[98] That is not to say that all future association agreements will be mixed agreements. Mixity will generally be facultative. The Trade and Cooperation Agreement (TCA) between the EU and the UK, which has been legally based on Art 217 TFEU, has for instance been concluded as a (facultative) 'EU-only' agreement. On that agreement see G Kübek, CJ Tams and JP Terhechte (eds), *Handels- und Kooperationsvertrag EU/GB* (Baden-Baden, Nomos, forthcoming 2022 in both German and English).

[99] On the mixed character of CETA see further the chapter by Manon Damestoy and Nicolas Levrat in this volume.

[100] F Kaiser, *Gemischte Abkommen im Lichte bundesstaatlicher Erfahrungen* (Tübingen, Mohr Siebeck, 2009) 3.

[101] See also CD Ehlermann, 'Mixed Agreements: A List of Problems' in O'Keeffe and Schermers (n 6) 3–21, 6. On mixity in the context of international organisations see further the chapter by Julija Brsakoska and Elaine Fahey in this volume.

their prior contracting party status enabled both them and the European Communities to become original members of the World Trade Organization (WTO) in 1994.[102] The Court's decisions in *Daiichi Sankyo*[103] and *Conditional Access Convention*[104] highlighted that the WTO Agreements fall within the Union's exclusive competence post-Lisbon. Nevertheless, the Member States' independent status in the WTO is not merely nominal, as Brexit illustrates. Due to its independent contracting party status, the United Kingdom could remain a member of the WTO despite its decision to withdraw from the Union.[105] The same cannot be said about the UK's membership in bilateral mixed EU agreements post-Brexit, as will be further outlined in another contribution to this volume.[106]

The recourse to mixity for multilateral agreements is sometimes not only a legal requirement or legitimate policy choice under EU law, but predetermined by the multilateral agreement itself by means of 'a subordination clause'. Article 3 of Annex IX UNCLOS, for example, stipulates that the Union may only deposit its ratification instrument after the majority of its Member States have deposited theirs.[107] In other instances, mixity is *implied* in the decision-making framework of multilateral agreements. Many multilateral agreements specify that the EU may cast a number of votes equal to the number of Member States that are contracting parties, implying that the EU cannot exercise (full) voting rights without the Member States, and that the number of EU votes is highest if mixity is 'complete'.[108] In the multilateral context, mixity therefore remains 'here to stay'[109] – for political, legal, and practical reasons.

IV. Conclusion

We conclude with a small reminder of how one should treat the above typology (and, indeed, any typology of mixed agreements). Any user of a typology of mixed agreements should be aware of the purpose as well as the limitations of such an exercise of classification. At best, typologies of mixed agreements may serve as a shorthand for describing

[102] Art XI:1 WTO Agreement. On the EU's and the Member States' joint membership in the WTO see esp C Herrmann and T Streinz, 'Die EU als Mitglied der WTO' in A von Arnauld (ed) *Enzyklopädie Europarecht*, Band 10 (Baden-Baden, Nomos, 2014) § 11; and in the context of WTO dispute settlement J Heliskoski, 'Joint Competence of the European Community and its Member States and the Dispute Settlement Practice of the World Trade Organization' (1999) 2 *Cambridge Yearbook of European Legal Studies* 61.

[103] Case C-414/11, *Daiichi Sankyo*, EU:C:2013:520. As explained above, one might therefore question whether the Agreement establishing the WTO has become a false mixed agreement (section II.D).

[104] Case C-137/12, *Commission v Council*, EU:C:2013:675.

[105] On the problems that Brexit nevertheless creates for the UK's WTO membership see esp. C Herrmann, 'Brexit and the WTO: challenges and the solutions for the United Kingdom (and the European Union)' in (2017) *ECB Legal Conference Volume* 165; and F Baetens, "No deal is better than a bad deal'? The fallacy of the WTO fall-back option as a post-Brexit safety net' (2018) 55 *CML Rev* 133.

[106] See the contribution by Habib Touré and Christine Kaddous to this Volume.

[107] See also n 22.

[108] See eg Art IX:1 WTO Agreement or Art 9(2) Conditional Access Convention. Indeed, for this reasons, some Member States did not denounce the Conditional Access Convention after Case C-137/12, *Commission v Council*, EU:C:2013:675, turning it into a false mixed agreement (see above section II.D.).

[109] A Rosas, 'The Future of Mixity' in Hillion and Koutrakos (n 1) 376.

the complex reality of mixed agreements through classifying such agreements into certain more general groups or categories and, by so doing, help one to understand the phenomenon of mixity. No more, no less. For instance, a typology may serve as illustrating the fundamental significance of the distinction between the existence and nature of the Union's external competence for the practice of concluding and applying mixed agreements and, as a corollary, the distinction between mandatory and facultative mixed agreements. Likewise, the categories of bilateral and multilateral mixed agreements each have a set of distinct characteristics of their own that may usefully be illustrated by means of typology. The same applies to the phenomenon of incomplete mixed agreements which involves a specific set of legal issues that do not arise with complete mixed agreements. Therefore, a typology may shed light on the complex and varying landscape of mixity for the purpose of either a further study or gaining a more general understanding of the practice of mixed agreements. In that sense, a chapter on a typology of mixed agreements would seem as an appropriate opener for a collection of more specific studies on the topic.

In our submission, however, one would be ill-advised to rely on a typology for the purpose of ascertaining what the state of the law is in respect of specific legal problems arising in the context of mixed agreements. To us, certain categories of mixed agreements established within a given typology have no normative content of their own. In that regard, the sources of law are what they are: the Treaties, legislation, including international agreements, and the case law of the Court. Typologies may only serve as a tool of describing those sources and their implications in a more user-friendly manner. Whether they succeed in serving this purpose depends solely on the merits of a given typology in the eyes of both scholars and practitioners. This chapter has sought to provide one such tool of description. In principle, there may be an infinite number of others, and the authority of each of them will be decided on how well or badly they are conceived of as serving the task describing the legal complexities of mixity.

2

The Continuing Contestation of *ERTA*

*Conferral, Effectiveness and the Member States' Participation in Mixed Agreements**

MIRKA KUISMA AND JORIS LARIK

I. Introduction

On 31 March 1971, the Court of Justice of the European Union (CJEU) dismissed the European Commission's action for annulment in a case concerning the European Road Transport Agreement (ERTA).[1] It is easy to forget sometimes that the Council actually won the *ERTA* case due to technical and timing issues, given the decades of legal headaches it seems to have caused the Member States. *ERTA* was their wake-up call to the reality that balancing the three different hats of 'Masters of the Treaties', co-legislator alongside the European Parliament, and international legal subjects all at the same time can severely curtail their freedom of action on the international scene.

The *ERTA* case and the ensuing doctrine named after it remain central to determining the scope and nature of the Union's international treaty-making powers and, correspondingly, the ability of the Member States to conclude international agreements in their own name, including at times alongside the Union ('mixed agreements'). The *ERTA* doctrine ushered in the concept of 'supervening exclusivity'[2] of the Union's external competences. After having emerged in the *ERTA* ruling and subsequently – more or less – codified in Article 3(2) TFEU, the *ERTA* doctrine entails that the Union shall have an exclusive competence to conclude an international agreement where its conclusion may affect common rules or alter their scope. Where this is the case, Member States are pre-empted from exercising their own treaty-making powers on the

* This chapter draws on research from Mirka Kuisma's doctoral thesis entitled 'Confronting Realities with the Legal Rule: On Why and How the European Court of Justice Changes Its Mind', defended at the University of Turku on 7 May 2021.

[1] Case 22/70, *Commission v Council (ERTA)*, EU:C:1971:32.

[2] Supervening exclusivity refers to exclusivity of competence that is not directly based on a Treaty provision (the latter being known as a priori exclusivity) but that emerges as a result of the Union's internal use of its powers. The term originates with Alan Dashwood, 'Mixity in the Era of the Treaty of Lisbon' in Christophe Hillion and Panos Koutrakos (eds), *Mixed Agreements Revisited: The EU and its Member States in the World* (Oxford, Hart Publishing, 2010) 360.

international stage, which is known as the '*ERTA* effect'. Since its inception, the doctrine has been at the heart of recurring competence disputes between the Commission and the Council and/or Member State governments, each seeking to steer the Court of Justice towards their own preferred interpretation.

This chapter analyses the Member States' disagreement with the Court's approach by means of charting their calls for change of the *ERTA* doctrine in pre- and post-Lisbon case law. Whilst the Council and the Member States have accepted the overall premises of the *ERTA* doctrine, they have tended to differ with the Court as to how it should be applied in practice. The crux of their opposition is that *ERTA*-based exclusivity is seen as limiting Member State participation in external action in a manner that is inconsistent with the principle of conferral. The attempt to codify the *ERTA* doctrine with the Lisbon Treaty, understood by some as an attempt to prune the *ERTA* doctrine, added a new spin to the argument. Yet, calls for change have consistently been rejected by the Court, implying a deeper divide in how the Member States and the Court perceive the implications of the principle of conferral. This creates a dissonance between the Member States' self-perceived prerogative to participate in the conclusion of international agreements and the participation rights actually protected by the Court.

As this chapter argues, the Court is right to rebuff the Member States' attempts to roll back the *ERTA* effect through litigation – not despite the principle of conferral, but partly because of it. Exclusivity is to be understood as premised on both the respect of the principle of conferral and the effectiveness of the Union's action through legislation and international action: *ERTA* exclusivity can only arise as a result of the exercise of powers conferred upon the Union, specifically through legislative procedures, in which the Member States play a crucial part through the Council. At the same time, the *ERTA* doctrine in itself serves as a mechanism for establishing that the Union enjoys competence, resting on the rationale of protecting the integrity of the rules created through the Union's co-legislators' activity. Where the protection of rules thus created is necessary, the width of *ERTA* exclusivity need not fully coincide with the scope of the common rules. This consequently limits the Member States' ability to demand joint participation in international agreement concluded by the EU. In particular, it means that when some aspects of an agreement fall within the scope of the Member States' retained powers, this does not prevent them from being subsumed under (exclusive) Union competence.

To elaborate on this argument, the chapter starts with a brief exploration of the premises of the *ERTA* doctrine (section II). Subsequently, it discusses pre- and post-Lisbon calls for change (sections III and IV), following which the discrepancy between how the Member States and the Court understand the import of the principle of conferral for *ERTA*-based exclusivity is analysed (section V). The conclusion highlights the importance of the findings for Member State (non-)participation in international agreements (section VI).

II. A Reading of *ERTA* Premised on the Protection of the Union's Policy-Setting Space

It is appropriate to begin by recalling the basic tenets of the *ERTA* doctrine and formulating the interpretation of the doctrine upon which the present account is built. It is posited that the key rationale of *ERTA*-based exclusivity is, and has been since its inception, the *protection of the integrity of the Union's internal policy-setting space*. As the Court noted in *ERTA*:

> … each time the Community [now the Union], with a view to implementing a common policy envisaged by the Treaty, adopts provisions laying down common rules, whatever form these may take, the Member States no longer have the right, acting individually or even collectively, to undertake obligations with third countries which affect those rules.[3]

As explained later in the judgment, any 'concurrent powers on the part of the Member States' for concluding international agreements in these situations is excluded 'since any steps taken outside the framework of the Community institutions would be incompatible with the unity of the common market and the uniform application of Community law'.[4]

The *ERTA* test, as clarified also by subsequent case law, contains three elements which jointly determine whether the Union holds exclusive external competence: (1) there needs to be a concrete use of an internal competence,[5] (2) bringing about a (foreseen[6]) body or system of rules,[7] (3) and a coincidence in terms of substance or objectives between these rules and an envisaged international commitment, which one or several Member States intend to conclude, which has the potential of jeopardising the autonomous functioning of the Union rules.[8] Once a sufficient overlap has been identified, the test of whether the international commitment affects Union action is relatively easy to satisfy.[9] The case law appears to have constructed a strong, yet not automatic,[10] assumption that this is the case as soon as a parallelism can be established between a system of Union rules and an international obligation. *ERTA*-based exclusivity seeks to remove obstacles to 'the correct functioning and, possibly, the future development of EU law'.[11] What is thus key in the application of the *ERTA* test is whether '*the discretion enjoyed by the Union legislature is reduced* where commitments are entered into vis-à-vis third countries'.[12]

[3] *ERTA*, para 17.

[4] *ERTA*, para 31.

[5] Opinion 1/94, *WTO Agreements*, EU:C:1994:384, para 77; Opinion 2/91, *ILO Convention*, EU:C:1993:106, para 11.

[6] Opinion 2/91, para 25; Opinion 1/03, *Lugano Convention*, EU:C:2006:81, para 126; Case C-66/13, *Green Network*, EU:C:2014:2399, paras 61–64. See further the chapter by Marja-Liisa Öberg and Marcus Klamert in this volume.

[7] On the systemic approach, see eg Opinion 1/03, para 151; Case C-114/12, *Commission v Council (Neighbouring Rights)*, EU:C:2014:2151, para 78–80; Opinion 1/13, *Hague Convention*, EU:C:2014:2303, para 78; *Green Network*, para 42; Opinion 2/15, *EUSFTA*, EU:C:2017:376, para 182.

[8] For examples of coincidences, interlinkages, contradictions, or functional restrictions which have triggered the *ERTA* effect, see *Opinion 1/03*, para 151; Case C-467/98, *Commission v Denmark (Open Skies)*, EU:C:2002:625, para 101; *Neighbouring Rights*, para 84; *Opinion 1/13*, para 85–89; *Opinion 2/15*, paras 188–92; Opinion 3/15, *Marrakesh Treaty*, EU:C:2017:114, paras 127–28.

[9] Allan Rosas, 'EU External Relations: Exclusive Competence Revisited' (2015) 38 *Fordham Int'l LJ* 1073, 1091.

[10] See Opinion 2/91, *ILO Convention*, para 21; and Case C-316/91, *Parliament v Council (Lomé Convention)*, EU:C:1994:76.

[11] Opinion of AG Wahl in *Opinion 3/15*, EU:C:2016:657, paras 125–35.

[12] Opinion of AG Kokott in Case C-137/12, *Commission v Council (Conditional access services)*, EU:C:2013:441, para 101 (emphasis added).

Seen in this light, the Court's take on *ERTA* centres on the protection of the Union's internal policy-setting space. Drawing upon the reflections of Robert Post on the *ERTA* doctrine,[13] Marise Cremona has argued that the Court's focus within external relations law more broadly is in 'establishing and protecting an institutional space within which policy may be formed, in which the different actors understand and work within their respective roles'.[14] This goal can be recognised at the heart of the *ERTA* doctrine: that of protecting the effectiveness of the Union's internal policy-setting within the constitutional bounds formed by the Union's powers and objectives.[15]

This conceptual foundation has consequences for how the development of the *ERTA* doctrine should be evaluated. The Union's international treaty-making is often portrayed as showcasing a dichotomy of conflicting interests: the Member States' interest in acting in their own name, including alongside the Union in mixed agreements, and the Commission's wish for unity in the external representation of the EU and effectiveness of EU external action that is unencumbered by concurrent Member State activity.[16]

As a result, a commonplace approach to construing the development of the *ERTA* doctrine is to analyse which camp is 'winning' the competence battle, the implication being that the Court is 'taking sides' between the Commission and the Member States or the Council,[17] or alternates between presumptions of exclusivity or shared competence.[18] If we rather perceive *ERTA* as stemming from the need to protect the integrity of the Union legislator's work, in which the Member States participate through the Council, the aims of ensuring that 'the institutions act within their powers' and that 'the Member States do not obstruct the formation and implementation of EU policy' must be accepted as two sides of the same coin.[19]

Rather than evidencing the Court's 'manoeuvring between principle and pragmatism' in deciding external powers disputes,[20] its findings should be seen to result from reconciling the separate interests inherent in the *ERTA* doctrine in accordance with the circumstances of each case: on the one hand, observance of the principle of conferral, and, on the other, furthering Union objectives, including the protection of its internal rules and the effectiveness of its external action.[21] Pre-Lisbon, the distinction between

[13] Robert Post, 'Constructing the European Polity: *ERTA* and the *Open Skies* Judgments' in Miguel Maduro and Loïc Azoulai (eds), *The Past and Future of EU Law: The Classics of EU Law Revisited On the 50th Anniversary of the Rome Treaty* (Oxford, Hart Publishing, 2010) 234.

[14] Marise Cremona, 'A Reticent Court? Policy Objectives and the Court of Justice' in Marise Cremona and Anne Thies (eds), *The European Court of Justice and External Relations Law: Constitutional Challenges* (Oxford, Hart Publishing, 2013) 30.

[15] See Marise Cremona, 'Internal Differentiation and External Unity' in Fabian Amtenbrink et al (eds), *The Internal Market and the Future of European Integration: Essays in Honour of Laurence W. Gormley* (Cambridge, Cambridge University Press, 2019) 607.

[16] Eg Joni Heliskoski, *Mixed Agreements As a Technique for Organizing the International Relations of the European Community and its Member States* (The Hague, Kluwer Law International, 2001) 10.

[17] See eg 'Introduction' in Piet Eeckhout and Manuel Lopez-Escudero (eds), *The European Union's External Action in Times of Crisis* (Oxford, Hart Publishing, 2016) 5.

[18] See eg Thomas Verellen, 'The ERTA Doctrine in the Post-Lisbon Era: Note under Judgment in Commission v Council (C-114/12) and Opinion 1/13' (2015) 21 *Columbia Journal of European Law* 383, 408.

[19] Cremona (n 14) 29–30.

[20] Verellen (n 18) 384. The dichotomy originates in Takis Tridimas and Piet Eeckhout, 'The External Competence of the Community and the Case-Law of the Court of Justice: Principle versus Pragmatism' (1994) 14 *Yearbook of European Law* 143.

[21] This is not to say, however, that the case law did not bear signs of pragmatism; see section V below.

competences and objectives remained somewhat blurred, with the TEC stating that the 'Community shall act within the limits of the powers conferred upon it by this Treaty *and* of the objectives assigned to it therein.'[22] Post-Lisbon, the TEU makes clear that these are two separate norm categories: 'the Union shall act only within the limits of the competences conferred upon it by the Member States in the Treaties *to attain* the objectives set out therein.'[23]

III. Member State Challenges in Pre-Lisbon *ERTA* Litigation

The following paragraphs chart the reception of the *ERTA* doctrine by the Council and Member State governments in the periods before and after the entry into force of the Lisbon Treaty in 2009. The analysis shows a disagreement between the Court and the Member States over the question of whether the external protection of the internal policy-making space must strictly correlate with the limits of the Union's conferred powers.

In pre-Lisbon case law, despite accepting supervening exclusivity as a concept, the Council and Member State governments consistently suggested more lenient versions of the *ERTA* doctrine.[24] Their views were underpinned by a two-fold claim: first, that independent or participatory Member State external activity is not harmful to the Union's policy aims; and second, that it is even constitutionally mandated by the principle of conferral.

The view that Member State participation is not harmful to the effective pursuit of the Union's objectives should be observed in light of the competing claims occasionally presented by the Commission, maintaining that the Member States' presence is bound to impair the *effectiveness* of internal and/or external Union action.[25] The Member States' view is illustrated by the arguments presented by some governments in the *Open Skies* cases. In defence of their independent conclusion of air traffic agreements with the United States, the Member State governments referred to the inclusion in the agreements of clauses that sought to remove any discrepancy between the agreement and secondary Union legislation on air traffic.[26] The Member States thus effectively suggested that common rules would not be 'affected' unless an actual conflict arose between the international commitment and Union rules. This view alone betrays a difference of perception as regards the level of autonomy necessary for the Union's interests to be protected.

[22] Treaty establishing the European Community (Consolidated version 2006) [2006] OJ C321E/3, Art 5(1) (emphasis added).

[23] Art 5(2) TEU (emphasis added). See further Joris Larik, 'From speciality to a constitutional sense of purpose: On the changing role of the objectives of the European Union' (2014) 63 *International & Comparative Law Quarterly* 935.

[24] Allan Rosas, 'The European Union and Mixed Agreements' in Alan Dashwood and Christophe Hillion (eds), *The General Law of E.C. External Relations* (London, Sweet & Maxwell, 2000) 201–202.

[25] See eg Opinion 1/94, *WTO Agreements*, paras 78 and 106; Opinion 1/08, *Modification of GATS Schedules*, EU:C:2009:739, para 127.

[26] *Open Skies Denmark*, para 73.

A more pressing disagreement, however, has concerned the constitutional mandate of Member State participation in international agreements. Building upon a strict interpretation of the principle of conferral, the Council and Member State governments have repeatedly argued that Member State participation in Union agreements should not be foreclosed lightly. The disagreement has centred around the 'covered to a large extent' concept stemming from *Opinion 2/91 (ILO Convention)*. According to this notion, a risk of common rules being affected, and thus the triggering of supervening exclusive Union competence, does not require total harmonisation but could exist also where a regulatory field is covered 'to a large extent'.[27]

The Member States' rejection of the 'covered to a large extent' part of the *ERTA* doctrine has been profound. In its crudest form, it meant that this element simply was omitted in the Member State governments' renditions of the *ERTA* test. The approach has been supported by close attachment to the Court's language in *Opinion 1/94 (WTO Agreements)*, where the Court could be understood to have laid down a three-part enumeration of circumstances where *ERTA*-based exclusivity could be triggered.[28] In particular, the reference in *Opinion 1/94* to 'complete harmonisation' as a situation where common rules can be affected has been (mistakenly) grasped by the Member State governments as an implicit reversal of the 'covered to a large extent' doctrine.[29] Thus, the Member States did not accept exclusivity that does not abide by the strict limits of the prior use of internal powers as part of the *ERTA* case law.

Even express calls for reconsideration of the 'covered to a large extent' doctrine were made in the pre-Lisbon period by the Member States. In *Opinion 1/03 (Lugano Convention)*, two approaches to the level of scrutiny required by the *ERTA* test were on offer. On the one hand, the foreseen Lugano Convention on jurisdiction and the recognition and enforcement of judgments in civil and commercial matters could either be examined in minute detail, as suggested by the Council and a host of Member State governments, in order to establish whether the substance of the individual provisions of the Convention was encompassed by common rules. On the other, a more systemic approach could be adopted, whereby the evaluation would observe the Union rules as a body of rules whose overall functionality was to be safeguarded.[30]

In this context, the government of the United Kingdom (which was then still an EU Member State) directly 'invited the Court to reconsider' the 'covered to a large extent' doctrine with reference to 'the general principles of the Treaty governing the limits of Community competences and the internal consistency of the case law on the effect of an international agreement within the meaning of the ERTA judgment.'[31] The reference to the limits of Union competences is to be understood as pertaining to a strict understanding of the principle of conferral and its repercussions for the vertical division of powers: according to the UK government, the 'covered to a large extent' doctrine

[27] *Opinion 2/91*, para 25.

[28] *Opinion 1/94*, paras 95–96. This reading, however, is mistaken as the Court's language should be read with reference to the specific claims made by the Commission in the case.

[29] See eg *Open Skies Denmark*, para 72; Case C-468/98, *Commission v Sweden (Open Skies)*, EU:C:2002:626, paras 68–69.

[30] *Opinion 1/03*, paras 59–63.

[31] *Opinion 1/03*, para 46.

resulted in 'unacceptable' imprecision in the conferral of powers to the Union.[32] The alleged problems relating to the 'internal consistency of the case law' in turn arise from the above-noted perception of *Opinion 1/94* as having reformed the criteria of the *ERTA* doctrine under which common rules can be considered as being affected.[33] Also here, the justifiability of *ERTA*-based exclusivity was not, as such, contested; instead, the resistance was due to a conviction that the triggering of the *ERTA* effect even in situations of partial harmonisation *à la Opinion 2/91* stood in conflict with the principle of conferral and the *ERTA* doctrine itself.

The Court disagreed with the Member State governments' views both with regard to the harmlessness and constitutional mandate of Member State participation. The no-discrepancy defence in *Open Skies* was rejected by the Court on the grounds that the mere existence of international commitments could affect common EU rules.[34] Moreover, the analysis was not only to include the rules as they stood at that moment in time, but also 'their foreseeable future development'.[35]

As for the disagreement over the implications of the principle of conferral, in *Opinion 1/03* the Court confirmed that full identity between the scopes of the international agreement and common rules was not required for *ERTA*-based exclusivity to be triggered. It emphasised that the decisive test was whether Member State external action jeopardised the attainment of the Union's objectives; this was not a question the answer to which was determined by the *scope* of the Union's prior use of its power to adopt common rules, but rather by the 'nature and content' of, and the 'proper functioning of the system' established by those rules.[36] This revealed a marked difference to the Member States' view according to which the limit of exclusivity should lie where internal action has produced actual Union rules.

IV. Member State Challenges in Post-Lisbon *ERTA* Litigation

The Council's and Member State governments' disagreement with the Court's understanding of the *ERTA* doctrine was carried over to the post-Lisbon period in largely unaltered form. With the entry into force of the Lisbon Treaty in late 2009, the EU Treaties now contain a 'competence catalogue' (Articles 3–6 TFEU) as well as a number of provisions on the distinctions between different types of competences. To some extent, this was also an attempt to codify the Court's existing case law, including as regards *ERTA*. According to Article 3(2) TFEU, which follows an enumeration of the EU's explicit exclusive competences, the 'Union shall also have exclusive competence for the conclusion of an international agreement … in so far as its conclusion may affect

[32] *Opinion 1/03*, para 47.

[33] *Opinion 1/03*, para 48.

[34] *Open Skies Denmark*, paras 101 and 105; confirmed in *Opinion 1/03*, para 129. But note also Loïc Grard, 'Les accords ciel ouvert: Vers un ordre juridique aérien international "postbermudien". Bientôt un ordre juridique "post-libéral"' (2004) 54 *Revue française de droit aérien et spatial* 267, 272, who remarks that the Commission had failed to convince the Court to hand down an even more sweeping judgment.

[35] *Opinion 1/03*, para 74. See further the chapter by Marja-Liisa Öberg and Marcus Klamert in this volume.

[36] *Opinion 1/03*, paras 124–28.

common rules or alter their scope'. Moreover, Article 216(1) TFEU states that the 'Union may conclude an agreement with one or more third countries or international organisations where … the conclusion of an agreement … is likely to affect common rules or alter their scope.' These two provisions (attempt to) 'codify in two sentences fundamental elements of the case law on (external) competences, dating back from dozens of cases between the *ERTA* case (1971) until the *Open Skies* judgments (2002).'[37]

In Article 2(2) TFEU on shared competences, moreover, it is noted that the 'Member States shall exercise their competence to the extent that the Union has not exercised its competence.' How these different provisions relate to each other has been a major source of debate. For the Member States and Council in particular, it has been an opportunity for trying to rein in the *ERTA* doctrine. After all, it was them in their capacity as Masters of the Treaties who brought about these amendments.

On the one hand, some Member State governments have continued to build on an expansive reading of *Opinion 1/94*, portraying the 'covered to a large extent' doctrine as inconsistent with the *ERTA* doctrine. This is exemplified by the competence dispute between the Commission and the Council culminating in *Opinion 3/15 (Marrakesh Treaty on access to published works)*,[38] where numerous Member State governments argued that the 'covered to a large extent' doctrine stood in conflict with the premise that exclusivity was to be strictly limited to the occasions where the Union had adopted internal legislation.[39]

On the other hand, a new line of argumentation emerged in post-Lisbon *ERTA* litigation which drew from the alleged will of the 'Masters of the Treaties' when formulating the system of Union competences in the EU Treaties as amended by the Lisbon Treaty. According to members of the External Relations Team of the Council Legal Service, the Council has perceived the added references to the principle of conferral in the Treaties to produce a normative requirement for a stricter delimitation of the Union's competences.[40] In its view, the attempted codification of the *ERTA* doctrine in Article 3(2) TFEU should be read in light with the new emphasis on the principle of conferral in Article 4(1) TEU as well as Articles 2(2), 4(3) and 4(4) TFEU. This would mean that the Court's pre-Lisbon case law should be re-evaluated in the post-Lisbon context.[41] Thus, in the first wave of post-Lisbon *ERTA* litigation, the Council and some Member State governments sought to challenge the 'covered to a large extent' doctrine by way of relying on a joint reading of Articles 2(2) and 3(2) TFEU.

[37] Andrea Ott, 'EU External Competence' in Ramses A Wessel and Joris Larik (eds), *EU External Relations Law: Text, Cases and Materials*, 2nd edn (Oxford, Hart Publishing, 2020) 64; also Jean-Paul Jacqué, 'Les Changements Apportés par le Traité de Lisbonne' (2011) 21 *Swiss Review of International and European Law* 29, 69.

[38] This was argued by the governments of CZ, FI, FR, DE, RO, SK and SL in the pre-litigation stage: see '"I/A" Item Note from the General Secretariat of the Council to COREPER on the Council Decision on the signing, on behalf of the European Union, of the Marrakesh Treaty to Facilitate Access to Published Works for Persons who are Blind, Visually Impaired, or otherwise Print Disabled', 8305/14 ADD 1, 31.3.2014; for the argumentation of the governments of FR, HU and RO before the Court, see *Opinion 3/15*, EU:C:2017:114, para 54.

[39] For analogous claims in the context of Art 216(1) TFEU, see even Opinion of AG Saugmandsgaard Øe in Case C-687/15, *Commission v Council (CMR-15)*, EU:C:2017:645, para 49.

[40] Ricardo Gosalbo-Bono and Frederik Naert, 'The Reluctant (Lisbon) Treaty and Its Implementation in the Practice of the Council' in Piet Eeckhout and Manuel Lopez-Escudero (eds), *The European Union's External Action in Times of Crisis* (Oxford, Hart Publishing, 2016) 17–18.

[41] Ibid, 22–23.

The joint reading of the two Articles appears to have first emerged in the early comments on the Draft Constitutional Treaty by legal academia.[42] Prominent commentators of EU external relations law saw the codification of *ERTA*-based exclusivity in Article 3(2) TFEU at odds with the pre-emption rule of Article 2(2) TFEU. Whereas the pre-emption arising from the Union's use of its shared competence under Article 2(2) TFEU is limited to the actual scope of Union action, the pre-emptive effect associated with the *ERTA* doctrine extends over larger areas. This is, in particular, due to the 'covered to a large extent' doctrine: where a field was covered 'to a large extent', Member State action could be barred even with respect to aspects as of yet unregulated by the Union. This was seen to create incoherence in the system of competences laid down in the Treaties. The question was thus raised whether, on a systemic reading, the codification of *ERTA* in Article 3(2) TFEU had excluded the 'covered to a large extent' doctrine.[43]

This line of argumentation was seized upon by the Council and some Member State governments[44] in *Neighbouring Rights*,[45] *Conditional Access Services*,[46] and *Opinion 1/13 (Hague Convention)*,[47] delivered in strong terms likely 'meant to enforce compliance by the ECJ with the Member States' interpretation of the Treaties'.[48] The claim was, essentially, that the way in which the rule of pre-emption was laid down in the context of Article 2(2) TFEU on the use of shared competences had repercussions even for how pre-emption could take place in the context of Article 3(2) TFEU. The new Article 3(2) TFEU should be read in conjunction with Article 2(2) TFEU and Protocol No 25 on the exercise of shared competence annexed to the Treaties, which were seen to delimit the scope of pre-emption to the exact material breadth of the common rules adopted. The Treaty provisions on pre-emption in the context of shared competence were thus relied upon as a proxy for invoking a strict reading of the principle of conferred powers. As a result, it was considered by the Council that the purpose of the language of Article 3(2) TFEU was to exclude the 'covered to a large extent' doctrine.[49]

[42] Marise Cremona, 'Defining Competence in EU External Relations: Lessons from the Treaty Reform Process' in Alan Dashwood and Marc Maresceau (eds), *Law and Practice of EU External Relations: Salient Features of a Changing Landscape* (Cambridge, Cambridge University Press, 2008) 61; and Dashwood (n 2) 361–62.

[43] Marise Cremona, 'EU External Relations Law: Unity and Conferral of Powers' in Loïc Azoulai (ed), *The Question of Competence in the European Union* (Oxford, Oxford University Press, 2014) 72–73.

[44] Notably the CZ, DE, NL, PL and the UK governments.

[45] *Neighbouring Rights*, para 51–52.

[46] Opinion of AG Kokott in *Conditional access services*, para 111.

[47] *Opinion 1/13*, para 63. It emerges from para 71 of the View of AG Jääskinen in the case, EU:C:2014:2292, that the claim has been advanced at least by the DE, EE, LV, AU, SE and UK governments.

[48] Inge Govaere, '"Setting the International Scene": EU External Competence and Procedures Post-Lisbon Revisited in the Light of ECJ Opinion 1/13' (2015) 52 *CMLRev* 1277, 1292.

[49] In the context of *Opinion 1/13*, the Council made the following remarks in its written observations: 'Le texte de la troisième alternative de l'article 3, paragraphe 2, TFUE est inspiré par la jurisprudence de la Cour de Justice, cet article ayant codifié et précisé la jurisprudence "AETR". Cette troisième alternative doit être lue avec l'article 2, paragraphe 2, TFUE et le protocole (n° 25) … comme signifiant que la compétence exclusive de l'Union doit être limitée aux situations où la conclusion d'un accord international est susceptible d'aboutir à une affectation ou à une altération de la portée des règles existantes de l'Union, pour ce qui concerne les éléments régis par les règles en question. Ces dispositions reflètent le choix de ne pas inclure expressément dans le TFUE le critère jurisprudentiel du "*domaine déjà couvert en grande partie*" par des règles de l'Union' (citations omitted). Observations écrites présentées par le Conseil de l'Union européenne dans l'affaire A-1/13, 16.9.2013, SGS13/09860, para 21.

Both strategies for challenging the *ERTA* doctrine have been rejected by the Court in its post-Lisbon case law.[50] As noted, the present account has construed the pre-Lisbon *ERTA* doctrine as building upon the rationale of protecting the Union legislator's policy-setting space. The triggering of *ERTA*-based exclusivity is thus understood as premised on both the respect for the principle of conferral and the effectiveness of the Union's action: exclusive external competence could only arise as a result of the Union legislator's activity, but where the protection of the autonomy of the rules thus created so necessitates, its width need not fully coincide with the scope of the common rules. A similar philosophy appears to guide the Court in its post-Lisbon case law: in fact, it appears to have carried over its pre-Lisbon approach to the post-Lisbon setting in its entirety.[51]

As before, the Court has rejected the arguments advanced by some Member State governments challenging the tenability of the 'covered to a large extent' doctrine by summarily remarking that complete harmonisation is only one of the situations in which *ERTA*-based exclusivity may arise.[52] Drawing on what emerges from the Treaty text and the *travaux préparatoires*, the Court has also rejected the claim pertaining to the intent of the Treaty drafters to abolish the 'covered to a large extent' doctrine.[53] There is indeed little support for the alleged codification intent in the preparatory materials of the Convention on the Future of Europe and later on the Lisbon Treaty. In fact, the Council and the supporting Member State governments have failed to produce any evidence to that effect before the Court.[54]

According to the Court, its findings are not affected by the arguments drawn from the alleged relation between Articles 2(2) and 3(2) TFEU, which the Court considered to be erroneous on the grounds of a purely textual-systemic review.[55] This reading is to be deemed the correct one. As emphasised by Fernando Castillo de la Torre, the different roles played by Articles 2(2) and 3(2) TFEU render the reading suggested by some Member States untenable as Article 2(2) TFEU 'does not define competences, but explains the consequence of the exercise of *one type of competence*', ie the shared competence; Article 3(2) TFEU, for its part, 'creates a specific and independent source of competence for the EU'.[56] It would go against the apparent logic of separating the

[50] At the time of writing, the Court has delivered eight rulings in the post-Lisbon period which have in some way touched upon the *ERTA* principle: *Neighbouring Rights*; Case C-370/12, *Pringle*, EU:C:2012:756; *Opinion 1/13*; *Green Network*; Case C-600/14, *Germany v Council (Amendment of the COTIF Convention)*, EU:C:2017:935; *Opinion 3/15*; *Opinion 2/15*; and Joined Cases C-626/15 and C-659/16, *Commission v Council (AMP Antarctic)*, EU:C:2018:925.

[51] This understanding is also reflected in commentary from within the Court: see Rosas (n 9). For contrary views alleging an 'eagerness' to find exclusivity in post-Lisbon case law, see eg Merijn Chamon, 'Implied Exclusive Powers in the ECJ's Post-Lisbon Jurisprudence: The Continued Development of the *ERTA* Doctrine', 55 *CMLRev* 1101 (2018), 1133*ff*, and Joni Heliskoski, 'The Exercise of Non-Exclusive Competence of the EU and the Conclusion of International Agreements' in Koen Lenaerts et al (eds), *An Ever-Changing Union: Perspectives on the Future of EU Law in Honour of Allan Rosas* (Oxford, Hart Publishing, 2019) 302–303.

[52] *Opinion 3/15*, paras 105–108 and 115–18.

[53] *Neighbouring Rights*, paras 66–67, 70.

[54] Opinion of AG Kokott in *Conditional Access Services*, para 111; View of AG Jääskinen in *Opinion 1/13*, para 70.

[55] *Neighbouring Rights*, paras 72–73; and *Opinion 1/13*, para 73.

[56] Fernando Castillo de la Torre, 'The Court of Justice and External Competences After Lisbon: Some Reflections on the Latest Case Law' in Piet Eeckhout and Manuel Lopez-Escudero (eds), *The European Union's External Action in Times of Crisis* (Oxford, Hart Publishing, 2016) 158.

different competence types in their own Articles to extend the effect of Article 2(2) TFEU beyond shared competence to the realm of exclusive competence.[57] Lacking proof of a codifying intent or any factor in the Treaty text imposing upon it a reconsideration of the 'covered to a large extent' doctrine,[58] the Court has remained free to 'shrug its shoulders and proceed with further developing the ERTA doctrine'.[59]

V. The Lingering Dissonance: Can the Principle of Conferral Rein in Supervening Exclusivity?

The recurrent theme of Council and Member State calls for changing the *ERTA* doctrine is clear: it is the refusal to accept that the protection of the Union's internal policy-making space could justify pre-emption of Member State action in fields larger than those touched by pre-existing common rules. According to this view, all competence enjoyed by the Union ought to be based on a strict notion of conferral, understood as a sector-based or *spatial* assignment of fields of governance (which is well captured in the German rendition of the principle of conferral: *Prinzip der begrenzten Einzelermächtigung*) which, as a result, also necessitates that the preclusion of Member State action be similarly spatially defined.

The approach of the Court, in contrast, equally acknowledges the importance of the principle of conferral, but is more nuanced with regard to the manners in which non-explicit powers may be established. Ever since the judicial 'discovery' of the Union's implied external competences, the Court's understanding of external competence has been *purposive*: it has drawn an external capability to act from a teleological reading of the Treaties, initially linked to the development of the internal market. The preclusion of Member State action associated with exclusive external competence has, likewise, been understood in such purposive terms. In the case of *ERTA*, the limits of the Union's exclusive competence are drawn with reference to what is necessary for the protection of what has already been achieved by the Union. *ERTA*-based exclusive competence therefore exemplifies a 'criterion of pragmatic necessity leading to exclusivity'.[60]

To a certain extent, the Member States are therefore correct in underlining the importance of the principle of conferral. In the words of Eleftheria Neframi, '[t]he fact

[57] Suggesting that the pre-emption effect under Art 3(2) TFEU should be seen as a *lex specialis* in relation to Art 2(2) TFEU, see Allan Rosas, 'Exclusive, Shared and National Competence in the Context of EU External Relations: Do Such Distinctions Matter?' in Inge Govaere, Erwan Lannon, Peter van Elsuwege and Stanislas Adam (eds), *The European Union in the World: Essays in Honour of Professor Marc Maresceau* (Leiden, Brill/Nijhoff, 2014) 23.

[58] The Article neither uses a 'covered to a large extent' type of language to signal the continued relevance of the Opinion 2/91 (*ILO Convention*) doctrine, nor does it refer to 'complete harmonisation of a field' à la Opinion 1/94 (*WTO Agreements*) in order to limit it. See eg Govaere (n 48) 1306; and Rosas (n 9) 1086.

[59] Pieter Jan Kuijper, 'The Court and the New EU Foreign Relations Law: Institutional Balance?' in Jenő Czuczai and Frederik Naert (eds), *The EU as a Global Actor Bridging Legal Theory and Practice: Liber Amicorum in Honour of Ricardo Gosalbo Bono* (Leiden, Brill Nijhoff, 2017) 49.

[60] Eleftheria Neframi, 'Vertical Division of Competences and the Objectives of the European Union's External Action' in Marise Cremona and Anne Thies (eds), *The European Court of Justice and External Relations Law: Constitutional Challenges* (Oxford, Hart Publishing, 2014) 84.

that exclusive implied external competence of the Union derives from the consideration of its internal objectives shows that the general external action objective to promote international cooperation and to be a globally influential actor *is not to be considered beyond the principle of conferral*.'[61] This is true in the sense that *ERTA*-based competence must be anchored to existing and foreseeable internal rule-setting. But it does not mean that *ERTA*-based exclusivity would be strictly limited to the exact scope of a prior use of competence in a similar manner as the pre-emption caused by Article 2(2) TFEU would demand.

The pre-Lisbon disagreements show that the Member States have struggled all along with such a dynamic, necessity-based preclusion of Member State action. After the entry into force of the Lisbon Treaty, the Member States' approach seems to have been to accept that such a doctrine created by the Court may have existed historically; but once implied competences have been made explicit through codification and thus formally conferred to the Union through the Treaties, their use should be strictly delimited in accordance with the more protective pre-emption rule applicable in the field of shared competences. After all, '[c]ompetences not conferred upon the Union in the Treaties remain with the Member States' (Article 5(2) TEU).

The Member State claim misses the difference in the *functions served* by the two pre-emption rules, which have direct repercussions for the tests triggering pre-emption under each rule. On the one hand, the Article 2(2) TFEU-based pre-emption rule embodies the legislative task-sharing between the Union and Member State legislators. It is governed by a clear-cut *exercise* rule reserving to the Member States all residual legislative power. On the other hand, the pre-emption under the *ERTA* doctrine under Article 3(2) TFEU serves the task of protecting the Union legislator's internal policy-setting autonomy, which is governed by the concept of Union rules being *affected*.

As a result, the pre-emption of Member States' international action is not governed by such strictly pre-determined either/or rules as called for by the Member States. The pre-emptive effects produced under each Article therefore need not be identical.[62] The Court's post-Lisbon case law suggests that by codifying the Court's judicial constructs in *ERTA*, the Treaty Drafters are understood to have embraced the underlying functionalist foundation of a broad notion of pre-emption. The Treaties now therefore directly confer an exclusive external competence, the delimitation of which is measured on a looser metric based on teleology, and not on a rigid spatial delimitation.

It is perhaps helpful to note that *ERTA* is in this sense not an isolated incident. An analogous approach can be found in the Court's use of the 'centre of gravity' test in the determination of the relevant Union competence bases for envisioned international commitments, equally contested by the Member States to this day. Stemming already from the pre-Lisbon period, the point of contestation has emerged in post-Lisbon case law, eg in *Opinion 2/15 (EUSFTA)* and *AMP Antarctique*. According to the summary provided by AG Sharpston in *Opinion 2/15*, 'the Council and a number of Member States consider that *the allocation of competences between the European Union and the Member States … must first be established* before determining, as a subsequent step, the

[61] Ibid.

[62] Similarly, see Opinion of AG Kokott in *Conditional access services*, paras 114–17.

legal basis on which the European Union's [action] should rest.'[63] In other words: the evaluation of the Union's international commitments should begin with the identification of the substantive fields within which each provision of an international agreement falls. Crucially, any aspects of an international agreement, no matter how minuscule, which do not coincide with a field occupied by the Union should be left outside the Union's (exclusive) competence. This contention betrays a similar *spatial* approach to conferral as has been identified above in the calls for overturning the *ERTA* doctrine: the Union is only to gain (exclusive) external powers in areas strictly coinciding with a spatially understood division of powers. Moreover, the Member States should be guaranteed a right of participation every time the spatial scope of a competence shared between the Union and Member States or retained by the latter is touched.

The Court, however, has not adopted such a rigid approach. Its case law has built on the general principle applicable in the determination of legal bases, known as the centre of gravity test. According to that test, Union acts should preferably have as few legal bases as possible and rely on on the legal basis that corresponds to the predominant purpose of the act at hand; any other purposes that are merely incidental or extremely limited in scope thus not necessitating the use of further legal bases. As a result, an act the predominant purpose of which relates to a legal basis under which the Union enjoys (exclusive) competence can be subsumed, in its entirety, under that legal basis.[64] This approach, in turn, operates on the basis of an effectiveness-based logic of *necessity*.

The Member States' view has received some support from different Advocates General, holding that the centre of gravity test should only be applied in the context of the *horizontal* delimitation of the Union's powers (ie situations where a delimitation between different Union competence bases is at stake) and should not disturb the *vertical* division of powers between the Union and the Member States.[65] However, the Court has accepted in its pre-Lisbon case law that the centre of gravity test may entail limited consequences in the vertical relation as well.[66] This is even shown by its established doctrine according to which ancillary provisions in an international agreement are subsumed under the legal basis of its material provisions, which has also been employed in situations where matters falling within the spatial scope of shared or retained competences have been at stake.[67]

This approach to questions of legal basis may also have the effect of extending the material scope of *ERTA*-based exclusivity: post-Lisbon case law confirms that ancillary

[63] Opinion of AG Sharpston in *Opinion 2/15*, EU:C:2016:992, para 88. See further the chapter by Merijn Chamon and Marise Cremona in this volume.

[64] See eg Case C-263/14, *Parliament v Council (Pirate Transfer Agreements)*, EU:C:2016:435, paras 43–44 with references; and, for a delimitation between CFSP and non-CFSP legal bases, Case C-244/17, *Commission v Council (Agreement with Kazakhstan)*, EU:C:2018:662, paras 36–46. For discussion, see eg Heliskoski (n 51) 299–301.

[65] Opinion of AG Kokott in Case C-13/07, *Commission v Council (Vietnam)*, EU:C:2009:190, para 113, echoed by AG Sharpston in *Opinion 2/15*, para 78; as well as Opinion of AG Kokott in *AMP Antarctic*, EU:C:2018:362, para 82.

[66] For discussion, see Luca Prete, 'The constitutional limits to the choice of mixity after *EUSFTA*, *COTIF I*, *MPA Antarctic* and *COTIF II*: towards a more constructive discourse?' (2020) 45 *ELRev* 113, 117–19.

[67] Pre-Lisbon, see Opinion 1/78, *International Agreement on Natural Rubber*, EU:C:1979:224, para 56, and Case C-268/94, *Portugal v Council (Co-operation agreement with India)*, EU:C:1996:461, paras 56–68. In analogy, see even Opinion of AG Kokott in *Vietnam*, para 114. Post-Lisbon, see *Opinion 2/15*, paras 97–109 (investment protection), 214–17 (internal waterways transport), and 281–84 (transparency).

provisions may be subsumed under the *ERTA*-based exclusive competence governing the material provisions of an international agreement even in situations where the ancillary provisions in and of themselves would not fulfil the conditions of the *ERTA* test, if considered independently.[68] This evidences a judicial choice in favour of the effectiveness of Union action: the importance of the principle of conferral is not denied, but is construed in functional terms as opposed to a spatial delimitation.

The choice is further emphasised if we consider the asymmetry in the way in which the subsumption effect works. Whilst the Member States' retained competences may be subsumed, this appears not to be the case of the Union's *ERTA*-based exclusive competence. This results from *Opinion 1/03*, where the Court found that the legal basis of common rules should not be decisive in the application of the *ERTA* test as 'the legal basis of internal legislation is determined by its principal component, *whereas the rule which may possibly be affected may be merely an ancillary component of that legislation*.'[69] In other words, the *ERTA* effect cannot be cancelled by the circumstance that the common rules at risk of being affected are 'merely ancillary' to a body of Union rules the legal basis of which does not coincide with the field of the international commitments envisaged. If an international commitment affects common rules, the Union gains exclusive competence in all circumstances.

The above reveals how the construction of the principle of conferral adopted in the evaluation of Union competences is crucial for determining the Member States' (in-) ability to act externally. Because of their insistence on a spatially construed principle of conferral, the Member States see it as an aberration that the Union should gain exclusive external powers in entire areas of law where it has only made use of its internal competence sporadically. According to this view, due adherence to the principle of conferral would entail that Union powers should become exclusive only under strictly spatially defined terms.[70] The Court, however, approaches the question from a different vantage point: in its thinking, the protection of the internal policy-making space may necessitate the pre-emption of Member State action on the international stage in fields surpassing the bounds of the Union's actual use of its internal competences, or, with ancillary provisions, even the limits of its policy-making mandate.[71]

Thus, every time the Member States exercise their role as the EU co-legislators, they contribute to a potential de facto conferral of new external competences to the Union. Although *ERTA* exclusivity has been traditionally attached to the use of *internal* competence,[72] one may wonder whether the wording of Article 3(2) TFEU even prevents the triggering of exclusivity by 'common rules' created *through external*

[68] *Conditional access services*, para 70, and *Opinion 2/15*, para 217. See also Opinion of AG Sharpston in *Opinion 2/15*, paras 88–94, esp 93; and Opinion of AG Wahl in *Opinion 3/15*, paras 30–35. For discussion, see Rosas (n 9) 1083.

[69] *Opinion 1/03*, para 131 (emphasis added). See even AG Kokott in *AMP Antarctic*, paras 131–32. Cf Prete (n 66) 120–21.

[70] For support within the Court, see AG Sharpston in *Neighbouring Rights*, EU:C:2014:224, paras 89, 111; and in *Opinion 2/15*, paras 235–41.

[71] See Eleftheria Neframi, 'The Dynamic of the EU Objectives in the Analysis of the External Competence' in Eleftheria Neframi and Mauro Gatti (eds), *Constitutional Issues of EU External Relations Law* (Baden-Baden, Nomos, 2018) 74–77.

[72] *Opinion 2/15*, paras 233–34.

action, especially in non-mixed settings: that is, the Union's adoption of international commitments, which potentially themselves already build on the expansive *ERTA* logic, could create a further purposive external competence necessary to protect such rules.[73] Pending future case law, it remains to be seen whether the Court will grant exclusive Union competence even more often than the Member States are willing to accept.[74]

VI. Conclusions: Understandings of Conferral as a Source of Dissonance in Mixed Agreements

This chapter has explored the *ERTA* case law and calls for change made by Member State governments and the Council in order to underline a fundamental difference between the Member States and the Court as regards the import of the principle of conferral for Member States' participation rights.

In sum, for the Member States, the principle of conferral is the beginning and the end of the Union's powers. In addition, only one version of the principle of conferral is accepted: one conditioned by an understanding of conferral in a spatial sense, entailing that competence in a substantive field is conferred to the Union in accordance with the exact limits of prior use of internal powers. This becomes visible in the Member States' recurring insistence on a 'screening of [international agreements], provision by provision, in order to establish the nature of [the Union's and the Member States'] respective competences.'[75]

For the Court, the principle of conferral equally governs the Union's use of powers. However, it is accepted that powers can also be conferred on a looser metric based not on a predetermined assignation of substantive fields, but on a needs-based evaluation where the limits of a competence are rather determined situationally and functionally. As a result, it has not granted the principle of conferral such restrictive effect as the Member States have sought to enforce.

These different approaches give rise to an important dissonance between the Member States' self-perceived prerogative to participate in the conclusion of mixed agreements, and the participation rights protected by the Court. The dissonance has concrete

[73] See *Opinion 2/15 (EUSFTA)*, para 230, referring to 'a rule adopted on the basis of the FEU Treaty' as the 'common rules' intended in Art 3(2) TFEU. This has been referred to at times as a 'reverse ERTA effect', see Merijn Chamon, 'Provisional Application of Treaties: The EU's Contribution to the Development of International Law' (2020) 31 *European Journal of International Law* 883, 900 (fn 81); Marianne Dony, 'Retour sur les compétences externes implicites de l'Union' (2018) 54 *Cahiers de droit européen* 109, 163–64; and Jean-François Brakeland, 'Politique commerciale commune, coopération avec les pays tiers et aide humanitaire' in Giuliano Amato et al (eds), *Genèse et destinée de la Constitution européenne* (Bruxelles, Bruylant, 2007) 863. However, the term 'reverse' is somewhat misleading if it is used in the sense of EU external treaty-making potentially creating an *ERTA* effect on the external relations of the Member States.

[74] A readiness to expand *ERTA* beyond its origins can be seen in *Pringle*, paras 99–101, where the Court accepted that the doctrine originally attaching to Member States' obligations with *third countries* could even be applied in the context of a Member State *inter se* international agreement. Cf View of AG Kokott in *Pringle*, EU:C:2012:675, paras 98–99.

[75] In the context of the Istanbul Agreement, Sacha Prechal, 'The European Union's Accession to the Istanbul Convention' in Koen Lenaerts et al (eds), *An Ever-Changing Union? Perspectives on the Future of EU Law in Honour of Allan Rosas* (Oxford, Hart Publishing, 2019) 285.

repercussions. First, it limits the Member States' ability to demand mixed action in fields where the Union and the Member States share powers;[76] second, it entails that the fact that some aspects of an international commitment fall within the scope of the Member States' retained powers does not prevent them from being subsumed under (exclusive) Union competence. As illustrated through examples above, both are claims that the Member States have tended to make in the context of external competence disputes.

As long as these discrepancies reign between the approaches adopted by the Council and Member State governments on the one hand and by the Court on the other, Member State claims to the effect that an international commitment should be undertaken as a mixed agreement will therefore not necessarily enjoy judicial protection. If the Member States wanted to really rein in the *ERTA* effect, they could either restrain themselves from producing more and more common rules, or, as Masters of the Treaties, choose much clearer language. They have thus far not chosen either of these routes.

[76] For the sake of clarity, it should be emphasised that in such situations, moreover, mixity often is facultative rather than obligatory; see eg Prete (n 66).

3

Foreseeability and Anticipation as Constraints on Member State Action under Mixed Agreements

MARJA-LIISA ÖBERG AND MARCUS KLAMERT

I. Introduction

Mixed agreements are complicated legal constructions created with the aim of reconciling the division of competences in the European Union (EU) on the one hand with the need to uphold effective external representation of both the Union and its Member States on the other. The management of mixity is particularly intricate because of, (1) the need to establish the division of competences between the EU and the Member States and, (2) the need to ensure the proper functioning of a mixed agreement while protecting the interests of all parties. In both of these broad aspects, the Member States' external action is constrained by an obligation not only to conform to EU law as it is but also to foresee or anticipate its future development.

By definition, foreseeability is anticipation or awareness, knowing in advance the likelihood of some future event or circumstance occurring.[1] It does not necessarily entail taking any action. Compared to this rather neutral term, anticipation has a more positive connotation, meaning a feeling of excitement about something that is going to happen in the near future.[2] It can allude to a prior action that takes into account or forestalls a later action.[3] The aim of this chapter is to show the relevance of both concepts in EU law generally and EU external relations law particularly, especially with regard to the conclusion of mixed agreements – an issue that has not yet received comprehensive analysis.

The development of EU law, which the Member States are expected to anticipate, may concern either changes in legislation or policy or the case law of the Court of Justice ('the Court'). From the perspective of the principles of conferral as well as

[1] See Oxford Dictionary, www.oxfordreference.com/view/10.1093/oi/authority.20110803095828690.
[2] See Cambridge Dictionary, dictionary.cambridge.org/de/worterbuch/englisch/anticipation.
[3] Merriam Webster Online, www.merriam-webster.com/dictionary/anticipation.

legal certainty, an excessively wide construction of the duty of loyal cooperation is highly problematic whereas an overly narrow interpretation will undermine the achievement of the Union's external policy objectives, as will be shown in the following.

Section II of this chapter shows that Union institutions must foresee certain future developments and events when taking action both internally and externally. Section III, in contrast, deals with aspects of anticipation that are relevant for Member States' obligations, both internally and externally, resulting from Article 4(3) of the Treaty on European Union (TEU). Section IV discusses whether a similar role for foreseeability and anticipation also exists with regard to mixed agreements and the case law of the Court specifically, involving, in particular, the opinion procedure under Article 218(11) of the Treaty on the Functioning of the European Union (TFEU).

II. Foreseeability in EU Law

A. External Competence

One of the few occasions on which the Court has used the term 'foreseeable' is in connection with the *ERTA/AETR* principle that was codified by the Lisbon Treaty in Article 3(2) TFEU on exclusive external competence.[4] Under this provision, the scope of common EU rules may also be affected or altered by commitments that fall within an area, which is already largely covered by such rules.[5] According to this part of the *ERTA* test, there must be a 'comprehensive and detailed' as well as 'specific' analysis of the relationship between the international agreement envisaged and Union law, 'from which it is clear that such an agreement is capable of affecting the common EU rules or of altering their scope'.[6] Such analysis must take into account the current status of the law in the areas covered, respectively its future development 'insofar as that is *foreseeable* at the time of that analysis'.[7]

The test of an area largely covered was also applied in *Étang de Berre* on the jurisdiction of the Court to hear a case on the pollution of the eponymous salt-water lake

[4] Art 3(2) TFEU states: 'The Union shall also have exclusive competence for the conclusion of an international agreement when its conclusion is provided for in a legislative act of the Union or is necessary to enable the Union to exercise its internal competence, or in so far as its conclusion may affect common rules or alter their scope.' See also Case 22/70, *Commission v Council (AETR)*, EU:C:1971:32. See, generally, Marise Cremona, 'Defining Competence in EU External Relations: Lessons from the Treaty Reform Process' in Alan Dashwood and Marc Maresceau (eds), *Law and Practice of EU External Relations: Salient Features of a Changing Landscape* (CUP 2008), 58. See Mirka Kuisma and Joris Larik in this volume.

[5] Opinion 2/15 *FTA Singapore*, EU:C:2017:376, para 181; Case C-114/12, *Broadcasting Organisations*, EU:C:2014:2151, paras 69–70; Opinion 2/91, *ILO Convention 170*, EU:C:1993:106, para 25; Case C-467/98, *Open Skies*, EU:C:2002:625, para 82; Opinion 1/03, *Lugano Convention*, EU:C:2006:81, paras 120 and 126; Case C-66/13, *Green Network*, EU:C:2014:2399, paras 30–31.

[6] Case C-66/13, *Green Network* (n 5) para 33; Case C-114/12, *Broadcasting Organisations* (n 5) para 74.

[7] Case C-66/13, *Green Network* (n 5) para 33 (emphasis only here); Opinion 1/03, *Lugano Convention* (n 5). For examples of such analysis, see Case C-114/12, *Broadcasting Organisations* (n 5) paras 76-102; Case C-467/98, *Open Skies* (n 5) paras 82–112; Opinion 1/13, *Convention on the civil aspects of international child abduction*, EU:C:2014:2303, paras 75–90. See also Opinion by AG Wahl in Opinion 3/15, *Marrakesh Treaty*, EU:C:2016:657, paras 131–34.

in Provence.[8] France objected to the Court's jurisdiction over the mixed Barcelona Convention for the Protection of the Mediterranean Sea against Pollution and over a protocol to this Convention, which allegedly prohibited such pollution.[9] France argued that the obligations on issue did not fall under Community law. The Court rejected the argument and affirmed its jurisdiction, despite the fact that the Union had not yet legislated on matters that were at issue in that action.[10] The Court claimed that environmental protection had 'in very large measure' been regulated by Union legislation,[11] and, therefore, there was a Union interest in compliance by both the Community and its Member States with the commitments entered into.[12]

Under the test on exclusive competence, this element of foreseeability does thus not primarily address the Member States but must be heeded by the Union institutions when taking action. This can concern the Commission when making a proposal for concluding an international agreement, or the Council when adopting the respective decision under Article 218 TFEU. Yet it can also concern the Court, not only when adjudicating on the matter of external competence but also when deciding on the scope of its own jurisdiction.

B. Internal Competence

Foreseeing future events also plays a role with regard to internal competences. Article 114(1) TFEU establishes that the Parliament and the Council are to adopt the measures for the approximation of the provisions laid down by law, regulation or administrative action in Member States which have as their object the establishment and functioning of the internal market. The Court has held that recourse to Article 114 TFEU as a legal basis is possible if the aim of the legal act is 'to prevent the emergence of future obstacles to trade as a result of divergences in national laws', provided that the emergence of such obstacles is likely and the measure in question designed to prevent them.[13] In this connection, one can also consider the precautionary principle that flows into proportionality assessment when proposing a certain level of protection under legislative measures. Accordingly, where preliminary objective scientific evidence indicates the existence of reasonable grounds for concern about possible negative effects

[8] On the connection between the establishment of exclusive competence and the establishment of exclusive jurisdiction, see Marcus Klamert, 'Dark matter: Competence, Jurisdiction and the Area Largely Covered by EU Law – Comment on *Lesoochranárske*' (2012) 37 *EL Rev* 340.

[9] Case C-239/03, *Commission v France (Étang de Berre)*, EU:C:2004:598. See also Case C-53/96, *Hermés International*, EU:C:1998:292, para 32; Joined Cases C-300/98, *Christian Dior* and C-392/98, *Assco Gerüste*, EU:C:2000:688.

[10] Case C-239/03, *Commission v France (Étang de Berre)*, (n 9) para 30.

[11] See ibid para 28.

[12] ibid para 29. See Pieter-Jan Kuijper, 'Annotation to Case C-239/03, *Commission v France*' (2005) 42 *CML Rev* 1491, 1495–96, who however seems not to assume exclusive competence in the present case (1498). See also Marise Cremona, 'Defending the Community Interest: the Duties of Cooperation and Compliance' in Marise Cremona and Bruno de Witte (eds), *EU Foreign Relations Law: Constitutionals Fundamentals* (Hart, 2008) 148.

[13] Case C-358/14, *Poland v Parliament and Council*, EU:C:2016:323, para 33 with further references. See also Case C-359/92, *Germany v Council*, EU:C:1994:306.

of an activity or product on public health, including future negative effects, this would argue against their conduct or use.[14] The precautionary principle, therefore, includes a prospective element that must be taken into consideration by Union organs when initiating or enacting legislation.

C. Competition Law

In the area of competition rules, too, there are pertinent elements of foreseeability. The Court has interpreted Article 101(1) TFEU on the prohibition of cartels as not requiring that the arrangements referred to in that provision have actually affected trade between Member States, but that it be established that the arrangements are capable of having that effect. It would thus be 'necessary to take account of the foreseeable development in the conditions of competition and in the pattern of trade between Member States'.[15] Referring national courts must, for example, take into consideration possible developments in cross-border activities and the foreseeable impact of any policy or legislative initiatives designed to reduce legal or technical barriers to trade.[16] Similarly, under Article 107 TFEU on state aid, when the Commission establishes the existence of state aid, it is not strictly bound by the conditions of competition existing at the date on which its decision is adopted, but 'must carry out an assessment in a dynamic perspective and take account of the foreseeable development of competition and the effects which the aid in question will have upon it'.[17]

D. Interim Conclusion

Foreseeability is, thus, a factor to be considered by the Union institutions when taking action externally, internally, and specifically in the field of competition law. While the aspects to be foreseen by the Union in the context of external competence pertain to future *Union* measures, in the internal dimension they rather concern *Member State* measures. In both constellations, foreseeability and the future developments it relates to primarily affect the Union's (and not the Member States') right to act.

Notably, the case law discussed above does not concern the general principle of loyalty,[18] of which the duty of (sincere or loyal) cooperation is a subcategory.[19] In the following, we will now turn to the relevance of anticipation in case law, which is rooted in sincere cooperation under Article 4(3) TEU.

[14] Case C-333/08, *Commission v France*, EU:C:2010:44, paras 91–96. See further Marcus Klamert, 'Public Health' in Herwig CH Hofmann, Gerard C Rowe and Alexander H Türk (eds), *Specialized Administrative Law of the European Union* (OUP, 2018). See also the Communication from the Commission on the precautionary principle, COM/2000/1 final.

[15] Case C-238/05, *Asnef-Equifax*, EU:C:2006:734, para 43 with further references.

[16] Ibid, para 44.

[17] Joined Cases C-57/00 P and C-61/00, P *Freistaat Sachsen*, EU:C:2003:510, para 211.

[18] With the exception of the ERTA principle, which was introduced by the Court with reference to the now Art 4(3) TEU. See Case 22/70, *Commission v Council (AETR)*, EU:C:1971:32, para 21.

[19] See also Eleftheria Neframi, 'The Duty of Loyalty: Rethinking its Scope Through its Application in the Field of EU External Relations' (2010) 47 *CML Rev* 323, 325.

III. Anticipation in EU Law

A. Introduction

The principle of loyalty as prescribed by Article 4(3) TEU has various functions in EU law, including in connection with the 'constitutionalisation' of Union law and with the duty of the Member States to comply therewith.[20] The case law based duty of loyalty discussed below, in both EU internal and external contexts, imposes duties of abstention in anticipation of future action by the Union relating to directives, Council negotiation mandates, Council common positions and concerted Union actions more generally. While this places the focus on the starting point of obligations imposed by loyalty, it is also relevant when these duties end.

B. Directives

Based on Article 4(3) TEU and Article 288 TFEU, the Court has imposed a duty of abstention in relation to Union directives. During the period provided for the transposition of a directive, the Member States must refrain from taking any measure liable to seriously compromise the attainment of the result prescribed by the directive.[21] This includes interpretations of national law likely to have such effect.[22] In *Inter-Environnement Wallonie*, the Court instructed that the national court must contemplate on whether the provision in question constitutes full transposition of the directive, what would be the practical effects of applying incompatible provisions, and whether the timeframe would allow for possible amendments.[23] With the judgment in *Impact*, this duty of abstention was extended to the period between the expiry of the transposition deadline and the entry into force of the national implementing legislation.[24]

The case law referred to addresses primarily the Member States and places upon them an obligation to consider the implications of measures taken during the transposition period of a directive.[25] The Member States must anticipate the end of the transposition

[20] See Marcus Klamert, 'Commentary on Art 4 TEU' in Manuel Kellerbauer, Marcus Klamert, and Jonathan Tomkin (eds), *The EU Treaties and the Charter of Fundamental Rights – A Commentary* (OUP, 2019), paras 60–79.

[21] Case C-129/96, *Inter-Environnement Wallonie*, EU:C:1997:628, para 45; Case C-14/02, *ATRAL*, EU:C:2003:265, para 58; Case C-144/04, *Mangold*, EU:C:2005:709, para 67; Case C-157/02, *Rieser*, EU:C:2004:76, para 67; Joined Cases C-378-380/07, *Angelidaki*, EU:C:2009:250, 206.

[22] Case C-212/04, *Adeneler*, EU:C:2006:443, para 123. It has also been argued that the Member State courts must consider the objectives of a directive when interpreting national law even before the expiry of the transposition deadline based on Art 4(3) TEU ('anticipatory indirect effect'). See Marcus Klamert, 'Judicial Implementation of Directives and Anticipatory Indirect Effect: Connecting the Dots' (2006) 43 *CML Rev* 1251, 1252.

[23] Case C-129/96, *Inter-Environnement Wallonie* (n 21) para 47.

[24] Case C-268/06, *Impact*, EU:C:2008:223, paras 90–91, based on ex Art 10 EC, ex Art 249(3) EC, and Directive 1999/70. On this case, see also Marcus Klamert and Bernhard Schima, 'Commentary on Article 19 TEU' in Manuel Kellerbauer, Marcus Klamert and Jonathan Tomkin (eds), *The EU Treaties and the Charter of Fundamental Rights – A Commentary* (OUP, 2019), 31–39.

[25] For an, arguably misguided, comparison of this Case law with Case T-115/94, *Opel Austria*, EU:T:1997:3, see AG Poiares Maduro's Opinion in Case C-422/05, *Commission v Belgium*, EU:C:2007:62, para 39. See also Jan Klabbers, 'Restraints on the Treaty-Making Powers of Member States deriving from EU Law: Towards a

deadline, respectively the time of the entry into force of the national implementing measures, and, in view of this future event, must choose their actions accordingly. The start of the duties imposed on the Member States under this line of case law is clearly the entry into force of a Union directive.

The anticipatory effect of directives has been proposed to also apply prior to the exercise of shared competences by the Union, and it has been suggested that the fact that the Court has not yet done so is 'purely a matter of chance'.[26] In support of this claim, it has been pointed out that in both cases 'a conflict with national legislation can occur only after a certain point in time, respectively the end of the period for transposition and the exercise of Community competence'.[27] This view has rightly not gained much traction. First, the case of directives is distinct from the question of shared competences in that the expiry of the transposition period and, thus, the graduation of the legal norm is certain, whereas the exercise of a shared competence remains a mere possibility.[28] In the same vein, it is relevant that competence norms provided in the Treaty require an actual activation by the Union legislator, whereas directives by themselves constitute such activation.[29] Article 4(3) TEU third sentence speaks, generally, of the objectives of the Union as the reference for duties of abstention of the Member States. It should not, however, be read as implying that the 'naked' Treaty objectives are a sufficient basis for such duties of abstention.[30] There is, thus, a decisive difference between the 'result prescribed' in a directive, which is the cause of the abstention duty in *Inter-Environnement Wallonie*, on the one hand, and the regulatory objective expressed in the legal basis for a shared competence, on the other.[31] While the former is the activation of a Union competence thereby realising a Union objective, the latter is an objective not yet realised.

C. Concerted Actions by Union Organs

In light of the *Sea Fisheries* and *Waterways* jurisprudence discussed below, it is arguably relevant that in the case of shared competences the Union legislator has not yet expressed the intent to activate its powers, ie has not taken 'Union action' and, thereby, concretised the Union interest.

Framework for Analysis' in Enzo Cannizzaro (ed), *The European Union as an Actor in International Relations* (Kluwer, 2002), on a comparison with the so-called interim obligation under Art 18 of the first Vienna Convention on the Law of Treaties (VCLT) 1969. See further Marcus Klamert, 'Legal Certainty and Customary International Law: *Opel Austria*' in Graham Butler and Ramses A Wessel (eds), *EU External Relations Law: The Cases in Context* (Hart, forthcoming 2021).

[26] Opinion of AG Poiares Maduro in Joined Cases C-205/06, *Commission v Austria* and C-249/06 *Commission v Sweden*, EU:C:2008:391, para 38.

[27] Ibid para 37.

[28] Ibid para 39.

[29] Ibid. A directive's objective is binding from the moment the instrument has been passed by the Union legislator. The fact that the Member States are given a 'grace period' to adapt their national laws should not distract from this.

[30] But see ibid para 38.

[31] See further Marcus Klamert, *The Principle of Loyalty* (OUP, 2014), 161–63. See also Panos Koutrakos, 'Annotation to Case C-205/06, Commission v. Austria and Case C-249/06, Commission v. Sweden' (2009) 46 *CML Rev* 2059, 2066–67.

The *Sea Fisheries* cases concerned a failure by the Council to adopt certain measures for the conservation of fisheries resources which the Commission had proposed and which fell within the Union's exclusive competence. Subsequently, the United Kingdom, which had blocked decision-making in the Council, adopted corresponding national measures after informing the Commission of its intentions but not receiving a verbatim approval. The Court prescribed that the Member States have 'special duties of action and abstention' in situations where 'concerted Community action' has started, such as, in these cases, the submission by the Commission to the Council of proposals, although not yet adopted by the latter.[32] The Court made clear that although the Council had not fully regulated in the pertinent field, it had done enough to express its 'intention to reinforce the authority of the Commission's proposals as well as its intention to prevent the conservation measures in force from being amended by the Member States without any acknowledged need'.[33] The plans and initial steps taken on the path to regulate could, rather than adopting legislation, thus give rise to a duty of abstention on behalf of the Member States.

The starting point of the duty of loyalty was also central in the cases *Commission v Germany* and *Commission v Luxembourg* (the *Inland Waterway* cases) concerning infringement proceedings in the field of transport policy.[34] Germany and Luxembourg had negotiated, and respectively concluded, with certain Central and Eastern European states, which at the time were not yet members of the Community, bilateral agreements on the transport of passengers and goods between the parties by inland waterways, and the reciprocal use of their inland waterways in general. After the start of negotiations on the bilateral agreements but prior to their ratification, a Council decision mandated the Commission to negotiate a corresponding Community agreement with the same non-Member States. Consequently, the Commission called on the Member States to 'abstain from any initiative likely to compromise the proper conduct of the negotiations initiated at Community level and, in particular, to abandon ratification of agreements already initialled or signed, and to forgo the opening of further negotiations with the countries of Central and Eastern Europe relating to inland waterway transport',[35] to ensure that Member State action does not compromise the Community's external action.[36]

The Court stated that the adoption of the Council decision authorising the Commission to negotiate the international agreement 'marks the start of a concerted Community action at international level' requiring 'if not a duty of abstention on the part of the Member States, at the very least a duty of close cooperation' with the Community institutions to 'facilitate the achievement of the Community tasks and to ensure the

[32] Case 804/79, *Commission v United Kingdom (Sea Fisheries)*, EU:C:1981:93, para 28. See also Case 325/85, *Ireland v Commission (Sea Fisheries)*, EU:C:1987:546, para 15; Case 326/85, *Netherlands v Commission (Sea Fisheries)*, EU:C:1987:547, para 21; Case 332/85, *Germany v Commission (Sea Fisheries)*, EU:C:1987:549, para 20.

[33] Case 804/79, *Commission v United Kingdom (Sea Fisheries)* (n 32) para 25.

[34] Case C-266/03, *Commission v Luxembourg (Inland Waterway)*, EU:C:2005:341, and Case C-433/03, *Commission v Germany (Inland Waterway)*, EU:C:2005:462.

[35] Case C-266/03, *Commission v Luxembourg (Inland Waterway)* (n 34) para 18.

[36] On the reluctance of the Member States to cede treaty-making powers to the Union, see Robert Post, 'Open Skies? Constructing the European Polity: ERTA and the Open Skies Judgments' in Miguel Poiares Maduro and Loïc Azoulai (eds), *The Past and Future of EU Law: The Classics of EU Law Revisited on the 50th Anniversary of the Rome Treaty* (Hart, 2010), 244.

coherence and consistency of the action and its international representation'.[37] The Court thus drew an analogy between the Commission proposal in the *Sea Fisheries* case and the negotiating mandate in the *Inland Waterway* cases, both of which denote 'points of departure for concerted Community action'. The Court held that the Member States' failure to cooperate or consult with the Commission after the Council Decision and before implementing and ratifying their own agreements 'compromised the achievement of the Community's task'[38] and the Treaty objectives,[39] and deemed both Germany and Luxembourg to have violated what is now Article 4(3) TEU.[40]

In the above cases, no Union law in the sense of Article 288 TFEU had yet been adopted and there was 'only' a mandate to negotiate for the Commission. Since, however, the Commission would have dictated the conditions on Germany and Luxembourg for concluding these agreements, and a commitment on behalf of the two Member States to denounce their agreements once the Community agreements would enter into force would not have sufficed, a de facto duty of abstention was, indeed, placed on the Member States concerned.[41]

D. Common Positions in International Fora

It seems logical that Council decisions authorising the signing of an international agreement by the Union under Article 218(5) TFEU, or Council decisions authorising their conclusion under Article 218(6) TFEU, would essentially have the same effect on the Member States as the passing of internal legal acts by the Union legislator. Differently from directives, however, in the case of international agreements there is no implementation period where the Member States still enjoy a certain degree of autonomy, warranting the imposition of duties of loyalty as established above.

The situation is different with common positions under Article 218(9) TFEU. Under this provision, the Council, on a proposal from the Commission or the High Representative of the Union for Foreign Affairs and Security Policy, can adopt a decision establishing the positions to be adopted on the Union's behalf in a body set up by an agreement, when that body is called upon to adopt acts having legal effects, with the exception of acts supplementing or amending the institutional framework of the agreement. Such positions regarding acts having legal effects must be adopted by way of formal decisions.[42]

[37] Case C-266/03, *Commission v Luxembourg (Inland Waterway)* (n 34) para 60; Case C-433/03, *Commission v Germany (Inland Waterway)* (n 34) paras 60–74. See Pieter-Jan Kuijper, 'Re-reading External Relations Cases in the Field of Transport: The Function of Community Loyalty', in Mielle Bulterman et al (eds), *Views of European Law from the Mountain. Liber Amicorum for Piet Jan Slot* (Kluwer, 2009), 300, who sees a violation of ex Art 300 EC instead of a breach of ex Art 10 EC.

[38] See Case C-433/03, *Commission v Germany (Inland Waterway)* (n 34) para 62.

[39] Ibid paras 69–70.

[40] See ibid para 72.

[41] It has been argued that to impose a duty of abstention in this situation would amount to 'an AETR effect by anticipation'. See Christophe Hillion, 'Mixity and Coherence in EU External Relations: The Significance of the "Duty of Cooperation"' (2009) 2 *CLEER Working Papers* 15.

[42] Case C-687/15, *Commission v Council (ITU)*, EU:C:2017:803, paras 40–53. The Court has clarified that these acts produce legal effects within the EU legal order already when they make a (dynamic) reference to acts of

The *PFOS* case showed that a decision not to take such a common position has effects on the Member States.[43] The case concerned a unilateral proposal by Sweden to add to an Annex of the mixed Stockholm Convention on Persistent Organic Pollutants (POPs) a new group of substances, perfluoroctane sulfonates (PFOS). Both the EU and, among other Member States, Sweden were parties to the Stockholm Convention. No agreement on a common proposal concerning PFOS to be submitted on behalf of the Union had been reached in the Council. At the time, a Union regulatory framework was in place but it did not yet include PFOS.[44] Thus, it was assumed that the proposal concerned a matter for which the Union was not exclusively competent.[45]

In the judgment, the Court stated that a common position of the Union to preclude Member State individual action must not take a specific form in order to breach the duty of loyalty.[46] For a common position to exist one must, however, have established some kind of an agreement on the course of action. In the case at hand, PFOS would have been nominated under another agreement, the Aarhus Protocol, once the Commission had submitted a proposal for Community legislation on the substance; the latter was, in fact, under way.[47] The concrete events indicating the upcoming nomination were the adoption of a Council's decision, the submission of a proposed amendment to Directive 76/769 as well as a proposal to list PFOS in the relevant Annexes to that protocol.[48] The Court held that there was, thus, 'a common strategy' to refrain from proposing to list PFOS in Annex A to the Stockholm Convention, and to propose it instead to be listed in the Aarhus Protocol.[49] It was not a question of a 'decision-making vacuum' or even a 'waiting period equivalent to the absence of a decision'.[50] The Court, thereby, extended the precluding effect of the pre-stages of the legislative procedure to also include a 'concerted common strategy within the Council'.[51] The claim for infringement in this case was based on ex Article 10 EC (now Article 4(3) TEU) in combination with 'the principle of unity in the international representation of the Union and its Member States' and the weakening of the Union's negotiating power.[52]

E. The Commencement and End of Duties of Loyalty

In most of the external constellations examined above, the decisive element triggering a constraint for Member State action is the outline of a 'concerted action' or a 'common strategy' of the Union. Such action or strategy appears to require some involvement of

international organisations, or when there exists an obligation of Union institutions to consider these acts when defining Union policy. See Case C-399/12, *Germany v Council (OIV)*, EU:C:2014:2258, paras 56–64.

[43] Case C-246/07, *Commission v Sweden (PFOS)*, EU:C:2010:203.

[44] The question of exclusive competence was not raised in the case. AG Poiares Maduro in his opinion in Case C-246/07, *PFOS*, EU:C:2009:589, paras 28–30, qualifies the Community rules as minimum regulation, which prevented the application of the pre-emptive effect.

[45] ibid paras 29–31.

[46] Case C-246/07, *Commission v Sweden (PFOS)* (n 43) para 77.

[47] Ibid para 85.

[48] Ibid.

[49] Ibid paras 89–90.

[50] Ibid para 87.

[51] Ibid para 91.

[52] See ibid para 104.

the Council, by expressing its interest to regulate and the objectives of its policy in the *Sea Fisheries* case, by issuing a negotiating mandate in the *Waterway* cases, or by adopting a certain strategy for action within the Council in the *PFOS* case. By these actions, the Council arguably concretised the Treaty objectives now listed in Article 3 TEU and expressed, thereby, a Union interest in a sufficiently concrete form. In the case of directives, by contrast, the Member States are constrained because of the entry into force of the directive per se as a legal act under Article 288 TFEU. A Commission proposal by itself will normally not have a precluding effect on the Member States. The beginning of duties of loyalty thus appears to depend on the involvement of the Council and its expression of a position in the name of the Union.

The case law discussed above has primarily concerned the question of the point of time at which Member State obligations set in. Another question, which has not yet received particular attention by the Court, in contrast, concerns the end of the period during which the duty of loyalty requires the Member States to patiently 'wait' for a certain Union action and to hold back their own. In *PFOS*, Advocate General (AG) Poiares Maduro suggested that the duty of loyalty entails that the Member States refrain from individual action 'for a reasonable time' until the Union's decision-making process has been concluded.[53] How long such reasonable time could be remains unclear. It is submitted that before the Member States would be allowed to act, they would need to extensively coordinate with the relevant institution of the Union, and leave ample room for the latter to take the required action. Only if a Member State were in jeopardy of having its interests damaged or of suffering a non-retractable loss, would it arguably be apposite to release it from any duties of abstention.

IV. The Rulings of the Court of Justice and Article 4(3) TEU

A. Introduction

The Court of Justice has repeatedly held that the duty of cooperation applies where an agreement falls in part within Union competence and in part within Member State competence, as is the case with mixed agreements.[54] Duties of cooperation apply throughout the life cycle of mixed agreements, namely the negotiation of a mixed agreement, its conclusion, the fulfilment of the commitments entered into,[55] as well as the ratification process.[56]

The case law discussed above in section III shows that the duty of loyalty vis-à-vis the Member States can be triggered at a very early stage with the start of a concerted Union action. As explained, this can be theorised as representing a sufficiently concrete

[53] See Opinion of AG Poiares Maduro in Case C-246/07, *Commission v Sweden (PFOS)* (n 44) at para 49.

[54] See Ruling 1/78, *IAEA*, EU:C:1978:202, paras 34–36; Opinion 2/91, *ILO Convention 170* (n 5) para 36; Opinion 1/94, *WTO*, EU:C:1994:384, para 108; and Opinion 2/00, *Cartagena Protocol on Biosafety*, EU:C:2001:664, para 18.

[55] Opinion 1/94, *WTO* (n 54) para 108.

[56] Opinion 2/91, *ILO Convention 170* (n 5) para 38.

manifestation of the Union interest by a Union institution. Consequently, the Member States are under an obligation to 'wait' and to temporarily abstain from acting on their own, based on Article 4(3) TEU.

Recent case law has raised the question of whether such obligation might also result not from an action by the Commission or the Council, but from a ruling by the Court of Justice in the context of mixed agreements. In the following, we start by discussing a recent judgment and a recent opinion by the Court on agreements featuring clauses on an investor-state dispute settlement system (ISDS). This is followed by a discussion on the effect of Court rulings generally. In the final subsection, it is examined whether national authorities must adapt their actions to rulings that the Court might render in the future.

B. *Achmea*, CETA, and ISDS

The question of Member State obligations regarding the foreseeability and anticipation of the Union's actions through judgments of the Court has surfaced most sharply in the relationship between *Achmea* and Opinion 1/17 in connection with the Union's old and new, intra- and extra-EU investment treaties and the dispute settlement mechanisms provided therein.

On 6 March 2018, the Court rendered a preliminary ruling in *Achmea* concerning an arbitration clause in the bilateral investment treaty (BIT) in force between the Netherlands and Slovakia, concluded before the accession of the latter to the EU.[57] The Court was called upon by the German Federal Court of Justice – Germany being the place of arbitration pursuant to Article 8 of the BIT for disputes arising from the subject matter of the BIT – to provide a preliminary ruling on the lawfulness under Articles 18, 267 and 344 TFEU to submit disputes arising from an 'intra-EU BIT' to arbitration. The Court's judgment was negative. According to the Court, Article 8 of the BIT jeopardised the principle of mutual trust between the Member States as well as the 'preservation of the particular nature of the law established by the Treaties [and] ensured by the preliminary ruling procedure' and, therefore, breached the principle of sincere cooperation and affected adversely the principle of autonomy of the EU legal order.[58] In particular, the BIT tribunal was not integrated in the Union's judicial system and fell, therefore, outside of the preliminary ruling system,[59] whereas the Court deemed the disputes falling within the jurisdiction of the arbitral tribunal to potentially concern the interpretation of both the agreement and EU law.[60]

In the subsequent Opinion 1/17,[61] the Court was called upon by Belgium under Article 218(11) TFEU to review the compatibility with the Treaties of the envisaged Comprehensive Economic and Trade Agreement between Canada, of the one part, and the EU and its Member States, of the other part (CETA).[62] The decisive issue was

[57] Case C-284/16, *Achmea* EU:C:2018:158.
[58] Ibid paras 58 and 59.
[59] Ibid para 49.
[60] See chapter by Bartosz Soloch and Makane Moïse Mbengue in this volume.
[61] Opinion 1/17, *CETA*, EU:C:2019:341.
[62] [2017] OJ L11/23.

whether the Court itself would be able to maintain the exclusive jurisdiction to give definitive interpretations of EU law in the light of the planned ISDS with an arbitral tribunal 'that would be called upon to give rulings on disputes that might concern the interpretation or application of EU law'.[63]

Opinion 1/17 was anticipated to clarify the compatibility of ISDS with the Treaties, in particular with the principle of autonomy. Before Opinion 1/17 was handed down, the ruling in *Achmea* was 'the only judicial authority to date on the principle in the area of international investment law'[64], but did not necessarily foreshadow its outcome. Differently from *Achmea*, Opinion 1/17 dealt with a dispute settlement mechanism set up by an agreement between the EU and a third country. Whereas in *Achmea*, the Court had condemned the arbitration mechanism in intra-EU BITs, the ruling nevertheless had left a door open for ISDS in bilateral trade agreements.[65]

At a specific point of time, after the ruling in *Achmea* and before the Opinion on CETA, it was questioned whether *Achmea* might pave the way for an equally negative outcome for the ISDS featured in CETA.[66] Both agreements under scrutiny contained similar investor-state arbitration clauses, albeit in different contexts. A negative Opinion of the Court would have caused a halt to the ratification process and likely resulted in the renegotiation of CETA. Most pronouncedly, the question was raised whether proceeding with the ratification of CETA might entail, on behalf of the Member States, a violation of the principle of loyalty in anticipation of Opinion 1/17.[67]

At that time, not only CETA but all new generation free trade agreements (FTAs) of the EU containing ISDS, such as those concluded with Singapore and Vietnam, were put in doubt.[68] The multitude of 'new generation agreements' with uniform features, such as bilateral FTAs and Association Agreements/Deep and Comprehensive Free Trade Areas (AA/DCFTAs) are concluded as mixed agreements.[69] Because of their commonalities, a ruling by the Court declaring any such agreement to be incompatible with the Treaties

[63] Opinion 1/17, *CETA* (n 61) paras 126–27.

[64] Panos Koutrakos, 'The autonomy of EU law and international investment arbitration' (2019) 88 *Nord J Int Law* 41.

[65] See Mauro Gatti, 'Opinion 1/17 in Light of Achmea: Chronicle of an Opinion Foretold?' (2019) 1 *European Papers* 109.

[66] See Opinion 1/17, *CETA*, Opinion of AG Bot, EU:C:2019:72, paras 95-114. See also Daniel Thym, 'The CJEU ruling in Achmea: Death Sentence for Autonomous Investment Protection Tribunals', *EU Law Analysis*, 9 March 2018, eulawanalysis.blogspot.se/2018/03/the-cjeu-ruling-in-achmea-death.html; Szilárd Gáspár Szilágyi, 'The CJEU Strikes Again in Achmea. Is this the end of investor-State arbitration under intra-EU BITs?', *International Economic Law and Policy Blog*, 7 March 2018, worldtradelaw.typepad.com/ielpblog/2018/03/guest-post-the-cjeu-strikes-again-in-achmea-is-this-the-end-of-investor-state-arbitration-under-intr.html.

[67] Quentin Declève and Isabelle Van Damme, 'Achmea: Potential Consequences for CETA, the Multilateral Investment Court, Brexit and other EU trade and investment agreements', *International Litigation Blog*, 13 March 2018, international-litigation-blog.com/achmea-sconsequences-ceta-mic-brexit/; Christina Eckes, 'Don't Lead with Your Chin! If Member States continue with the Ratification of CETA, they violate European Union law', *European Law Blog*, 13 March 2018, europeanlawblog.eu/2018/03/13/dont-lead-with-your-chin-if-member-states-continue-with-the-ratification-of-ceta-they-violate-european-union-law/.

[68] Both have in the meantime been 'split' into a free trade agreement and a separate investment protection agreement. See trade.ec.europa.eu/doclib/press/index.cfm?id=1437 and trade.ec.europa.eu/doclib/press/index.cfm?id=961.

[69] See, for an overview, Rainer Arnold and Marcus Klamert, 'Außenhandelsrecht, K. I. Grundlagen' in Manfred A Dauses and Markus Ludwigs (eds), *Handbuch des EU Wirtschaftsrechts* (Beck, 2020), para 48.

could raise doubts as to the legality of other agreements of the same kind, including those under negotiation, those concluded, and those already in the ratification process.

C. The Effect of the Rulings of the Court According to Case Law

The precedent value of the judgments of the Court of Justice is an intricate issue. Preliminary rulings of the Court are binding on the requesting court.[70] The results of an annulment procedure are binding also on other national courts and administrations,[71] as required by the principles of the unity of the EU legal order and legal certainty.[72] However, analogies may not be drawn by national courts to set aside similar provisions in other Union acts.[73] In the same vein, interpretations given by the CJEU are binding on all national courts and authorities alike.[74] When the Court renders a ruling, its effects stretch to the parties of the case, the national courts concerned in the preliminary reference procedure, as well as the other Member States' courts and national authorities, insofar as the Court lays down an authoritative interpretation of EU law. The Court can, however, exclude the precedent effect that its judgments may have on future case law by conditioning a ruling to the (very) specific circumstances of the case a hand, such as in the *Achmea* judgment.

In the context of preliminary rulings, an unequivocal interpretation by the Court constitutes an *acte clair* or *acte éclairé*. For example, in *CILFIT*, the Court held that a national court of last instance is under no obligation to request a preliminary ruling from the Court if the 'correct application of Community law [is] so obvious as to leave no scope for any reasonable doubt as to the manner in which the question raised is to be resolved'.[75] Such determination must, however, be based on a correct assessment of the 'characteristic features of [EU] law and the particular difficulties to which its interpretation gives rise',[76] considering specifically the different language versions and the EU-specific terminology.[77] A national administrative authority or court, or, indeed, a Member State government or national parliament does not, should they deviate from the Court's interpretation, commit a breach of the duty of loyalty. However, their interpretation can be challenged in front of a national court and once again reach the Court via a preliminary reference procedure, or the Member State may be subjected to infringement proceedings.

Under the *acte éclairé* doctrine, a national court of last instance may refrain from requesting a preliminary reference from the Court if the question is 'materially identical with a question which has already been the subject of a preliminary ruling in a similar case'.[78] A wrong determination of 'materially identical' may eventually lead to

[70] Case 69/85, *Wünsche*, EU:C:1986:104, para 13.
[71] Case 66/80, *International Chemical Corporation*, EU:C:1981:102, paras 12–13.
[72] Case 314/85, *Foto-Frost v Hauptzollamt Lübeck-Ost*, EU:C:1987:452, para 15.
[73] Case C-461/03, *Gaston Schul*, EU:C:2005:742, para 25.
[74] Case C-453/00, *Kühne & Heitz*, EU:C:2004:17.
[75] Case 283/81, *CILFIT*, EU:C:1982:335, para 16.
[76] Ibid para 17.
[77] Ibid paras 18–20.
[78] Joined Cases 28-30/62, *Da Costa* EU:C:1963:6.

infringement proceedings against the Member State whose court of last instance fails to make the necessary reference to the Court of Justice.[79]

In order to avoid a situation on the international plane where an international agreement concluded under a wrongful legal basis or by recourse to a wrongful procedure must, in order to remedy these faults, be denounced and renegotiated, the TFEU includes Article 218(11) TFEU and the possibility to request the Court to assess the compatibility with the Treaties of a draft international agreement to be concluded by the Union. Such situations might possibly undermine the Union's negotiating position and reputation as a treaty partner, causing 'serious difficulties and … adverse consequences' to all parties involved.[80] Opinions given under this provision have binding effect insofar as an adverse opinion by the Court precludes the entry into force of the agreement unless the latter is amended or the Treaties revised. Article 218(11) TFEU is essentially a constitutional safeguard mechanism for securing the effectiveness of the Union's external action, as is the duty of loyalty.

Hence, under normal circumstances, assessing the effects of rulings or opinions of the Court does not involve elements of foreseeability or anticipation. Instead, Member State courts are themselves required to interpret the judgments of the Court and draw the correct conclusions. It is a different matter whether national authorities must adapt their actions to rulings which the Court might render in the future. This is discussed in the following section.

D. The Effect of Court Rulings and the Duty of Loyalty

Trying to predict the holding of the Court based on previously decided cases, such as explained above in the example of *Achmea* and Opinion 1/17, is common practice and, in fact, constitutes an example of dealing with the developing case law of the Court. *Achmea* and Opinion 1/17 belong to a sequence of cases assessing the compatibility of international agreements with the principle of autonomy.[81] Whereas predicting the direction of the Court's case law can be an ungrateful job despite major efforts to carve out, consider and apply the patterns of previous case law shaping the contours of a provision or principle of EU law, the Court's rulings are, to a certain degree, unpredictable. In the absence of a formal doctrine of precedent, the Court is generally consistent in its case law but does occasionally, in more or less explicit forms, depart from its previous decisions.[82]

In view of the case law discussed in section III above, it can be asked whether the rulings of the Court could constitute Union acts which mark the start of concerted

[79] For example, Case C-173/03, *Traghetti del Mediterraneo*, EU:C:2006:391; Case C-416/17, *Commission v France*, EU:C:2018:811.

[80] Opinion 1/75, *Local Cost Standard*, EU:C:1975:145.

[81] See Panos Koutrakos, 'The Autonomy of EU law' (n 64); and more generally on autonomy, Marcus Klamert, 'The Autonomy of the EU (and of EU Law): Through the Kaleidoscope' (2017) 42 *EL Rev* 815; and Marja-Liisa Öberg, 'Autonomy of the EU Legal Order: A Concept in Need of Revision?' (2020) 26 *Eur Public Law* 705.

[82] See Anthony Arnull, 'Owning up to fallibility: Precedent and the Court of Justice' (1993) 30 *CML Rev* 247; Marc Jacob, *Precedents and Case-Based Reasoning* (CUP, 2014).

Union action. The latter trigger the duty of loyalty in order to ensure the effectiveness of the Union's external action, going beyond the obligation to observe the binding rulings of the Court. A very broad reading of the principle of loyalty would, in effect, interpret the second sentence of Article 218(11) TFEU not only to preclude the entry into force of an envisaged agreement when an adverse opinion of the Court has been rendered, but also when such opinion can be anticipated.

In the particular case of CETA outlined above, the possible breach of the duty of loyalty on behalf of the Member States would have concerned the ratification process of the mixed agreement. Ratification by all parties to a bilateral mixed agreement concluded by the EU and its Member States, of the one part, and a third country, of the other part, is required for the entry into force of the treaty, whereas certain provisions thereof may be applied provisionally between some of the parties pending ratification by others.[83] In case of a multilateral agreement to which the Union cannot become party but whose subject matter falls within the Union's competence, the duty of loyalty obliges the Member States to ratify the treaty in their capacity of trustees of the Union.[84] In other cases concerning multilateral mixed agreements, which would result in 'incomplete' mixed agreements,[85] the duty of loyalty requires close cooperation between the Union and the Member States but cannot be construed as to forbid non-ratification altogether,[86] at least if compelling reasons to refrain from ratification are present.[87]

This arguably does not change if there exists a judgment by the Court that suggests that certain elements which are common to multiple agreements do not conform with EU law, albeit none of the other relevant agreements were the subject of the ruling itself. This was the situation with *Achmea* and Opinion 1/17 as explained above. Thus, the Member States were not required under Article 4(3) TEU to refrain from ratifying CETA, irrespective of the preceding judgment in *Achmea* that may have hinted at a possible incompatibility.

In order to establish such a scenario, according to the logic of the case law discussed under section III above, we would need to understand the rulings of the Court as expressions of a Union interest, which would require the Member States to refrain from concluding a certain mixed agreement. It is submitted that this is not convincing, for the following reasons.

Firstly, the nature of the Court's rulings and opinions cannot be equated with the nature of the actions of the Union's political organs. The latter express the Union's interest which have been concretised through the exercise of the competences conferred on the EU by the Member States. This is different from the rulings of the Court, whose task

[83] See Notice concerning the provisional application of the Comprehensive Economic and Trade Agreement (CETA) between Canada, of the one part, and the European Union and its Member States, of the other part [2017] OJ L 238/9. On the provisional application of the CETA, see further Luca Pantaleo, 'The provisional application of CETA: Selected issues' (2017) 41 *Questions of International Law* 59.

[84] See Opinion 2/91, *ILO Convention 170* (n 5) paras 37–38.

[85] Henry G Schermers, 'A typology of mixed agreements' in David O'Keeffe and Henry G Schermers (eds), *Mixed Agreements* (Kluwer, 1983).

[86] See Guillaume Van der Loo and Ramses A Wessel, 'The non-ratification of mixed agreements: Legal consequences and solutions' (2017) 54 *CML Rev* 735, 744–45.

[87] Marcus Klamert, *The Principle of Loyalty* (n 31) 202–203.

pursuant to Article 19 TEU is to 'ensure that in the interpretation and application of the Treaties the law is observed'.

Secondly, whereas the Member States' individual or joint action during the conclusion of international agreements or in international organisations may interfere with the Union's interests and impede with fulfilling the Treaty objectives, the rulings of the Court do not entail these broader consequences. The Union's concerted action triggers a duty of loyalty with respect to the entire proposed field of action the scope of which is discernible, whereas the Court's rulings are so tied to the circumstances under scrutiny that its later effects cannot be predicted with any degree of certainty and cannot, thus, be considered reasonable for the Member States to anticipate.

Thirdly, as discussed above in section III, the duty of loyalty safeguards the effectiveness of the Union's external action and the unity of its external representation. A mixed agreement cannot be (wrongfully) ratified by one or more Member States without the active participation of the Union, often including all of its law-making institutions – the Commission, the Council and the European Parliament. The Union initiates and carries out the negotiations, signs the treaty, ratifies it and sanctions its provisional application. Union ratification usually takes place last after the Member States have ratified the mixed agreement in question.[88] The Union and its institutions are, thus, in control of every step of the conclusion of a mixed agreement, rendering it in practice impossible for one or more Member States to jeopardise the Union's interests by ratifying rather than refraining from ratifying a mixed agreement.[89]

Finally, an interpretation of Article 218(11) TFEU to the effect of extending the constraining force of the provision to situations where an opinion has not yet been given would not only run afoul of the clear wording of the Treaty, but could also possibly only affect actions by the Union institutions. Article 218(11) TFEU, such as the remainder of Article 218 TFEU, is primarily concerned with the Union's side of agreements, rather than the Member States'. It does not govern the specific case of mixed agreements and even less the part of mixed agreements that falls within the competence of the Member States.

V. Conclusion

We have distinguished between elements of foreseeability and elements of anticipation resulting from the Treaties and the Court's case law. While the former notion relates to assessments that must be undertaken by Union institutions, the latter relates to duties of abstention, or at least coordination by the Member States.

These duties of abstention imposed on Member States in case law have been founded on concretisations of the Union interest by at least a concerted strategy in the Council. It has been argued that this logic cannot be transferred to rulings by the Court, which

[88] See the pending request for an Opinion by the Court submitted by the European Parliament (1/19), *Istanbul Convention*. See the contribution by Panos Koutrakos and Viktorija Soņeca in this volume.

[89] The Union's own institutions may, however, conclude and ratify an international agreement in breach of the Treaties leading to both internal and external repercussions.

serve a different purpose under the Treaties. This means that based on Article 4(3) TEU and analogies to case law decided on its basis, it is not plausible to argue that Member States are obliged to refrain from ratifying a mixed agreement, even though elements of such agreement could be considered potentially unlawful in light of a previous judgment or opinion by the Court.

Nobel laureate in physics, Niels Bohr, is quoted as saying: 'Prediction is very difficult, especially if it's about the future.'[90] While Union law does contain a number of 'prospective' elements influencing actions by both the Union and the Member States, it thus seems sound not to involve the case law of the Court in this.

[90] en.wikiquote.org/wiki/Niels_Bohr.

4

The Mixed Nature of the EU-Canada FTA

Between Competences Distribution and Democratic Legitimacy

MANON DAMESTOY AND NICOLAS LEVRAT

I. Introduction

Recent negotiations between the European Union and its transatlantic partners, Canada and the United States, have highlighted the potential democratic tensions through the lens of the division of competences between the EU and its Member States. The remarkable demonstrations surrounding the CETA (Comprehensive Economic and Trade Agreement) and TTIP (Transatlantic Trade and Investment Partnership) negotiations between 2013 and 2017, and the blocking of the Walloon parliament led by Magnette, were signs not only of a questioning of the EU trade policy orientation, but also of a wider and significant mistrust by citizens of some EU decision-making processes. By looking at this empirical case we will analyse the mechanics and the process of trust/distrust regarding the EU external action. It will lead us to conclude that on the one hand, the current negotiation process lacks legitimacy, and on the other, that leaving a veto right on the outcome of such complex year-long negotiations to each national (or even subnational, as in the present case) parliament is a 'sword of Damocles', incompatible with the EU's wish to present itself as a strong and resolute commercial partner on the world stage. This is why we suggest the involvement of national parliaments at an earlier stage, inspired by the existing mechanisms for the implementation of shared competences within the EU. We argue this could bring a certain democratic rebalancing and a renewed legitimacy to the common commercial policy.

II. The EU Trade Policy: A European Common Policy that Divides

Trade policy is undoubtedly one of the European Union's most integrated policies. Having quickly become a common policy of the Union,[1] the 2009 Treaty of Lisbon confirmed the Union's extensive exclusive competence in trade matters.[2] However, from a single competence to trade in goods inaugurated in 1958 to the allocation of a competence on foreign direct investment in 2009,[3] the road to a common EU trade policy has not been so smooth. Taking a quick look at this process of economic integration will allow us to explain some of today's political blockages. Partly based on the research of the political scientist Sophie Meunier,[4] we support the idea that the gradual transfer of trade competences from the Member States to the Union has taken place according to two different but complementary dynamics. An initial intergovernmental dynamic saw a shift of competences agreed by the Member States and responding to both political and economic interests. Then a neo-functionalist dynamic led by the Commission, under pressure from the ECJ which pointed out the limits of the CCP scope,[5] drove an incremental transfer of competences to the Union without a genuine Member States and citizens will. This second dynamic could explain the current blockages in the implementation of the Union's new trade competences through its 'new generation trade agreements'.

Until the 1980s, the European Union was able to rely on a permissive consensus to quietly run its economic integration, but the end of this situation gave way to a less consensual dynamic, described as an 'integration by stealth'.[6] By negotiating an extensive and living 'new generation' trade agreement[7] with Canada from 2009, the European Commission has finally shed light on the issue of the distribution of trade competences between the EU and its Member States as regard legitimacy to negotiate on a wide number of related areas (social, environmental, health) on behalf of the Union, its Member States and citizens.

A. The 'Integration by Stealth' of EU Trade Policy

In 1957, aware that the Community had to speak with a single voice if it wished to play a role in international trade and comply with GATT rules, the six founding states resolved

[1] Consolidated version of the Treaty on the Functioning of the European Union [2012] OJ C 326/47, Art 3 para 1 (TFEU).

[2] ibid Art 207.

[3] See in this volume the chapter by Bartosz Soloch and Makane Moïse Mbengue.

[4] Sophie Meunier, 'Integration by Stealth: How the European Union Gained Competence over Foreign Direct Investment' (2017) 55 *Journal of Common Market Studies* 593.

[5] Opinion 1/94, (Competence of the Community to conclude international agreements concerning services and the protection of intellectual property), EU:C:1994:384.

[6] See Meunier (n 4) 593.

[7] ie a generation of comprehensive agreements based on continuous regulatory cooperation aiming at the progressive removal of all non-tariff barriers to trade (sanitary, environmental measures etc). The 'new generation trade agreements' are qualified as 'living agreements', meaning that they have a dynamic or evolving aspect. Their content may and will be detailed and completed by the cooperation bodies it creates and to which it assigns real decision-making powers.

to create a Customs Union and adopted a common customs policy towards foreign states. To give substance to this single voice, they decided to transfer the power to negotiate on trade in goods to the European Commission in accordance with their economic interests. Following the idea of supranational efficiency, the Member States have gradually agreed to new transfers.[8] Thus, until the 1990s, benefiting from a permissive consensus, the Union and the Member States were able to continue this dynamic. However, since the conclusion in 1994 of the Uruguay round which led to the institution of the World Trade Organization (WTO) encompassing new multilateral agreements (such as TRIPS), the face of international trade has changed and the Commission is asking EU Member States for new competences in order to adapt, particularly in the fields of services and intellectual property. Unlike past transfers, these sovereignty negotiations will not take place quietly and easily, but with a strong opposition from several Member States.[9] The ECJ also pointed out the limits of the scope of the existing CCP competence.[10]

Thus, if the early stages of the common commercial policy can be read in terms of a rational will of the states to be more efficient at the European level,[11] the last major shift of competences to the Union in 2009, that of foreign direct investment, is rather 'the result of a combination of neo-functionalist Commission entrepreneurship and historical accident, against the preferences of the Member States',[12] or what Meunier calls a form of 'integration by stealth'. By pursuing integration without the strong support of the Member States, the European Commission has gained competences and thus considers it can negotiate agreements of a much broader scope.

However, since this latest shift of competences has not been the outcome of a genuine willingness on the part of the Member States or by an in-depth political debate, it is now – during the implementation phase and the negotiations of the 'new generation' free trade agreements – that the debate occurs, leading to the Union being at risk of losing its much sought-after single voice. The reason is that states need to express, either indirectly or in a remote procedural arrangement, consent to rules that will become binding for them and their citizens. It is a fundamental requirement of liberal democratic theory that the legal rules enforceable by authorities have received consent from the members of the polity (usually citizens). This provides legitimacy to the authorities in charge of implementing the norms.[13] Naturally, not all citizens need to consent directly,[14] a chain of delegation which allows some democratically elected authority, usually Parliament, to consent on behalf of the whole community being the most common institutional arrangement.

[8] See especially Sophie Meunier, *L'Union fait la force: L'Europe dans les négociations commerciales internationales* (Presses de Sciences Po, 2005).

[9] See Sophie Meunier and Kalypso Nicolaïdis, 'Who Speaks for Europe? The Delegation of Trade Authority in the European Union' (1999) 37 *Journal of Common Market Studies* 477.

[10] See Opinion 1/94 (n 5).

[11] We could also refer here to the work of Andrew Moravscik, *The Choice for Europe: Social purpose and State power from Messina to Maastricht* (Cornell University Press, 1998) to explain the agreement of the Member States to delegate more sovereignty to the EU.

[12] See Meunier (n 4) 593.

[13] See for a very thorough and subtle analysis of such mechanisms, Jean-Marc Coicaud, *Legitimacy and politics: a contribution to the study of political right and political responsibility* (Cambridge University Press 2002).

[14] However, it may also happen. In Switzerland, international agreements may be submitted to referendum for approval (Federal Constitution of the Swiss Confederation of 18 April 1999 (Status as of 1 January 2021) AS 1999 2556 Art 141.1.d).

B. The 'Community Method' and the Legitimacy of Norms of International Origin

This legitimacy theory functions well for unilaterally adopted legal norms, but it becomes more complex when the norms are embedded in an international agreement, that shall simultaneously bind several sovereign polities under the same rules.[15] The consent of each sovereign polity can only be expressed on a single common text embedding the rules. This is why the legitimation of international agreements usually only comes at the end of the drafting process – which takes place at the international level between delegates of the different sovereign polities (diplomats) – through a process of ratification from each sovereign polity.[16] It is only after such ratification that the internationally originated rules become binding and enforceable within the legal order of each polity, having received proper democratic consent.

One of the most striking feature of EU law-making capacity is that it has supressed this two-step process, through the principle of 'direct effect of EU law'. Initially limited to Regulations, it was quickly extended by the ECJ to most areas of EU law,[17] with the consequence that ex-post ratification by national parliaments is no longer needed for EU law to be enforceable by national authorities.[18] This is the origin of what Marquand termed 'democratic deficit',[19] since, up to 1994 at least, EU normative acts were adopted without the formal consent of any parliament, not even the European Parliament (EP). The European Economic Community (EEC), at the time, tried to remedy this difficulty by improving the democratic legitimacy of EEC institutions; the European Parliament is thus since 1979 directly elected and is now 'composed of representatives of the Union's citizens'.[20] Through incremental revisions of EC-EU decision-making procedures, EP is now genuinely exerting legislative and budgetary functions – jointly with the Council – at the EU level.[21] The second guarantee offered to national polities in exchange for the delegation of direct law-making capacity to EU institutions, is to bind such exercise of normative power by a strict principle of conferral.[22] As stated in Article 5§2 TEU, 'under

[15] Hilary Charlesworth and Jean-Marc Coicaud (eds), *Fault lines of international legitimacy* (Cambridge University Press, 2010).

[16] Such process may be found in EU law as regards the acceptation of a treaty modifying the EU treaty at Art 48 para 4 al. 2 TEU. As regard agreements concluded by the EU, see Art 218 para 6 TFEU. More generally, see the Vienna Convention on the Law of Treaties of 1969, Art 14.

[17] Case 26/62, *NV Algemene Transport- en Expeditie Onderneming van Gend & Loos v Netherlands Inland Revenue Administration*, EU:C:1963:1.

[18] See Case 106/77, *Amministrazione delle Finanze dello Stato v Simmenthal SpA*, EU:C:1978:49.

[19] David Marquand, *Parliament for Europe* (London, J. Cape, 1979).

[20] Consolidated version of the Treaty on European Union [2012] OJ C 326/13, Art 14 para 2 (TEU).

[21] Ibid Art 14 para 1.

[22] International organisations are always bound by a principle of specialty, meaning that they may not act beyond the aim they were constituted for by their Member States (see ICJ, 11 April 1949, 'Reparation for injuries suffered in the service of the United Nations, Advisory Opinion': *ICJ Reports* 1949, 174. And ICJ, 8 July 1996, 'Legality of the Use by a State of Nuclear Weapons in Armed Conflict, Advisory Opinion', *ICJ Reports* 1996, 66). However, since no international organisation other than the EU has the capacity to adopt normative acts which would become binding without proper ex-post state consent, the control of this principle of specialty is rather loose. It is not so for the EU principle of conferral. Even though the wording 'principle of conferral' only appears with the Lisbon Treaty (2009), the principle was already embedded in Art 5 TEC, and the ECJ since 1957 has had the power to declare an EU normative act void (art 174 TEC, now Art 264 TFEU) on the ground of a lack of EU competences (Art 173 TEC, now Art 263 TFEU).

the principle of conferral, the Union shall act only within the limits of the competences conferred upon it by the Member States in the Treaties to attain the objectives set out therein. Competences not conferred upon the Union in the Treaties remain with the Member States.'

C. The Distribution of Competences within the EU and Democratic Legitimacy

The boundary between EU and Member States competences is not clearly defined, all the more since the Treaties (which confer competences to the EU) introduced the concept of non-exclusive competences,[23] now referred to as 'shared competences'.[24] This recognition of intertwined competences between the EU and its Member States reflects the genuine nature of the EU as a multilevel polity, or a *demoïcracy*.[25] If the adoption of EU norms still excludes national parliament (thanks to the direct effect principle), the exercise of shared competences by the EU is subordinated to the respect of a 'principle of subsidiarity'.[26] Described only briefly in the Treaties, the principle was operationalised through Protocols,[27] appended to the Treaty of Amsterdam and the Treaty of Lisbon. Both, but in different ways, recognise the necessity of a role for national Parliaments in the exercise of this category of competences.[28]

The Amsterdam Protocol 'on the application of the principles of subsidiarity and proportionality' stated that in the domain of shared competences, if the EC was to adopt normative acts after having fulfilled the conditions set forth in Article 5 TEC, then 'the form of Community action shall be as simple as possible, consistent with satisfactory achievement of the objective of the measure and the need for effective enforcement. The Community shall legislate only to the extent necessary. Other things being equal, directives should be preferred to regulations and framework directives to detailed measures.'[29] A directive, and a fortiori a framework directive, leaves room for national legislator to translate (and eventually adapt) the provisions of EU law into national law provision, guaranteeing thus a legitimation through the formal adoption of a normative act by the national (or subnational) Parliament. According to the 'Amsterdam scheme', there is therefore an ex-post national democratic appropriation of the EU normative

[23] Treaty of Maastricht on European Union [1992] OJ C 191, Art G para 5 instituting a new Art 3B in the Treaty instituting the European Community (Maastricht Treaty).

[24] TFEU, Art 2 para 2.

[25] The term seems to have been first used to describe the EU by Kalypso Nicolaidis, in a 2004 piece published in *Foreign Affairs* ('We, the Peoples of Europe …' (2004) 83(6) *Foreign Affairs* 97). For more developments on the same issue, see Francis Cheneval, *The Government of the Peoples. On the idea and principles of multilateral democracy* (New York, Palgrave Macmillan, 2011).

[26] See Maastricht Treaty (n 23). It then became Art 5 TEC and is now found as Art 5 para 3 TEU.

[27] According to Art 51 TEU, 'The Protocols and Annexes to the Treaties shall form an integral part thereof'. Protocols thus have the same legal force as treaty provisions.

[28] In countries where the legislative power is distributed between several tiers of authorities, such authority may also be recognised to sub-national Parliaments, as is for example the case in Belgium.

[29] Protocol on the application of the principles of subsidiarity and proportionality, para 6, *in European Union, The Treaty of Amsterdam*, (Luxembourg: Office for Official Publications of the European Communities 1997) 106.

act – but not a formal approval, the directive being from its entry into force binding on Member States, including their parliaments – which accompanies the exercise of a shared competence by the EU institutions.

The Lisbon Protocol no 2, which replaces the Amsterdam Protocol no 30, proposes a quite different path for involving national parliaments in the exercise of shared competences. The reference to specific forms of normative EU acts (directives) is dropped. The strongly suggested post-adoption intervention of national parliaments (through transposition of the directive) to generate democratic legitimacy when the transfer of normative competences to the EU was not unconditional is replaced by an ex-ante capacity, on the part of national parliaments, to challenge the appreciation of EU institutions as regards the subsidiarity principle. Thus, 'any national Parliament or any chamber of a national Parliament may, within eight weeks from the date of transmission of a draft legislative act, in the official languages of the Union, send to the Presidents of the European Parliament, the Council and the Commission a reasoned opinion stating why it considers that the draft in question does not comply with the principle of subsidiarity.'[30] Thereafter, 'The European Parliament, the Council and the Commission … shall take account of the reasoned opinions issued by national Parliaments or by a chamber of a national Parliament.'[31] This ex-ante mechanism extends democratic legitimacy from the national level to the exercise of shared competences by the EU, since by not issuing a negative reasoned opinion, the majority of national parliaments consent to the implementation of a shared competence by EU institutions alone.

Isn't it the same type of issue that is a stake with EU mixed agreements? The CETA saga and the numerous political and academic debates it generated seems a proper case study to address this question.

III. The CETA Saga: a Contribution of National Parliaments to the Legitimisation of Trade Agreements

Since 2009, stimulated by its new competences and facing a paralysed WTO, the EU has embarked on numerous bilateral trade negotiations in order to modernise some outdated agreements and pave the way to a new generation of agreements whose objective is not limited anymore to the elimination of tariff barriers to trade, but also aiming at a degree of harmonisation of 'conditions' in which goods object of the free-trade are produced. These notably include social rights of workers or respect of normative environmental constrains, both understood as factors that could distort fair competition in a free trade agreement. Let us on this specific point underline that up to the Single European Act (1987), such measures within the EU required unanimous consent. This is the illustration that such measures call for a higher threshold of legitimacy.

[30] Protocol (no 2) on the application of the principles of subsidiarity and proportionality, [2016] OJ C 202/207 Art 6.

[31] Ibid, Art 7 para 1, if the number of reasoned opinions represent one third of parliamentary chambers or more than half of them, the EU institutions will be compelled to formally decide on the national parliaments 'objections' (see Art 7 para 2 and 3 of the aforementioned Protocol).

In line with this objective, in 2009 the EU launched new negotiations with Canada (CETA) to sign what will be one of the first and deeper agreements of this new generation and, as a consequence, one of the most contested. Indeed, while the relative secrecy inherent to trade negotiations allowed the Commission to negotiate this agreement smoothly for years (almost until the adoption of a final text in 2014), CETA became a political issue at a very late stage. The relative opacity of the negotiation process, the new awareness of civil society of the possible impact of technical provisions on their daily life,[32] the new pre-eminence of the climate issue and, above all, the new extension of the negotiating mandates to areas affecting national (or European) democratic choices,[33] led to the contestation of the CETA. Significant demonstrations have thus brought hundreds of thousands of citizens to the streets of Europe.[34]

If the supposed neo-liberal orientation of the trade policy pursued by the Commission has been called into question, very quickly the issue of legitimacy of new binding rules embedded in the CETA has also been put forward by its critics, both with regard to the content of the agreement, as well as with the way in which it was negotiated.[35] On the one hand, the regulatory cooperation chapter and the protection of investment chapter – which creates a new Investment Court System (ICS) – have drawn fire from critics, considering them as threats to European *demoïcracy* and national democratic choices over environmental, social or sanitary measures. On the other hand, the relative opacity of the negotiating rounds, the limited power of the European Parliament in the process and the fact that the national parliaments have been side-lined despite the breadth of the areas concerned, has once again brought the debate on the Union's 'democratic deficit' back to the forefront.

It is on the strength of this exceptional mobilisation of European civil society and his national specific right of veto[36] that Paul Magnette, then Minister-President of the Walloon region (Belgium), opposed head-on the signing of the CETA in 2016, working for the reopening of the negotiations and the recognition of the key role of national parliaments in view of the mixed nature of this agreement.[37] By doing so, Magnette relaunched the academic debate on the democratic legitimacy of the European Union, a debate often presented by the media in these terms: can a small village of die-hard Walloons[38] single-handedly block a trade agreement negotiated for years by

[32] At the international level, we can date this increasing politicisation of international trade policy to the 1999 Seattle WTO protests which saw the emergence of new, highly structured anti-globalisation movements that have led to the premature failure of this WTO new millennium round.

[33] We could also cite here the launch of new negotiations with the United Stated in 2013 which will, de facto, put the spotlight on the almost completed CETA negotiations and will be the starting point of its contestation.

[34] A substantial literature has emerged in recent years around the particular mobilisation and politicisation of CETA and its American cousin TTIP. See, for a comprehensive example, Dirk De Bièvre, Patricia Garcia-Duran, Leif Johan Eliasson and Oriol Costa (eds), 'Politicization of EU Trade Policy Across Time and Space' (2020) 8 *Politics and Governance* 239.

[35] For an example of civil society petition explaining the rejection of CETA, see, 'European and Canadian civil society groups call for rejection of CETA' (*S2B Network*, November 2016), www.s2bnetwork.org/wp-content/uploads/2016/11/Transatlantic-CETA-statement.pdf.

[36] See section III.A.

[37] For a complete story of this 'Walloon saga', see, Paul Magnette, *CETA: Quand l'Europe déraille* (Waterloo, Editions Luc Pire, 2017).

[38] This is a reference to *Asterix and Obelix*, a famous Belgian cartoon strip (from Gosciny and Uderzo) which depicts the resistance of 'a small village of die-hard gauls' against the whole Roman Empire, at the time of Julius Caesar.

the European Union?[39] By opposing the signing of the CETA on behalf of a European region, Paul Magnette has finally made the juridical issue of mixed agreement, and thus the involvement of national parliaments, a question of prominent democratic issue. Can a small European region alone block such a European agreement without endangering European democracy? Naturally, the opposite question is as legitimate: can the European Union negotiate such an agreement alone, without the clear consent of all its citizens, expressed through democratic institutions such as national or subnational parliaments, and yet be considered as legitimate to do so? As we will see below, depending on how academics have framed the question, they have adopted very different perspectives. We shall try to understand why.

A. Magnette and the Walloon Veto of CETA: A Three-Level Interest Game

Due to institutional singularities of Belgium, the federal government needed the consent of its regional governments to sign the CETA – something the government of Wallonia, supported by its parliament, refused to give in 2016. By doing so, regional President Magnette incurred the wrath of his federal government, the European Commission – not to mention the Canadian government – but also the vast majority of Member States which supported the agreement as it stood. What were Magnette's motives for standing alone against this agreement?

In October 2016, as Member States prepared to sign the CETA in Brussels, Magnette in consultation with his parliamentary majority decided to oppose the Walloon veto. At that time, Magnette was Minister-President of Wallonia; however, he had in the past served several times as a federal minister. As Minister-President, he was excluded from the decision-making Council to which he had had access as a federal minister; therefore, the only leverage he had to oppose the outcome of negotiations with Canada was his regional veto on external affairs, as allowed by Belgian constitutional arrangements. At first glance, it seems possible to hypothesise that the Walloon parliament would not have had the central role it had in 2016 if Magnette had had direct access to the Council of the Union. However, without this direct access, it was in his interest to support his parliament, and therefore the citizens, in order to legitimise his opposition and gain visibility. Thus, by a first reading by interests, it is therefore possible to put forward the hypothesis that the Walloon President was playing a kind of three-level political game in this 'CETA-saga'.

- *At the regional level*, by relying on his parliament to oppose his veto to the signing of the CETA, which he wasn't legally required to do at this stage, Magnette strengthened its legitimacy with the Walloon parliament and the highly organised and mobilised Walloon civil society whose interests he defended.

[39] For example, see, 'CETA: la Wallonie, « irréductible résistante », au centre du monde (médiatique)' *RTBF*, (Brussels, October 2016), www.rtbf.be/info/dossier/ceta-la-wallonie-defie-l-europe-et-le-canada/detail_ceta-la-wallonie-irreductible-resistante-au-centre-du-monde-mediatique?id=9439597.

- *At the federal level*, he also enabled Wallonia, a Belgian region with relatively minor weight in the Belgian institutional game, to regain a singular role at the federal level and influence important decisions.
- *At the EU level*, his landmark opposition to an international treaty negotiated for years by the European Commission (2009–14) gave opposition social movements an audible political voice and thus led to the questioning of both the European trade model and the EU governance of external affairs.

Some voices have accused the President of Wallonia of simply wanting to serve his political interests through this opportunistic opposition.[40] Some others read in this frontal opposition an anti-European position, a rejection of the European project and support for anti-capitalist or even national-sovereigntist movements.[41] However, this first reading tends to deny or obscure 'the second hat' of Magnette, who, much more than a politician, is also recognised as a brilliant EU scholar.[42] Thus, *reading by interests* cannot dispense with an even more important *reading by ideas*. Focusing on the ideas that he defended during his academic career and those that he decided to put forward in his famous 'Namur Declaration' in December 2016, we will highlight a particular vision of European construction which, far from being anti-European, simply tends to defend a vision of European project and governance that is different from those promoted by the European Commission and Member States' governments. The publication of this declaration brought back to the forefront the now old debate on the democratic legitimacy of the Union and the particular role of national parliaments in this respect.

B. The 'Namur Declaration': Advocacy for Democratic European Governance

On 5 December 2016, a few months after the signing of the CETA – finally conceded to by Wallonia at the price of some modifications to the agreement[43] – Paul Magnette,

[40] According to Magnette's account of his discussions with Canadian Minister Chrystia Freeland during the Walloon blockade, Freeland seemed to see his opposition as nothing more than a political strategy to be 'leader of the European left' and be able to return to his parliament with a 'hunting trophy'. (Magnette, *Ceta: Quand l'Europe déraille*, 83-84.) See also, for an example among numerous media debates on the meaning of this opposition, 'La fronde des Wallons contre l'accord CETA avec le Canada, un combat précurseur?', a discussion between Yuliya Kaspiarovich and Cenni Najy, *Le Temps* (Geneva, 5 November 2016, www.letemps.ch/opinions/fronde-wallons-contre-laccord-ceta-canada-un-combat-precurseur.

[41] In France, the indirect support of Marine Le Pen (From the extreme right Rassemblement National party) through the social networks and media may have played in favour of this anti-European interpretation of Magnette's opposition, to the point of making him 'the anti-CETA hero' in the media. See, for an example, Céline Boff, 'Qui est Paul Magnette, le nouveau héros des anti-Ceta?', *20 minutes* (24 October 2016), www.20minutes.fr/economie/1948855-20161024-paul-magnette-nouveau-heros-anti-ceta.

[42] Paul Magnette has spent his academic career studying European construction and the theories of democracy, becoming a noted contributor in the field of European studies.

[43] See 'Joint Interpretative Instrument on the Comprehensive Economic and Trade Agreement (CETA) between Canada and the European Union and its Member States' [2017] OJ L 11/3.

supported by some 40 international researchers,[44] decided to elaborate a 'Namur Declaration'. This Declaration, published as a follow-up to the 'CETA-saga' and the new politicisation of EU trade policy, calls on the Union to respect democratic procedures and to ensure a more social, sustainable and responsible trade policy.[45] By publishing it, the signatories of this declaration attempted to propose a decision-making process that would be more democratic than today, by giving a central role to parliamentary scrutiny, publicity and deliberation. By analysing signatories' research work and the content of the Namur declaration text in the following paragraphs, we will demonstrate that, far from being an anti-European position or an attempt to renationalise the EU trade policy, the position defended by this academic collective proposes to rely on the national parliaments to reinforce the European democratic process.

First of all, we can read Magnette's positioning on the CETA as a two-step reflection. Not going so far as to subscribe to the myth of the European democratic deficit advanced by the political scientist Andrew Moravscik,[46] Paul Magnette tends, however, to see the democratic deficit more as 'a feeling of dispossession [of European citizens] in the face of a political process in which neither the ideological orientations nor the way in which they are formed are clearly perceived'[47] than as a real structural problem. He considers that this feeling, which is reflected in the discourse around the 'democratic deficit', must be taken seriously. Accordingly, the Namur Declaration should not be seen as an attempt to respond to a structural problem of a Union which would be undemocratic in its form, but rather to respond to a particular situation that is considered by the signatories as illegitimate, namely, the signing of the mixed agreements without proper national debates.[48]

Indeed, Magnette considers that the Union alone – through its Council and the European Parliament – does not have the legitimacy to negotiate 'new generation' agreements such as the CETA. Quite simply because these comprehensive and 'living' agreements deal with the capacity of national (or *in casu* sub-national) parliaments to make and implement choices reflecting the political preferences of their voters[49] (on issues such as social rights or environmental policy) and is not limited to EU exclusive competences; they therefore remain, at least in part, a matter of national sovereignty.

[44] It should be noted that Nicolas Levrat, co-author of this chapter, was one of the first signatories of this declaration. A careful analysis of the profiles of all the first 40 signatories reveals several interesting things: 1) the majority of signatories are political scientists or economists, as well as some jurists; 2) a very large majority of signatories are interested in European construction and are teaching European integration; 3) finally, we can identify a social-democratic political trend in the profiles of the signatories.

[45] 'Namur Declaration' (Namur, 5 December 2016).

[46] See especially, Andrew Moravcsik, 'Reassessing legitimacy in the European Union' (2002) 40 *Journal of Common Market Studies* 603.

[47] Paul Magnette, *Le régime politique de l'Union européenne*, 4th edn (Paris, Presses de Sciences Po, 2017) 233 (our translation from the French version).

[48] Note that a semi-directive interview conducted on 20 February 2020 with Paul Magnette at the Belgian Socialist Party headquarters in Brussels has enabled us to substantiate the position briefly defended in the Namur Declaration.

[49] For considerations on such issue, see Steve Charnovitz, 'An analysis of Pascal Lamy's proposal on collective preferences' (2005) 8 *Journal of International Economic Law* 449.

If the Union wishes to legislate alone in this area, as it could do based on an exclusive competence, it must have the consent of its Member States and their citizens: 'But progressive erosions without real deliberation, and without consent, pose a real problem of democratic legitimacy.'[50] The end of the permissive consensus no longer allows the Commission to move forward incrementally without the agreement of European citizens, even with the approval of the European Parliament. The neo-functionalist (or spillover) thesis seems outdated; a political and public debate is unavoidable if the Union wishes to negotiate such wide-ranging agreements. Thus, Magnette will say 'the Namur declaration was quite objectively and quite openly transnational or even multinational, saying that we have to come back to real debates in national parliaments, if you want a broad spectrum. Otherwise you have to stick to the competences you have been given and not try to conquer others.'[51] From this response, and from the text of the Declaration, emerges a second element essential to legitimisation, namely the need of public deliberation.

We can thus draw one short conclusion from this Declaration: of a rather defensive nature, this Declaration pleads for a procedure of open dialogue that is better framed and respectful of civil society while remaining within the representative framework. It is finally a rather simple plea for a more open and transparent dialogue. Nevertheless, beyond this rather political posture, the ultimate theoretical expression aimed at by this declaration and which is expressed through the work of several of its signatories (Jean-Marc Ferry and Kalypso Nicolaidis, in particular), seems to be the transnational or cosmopolitan vision of the European Union.[52] Thus, Jean-Marc Ferry – a former Magnette professor – as early as 2000, in *La Question de l'Etat européen*, proposed close cooperation, both vertical and horizontal, between national parliaments and the European Parliament. In this way, the national parliaments, closer to the citizens, could bring forward the demands of civil society, exchange information, thus leading to a real multi-site European debate, instead of multiple national debates on Europe. The European Parliament would then be the 'sounding board' of the non-institutionalised public arena.[53] Subscribing to the Declaration but with a more critical vision of the current Union than Magnette's one, Jean-Marc Ferry called for the end of the 'privatisation of European polity'.[54]

This cosmopolitan or transnational project of Kantian inspiration is largely based on a deliberative Habermassian vision of democracy. It is through public and contradictory deliberation that a decision emerges that would be accepted or socially acceptable by a majority of citizens. But this democratic process takes time. Reacting to the Walloon

[50] Interview with Paul Magnette, President of the Socialist Party and Bourgmestre of Charleroi (Belgian Socialist Party Headquarters, Brussels, Belgium, 20 February 2020).

[51] Ibid.

[52] It should be noted, however, that not all the signatories of the declaration support the same vision of the Union. The analysis that follows therefore reflects what emerges from the declaration itself and its main initiators research and does not reflect the complexity of the positions of all its signatories. The same observation can be made with regard to the following analysis of the statement 'Trading together'.

[53] Jean-Marc Ferry, *La Question de l'Etat Européen* (Paris, Gallimard 2000).

[54] Jean-Marc Ferry, 'Non à la privatisation du politique européen' *Le Monde* (Paris, 7 November 2016), www.lemonde.fr/idees/article/2016/11/07/non-a-l-europe-des-portes-closes_5026520_3232.html.

veto, Ferry will thus plead in *Le Monde* for democratic patience: 'Being effective in politics does not mean bypassing deliberative processes under the assumption that they would be a waste of time. It is already a mistake at the national level and, even more so, at the level of a Union of co-sovereign states. Rather, political effectiveness requires democratic patience, which consists in ensuring that all partners reach an agreement without violence of reason and will.'[55]

C. The 'Trading Together Declaration': Let's Continue Business as Usual

A few weeks after the publication of Namur Declaration, on 25 January 2017, a collective of 70 European researchers[56] decided, in a competing statement, to respond directly to Namur. Called, 'Trading Together: For strong and democratically legitimised EU international agreements', this declaration sees in Namur a real threat to the 'EU's international standing'[57] as well as a call for the renationalisation of European trade policy. In their view, the European decision-making process, as provided for in the Treaties, fully guarantees the democratic legitimacy for the EU's international agreements.[58] On the basis of this Declaration, we can notice two different criteria of legitimacy for these agreements: first, the elective legitimacy of the European Parliament and of the Council of the Union (an indirect elective legitimacy) and secondly, the legitimacy through participation of the organised civil society though the creation of several tools of participatory democracy.[59]

Just as the Namur Declaration did not explicitly express a cosmopolitan theory of Europe, by its primarily political and reactive nature, the vision developed by the signatories of the 'Trading Together' declaration is not openly 'federalist'. However, it is clear that the underlying logic is federalist or more correctly, statist and really close to the vision held by the European Commission and a number of political actors in the EP. This Union mainly draws on the democratic canons of its nation-states to build its legitimacy and thus has certain limits induced by a European construction that is far from state-building.

[55] Ibid. Our translation from French.

[56] Contrary to the Namur Declaration, the 70 researchers are mostly jurists (≈80%) and for the most part of them, specialists in international law or trade law. Some of them are also lawyers or arbitrators. As specified in note 44 as regards author involvement in the 'Namur Declaration', it should here be noted that Christine Kaddous, one of the co-editors of the book, is among the signatories of this Declaration.

[57] 'Trading Together: For strong and democratically legitimized EU international agreements' (Brussels, 25 January 2017).

[58] See on this trend, Christine Kaddous, 'Un nouvel élan en matière de politique commerciale: vers une redynamisation de la Commission européenne' in Josiane Auvret-Finck (ed), *La Commission européenne en voie de redynamisation*, (Paris, Pedone, 2017) 295–308.

[59] As for the Namur Declaration, we summarise these two positions in Figure 4.1 below.

First of all, the elective legitimacy provided by the EP and the Council seems insufficient to legitimate the process in the eyes of European citizens. The relative opacity of the functioning of the Council and the low turnout at European Parliament elections make elective legitimation not as effective at the European level as it used to be at the national level. In that line, numerous researchers have shown the failure of the parliamentarisation of the EU as a remedy for democratic deficit.[60]

Secondly, by making participatory democracy the ideal to be achieved or followed, the Commission (supported in this idea by this declaration) tends to instrumentalise the participation of civil society for democratic legitimisation purposes. It thus creates a whole range of procedural tools supposed to respond to the organised civil society (or interest groups representation) demand.[61] However, these tools give the illusion of a participatory democracy that operates on the self-exclusion of the vast majority of citizens. These tools are not part of a deliberative democracy either because they generate micro-debates in highly professionalised circles, and not a debate of general interest at the level of European societies as a whole. In short, participation as conceived by the European institutions creates a technocratic Union that cannot acquire a more substantial political legitimacy in the eyes of the public.[62]

Finally, signatories consider that this demand for national parliament involvement is a threat to European integration and can be a breeding ground for populist movements, such as those that led to Brexit:

> What scared us most in the Namur Declaration was the desire to unravel exclusive competences that are conferred on the European Union by the treaties. We can always improve the system, but we are at an extremely dangerous historical moment for the construction of the Union. The 'take back control' that presided over Brexit in the United Kingdom may resonate elsewhere as well.[63]

By doing so, they finally prevent a real public debate on the European project for fear of disintegration of the Union.[64] We consider that continuing with trade policy as it was conceived 10 years ago, impacting more and more on the citizens' daily life but without approval or informed consent, would undoubtedly be more dangerous for European integration than listening to demands from below.

[60] See, for examples, Magnette, *Le régime politique de l'Union européenne* (n 47) or Nicolas Levrat, *La construction européenne est-elle démocratique?* (Paris, La Documentation française, 2012) 22; in English, Andreas Follesdal and Simon Hix, 'Why There Is a Democratic Deficit in the EU: A Response to Majone and Moravcsik' (2006) 44 *Journal of Common Market Studies*, 533.

[61] See for an unashamed presentation of such practice, the Commission 'White Paper on European Governance', [2001] OJ C 287.

[62] To go further on the impact of europeanisation on interest groups and/or the democratisation of the EU 'from below', see the important work of the political scientist, Sabine Saurugger. See also, Rosa Sanchez-Salgado, *Comment l'Europe construit la société civile* (Paris, Dalloz, 2007).

[63] Olivier Le Bussy, 'La puissance de négociation commerciale de l'Union européenne n'existe que parce que nous sommes unis' an interview with Pierre d'Argent, *LibreEco* (Brussels, 25 January 2017), www.lalibre.be/economie/decideurs-chroniqueurs/la-puissance-de-negociation-commerciale-de-l-union-europeenne-n-existe-que-parce-que-nous-sommes-unis-588907bbcd70ff671dcf135.

[64] Interview Paul Magnette (n 50). 'But under the pretext that they are hindering the "forward march", those who seek to put the Union on the rails of a great democracy are being looked at sideways.'

Figure 4.1 Pro-European visions of EU Trade Policy Governance[65]

	Namur Declaration	**Trading Together Declaration**
Observation	Legitimate protest from the Walloon Parliament	Dangerous blockade from the Walloon Parliament
Involvement of national and sub-national parliaments	Necessity to democratically legitimise mixed agreements = Shift of sovereignty not agreed by European citizens ('Competence creep'[66])	Threat to European integration and democracy Key role of governments
Legitimacy	Deliberative democracy	Extended representative legitimacy (consultations)
Efficiency	Through the inputs = democratic patience	Through the outputs = credibility as an international player
The test of discussion	European public space	European Parliament
Remedy	Construction of a European public space Public confrontation + deliberation	Parliamentarisation + Participation tools
Political form	Transnational Union	Federal Union (Statists)

[65] This figure and all the second part of this chapter focused on the pro-European debate. It deliberately sets aside the competing anti-European or national-sovereignist visions that have been strongly expressed around the CETA but which, however, have not been part of this public academic debate clearly opposing the two statements under consideration.

[66] This notion used in law is close to or could lead to an 'integration by stealth' – a concept developed by Sophie Meunier and quoted at the beginning of the chapter. To refer to the work of the jurist Sacha Garden, 'The phenomenon of "competence creep", [is the one] whereby the EU somehow manages to legislate and/or otherwise act in areas where it has not been conferred a specific competence'; Sacha Garden, 'Competence Creep Revisited' (2019) 57 *Journal of Common Market Studies* 205.

IV. Criteria and Procedure to Determine the Exercise of External Shared Competences by the EU and its Member States

As the title of our chapter indicates, multilevel democratic approval would give the CETA – or any other new generation FTA – great democratic legitimacy. On the other hand, such procedure allows any national government (or even subnational government, in the case of Belgium) to veto the signature. The same will be true at a later stage for any national or subnational Parliament, which could individually veto ratification for the whole of EU.[67] We fully acknowledge that this is not very democratic either! One can imagine solid majorities in all EU Member States, except a very small one (for example Cyprus (865,000 inhabitants)) which rejects ratification. In such case – and it did happen on 31 July 2020 – a majority of Cypriot Parliamentarians could block the adoption of an EU-Canada Treaty, against the democratically expressed will of elected representatives of some 450 million citizens in Europe.[68]

So, contrary to the domestic situation, where national parliaments are given a limited role in the adoption of normative acts in a domain of shared competences, it appears that as regard mixed agreements, Member States parliaments or governments will only be in a position to express a veto at the end of the norm-making process, potentially threatening years of negotiations. This observation leads us to raise the following question: why is it so different, as regard procedures and consequences, for the exercise of EU and Member States shared competences domestically and internationally?

A. Criteria for Choosing Between EU-Only or Mixed Agreement

First, it should be noted that mixed agreements had been used for the conduct of EEC external relations long before the concept of shared competences was included in the Treaties.[69] The reason to conclude mixed agreements was not to be found in the exercise of shared competences between the EEC and its Member States,[70] but actually in the necessary mobilisation of two sets of exclusive competences, one from the EEC, and another set of exclusive (not transferred to the EEC) competences from the Member States. On this longstanding practice, the ECJ introduced confusion in its recent case

[67] An incomplete mixed agreement could however in such case be envisaged. On incomplete mixed agreement, see the chapter by Joni Heliskoski and Gesa Kübek in this volume.

[68] See, Merjin Chamon and Thomas Verellen, 'Whittling Down the Collective Interest: CETA, Facultative Mixity, Democracy and Halloumi', (*VerfBlog*, 7 August 2020), https://verfassungsblog.de/whittling-down-the-collective-interest/>.

[69] The first mixed agreement was concluded between the EEC and its Member States on the one side, and Greece on the other, in 1961. See Council Decision 61/106/EEC of 25 September 1961 on the conclusion of the Agreement establishing an Association between the European Economic Community and Greece [1963] OJ 26/293.

[70] See in this volume the chapter by Joni Heliskoski and Gesa Kübek.

law. In its Opinion 2/15, rendered on 16 May 2017, the Court concluded, following a long and detailed examination of the EU-Singapore FTA, that

> It is apparent from paragraphs 80 to 109 and 226 to 242 of this opinion that the commitments contained in Section A of Chapter 9 of the envisaged agreement fall within the common commercial policy of the European Union and, therefore, within the latter's exclusive competence pursuant to Article 3(1)(e) TFEU in so far as they concern foreign direct investment of Singapore nationals in the European Union and vice versa. *On the other hand, those commitments fall within a competence shared between the European Union and the Member States pursuant to Article 4(1) and (2)(a) TFEU in so far as they concern other types of investment. It follows that Section A of Chapter 9 of the envisaged agreement cannot be approved by the European Union alone.*[71]

The wording used by the ECJ led part of the doctrine to conclude that shared external competences between the EU and its Member States means that the EU cannot conclude such agreement alone, or in other words, that international agreements in such fields should be concluded as mixed agreements.[72] It however took Marise Cremona's sharp eye to underline that the conclusion of the Court in that matter was linked to the specific circumstances of the case, in which all intervening Member States[73] in the case argued during the proceeding, that the EU should not conclude the Singapore FTA alone.[74] This is for that reason that, unless the examined FTA was entirely under the exclusive competence of the EU – in which case Member States would not be able, in legal terms, to claim participating to the conclusion of this agreement alongside the EU – Member States could legally claim their preference for a mixed agreement, with all the resulting procedural consequences, including individual Member States' veto right. Thus Cremona concluded on the matter:

> certainly there may be cases (although they are likely to be rare) where competence is shared in the sense that there are parts of the agreement which fall outside EU competence altogether; here, mixity would be required. But *where the EU possesses competence over the whole agreement albeit shared (in whole or part) with the member states, then mixity is a matter of political choice* and will depend on many factors, including the political importance of the agreement.[75]

This is, altogether, not so different than deciding whether the EU may or may not exert within the EU a shared competence unilaterally. In such case, it is also a political decision,[76] informed by the criteria set forth in Article 5§3 TEU, namely that 'the

[71] Opinion 2/15, *EU-Singapore FTA*, EU:C:2017:376, paras 243–244.

[72] For more developments on the issue, see in this volume the chapter by Merjin Chamon and Marise Cremona.

[73] All Member States, except Croatia and Estonia, were intervening parties to the procedure.

[74] See in this sense the opinion of AG Sharpston delivered on 21 December 2016 (ECLI:EU:C:2016-992) para 7.

[75] Marise Cremona, 'Shaping EU trade Policy post-Lisbon: Opinion 2/15 of 16 May 2017' (2018) 14 *European Constitutional Law Review* 249 (emphasis added); see also Isabelle Bosse-Platière and Marise Cremona, 'Facultative Mixity in the Light of the Principle of Subsidiarity', in Merijn Chamon and Inge Govaere (eds), *EU External Relations Post-Lisbon – The Law and Practice of Facultative Mixity* (Leiden, Brill, 2020) 48–85, esp 70.

[76] Early after the initial introduction of the subsidiarity principle, there was a huge literature discussing whether subsidiarity was a legal or political principle. A good presentation of this debate can be found in Antonio Estella De Noriega, *The EU principle of subsidiarity and its critiques* (OUP, 2002).

objectives of the proposed action cannot be sufficiently achieved by the Member States, either at central level or at regional and local level, but can rather, by reason of the scale or effects of the proposed action, be better achieved at Union level.' Such criteria will not be fit for deciding on the exercise of shared competences for external relations. But certainly some other, more relevant criteria could be agreed upon. And even better, a procedure to implement these criteria between EU institutions and Member States could be envisaged.

B. Proposal for an Early-Warning Procedure by National Parliaments

As we have seen above, the subsidiarity criteria set forth in the Treaty were considered too vague for proper implementation. Therefore, two different solutions, mixing the requirements of competence distribution and democratic legitimacy, were adopted by Protocols completing the Treaties. One of the difficulties of the choice about mixity or not for an EU international agreement, is that except in the case of EU exclusive competence, it may be made at any time, as long as the agreement is not signed. This is what happened as regards CETA, when under pressure from domestic political forces, some Member State governments required the CETA to be considered as a mixed agreement. For this reason, the initiation (at any time) of a mixity procedure may be seen by some as a procedural hazard.[77] However, completely banning democratic legitimation by national parliaments of EU international agreements, whose implementation may lead to strong constraints on the exercise of parliamentary democracy within Member States (in the interest of speediness of the process or 'credibility of the EU as an international actor'[78]), is a trade-off which makes too small a case for democratic legitimacy and will not be sustainable for long. The 'output legitimacy' so often relied upon by the EU institutions and their supporters, no longer convinces much; the time of a permissive consensus in favour of European integration is over.[79] This is why democratic legitimacy is no longer an academic chimera or an aesthetic option, but a central necessity for a sustainable European integration process. Further, Article 2 TEU requires both the EU and its Member States to respect a set of European values, including democracy.

For these reasons, we would suggest, in a likely future Treaty revision,[80] that Article 218 TEU be slightly modified. The current §2 of this article could be worded in a way that would allow national parliaments, in the case of an envisaged EU international agreement of wide scope and most likely covering areas of shared competences,[81] to be associated to the authorisation of the opening of negotiations. Procedural mechanisms – like for the implementation of the subsidiarity principle – could be dealt with in a

[77] See the 'Trading together declaration' (n 57), para 5 of the 'Analysis' section.

[78] Ibid.

[79] Gary Marks and Liesbeth Hooghe, 'A Postfunctionalist Theory of European Integration: From Permissive Consensus to Constraining Dissensus' (2009) 39 *British Journal of Political Science* 1.

[80] The Conference on the future of Europe was launched in May 2021. It can lead to Treaties revision proposals.

[81] It will be recalled that for agreements covering fields beyond EU competences, mixity is not an option but a legal requirement.

Protocol appended to the Treaties; or the Protocol no 2 'on the application of the principles of subsidiarity and proportionality' could be completed by specific provisions concerning potentially mixed agreements.[82]

It seems to us that such a proposal would have the advantage of striking a balance between EU interests as a credible trade partner on the international stage, and the legitimate worry of citizens that, under the cover of an international commercial agreement, their democratic rights – notably their capacity to express preferences as regards the socio-economic parameters applicable within their polity[83] – may have been forfeited. Such association of national parliaments would only concern the authorisation to open negotiation, eventually allowing a public debate on the scope of the negotiation mandate. For evident reasons, the precise negotiation mandate would not be the object of a public debate. If each national parliament, as under the 'Protocol on the implementation of the principles of subsidiarity and proportionality', could formulate a reasoned opinion stating why it considers that the proposed agreement would need to be ultimately submitted to an express approval by national parliaments (thus requesting the agreement from the outset to be envisaged as a mixed agreement), the procedural hazard would, in our view, appear much less random than it does nowadays. And naturally, if national parliaments failed to express such opinion at the opening of negotiations, or one parliament's opinion in favour of mixity of the envisaged agreement appeared very isolated, it would then have been democratically accepted (at least implicitly) that the envisaged agreement could be an EU-only agreement. We reckon that such a proposal falls short of meeting the most stringent standard of an open EU-wide public debate, but it would, in our view, strike a balance between the different known positions that have been exposed above.

V. Lessons and Conclusions

It thus clearly appears that the output legitimacy invoked by the Commission for a long time is no longer adequate in the eyes of citizens today to legitimise the imposition of a constraining normative regime. The attempt of the EU to regain legitimacy by better including national parliaments for scrutiny of internal acts (through the subsidiarity procedure) and by strengthening the European Parliament failed to convince. The CETA negotiations have shown the limits of the legitimisation of (mixed) international treaties by the European Parliament (still lacking proper legitimacy, despite the parliamentarisation of the EU) and the Council (opacity of discussions and unequal consultation of national parliaments by their governments). The ex-post legitimisation which may be appropriate at the national level, appears to be insufficient for extended EU agreements for which the transfer of sovereignty to the EU was the result of a neo-functionalist mechanism without real democratic consent of European citizens nor public debate on the project supported.

[82] See Bosse-Platière and Cremona (n 75) 57–58, who also consider such an option possible.
[83] See Steve Charnovitz (n 49).

By showing the limits of the statists' vision or the output legitimacy defended by the Commission, we finally highlight the interest and need to rely on the legitimacy of national parliaments to strengthen European democracy. Thus, the ex-ante involvement of national parliaments through an extension of a form of 'subsidiarity control'[84] defended in this chapter would allow us to:

1. put an end to the procedural uncertainty surrounding the legal qualification of new generation trade agreements (shared competences) – by determining the nature of the agreement at the beginning of the negotiations;
2. make it possible to ensure the consent of European citizens (through their parliaments) on the areas negotiated and thus the project defended by the Union on their behalf;
3. bring the debate back to the national level, closer to the citizens which would tend to deprivatise European politics and restore citizens' trust in the EU.

Our proposal therefore calls for democratic patience to be seriously put in balance with the effectiveness advocated by the Commission with a view to reconciling the different academic visions surrounding the need for legitimacy of international agreements in the domains of EU shared competences.

[84] This involvement shall be accompanied by the development of specific mechanisms to encourage a simultaneous transnational debate among national parliaments in cooperation with the EP.

5

The Representation of the EU and its Member States in Multilateral Fora

The AMP Antarctique Effect

MERIJN CHAMON AND MARISE CREMONA

I. Introduction

The present chapter will discuss the implications of the Court's ruling in *AMP Antarctique* for the question of the EU and the Member States' representation in international fora established pursuant to mixed multilateral agreements. While the Court itself as well as some commentators have presented *AMP Antarctique* as a special case with limited precedential value,[1] it is not clear yet what its ramifications will be for the practice of 'mixed' representation in international fora.

First the basic legal framework governing the EU's and Member States' joint participation and representation in international fora will be recalled. Subsequently, the relevant findings of the Court in *AMP Antarctique*, a case dealing with the issue of representation, will be summarised and it will be argued that the Court's reasoning fails to entirely convince in terms of both EU law and public international law (PIL). Next the key issues that determine the precedential value of the *AMP Antarctique* case will be identified. It will be shown how in principle *AMP Antarctique* could have significant repercussions for the EU's representation in international fora but that the ruling equally leaves enough flexibility for the Court to reduce the judgment's precedential value to zero. Given the questionable findings of the Court in *AMP Antarctique* that in itself would be positive, but it does mean that, notably, the Commission has missed an excellent opportunity to clarify the legal framework governing the joint representation

[1] Joined Cases C-626/15 and C-659/16, *Commission v Council*, EU:C:2018:925. See inter alia Fernando Castillo de la Torre, 'On 'Facultative' Mixity: Some Views from the North of the Rue de la Loi', in Merijn Chamon and Inge Govaere (eds), *EU External Relations Post-Lisbon – The Law and Practice of Facultative Mixity* (Leiden, Brill, 2020) 244; Stanislas Adam et al, 'Chronique de jurisprudence de l'Union – Les relations extérieures (1er Janvier 2017- 31 décembre 2019)', (2020) 56 *Cahiers de droit européen* 1, 342–43.

of the EU and its Member States under mixed multilateral agreements. Because of this the Court has not yet been pressed to address the question whether the Council has completely unfettered political discretion in deciding (not) to exercise EU shared competence. Finally, since the same principles govern the issues of both representation and participation, the question to which extent *AMP Antarctique* may shed light on the EU's participation in multilateral agreements will also be addressed.

II. The Basic Framework for the EU's Participation and Representation in Multilateral Fora

AMP Antarctique dealt with a problem of the EU's representation in an international forum. The question whether and when the EU must resort to mixed action in its representation pursuant to a mixed agreement should be distinguished from the question whether and when the EU must resort to mixed action when it concludes an agreement. Evidently, setting aside the possibility of participation in international fora as an observer, mixed representation is only possible when there is mixed participation, but it does not follow automatically from the latter. To recall, whether an international agreement should be concluded in mixed form (resulting in mixed participation) depends on the subject matter and the provisions of the international agreement. These will determine the existence and nature of EU competence, which in turn determines whether the mixed participation is obligatory, facultative or excluded.[2] Thus, as noted, mixed representation depends on but does not necessarily follow automatically from mixed participation. While the issues of participation and representation should thus be distinguished, and different legal rules may apply to both, they are governed by a single coherent legal framework.[3] This means that a case like *AMP Antarctique* which clarifies the rules on representation, might also be relevant to the issue of participation. This also follows from the Court's case law: as noted above, an agreement may be concluded as a mixed agreement depending on the nature of the EU's competence. But that it is indeed possible to conclude an agreement as facultatively mixed or facultatively EU-only when EU shared competences are in play is something which was only explicitly confirmed by the Court of Justice in the *COTIF I* case. That case dealt with the representation of the EU and the Member States in the Intergovernmental Organisation for International Carriage by Rail (OTIF (the acronym comes from the French name of the Organisation)) but has generally been interpreted as also applicable to the issue of participation, not in the least because the Court in *COTIF I* clarified (or corrected) one of its earlier statements on the possibility of facultative mixity in Opinion 2/15,[4] a case that dealt with the participation of the EU and the Member States in the Singapore FTA.[5]

[2] See on this also the chapter by Joni Heliskoski and Gesa Kübek in this volume.

[3] Ruling 1/78 re *the Draft Convention of the International Atomic Energy Agency on the Physical Protection of Nuclear Materials, Facilities and Transports*, ECLI:EU:C:1978:202, para 36.

[4] Case C-600/14, *Germany v Council*, ECLI:EU:C:2017:935, paras 66–68.

[5] Opinion 2/15 re *the EU-Singapore FTA*, ECLI:EU:C:2017:376.

In terms of representation, then, different approaches may be envisaged to determine whether the EU, the Member States or the EU and the Member States will speak on behalf of the mixed EU party for specific points on the agenda of an international forum. The basic approach and the one that is relied on in practice is to determine the representative depending on the competence at issue for the agenda item.[6] The FAO Arrangement at issue in the *FAO* case before the Court of Justice is a case in point.[7] A more recent example is the Code of Conduct adopted for the representation of the EU and the Member States in the framework of the UN Convention on the Rights of Persons with Disabilities (CRPD).[8] The Code of Conduct prescribes a different modus operandi depending on whether EU exclusive, shared, or Member State competence is at issue. The Code of Conduct therefore distinguishes between (i) Union, (ii) common and (iii) coordinated positions. In terms of procedure, it provides that each of the three types of position should be duly coordinated within the relevant Council working group, and at the initiative of either the (rotating) Presidency or at the request of the Commission or (one of) the Member States. Draft statements on coordinated positions are prepared by the Presidency, while Union and common positions are drafted by the Commission.

Of course, starting from the competence question, the framework governing representation should arguably be further refined. Indeed, in terms of the exercise of external competences, the subsidiarity principle should also play a role since an EU competence does not necessarily have to be exercised.[9] Likewise, the principle of sincere cooperation puts the emphasis on the achievement of the EU's objectives which cannot simply be equated with action by the EU (to the exclusion of action by the Member States).[10] Finally, as the *AMP Antarctique* case makes clear, international law may also be determinative of the question whether the EU should act together with its Member States (notwithstanding the EU having sufficient competence to act on its own).

[6] This is also reflected in Council of the European Union, General Arrangements for EU Statements in multilateral organisations, Doc 15901/11.

[7] Case C-25/94, *Commission v Council*, ECLI:EU:C:1996:114.

[8] Council of the European Union, Code of Conduct setting out internal arrangements for the implementation by and representation of the EU to the CRPD, 29 November 2010, Doc 16243/10.

[9] While subsidiarity is hardly explicitly in play when multilateral agreements are concluded, Bosse-Plattière and Cremona argue that subsidiarity could, and should, play a clearer role in how facultatively mixed multilateral agreements are implemented. See Isabelle Bosse-Plattière and Marise Cremona, 'Facultative Mixity in the Light of the Principle of Subsidiarity', in Merijn Chamon and Inge Govaere (eds), *EU External Relations Post-Lisbon – The Law and Practice of Facultative Mixity* (Leiden, Brill, 2020) 79–82. See also the chapter by Manon Damestoy and Nicolas Levrat in this volume.

[10] In this regard, Hillion and Chamon argue that while the principle of sincere cooperation is typically seen as promoting EU-only action, this is not necessarily so, precisely because there is not a perfect equation between EU-only action and 'achieving the EU's objectives'. They also argue that the specific requirements which flow from the principle of sincere cooperation are more restrictive in the phase of the implementation of a mixed agreement then in the phase of the conclusion (or before that, the negotiation) of an agreement. See Christophe Hillion and Merijn Chamon, 'Facultative Mixity and Sincere Cooperation', in Merijn Chamon and Inge Govaere (eds), *EU External Relations Post-Lisbon – The Law and Practice of Facultative Mixity* (Leiden, Brill, 2020) 99 and 103.

III. The Peculiar Case of the EU's Participation in the CCAMLR

The Canberra Convention (CAMLR) was negotiated by the consultative parties to the Antarctic Treaty and signed in 1980.[11] The EU (then EEC), which is not a party to the Antarctic Treaty, had requested to be an original signatory to the Convention, but eventually dropped this request after opposition mainly from the Soviet Union,[12] but also from a number of EU Member States.[13] Since Article XXVI of the Convention (on signature) only refers to states, it was decided to allow the EU to join the Convention after its signature, in accordance with Article XXIX paragraph 2.[14]

The Convention was originally set up by the parties to the Antarctic Treaty to prevent the ongoing development of commercial krill fishing in the Southern Ocean from prompting the UN Food and Agriculture Organisation to work out a global settlement for the Southern Ocean which would undermine their privileged position as parties to the Antarctic Treaty.[15] The dual approach of the Convention was then already clear during the negotiations: the Convention is not merely a traditional fishing treaty based on the rational use of biological resources (Article II), but it also follows a holistic ecosystem approach (Articles II and IX).[16]

As part of the ecosystem approach today, the concept of Marine Protected Areas (MPAs) plays a central role. MPAs are territorially defined parts of the sea and coast that enjoy specific legal protection in view of their ecological importance.[17] Yet, the establishment of Marine Protected Areas is not foreseen as such in the Convention. The fact that the Convention is nevertheless a forerunner in the creation of such areas on the high seas is primarily the result of the work done by the Scientific Committee to promote this approach within the Convention.[18] On the basis of this scientific work, the Commission of the CAMLR (CCAMLR) established an MPA in 2009 for the South Orkney Islands.[19] Two years later, at the 30th annual meeting of the CCAMLR, a general

[11] Convention on the conservation of Antarctic marine living resources 1980, UNTS 1329 (p 47). Bruce Davis, 'The legitimacy of CCAMLR', in Olav Schram Stokke and Davor Vidas (eds), *Governing the Antarctic* (Cambridge, Cambridge University Press, 1996) 234.

[12] William Bush, *Antarctica and international law: a collection of inter-state and national documents*, Vol I (London, Oceana Publications, 1982) 421.

[13] Belgium, Germany, France and the UK were the original EU parties to the Convention.

[14] Council Decision 81/691/EEC of 4 September 1981 on the conclusion of the Convention on the conservation of Antarctic marine living resources; [1981] OJ L 252/26. William Bush, *Antarctica and international law: a collection of inter-state and national documents*, Vol I (London, Oceana Publications, 1982) 422–23.

[15] Bruce Davis, 'The legitimacy of CCAMLR', in Olav Schram Stokke and Davor Vidas (eds), *Governing the Antarctic* (Cambridge, Cambridge University Press, 1996) 234.

[16] Ibid, 241. While *the* ecosystem approach does not exist, it is in any event holistic since fauna and flora are not approached individually (eg addressing each single fish species on its own) but in relation to each other and to abiotic factors. See Scott Parsons, 'Ecosystem Considerations in Fisheries Management: Theory and Practice' (2005) 3–4 *International Journal of Marine and Coastal Law* 382.

[17] Karen Scott, 'Conservation on the High Seas: Developing the Concept of the High Seas Marine Protected Areas' (2012) 4 *International Journal of Marine and Coastal Law* 850. There is however no fixed definition of what an MPA is; see Report of the 27th meeting of the Commission, CCAMLR-XXVII, para 7.16.

[18] See the Workshop on Bioregionalisation of the Southern Ocean organised in 2007 and reported in the Report of the 26th meeting of the Commission, CCAMLR-XXVI, p 32 et seq.

[19] See Conversation Measure 91-03 adopted at CCAMLR-XXVIII.

framework for the establishment of MPAs was adopted.[20] The actual expansion of the network of MPAs in the southern ocean is, however, very difficult and a recurring agenda item at the annual meetings of the CCAMLR.

For the 2015 and 2016 meetings of the CCAMLR there was a substantive agreement between the Council and the Commission on the position to be taken with regard to the establishment of MPAs for the Weddell and Ross Seas, but the European Commission considered that these positions should be adopted on behalf of the Union alone. The Council (COREPER) instead decided to submit them to the CCAMLR on behalf of the Union *and the Member States*.[21] This disagreement resulted from the difference in view over the competences at issue. According to the Commission, the discussions focused on fisheries matters (an exclusive Union competence), whereas the Council considered that the establishment of MPAs fell under environmental policy (a shared competence).

The Commission then went to Court to challenge the decisions of COREPER and the Council, which set out the positions of the Union and the Member States to be adopted in the context of the CCAMLR. The Commission relied on two pleas to show that what was at issue was in fact an exclusive EU competence.[22] However what is relevant for our present discussion is a third 'ghost plea' which the Commission had advanced but not properly elaborated. Indeed, apart from claiming an exclusive EU competence, the Commission also challenged the Member States' and the Council's political paradigm that shared competence by definition equates with mixed action. In other words, the Commission argued that even if a shared competence were at issue, this would not necessarily lead to mixed external action, since the EU could also exercise such a shared competence wholly on its own. In itself, this was uncontroversial, as the Court had already accepted this explicitly in the *COTIF I* case[23] where there had been an agreement within the Council to exercise certain EU shared powers externally in the framework of the OTIF without these powers having been exercised internally in the EU beforehand. However, that case was only decided after the Commission brought the *AMP Antarctique* case and, crucially, in *COTIF I* there was a clear agreement within the Council to make use of the EU's shared competence. Such an agreement appears to have been lacking in the decision-making resulting in the *AMP Antarctique* case.[24]

Of course, this issue ultimately boils down to the question whether in some scenarios or under some circumstances the Council could be legally obliged to opt for either EU-only or mixed action based on shared competences – and if so, on what legal grounds – or whether, instead, the choice is purely political and unfettered.

[20] See Conversation Measure 91-04 adopted at CCAMLR-XXX.

[21] Opinion of AG Kokott in Joined Cases C-626/15 and C-659/16, ECLI:EU:C:2018:362, paras 24–34.

[22] The Commission thus firstly argued that the issue came under EU a priori exclusive competence under Art 3(1) TEU or that alternatively it came under implied exclusive competence pursuant to the ERTA doctrine under Art 3(2) TEU. On the *ERTA* doctrine, see also the chapter by Kuisma and Larik in this volume.

[23] Case C-600/14, *Germany v Council*, EU:C:2017:296.

[24] According to AG Kokott there was no evidence that the Council had *not* wished to exercise EU powers, concluding that 'the only reason why the Council ultimately advocated joint action in the CCAMLR on behalf of the Union *and* its Member States in the contested 2015 and 2016 decisions is that the Council erroneously summarily equated shared competences and mixed action …'. Opinion of AG Kokott in Joined Cases C-626/15 and C-659/16, ECLI:EU:C:2018:362, para 116.

IV. The Court's Questionable Finding of Obligatory Mixed Representation in the CCAMLR

The Court's decision on the ghost plea was remarkable. This not simply because, having found that the decisions fell with shared environmental protection competence, it could have refrained from addressing a 'ghost' plea that had not been formally put forward, but also because through questionable legal reasoning it arrived at the conclusion that despite the competence at issue being shared, mixed action was in this case nonetheless *compulsory*. In the remainder of this paper this specific outcome will be referred to as the '*AMP Antarctique* effect'.

At the outset the Court uncontroversially noted that the Union must exercise its powers 'in observance of international law'.[25] What it subsequently deduced from this is less convincing however: in the specific system set up by the Antarctic Treaty System (ATS), of which the Canberra Convention forms part, it would be contrary to international law for the EU to act in such a way as to exclude the Member States from exercising their powers.[26] How does the Court come to this conclusion? First it notes the fact that the clause on participation by a regional economic integration organisation (REIO clause) in the Canberra Convention makes membership of the Union dependent on the membership of at least one of its member states. For the Court this means that the EU does not have fully autonomous status as a party to the Convention.[27] We will refer to this finding as *the autonomy condition* or *requirement*. The Court found further support for this in Article V of the Convention, which provides that parties to the Convention that are not parties to the Antarctic Treaty, like the EU, acknowledge the special position of the consultative parties to the Antarctic Treaty and their primary responsibility for developing the ATS and for ensuring its coherence.[28] This second element will further be referred to as the *international responsibility condition* or *requirement*.

Having invoked this international responsibility condition, one would expect the Court to go on to demonstrate how EU-only action pursuant to shared competence in the framework of the CCMALR would undermine the special obligations and the responsibilities that the EU Member State parties to the Antarctic Treaty derive from that treaty. However, this is not what the Court does. Instead, the Court notes that EU-only action 'might well … undermine the responsibilities and rights of those consultative parties – which could weaken the coherence of that system of agreements and, *ultimately*, run counter to Article V(1) and (2) of the Canberra Convention.'[29] Based on this, the Court (implicitly) concludes that as a matter of compliance with its obligations under the Canberra Convention, the EU should not act alone, and the positions were rightly adopted jointly by the EU and the Member States.

Before dissecting the reasoning of the Court, it is important to highlight the way in which the Court tries to limit the precedential value of its judgment in *AMP Antarctique*.

[25] Joined Cases C-626/15 and C-659/16, *Commission v Council*, EU:C:2018:925, para 127.
[26] Ibid, para 128.
[27] Ibid, para 130.
[28] Ibid, para 131.
[29] Ibid, para 133 (emphasis added).

The Court indeed starts its reasoning by emphasising 'the specific context of the system of Antarctic agreements',[30] following which it describes this specific context and adds that it is '[i]n those circumstances'[31] that the EU should not 'act without the participation of its Member States in an area of shared competence'.[32] One could therefore argue that the Court's ruling is, at the most, relevant only for multilateral treaties coming under the ATS and for situations in which shared EU competences are at issue. As will be shown below, however, the peculiar circumstances which the Court seems to find *in casu* are in fact not so peculiar at all but may be found in relation to many other multilateral treaties. First, the Court's reasoning will be scrutinised, following which we will assess to what extent *AMP Antarctique* could be applied analogously to other multilateral treaties despite the Court's best effort to 'contain' the relevance of its ruling.

A. The Public International Law Argument

Coming back to the remarkable reasoning of the Court, it must first be pointed out that a requirement in a REIO clause allowing an IO to become a party subject to at least one of its member states being a party to the multilateral treaty is not unusual.[33] In fact, it follows logically from an international legal order that emanates from sovereign states and that has only recently started to recognise the existence of REIOs as actors in their own right.

Apart from this contextual element, the REIO clause in the Canberra Convention only makes the *initial accession* of the Union to the agreement dependent on the presence of one of its member states among the parties. Once it has joined, the EU can act fully autonomously as a party. Even if all EU Member States that are currently parties to the Canberra Convention were to subsequently withdraw from the Convention, leaving the EU as the only 'European' party, this would not affect the EU's status as a party to the Canberra Convention. Indeed, the autonomous status of the EU in the Convention flows from its status as a REIO, a party separate from its Member States. This would only be different if the multilateral agreement were to somehow become (partially) inoperative as a result of the EU remaining a member while its Member States leave. For instance, if an international agreement prescribes recourse to the International Court of Justice for the settlement of disputes,[34] the agreement would become partially inoperative because the EU has no standing before the ICJ and any dispute it would find itself in with another party could not be resolved other than amicably. In Article XXV however, the Canberra Convention gives parties the choice to settle disputes either through the ICJ or through

[30] Ibid, para 128

[31] Ibid, para 133

[32] Ibid.

[33] See eg Art 1(2)(iii) of the Agreement establishing the General Fisheries Commission for the Mediterranean; Art 13(1) of the Agreement on the Conservation of African-Eurasian Migratory Waterbirds; Art 2 of the Constitution of the Food and Agriculture Organisation of the United Nations; Art 38 of the Convention concerning International Carriage by Rail (COTIF), etc.

[34] For instance, Art 66(2) of the UN Convention against Corruption, a mixed multilateral agreement, provides that parties may refer disputes to the ICJ if they cannot settle their dispute amicably and cannot agree on the organisation of arbitration.

arbitration. The same goes for the voting rights of the EU in the CCAMLR. Differently from other international agreements, the EU does not exercise the sum of its members' votes. Article XII(4) of the CAMLR provides that REIOs have only one vote. As a result, even if all the EU Member States were to withdraw from the Convention, the EU would still wield one vote and be able to act autonomously. In addition, even if the EU were to lose all its votes this would not show the EU's lack of autonomy but would at the most result in the EU being less effective in the international forum concerned.

That the Canberra Convention and the CCAMLR remain perfectly operative even if the EU were to act alone pursuant to shared competences is worth stressing. Govaere welcomed the Court's ruling in *AMP Antarctique*, finding that in its judgment the Court timidly but firmly seemed to embrace an approach that 'functionally integrate[s] and/or anticipate[s] international legal constraints when determining the issue of mixity under EU law'.[35] Govaere contrasts this with the Court's alleged lack of attention to the repercussions of the EU's inward looking approach in its dealings in the OIV.[36] However, while it may be accepted that the EU does indeed have a special responsibility not to frustrate or even paralyse the functioning of other international organisations, this was in reality never at issue in *AMP Antarctique*. Since EU-only action would not have had dysfunctional effects on the CAMLR or CCALMR, there was no need for mixity on functional grounds. Still, this type of dysfunctionality argument, on which, it should be noted, the Court did not rely in *AMP Antarctique*, could play in other circumstances depending on the votes allocated to the EU and how voting quorums are defined. For instance, the standard provision of a REIO clause in a multilateral agreement is that the REIO in question cannot vote simultaneously with its Member States and that its number of votes is equal to the combined votes of its Member States.[37] Depending on the number of other parties to a multilateral agreement, that standard provision may become unworkable and undermine the interests of the non-EU parties. The revision of the Data Protection Convention 108 provides an example. Initially the non-EU parties only wanted the EU to wield one vote but after protracted negotiations, special voting rules were agreed upon, specifically for the compliance mechanism.[38] When the Convention Committee reviews the implementation of the Convention by one of the parties pursuant to Article 23(h), a double majority is prescribed consisting of four-fifths of all parties and a majority of the non-EU parties. Furthermore if a decision pursuant to Article 23(h) comes within EU competence, both the EU and its Member

[35] Inge Govaere, 'Towards "Facultative" and "Functional Mixity" Consonant with the Principle of Partial and Imperfect Conferral', in Merijn Chamon and Inge Govaere (eds), *EU External Relations post-Lisbon – The Law and Practice of Facultative Mixity* (Leiden, Brill, 2020) 22.

[36] See Case C-399/12, *Germany v Council*, ECLI:EU:C:2014:2258. For a discussion, see Inge Govaere, 'Novel Issues Pertaining to EU Member States Membership of Other International Organisations: The OIV Case', in Inge Govaere et al (eds), *The European Union in the World – Essays in Honour of Marc Maresceau* (Leiden, Brill, 2014) 225–43. Govaere's criticism might also be reading too much in this case. After all, the political decision for EU action was clearly taken by the Council and the Court was only asked about the proper procedural legal basis for the Council's decision.

[37] See eg Art 15 of the Vienna Convention for the Protection of the Ozone Layer.

[38] See Jörg Polakiewicz, 'The European Union's External Action and International Law – the Council of Europe Perspective', Paper presented at the ESIL-ILAG Workshop on The European Union's External Action and International Law: A View From the Outside, 12/06/2020. pp 16–17.

States are precluded from voting.[39] These special arrangements were put in place to safeguard the Convention from dysfunctioning as a result of the EU's participation, but if they had not been in place a duty under EU law might still exist not to exercise its competences in such a way that the compliance mechanism would be undermined. Yet for the CCAMLR this is not an issue given the voting rules set out in Article XII of the Canberra Convention.

Secondly, the Court's finding that the parties under the Canberra Convention are obliged to recognise the obligations and responsibilities of the consultative parties to the Antarctica Treaty does not necessitate mixed action. As a preliminary point it should be noted here that the Court identifies problems on the basis of possible eventualities without making clear how the EU's action within the CCAMLR in any way makes it *impossible* (or even more difficult) for the consultative parties to further develop the ATS or to ensure its coherence. This is somewhat reminiscent of the Court's findings in Opinion 2/13 where mere theoretical possibilities led it to the finding that the draft accession agreement was contrary to the Treaties.[40] Assuming then that these unspecified eventualities do indeed materialise, the obligations of the consultative parties under the Antarctic Treaty would not, in any event, be legally compromised by the fact that the Union has acted alone within the CCAMLR. After all, the 'priority' of the Antarctic Treaty as well as the obligations of the consultative parties are safeguarded by the Canberra Convention itself in its Articles III and V, as a result of which the CCAMLR cannot adopt decisions that contradict the objectives or principles of the Antarctic Treaty or interfere with the responsibilities of the consultative parties. Moreover, should the CCAMLR adopt such a decision, then this would be a problem of international law rather than a problem of Union law. In short, contrary to the Court's finding, international law does not actually seem to prohibit the EU from acting on its own in the CCAMLR.

Although the Court refers to the *Kadi* case when it observes that the Union must respect international law when exercising its powers, the Court seems to ignore a further part of the *ratio decidendi* in *Kadi*, namely that 'an international agreement cannot affect the allocation of powers fixed by the Treaties or, consequently, the autonomy of the Community legal system.'[41] Although clearly *AMP Antarctique* did not concern the Court's jurisdiction it did involve the autonomy of the EU legal system, specifically the question on the division and exercise of (EU) competences. The problematic nature of the Court's reasoning is also evident when it is applied to a putative case in which the question is not of shared but of exclusive Union competence. Should the Union in such a case nonetheless act together with the Member States in an international body to which both are members? The Court preventively avoids this issue by referring to an inability of the Union to 'act without the participation of its Member States in an area of *shared* competence',[42] but this only highlights how unconvincing the reasoning is.

[39] See the Appendix to the Protocol amending the Convention for the Protection of Individuals with regard to Automatic Processing of Personal Data, CETS 223, 2018.

[40] See Opinion 2/13 re *the EU's accession to the ECHR*, EU:C:2014:2454.

[41] Joined Cases C-402/05 P and C-415/05 P, *Kadi and Al Barakaat v Council and Commission*, EU:C:2008:461, para. 282.

[42] Joined Cases C-626/15 and C-659/16, *Commission v Council*, EU:C:2018:925, para 133 (emphasis added).

After all, from an international law perspective, which the Court relies on to prescribe obligatory mixity, the internal division of powers between the Union and the Member States is not relevant at all.[43] If international law really did prevent the Union from acting autonomously, the Union could not escape this international law requirement by pointing to its exclusive competence under internal EU law.[44] Even if we read the Court's ruling as implying that whenever the internal EU rules on competence leave the Council with different options to act externally, the Council should pick the option that is most accommodating to international law, the requirement of mixed representation in this case is based on an unconvincing interpretation of the Convention. To be clear, our argument is not that the EU should ignore international law for the sake of the autonomy of its own legal order, but rather that in this case international law did not in fact require the EU to compromise its autonomy.

B. The Bad(?) Fit With Earlier External Relations Case Law

The international law reasoning elaborated by the Court therefore fails on the terms of international law itself. In addition, *AMP Antarctique* seems difficult to square with previous case law of the Court such as *Commission v Sweden* (*PFOS*), *Germany v Council* (*OIV*) and *Germany v Council* (*COTIF I*).[45] The *PFOS*, *OIV*, *COTIF I* and *AMP Antarctique* cases all involved the rights and obligations of the Member States in international organisations or fora in a situation of shared competence.[46] Unlike in *OIV* where the EU was not party to the agreement, in *PFOS*, *COTIF I* and *AMP Antarctique* both the EU and the Member States were Convention parties. While in *COTIF I* and *AMP Antarctique* there was no declaration of competences, in *PFOS* there was one, although it did 'not contain specific rules as regards the allocation of competence between itself and the Member States'.[47] Only in *PFOS* was the dispute of a substantive nature. In *OIV*, *COTIF I* and *AMP Antarctique* there was agreement on the course of action but the questions related respectively to whether the EU could rely on Article 218(9) TFEU to impose a position to be taken in an international organisation of which the EU is not a member (*OIV*), whether the EU could adopt a position pursuant to Article 218(9) TFEU in so far as it had not yet exercised the relevant shared competence internally (*COTIF I*) and lastly on whose behalf a position needed to be presented in the international forum (*AMP Antarctique*).

[43] As also reflected in Arts 27 and 46 of the VCLT.

[44] See Inge Govaere, 'Towards "Facultative" and "Functional Mixit" Consonant with the Principle of Partial and Imperfect Conferral', in Merijn Chamon and Inge Govaere (eds), *EU External Relations Post-Lisbon – The Law and Practice of Facultative Mixity* (Leiden, Brill, 2020) 43.

[45] See Case C-246/07, *Commission v Sweden*, EU:C:2010:203; Case C-399/12, *Germany v Council*, EU:C:2014:2258. *Commission v Greece* (*IMO*) could be mentioned here as well (see Case C-45/07, *Commission v Greece*, EU:C:2009:81). However, that case involved EU exclusive competences while the Court in *AMP Antarctique* seems to stress that its reasoning only applies to situations covered by shared competences. Yet as noted above, from an international law perspective, the distinction between exclusive and shared competences which is operated in the internal EU legal order is not relevant.

[46] In *OIV* AG Cruz Villalón assumed that an EU exclusive competence was at issue but Germany and the intervening Member States argued that the issue came under shared competence. The Court itself did not qualify the nature of the competence.

[47] Case C-246/07, *Commission v Sweden*, EU:C:2010:203, para 95.

In *PFOS* the Court identified a common strategy adopted by the Council not to immediately propose PFOS as a substance to be banned under the Stockholm Convention. It also went into the concrete consequences for the Union when a Member State (*in casu* Sweden) dissociates itself from such a common strategy.[48] On the other hand, it did not devote any attention to the repercussions of a Member State's duty to stay silent for the exercise by that Member State, state party to the Stockholm Convention, of its rights and obligations under that Convention. In *OIV* as well, the Court simply noted that the EU could implement a Common Agricultural Policy pursuant to Article 43 TFEU[49] and interpreted Article 218(9) TFEU broadly as also governing the scenario whereby the Council adopts positions to be defended in a body set up by an agreement to which the EU is not a party.[50] Similarly, in *COTIF I*, the Court accepted that once there is demonstrable shared external competence for the EU, it may exercise it regardless of whether it has already adopted internal rules on the matter. In these situations the effect of EU action on the rights and obligations of the Member States, state parties to the OIV and the OTIF Convention, was not taken into account. Although Sweden and Germany did not explicitly raise the issue of their position under those Conventions, that issue is implied in the competence question that the Court unreservedly resolved in favour of the Union. In a remarkable break with *PFOS*, *OIV* and *COTIF I*, the Court in *AMP Antarctique* all of a sudden attaches special importance to the Member States' rights and obligations under international law.[51] Unlike in *PFOS* however, where the Court certainly went into the repercussions of Sweden's unilateral action for the Union,[52] in *AMP Antarctique* it does not definitely show what the repercussions of the Union's actions for the Member States' rights and obligations would be.[53]

C. Containing the *AMP Antarctique* Precedent?

As already noted, the Court tried to limit the precedential value of its ruling by suggesting that it is only relevant in the context of the ATS and in so far as shared competences are being exercised. However, the context at issue in *AMP Antarctique* may not be as

[48] Ibid, paras 92–101.

[49] Case C-399/12, *Germany v Council*, EU:C:2014:2258, para 51.

[50] Ibid, para 55.

[51] Of course, the Court's apparent change of heart could also be welcomed, see Inge Govaere, 'Towards "Facultative" and "Functional Mixity" Consonant with the Principle of Partial and Imperfect Conferral', in Merijn Chamon and Inge Govaere (eds), *EU External Relations post-Lisbon – The Law and Practice of Facultative Mixity* (Leiden, Brill, 2020).

[52] Case C-246/07, *Commission v Sweden*, EU:C:2010:203, paras 92 et seq.

[53] If the rights and obligations of the consultative parties were the crux of the matter in *AMP Antarctique* it would further seem necessary to recognise that the mixed action in the CCAMLR is one of partial mixity. After all, only a few EU Member States are parties to both the Canberra Convention and the Antarctic Treaty. Belgium, Bulgaria, Finland, France, Germany, Italy, the Netherlands, Spain, Sweden and the Poland are parties to both Treaties. The Czech Republic is party only to the Antarctic Treaty, while Greece is party only to the CAMLR. The other Member States are not parties to either treaty. On this point, see also Anne Hamonic, 'L'Union européenne dans les enceintes internationales: La cour de justice souffle le chaud et le froid dans l'arrêt AMP Antarctique', (2020) 56 *Cahiers de droit européen* 1, 304–305.

peculiar as the Court implies. This is so essentially for two reasons: first, and as noted, a REIO clause that makes the initial accession of the EU dependent on at least one of its Member States being party to the agreement, while not a universal requirement,[54] is far from uncommon.[55] Secondly, while the Canberra Convention indeed refers to the 'special obligations and responsibilities' of the consultative parties to the Antarctic Treaty, this essentially refers to rights and obligations of third parties which the EU would be bound to respect in order to comply with international law. Whether the explicit cross-reference in the Canberra Convention to the Antarctic Treaty adds anything to this obligation is unclear.

One remarkable aspect of the Court's ruling is its silence on another peculiar aspect of the Canberra Convention, namely that it allows the EU and its Member States to act concurrently. Other multilateral agreements contain a rule that prohibits the EU and its Member States from both 'exercising their rights concurrently', or that prohibits 'an organization from exercising its right to vote if any of its member States exercises its right, and vice versa.' That this is not the case for the CCAMLR is indeed confirmed in Article XII(3) CAMLR and rule 4(c) of the CCAMLR's Rules of Procedure. It is therefore important to stress that the Canberra Convention, as compared with all other multilateral mixed agreements allows the Member States and the EU to vote concurrently.[56] At most, other agreements might allow the EU and its Member States to exercise some rights (but not voting rights) concurrently.[57] It is not clear how *AMP Antarctique* might be applied where mixed representation is not possible; presumably the EU and its Member States would adopt a joint position internally and this would then be represented either by the EU or by the Member States acting together (and also, in EU law terms, on behalf of the Member States, or the EU respectively) in the external forum.

[54] For instance Art 1(1)(k) of the Convention on the Conservation of Migratory Species of Wild Animals (Bonn Convention) only requires REIOs to be constituted by sovereign states and to have competence in matters covered by the Convention.

[55] See Art 38 of the OTIF; Art 17 of the Protocol against the Illicit Manufacturing and Trafficking in Firearms, Their Parts and Components and Ammunition, supplementing the United Nations Convention against Transnational Organised Crime; Art 6 of the Statute of the International Renewable Energy Agency; Art 67 of the United Nations Convention against Corruption; Art 13(1) of the Agreement on the Conservation of African-Eurasian Migratory Waterbirds; Art 21 of the Protocol Against the Smuggling of Migrants by Land, Sea and Air, supplementing the United Nations Convention Against Transnational Organised Crime; Art 16 Protocol to Prevent, Suppress and Punish Trafficking in Persons, Especially Women and Children, supplementing the United Nations Convention against Transnational Organised Crime; Art 25 of the OSPAR Convention; Art 305.1 of the United Nations Convention on the Law of the Sea even requires a majority of a REIO's member states to be signatories. In contrast, Art 20 of the Paris Agreement on Climate Change explicitly allows REIOs to be party without any of their Member States being parties.

[56] Art XII(3) CAMLR and r 4(c) of the CCAMLR's Rules of Procedure simply prohibits that the 'number of Contracting Parties so participating shall not exceed the number of Member States of the regional economic integration organization which are Members of the Commission.'

[57] Atypically, the text of the Bonn Convention itself would allow the EU and its Member States to exercise (voting) rights concurrently, but r 13 of the COP's Rules of Procedure provides that 'Regional economic integration organizations, in matters within their competence, shall exercise their right to vote with the number of votes equal to the number of their member States that are Parties. In such case, the member States of such organizations shall not exercise their right individually.'

V. *AMP Antarctique* and its Significance for the EU's Representation in Multilateral Fora

In light of the doubts on the uniqueness of the functioning of the CCAMLR, one should determine the precedential value of *AMP Antarctique*. For this, it will be necessary to clarify five issues:

1. Is the ruling relevant where EU exclusive competences are at issue?
2. Are the autonomy and rights and obligations conditions alternative or cumulative conditions?
3. What rights and obligations trigger the threshold resulting in obligatory mixed action?
4. In how far are the internal procedural rules of the international forum relevant?
5. Could the *AMP Antarctique* reasoning be applied to the conclusion of an international agreement?

A first issue is whether the PIL reasoning elaborated by the Court in *AMP Antarctique* would also require the EU and its Member States to act together where exclusive EU competences are at issue. For instance, when the CCAMLR is to adopt decisions that do squarely come under the Common Fisheries Policy. Above it was noted that the Court pre-emptively attempts to defuse this by stressing that shared powers are at issue. In this regard, Adam et al stress that

> [la] prise en compte du droit international dans le cadre de *l'exercice* d'une compétence externe n'est intervenue dans le raisonnement de la Cour qu'*après* que celle-ci avait tranché la question de la nature de ladite compétence. Rien dans l'arrêt AMP Antarctique ne permet donc de déduire que la Cour ait entendu remettre en cause le principe selon lequel l'existence et la nature de la compétence externe de l'Union doivent être exclusivement déterminées par référence au droit primaire de l'Union.[58]

However as was noted above, the internal (ie in the EU legal order) qualification of a certain competence (exclusive, shared, coordinating or supporting) is irrelevant from a public international law perspective, which still is the basis of the Court's reasoning. The Court might have an opportunity to clarify this issue in the currently pending Case C-161/20 in which the Commission reproaches the Council (Coreper) for having decided on a submission on behalf of the Member States and the Commission, in the context of the International Maritime Organisation on an issue allegedly coming under exclusive EU competence.

A second issue that has significant implications for the potential precedential value of *AMP Antarctique* is that related to the autonomy and rights and obligations-requirements. Is it sufficient to meet either one of these conditions result in the *AMP Antarctique* effect, or do these requirements have to be met cumulatively? As noted above, the autonomy-requirement applies to many multilateral agreements to which

[58] Stanislas Adam et al, 'Chronique de jurisprudence de l'Union – Les relations extérieures (1er Janvier 2017–31 décembre 2019)', (2020) 56 *Cahiers de droit européen* 1, 343 (emphasis added).

the EU is a party. Indeed, it also applies in the framework of the OTIF which provided the legal background for the Court to confirm, for the first time, in *COTIF I* that the EU can act 'autonomously' pursuant to shared powers. It is therefore doubtful that this constitutes a necessary and sufficient condition for requiring obligatory joint action. If it were, the autonomy of the EU on the international plane would be greatly affected and for instance the general rules on the EU's and the Member States' statements in international fora would surely have to be amended.[59] Today they take a wholly internal focus: who acts is entirely determined by the internal division of competences in the EU.[60] *AMP Antarctique* now requires these rules also to reflect the autonomy granted to the EU under the terms of the multilateral agreement itself.

If meeting the autonomy condition is not in itself sufficient to trigger obligatory joint action, it becomes even more critical to clarify the third issue, namely what balance of Member States' rights and obligations actually merit safeguarding? It follows from the discussion above that, unless the Court backtracked on its earlier case law (which is not assumed since the Court did not explicitly recognise this intention), not all rights which EU Member States enjoy under international agreements warrant obligatory joint action. A preliminary question to address here is whether it is relevant that in *AMP Antarctique* the rights which the Court had in mind were rights under a different treaty (Antarctic Treaty) to which the agreement in question (Canberra Convention) cross-referenced. While the Canberra Convention is not a formal protocol to the Antarctic Treaty, a similar constellation is not uncommon with main conventions and their protocols.[61] Another type of cross-reference is the type whereby generally an agreement confirms the right of the parties to conclude other agreements between themselves on the same subject matter. If the fact that the Canberra Convention explicitly cross-references to the Antarctic Treaty was determinative, the precedential value of *AMP Antarctique* is of course greatly reduced. At the same time if the cross-reference was determinative the above noted flaw in the Court's reasoning becomes even more glaring: since the Canberra Convention explicitly safeguards the Antarctic Treaty's consultative parties' rights and obligations, the risk of a CCAMLR decision undermining those rights and obligations is already catered for at international level within the CAMLR.

Alternatively, if the answer to the preliminary question identified above is that *any* right (or obligation) may potentially come into play, the issue of distinguishing relevant from irrelevant rights and obligations will be all the more pressing. In any event, the mere fact that by adopting an EU position pursuant to shared competences the Council can pre-empt Member States from voting or taking the floor in an international forum would not seem to be relevant. After all, the Court did not take issue with this in the *PFOS* case which related to the Stockholm Convention.[62] In *COTIF I* the Court did not

[59] See Council of the European Union, 'EU Statements in multilateral organisations – General Arrangements', Doc 15901/11.

[60] This focus on competences was criticised by Ramses Wessel and Bart Van Vooren, 'The EEAS's diplomatic dreams and the reality of European and international law', (2013) *Journal of European Public Policy* 1353–54.

[61] See also Anne Hamonic, 'L'Union européenne dans les enceintes internationals: La cour de justice souffle le chaud et le froid dans l'arrêt AMP Antarctique' (2020) 56 *Cahiers de droit européen* 1, 305.

[62] It must be noted however that the Stockholm Convention allows REIOs to become parties to the Convention without any of their member states being parties. See Art 25(2) of the Stockholm Convention.

take issue with Germany being pre-empted from exercising its rights in OTIF even if, admittedly, Germany also did not invoke these rights in one of its pleas (cf above).[63]

A fourth important issue relates to the question whether an international forum's procedural rules are relevant to determine the existence of an *AMP Antarctique* effect. In the reasoning as developed by the Court, what seems to be relevant are the REIO clause and/or the rights and obligations of the Member States. What the Court did not emphasise, as noted above, is the peculiar fact that in the CAMLR Commission, both the EU and the Member States are permitted to act concurrently and this differently from how joint action is regulated under the internal rules of other international fora. Two possible outcomes can be envisaged here: the internal rules of the CCAMLR were decisive for the Court's finding even if it did not draw attention to them. In this case *AMP Antarctique* would truly be a unique case. Alternatively, if the internal rules were not decisive for the Court's reasoning but merely allowed a joint action, the question becomes what happens when the autonomy and rights and obligations conditions are met but the international forum in question does not allow joint action. For instance, Article XIV of the Statute of the International Renewable Energy Agency provides that 'The provisions of this Statute shall not affect the rights and obligations of any Member deriving from any existing international treaty.' Article VI of the statute allows REIOs to accede on the condition that at least one of their Member States is a party to the Statute. These provisions combined would seem to correspond to the legal context that was also at issue in *AMP Antarctique*. Are we then to conclude that the EU cannot act alone in the IRENA and that mixed action is required? Yet under the same Article VI of the Statute a REIO and its constituent members are prohibited from exercising their voting rights concurrently, with the REIO being accorded the combined voting rights of its constituent members that are parties to the Statute. Does this then mean that the EU would have to completely leave the field to the Member States, resulting in compulsory MS-only action? Surely, the EU would also be able to act alone here (exercising the combined votes of its Member States) without this implying it would be affecting the rights and obligations which its Member States (parties to the IRENA Statute) derive from prior international treaties in the sense of Article XIV of the Statute.

Finally, there is the question of whether the *AMP Antarctique* reasoning could be applied to the conclusion of a multilateral agreement.[64] As already mentioned, the Court itself, in developing its reasoning on facultative mixity in the context of representation in *COTIF I*, referred to the operation of shared competence in the context of the conclusion of an agreement, suggesting that the same principles might apply.[65] Does this extend to the constraints apparently imposed by *AMP Antarctique*? First, it is clear that *AMP Antarctique*'s autonomy condition operates differently at the stage of conclusion or accession. Insofar as an international organisation or a projected multilateral agreement makes

[63] Case C-600/14, *Germany v Council*, EU:C:2017:296.

[64] Here, as throughout, our main focus is on multilateral fora; the conclusion of bilateral agreements raises different issues. On this distinction and its implications for facultative mixity, see further Isabelle Bosse-Platière and Marise Cremona, 'Facultative Mixity in the Light of the Principle of Subsidiarity', in Merijn Chamon and Inge Govaere (eds), *EU External Relations Post-Lisbon – The Law and Practice of Facultative Mixity* (Leiden, Brill, 2020).

[65] See above at n 4.

the participation of a REIO dependent on the participation of at least one of its Member States (and as we have seen, this is a common requirement), then mixed participation is required if the EU decides to exercise its competence; there is no 'EU-only' option. Instead of mixity flowing from the EU's status under the agreement (as in *AMP Antarctique*), its status as a participant is dependent on mixity. This is a different logic and not comparable to *AMP Antarctique* in its operation or effect. It is also sufficient to justify mixity: unlike *AMP Antarctique*, as argued above, the two conditions are not necessarily cumulative. On the other hand, where, exceptionally, the relevant REIO clause allows for REIO participation without any of its members being parties could there then still be an argument for mixity as imposed by international law? The Court will have the opportunity to clarify this in the currently pending case C-24/20. In 2017 the Court ruled that the Geneva Act came wholly under the EU's exclusive competence,[66] but when the Council adopted the decision allowing the EU to accede to the Act, it also authorised all Member States to accede to the Geneva Act.[67] The Commission is now challenging this decision since in its original proposal[68] it only foresaw EU participation. Yet, the Geneva Act prescribes that REIOs have as many votes in the assembly as the combined votes of their member states, parties to the Geneva Act. If the original proposal by the Commission had been adopted, the EU could have acceded but would have zero voting rights, potentially hindering the functioning of the assembly under the Geneva Act and the ability of the EU effectively to pursue its interests.[69]

The international responsibility condition suggests that a requirement of mixity – an '*AMP Antarctique* effect' – may arise where the rights and obligations of the Member States under international law are (potentially) impacted.[70] Bearing in mind the discussion above as to the scope of the relevant 'rights and obligations', we can limit ourselves here to the strongest case: where the projected agreement would itself amend or replace previously-existing rights and obligations of the Member States in international law. There are some precedents for accepting Member State participation in such cases, even in cases of exclusive competence. Thus, in Opinion 1/76 such a scenario was found to justify the participation of the relevant Member States in the new agreement, but only to the extent necessary to ensure the amendment of the prior agreements.[71] Any spill-over from that limited purpose to general mixed participation in the new agreement (and its organs) was found to be contrary to the EU's exclusive competence and 'a surrender of the independence of action of the Community in its external relations'.[72] Similarly, the Council authorised Member State participation in the Geneva Act on geographical indications on the ground of their participation in the pre-existing Lisbon Agreement,

[66] Case C-389/15, *Commission v Council*, ECLI:EU:C:2017:798.

[67] Council Decision 2019/1754 on the accession of the European Union to the Geneva Act of the Lisbon Agreement on Appellations of Origin and Geographical Indications, [2019] OJ L 271/12.

[68] See European Commission, COM (2018) 350 final.

[69] For an early discussion of this case, see Merijn Chamon, Analysis: 'Commission challenges authorisation granted to Member States to exercise EU exclusive competences', *EU Law Live*, 10 March 2020.

[70] See also the chapter by Delgado Casteleiro and Contartese in this volume.

[71] Opinion 1/76 re *the European Laying-up Fund*, EU:C:1977:63, paras 6–7. As the Court concluded, '[i]n these circumstances, the participation of the six Member States as contracting parties to the Agreement is not such as to encroach on the external power of the Community'.

[72] Ibid, para 12.

although this has been challenged by the Commission.[73] In contrast, albeit in a bilateral context, the Union's exclusive competence over foreign direct investment as part of the Common Commercial Policy was held in Opinion 2/15 to preclude the participation of Member States in a trade agreement for the purposes of terminating their previous bilateral agreements, since this competence now lay with the Union.[74]

In these examples from fields of exclusive competence, insofar as Member State participation was justified it was for specific limited purposes tied to earlier international agreements to which they were party. In cases of shared competence there is no presumption in favour of EU-only action; indeed, until recently some argued that shared competence presumed mixity, although this presumption was hardly born out in practice. Perhaps for this reason there has been little discussion as to an EU law *requirement* of mixity where Member States' rights and obligations under international law are at issue. It could be argued that mixed participation would avoid the possibility of conflict for a Member State between its earlier international law obligations and its obligations under a new EU-only agreement, binding on the Member States as a matter of EU law under Article 216(2) TFEU. However, this argument would equally apply to agreements concluded under exclusive EU competence. Indeed, EU law regulates such potential conflicts not via Member State participation in later agreements but through the principle of primacy accompanied by Article 351 TFEU, with its obligation to eliminate any inconsistencies, by denunciation of the earlier agreement if necessary.[75] There may be cases, depending on the nature of the pre-existing rights and obligations of the Member States, where mixed participation is desirable in order to achieve the objectives of the new agreement as a matter of international law. In other cases, the new agreement may make specific reference to earlier Member State agreements without the need for Member State participation.[76] Such a judgment would then form part of the general assessment as to the exercise of facultative mixity rather than a legal requirement as *AMP Antarctique* suggests.

VI. Conclusion

In sum, the Court's analysis, relying heavily on a PIL reasoning, cannot fully support the Court's conclusions. At the same time, an analysis of the legal context in which the

[73] Council Decision 2019/1754/EU of 7 October 2019 on the accession of the European Union to the Geneva Act of the Lisbon Agreement on Appellations of Origin and Geographical Indications, [2019] OJ L 271/12, recitals 8-10 and Arts 3 and 4. Notwithstanding EU exclusive competence (confirmed by Case C-389/15, *Commission v Council*, EU:C:2017:798) Member State participation was declared to be in the interests of the Union as well as ensuring 'continuity of rights' for the seven Member States concerned. The Council's authorisation has been challenged by the Commission: Case C-24/20, *Commission v Council*, pending.

[74] Opinion 2/15 re *the EU-Singapore FTA*, EU:C:2017:376, paras 246–52 (the Court here ignores the provisions of the Member States' bilateral investment treaties which concern non-direct investment).

[75] Note that Art 351 TFEU only protects the obligations of Member States towards third countries; it does not permit the Member States to maintain rights that are inconsistent with EU law. Case 812/79, *Attorney General v Burgoa*, ECLI:EU:C:1980:231; Case C-62/98, *Commission v Portugal*, ECLI:EU:C:2000:358; Case C-205/06, *Commission v Austria*, ECLI:EU:C:2009:118.

[76] See for example, in a bilateral context, the Agreement on extradition between the European Union and the United States of America, [2003] OJ L 181/27.

CCAMLR operates has shown that despite the Court not explicitly drawing attention to all of the distinguishing features of the CAMLR and CCAMLR, they can be qualified as truly unique in PIL. This thus leaves sufficient scope for the Court to reduce to zero the precedential value of *AMP Antarctique* in future cases.

It can be envisaged that *AMP Antarctique* will lead to new disputes (that might or might not end up at the Court). Not only may EU Member States invoke the specific wording of REIO clauses in other agreements in order to exclude an autonomous role for the Union, but it is also difficult to think of a multilateral agreement that does not somehow bestow rights and obligations on the contracting parties (including individual EU Member States). As set out above, *AMP Antarctique* then raises the question which rights and obligations should be taken into account, and which should not.

In the future the Court may simply defuse these thorny questions by ruling that the *AMP Antarctique* effect only applies in the context of the CAMLR. However, were it to do so this would only stress the fact that in this ruling the Commission has missed an opportunity to have the legal framework governing the joint action of the EU and the Member States under mixed agreements clarified.

PART II

Mixed Agreements from an International Law Perspective

6

EMU 'Mixity'

Overlap Between EU and Member States Action in Economic Governance

FLORE VANACKÈRE AND BRUNO DE WITTE

I. Introduction

Over the last 10 years, economic and monetary policy has been the object of inventive solutions, whose conformity with the constitutional order of the European Union (hereafter 'EU') was often dubious.[1] Those *sui generis* legal and institutional responses to the crisis also raised interrogations about the preservation of the balance between the more powerful and the economically weaker Member States.[2] Those measures gave rise, furthermore, to a series of reflections concerning the shift of economic policy towards the executive power, to the detriment of the legislative power and democratic representation in decision making.[3] Indeed, the measures that were justified by the economic urgency, in which certain Member States of the eurozone found themselves, often involved a strengthening of the intergovernmental approach. In the field of economic policy, we can clearly observe this tendency to go the intergovernmental way. In addition to the leading role taken by the EU's most intergovernmental bodies (the European Council and the Eurogroup), we have seen the conclusion of a number of international law treaties to support the stability of the EU's Economic and Monetary Union.

Unlike the other contributions in this book, this one does not concern the external action of the Union and its Member States, but their joint action 'internally', within the framework of a policy whose conduct involves a special form of cooperation based on a combination of EU law and international law. We will, however, draw a comparison between the field of joint external action of the Union and its Member States and the

[1] A Hinarejos, 'The Legality of Responses to the Crisis', in F Amtenbrink, C Herrmann and R Repasi (eds), *The EU Law of Economic and Monetary Union* (Oxford University Press, 2020) 1363–99.

[2] F Fabbrini, 'States' Equality v States' Power: the Euro-crisis, Inter-state Relations and the Paradox of Domination', *Cambridge Yearbook of European Studies*, Vol 17 (Cambridge University Press, 2015) 3–35; see also P Legrain, 'Eurozone Fiscal Colonialism', *The New York Times*, 21 April 2014.

[3] D Curtin, 'Challenging Executive Dominance in European Democracy' (2014) 77 *Modern Law Review* 1–32.

internal EU field of economic policy. Economic policy is a domain of EU action in which recourse to international agreements between groups of Member States, acting outside the EU legal framework, has been confirmed to be a valid option,[4] leading to forms of hybrid or mixed economic governance – thereby replicating, to some extent, the forms of governance created by mixed agreements. Such a comparison is relevant, in that it raises some interesting questions relating to the joint action of the EU and its Member States: in particular, as we shall see, the question of the allocation of responsibility and that of the distribution of competences between Member States and the EU. For this purpose, we will firstly (in section II) highlight the essentially shared nature of the EU's competence in the economic 'branch' of the Economic and Monetary Union (hereafter 'EMU'), allowing for a juxtaposition of EU action and Member States agreements, as mainly exemplified by the European Stability Mechanism (hereafter 'ESM'). We will then (in section III) examine two concrete examples of joint/mixed action of the EU and the Member States: that of the creation and operation of the Single Resolution Mechanism, which is part of the Banking Union; and that of the Memoranda of Understanding adopted in connection with financial assistance to eurozone states, in which we observe joint action by the ESM and by some EU institutions. This will enable us (in section IV) to highlight the eminently hybrid nature of this complex legal regime, and compare it with the equally hybrid character of the mixed agreements in the domain of external relations.

II. Economic Policy: Shared Competences Leading to Hybrid Institutional Solutions

Economic policy is not part of the general three-tiered system of Articles 2 to 6 TFEU, with its distinction between exclusive, shared and supplementary competences of the EU. Together with employment and social policy, it is described in a separate Article 5 TFEU. However, the text of Article 5 TFEU is rather deceptive in describing the Union's role as being some kind of passive container within which Member States 'coordinate *their* economic policies'. In fact, on a closer look at the economic policy chapter of the TFEU (Articles 120 to 126), it appears that this is a very complex competence domain, where *most* legal bases provide for coordination activities, but *some* legal bases provide for true law-making activities of the EU.[5] Therefore, some parts of economic policy fall within the domain of shared rather than supplementary competences. The policy response to the Euro crisis stimulated the development of a hybrid system combining rule-based and coordination-based forms of governance within a complex architecture of economic policy, in which the dividing line between shared and supplementary competences is very much blurred. We are therefore faced with what could be called a 'mixture' of EU competences in this field, which anyway leaves much room for national policy autonomy.

[4] B De Witte, 'Variable Geometry and Differentiation as Structural Features of the EU Legal Order', in B De Witte, A Ott, E Vos (eds), *Between Flexibility and Disintegration. The Trajectory of Differentiation in EU Law* (Edward Elgar Publishing, 2017) 24.

[5] See, for example, Art 121(6) TFEU and Art 122(2) TFEU.

The ESM is one of the hybrid outcomes of these intertwined competences.[6] Its operation is indeed highly unusual in that, being created as an international organisation and thus outside the legal framework of the European Union,[7] it nevertheless mobilises several EU bodies and institutions in its governance regime.[8] First of all, the ESM's central decision-making body, the Board of Governors, is in fact composed of the same persons who meet in the Eurogroup, namely the ministers responsible for financial affairs of the eurozone. As a matter of political practice, all decisions taken by the Board of Governors are predetermined by informal decisions adopted by the Eurogroup.[9]

Moreover, the concrete functioning of the ESM (and the realisation of its basic purpose to provide financial assistance) requires the intervention of the European Commission and of the ECB. Following a Eurogroup decision to grant financial assistance to the Member States requesting it, it is for the Commission (possibly assisted by the ECB) to negotiate and sign the Memorandum of Understanding (hereinafter 'MoU') containing the financial assistance programme and the elements relating to the conditionality of such assistance;[10] after the conclusion of the MoU, the same EU institutions monitor the compliance of the assisted Member States with the conditions it contains.[11] The ESM also mobilises the IMF in the negotiation and conclusion of, as well as the compliance, with the MoU.[12]

This mixed legal and institutional framework of the ESM was made possible by the shared nature of EU and Member States competences in the economic policy branch of EMU. In its *Pringle* judgment,[13] the Court of Justice chose to qualify the ESM as an economic policy instrument – thus not impinging on the EU's competence in the

[6] The ESM was preceded by the EFSF, which was formally set up, in May 2010, as a private law firm whose shareholders were the eurozone states. Its board of directors was composed of representatives of those states. On the EFSF, see F Martucci, 'Non-EU Legal Instruments (EFSF, ESM, and Fiscal Compact', in F Amtenbrink, C Herrmann and R Repasi (eds), *The EU Law of Economic and Monetary Union* (Oxford University Press, 2020) 293–325, at 296–99.

[7] Art 3 of the Treaty establishing the European Stability Mechanism defines the ESM as an 'international financial institution'. The current text of the treaty (as amended by later accessions of new Member States to the eurozone) can be found on the ESM's website, esm.europa.eu.

[8] See A Poulou, 'Financial Assistance Conditionality and Human Rights Protection: What is the Role of the EU Charter of Fundamental Rights?' (2017) 54 *Common Market Law Review* 991, 997–1003.

[9] The Eurogroup is mentioned in Art 137 TFEU and in Protocol 14 to the Treaties. It is stated in Protocol 14 that it is an informal body that cannot adopt formal decisions on behalf of the EU. In a recent judgment, the Court of Justice even denied that it is an EU body and stated that the Eurogroup 'was created as an intergovernmental body outside the institutional framework of the European Union' (Case C-597/18 P, *Council v Chrysostomides & Co. and Others*, EU:C:2020:1028, para 84). We disagree with this assessment and consider that there are good reasons for qualifying it as an EU body (see also, in this sense, M Markakis and A Karatzia; 'The Final Act on the Eurogroup and Effective Judicial Protection in the EU: *Chrysostomides*', Op-Ed in *EU Law Live*, 22-12-2020). The uncertainty about the true legal nature of the Eurogroup is yet another illustration of the 'mixed' character of economic policy.

[10] These economic adjustment programmes often contain measures relating to the restructuring of the banking sector or measures relating to certain systemic banks, and measures relating to labour law and entitlement to social benefits (thus, the Economic Adjustment Programme for Cyprus laid down in the MoU of 26 April 2013 – see n 38 below – states that 'Reforms of the labour market are designed to mitigate the impact of the crisis on employment and to support a strengthening of competitiveness').

[11] Art 13(7) ESM Treaty.

[12] Recital 8 of the preamble to the ESM Treaty gives particular importance to the role of the IMF in the functioning of the ESM.

[13] Case C-370/12, *Thomas Pringle v Government of Ireland*, EU:C:2015:400.

field of monetary policy – considering that the ESM is the logical complement to the EU instruments adopted in the context of strengthening budgetary surveillance and discipline. The Court added that financial assistance falls within the competence of the Member States – since the operation of the ESM affects the content of economic policies and not their coordination. Therefore, the eurozone Member States were entitled to set up the ESM by means of an international treaty as long as the content of that treaty would not conflict with their existing obligations under EU law which, according to the Court, was not the case here. The hybrid nature of the ESM's functioning (with the involvement of EU institutions) was challenged by the applicant in *Pringle* on the basis of Article 13(2) TEU, which states that 'each institution shall act within the limits of the powers conferred on it in the Treaties'. In this case, the powers were not conferred on the Commission and the ECB by 'the Treaties' (meaning the TEU and TEFEU) but by an agreement of public international law, the ESM Treaty. The Court found that Article 13(2) was not an obstacle to the hybrid solution adopted in the ESM Treaty.[14] The Court considered that the Member States may confer on the institutions of the Union tasks outside the Union's legal framework if, but only if, such tasks do not distort the powers conferred on the institutions by primary EU law. The Court considered that no such distortion occurred in this case: the tasks given to the EU institutions do not imply any decision-making power of their own, and they are an extension of the tasks which these institutions perform inside the EU legal order; indeed, that is the reason why the ESM Treaty gave them those tasks.[15]

The uniqueness (strangeness?) of such an institutional architecture, situated between Union law and international law, arose (and was legally justified) for several reasons. There is a structural reason, which relates to the nature of the EU's economic and monetary policy. These two policies are in fact inherently asymmetric in nature: they are of course complementary,[16] but different from the point of view of the division of competences, with monetary policy being an exclusive EU competence whereas economic policy is very much shared between the EU and its Member States. To this structural reason must be added the contingent reason of the emergency situation caused by the sovereign debt crisis. It appeared that the 'firepower' needed to stabilise the financial markets, and to solve the sovereign debt crisis, was simply not available in the EU budget, with its limited and heavily earmarked resources. The euro states had to provide that firepower through contributions from their national budgets, which led to the adoption of an international law instrument fully controlled by those states.

Whereas the creation of the ESM is an egregious example of the use of international law in the domain of European fiscal policy, it is not the only one. Another example

[14] *Pringle* judgment paras 153 to 177. Particularly as regards the role of the Commission, the Court ruled that '[b]y its involvement in the ESM Treaty, the Commission promotes the general interest of the Union' (point 164).

[15] Insofar as, according to Art 17 TEU, the Commission's main general task is to promote the general interest of the Union, this is what it does in negotiating and signing the MoUs. More specifically, the Commission has a task, under the TFEU, to monitor national fiscal and macroeconomic policies under the Stability and Growth Pact.

[16] The Court itself acknowledges this in one of the paragraphs of its judgment, when it considers that the (monetary) objective of price stability inevitably is impacted by that of maintaining the stability of the eurozone as a whole (*Pringle* judgment para 56).

is the Treaty on Stability, Coordination and Governance (the 'Fiscal Compact') whose subject matter could have justified EU action, but instead the eurozone states decided to use their fiscal policy competence to conclude a separate international agreement, which is also marked by a degree of hybridity between international law and EU law.[17] A later example was the project of setting up a new European financial instrument, the BICC, which aimed at supporting structural reforms in national economic policy.[18] This project would have been another example of joint action between the EU and (some of) its Member States, as it would have consisted of one or more EU regulations setting out its governance,[19] and an intergovernmental agreement concluded by the Member States of the eurozone contributing the funds out of their national budgets.[20] The project was abandoned shortly before its adoption because of the new context created by the COVID crisis. The adoption of the NextEU package, with its huge budget flowing to the EU as a whole, made the creation of a relatively small euro-specific fund like BICC superfluous, at least for the time being.

In the next section, we will look more closely at how EU/Member States hybrid action in the field of economic governance operates in practice, by examining two examples.

III. Two Examples of Hybrid (EU/Member States) Action: The Single Resolution Fund and the Conclusion of the MoUs for Financial Assistance

This section presents some examples of joint action by the Union and its Member States in the context of economic policy. First (in section A), we will examine the connection that was made between the Single Resolution Fund ('SRF', an EU law mechanism) and two international law instruments, namely the Intergovernmental Agreement on financial contributions to the Fund, and the Amended ESM Treaty that creates a 'backstop' for the Fund. Secondly (in section B), we discuss the way in which the ESM concludes a MoU with a Member States receiving its financial assistance; this may seem like an atypical instrument of international law, but in fact two EU institutions (the Commission and the ECB) play a crucial role in the formation of that instrument.

[17] On the Fiscal Compact's hybrid character, see F. Martucci (n 6 above), pp 318–22.

[18] BICC stands for Budgetary Instrument for Competitiveness and Convergence. The main content of the instrument, as politically agreed in October 2019, can be found in: Eurogroup, 'Term Sheet on the Budgetary Instrument for Convergence and Competitiveness', Council Press Release 642/19, 10 October 2019.

[19] European Commission, Proposal for a Regulation of the European Parliament and the Council on a governance framework for the budgetary instrument for convergence and competitiveness for the euro area.

[20] See Eurogroup report on a possible inter-governmental agreement for the budgetary instrument for convergence and competitiveness, Eurogroup press release of 17 February 2020. It may be noted that finding a consensus on such an agreement had been far from straightforward as it caused considerable tension between, on the one hand, France and Germany, which supported it, and, on the other hand, a group of so-called 'frugal' states, a group of fiscally conservative countries opposed to further solidarity, led by the Netherlands. See M Van Der Sluis, 'A Euro Area Budget: Another Seedling?', in D Fromage and B De Witte (eds), *Recent Evolutions in the Economic and Monetary Union and the European Banking Union: A Reflection*, Maastricht University, Faculty of Law Working Paper series, 2019/03, 18, 24.

A. The Single Resolution Mechanism: EU Law with an International Law Flavour

Alongside the single supervisory mechanism (SSM),[21] a single resolution mechanism (SRM) was set up by an EU regulation, as part of the Banking Union.[22] The SRM is a multilevel mechanism composed of an EU agency, the Single Resolution Board (SRB),[23] and the national resolution authorities of the Member States of the Banking Union.[24] A SRF was created in order to implement banking resolution operations. For the constitution of this fund, the Member States must raise funds from their banking institutions related to the size of their liabilities for eight years. The immediate objective of the Fund is to set up a reserve fund at the European level to ensure greater security for deposits in the event of bank failure and resolution; in addition, it pursues the systemic objective to stop the cascade effect of 'bank failure-sovereign failure' observed during the banking and then economic crisis of 2008–12.

The SRF is an example of joint action of the EU and its Member States. It was formed by a combination of an EU instrument with an intergovernmental one. Indeed, the SRF is created, as mentioned above, by the Regulation establishing the SRM; but the SRF, as it was said, 'steps on two boats':[25] the transfer and mutualisation of contributions by the banks to the SRF is regulated by an intergovernmental agreement (IGA)[26] concluded between 26 Member States.[27] In fact, the original Commission proposal for the banking resolution mechanism was entirely based on Article 114 TFEU, but it was split in two during the Council negotiations, with one part (the resolution mechanism itself) forming the object of an EU regulation, whereas the other part (the building of a fund to be used for resolution operations) was left to be created by the Member States by means of a separate international agreement. This splitting was requested by Germany by invoking legal arguments relating to the limited scope of Article 114, but there were above all important political reasons for this. It seems that the German government sought to ensure that it could abandon the Resolution Fund if the resolution rules themselves were

[21] Established by Council Regulation (EU) No 1024/2013 of 15 October 2013 conferring specific tasks on the European Central Bank concerning policies relating to the prudential supervision of credit institutions, [2013] OJ, L 287/63.

[22] Established by Regulation (EU) No 806/2014 of the European Parliament and of the Council of 15 July 2014 establishing uniform rules and a uniform procedure for the resolution of credit institutions and certain investment firms in the framework of a Single Resolution Mechanism and a Single Resolution Fund and amending Regulation (EU) No 1093/2010, [2014] OJ, L 225/1.

[23] The SRB is charged with the execution of the 'uniform rules and a uniform procedure for the resolution of the entities' placed under the SRM (Art 1 of the Regulation). Art 42 of the Regulation provides that 'The Board is hereby established. The Board shall be a Union agency with a specific structure corresponding to its tasks. It shall have legal personality.'

[24] Those are the eurozone states as well as non-euro states who wish to engage in 'close cooperation' with both the SSM and the SRM. At the time of writing, only Bulgaria and Croatia have done so.

[25] IG Asimakopoulos, 'International Law as a Negotiation Tool in Banking Union; the Case of the Single Resolution Fund' (2018) 21 *Journal of Economic Policy Reform* 120.

[26] Agreement on the transfer and mutualisation of contributions to the Single Resolution Fund, Council doc. 8457/14, 14 May 2014.

[27] That is, all the (then) Member States except Sweden and the United Kingdom. For some of the non-eurozone signatories, the IGA will apply only if and when they have joined the resolution mechanism. See Council press release 10088/14 of 21 May 2014, 'Member States sign agreement on bank resolution fund'.

to be later modified (under the qualified majority rule obtaining for Article 114-based measures) in contrast with German interests, for instance, by removing or reducing the bail-in provisions in the regulation. This aim of the German government may explain the curious reference, in Article 9(2) of the Agreement, to the 'fundamental change of circumstances' as a reason for terminating the agreement (this being a well-known, though controversial, rule of international treaty law). A similar termination clause would obviously not have been available to Germany if the whole mechanism had been created as an EU legal instrument.[28] We can thus see how the shadow of international law weighs on the future evolution of an EU law instrument: the adequate functioning of the SRM depends on whether the Member States comply with the IGA which they concluded among themselves, and if the IGA is not adequately implemented, or is terminated by one of the key participants, the SRF may lack the financial means to undertake its banking resolution operations.

A second connection between the SRM and an international law instrument is soon to come into being. Indeed, a forthcoming amendment of the ESM Treaty makes provision for joint action between the SRB (an EU agency) and the ESM (an international organisation of the eurozone states). A political agreement was reached in December 2018[29] that the ESM funds may be used as a safety net for the SRF, in order to give it more financial capacity so as to ensure the achievement of the two main objectives[30] of the resolution mechanism. This requires a revision of the ESM Treaty, so as to incorporate this financial backstop in the ESM 'toolkit'.[31] More specifically, the ESM would do so, in order to cover the expenses incurred by the SRF under Article 76 of the Regulation establishing the SRM,[32] through the issue of a revolving credit line to the SRB, an instrument that until now did not exist in the arsenal available to the ESM. Should the SRF be exhausted, the common backstop will be activated by the ESM to provide financing to the SRB, which then acts as a borrower under the backstop facility.[33] The principle of fiscal neutrality must be respected within the framework of such an operation: indeed, whereas the SFR is made up of funds from private credit institutions to face the possible failure of one of them, the capital of the ESM is made up of budgetary contributions from the Member States of the eurozone. In order to avoid transferring the cost of the bank failure to the budgets of the Member States, the SRF will have to recover and

[28] B De Witte and T Martinelli, 'Treaties between Member States as Quasi-Instruments of EU Law', in M Cremona and C Kilpatrick (eds), *EU Legal Acts: Challenges and Transformations* (Oxford University Press, 2018) 157, 175.

[29] Press release of the Eurogroup meeting of 4 December 2018, www.consilium.europa.eu/media/37268/tor-backstop_041218_final_clean.pdf.

[30] Namely protection of the deposits and avoidance of the cascade 'banking failure-sovereign failure'.

[31] Draft Art 18A of the revised ESM Treaty. Although a political agreement on the text of the amendments was reached already in December 2019, it took another year for ironing out all the remaining wrinkles. It was recently announced that the Amended ESM Treaty would be signed by the Parties in January 2021, after which the national ratification procedures can start: Letter of Pascal Donohoe, president of the Eurogroup, to the President of the European Council of 4 December 2020, consilium.europa.eu/media/47177/20201204-letter-to-president-Charles-Michel.pdf.

[32] Regulation (EU) No 806/2014 (n 22 above).

[33] See, on the content of the ESM reform: J Aerts and P Bizarro, 'The Reform of the European Stability Mechanism' (2020) 15 *Capital Markets Law Journal* 8; and G Zaccaroni, *The Future of the ESM within a Hybrid EMU Law*, BRIDGE Working Paper 6, September 2020.

reimburse, in the long term, the sums invested by the ESM. The hybrid nature of this solution implies that the activity of an EU body (the SRB) is being constrained by an international organisation controlled by the Member States (the ESM)[34] – at least if and when the backstop must be mobilised. On 27 January 2021, representatives from the Member States signed the amending agreements to the ESM Treaty on the one hand, and the SRF Intergovernmental Agreement on the other.[35]

Let us recapitulate. Although at first sight part of the EU legal order, the construction and functioning of the SRM also depends on the action of the EU Member States (not only from the eurozone) on the intergovernmental scene. Firstly, despite the adoption of a regulation by the EU legislator, the actual setting up of the SRF, by means of rules according to which contributions and pooling of funds from credit institutions in each Member States are set, is regulated by an intergovernmental agreement between the Member States of the eurozone, acting together with some other Member States. Secondly, the ESM (which is marked by the joint action of the EU and a group of its Member States) will be able to support the SRM, a mechanism which itself came about in this hybrid EU/international law mode.

B. The MoUs Concluded Between the ESM and its Member States: International Law with an EU Flavour

In EU law, a practice developed over the years whereby financial assistance granted by the Union to one of its Member States or to a third country was accompanied by a Memorandum of Understanding setting out the conditionality attached to the loans.[36] As was mentioned in section II, the MoUs that set out the conditions for the ESM's financial assistance are concluded outside the EU's legal framework, but they involve some of the EU institutions in their conception. That hybrid status raises the question whether the Commission and the ECB are bound by EU law (including fundamental rights) when helping to conclude those MoU. The Court of Justice partially answered those questions in its *Ledra Advertising* judgment of September 2016.[37]

This case had its origin in the terms of the MoU negotiated between the Commission, the ECB and the IMF on behalf of the ESM on the one hand, and the republic of Cyprus on the other hand.[38] The application of some of the provisions of the MoU had imposed

[34] Keppenne et al call this 'a difficult marriage', especially for its consequences for the accountability of the SRB under EU law: JP Keppenne, TM Rusche and LE Blaya, 'An ESM Backstop Facility to the Single Resolution Board: The Difficult Marriage of an EU Mechanism and an Intergovernmental Institution', in *Recent Evolutions in the Economic and Monetary Union and the European Banking Union* (n 20 above) 38.

[35] Statement by the Eurogroup President, Paschal Donohoe, on the signature of ESM Treaty and the Single Resolution Fund Amending Agreements, www.consilium.europa.eu/en/press/press-releases/2021/01/27/statement-by-the-eurogroup-president-paschal-donohoe-on-the-signature-of-esm-treaty-and-the-single-resolution-fund-amending-agreements/.

[36] A De Gregorio Merino, 'Memoranda of Understanding: A Critical Taxonomy', in *Building Bridges: Central Banking Law in an Interconnected World, ECB Legal Conference 2019* (ECB, 2019) 253.

[37] Case C-8/15 P, *Ledra Advertising v Commission and ECB*, EU:C:2016:701.

[38] Memorandum of Understanding on Specific Economic Policy Conditionality concluded between the Republic of Cyprus and the European Stability Mechanism (ESM). The text of the MoU can be found in European Commission, *The Economic Adjustment Programme for Cyprus*, European Economy Occasional Papers 149, May 2013, p 68.

the restructuring of two Cypriot banks – the Cyprus Popular Bank (Laïki) and the Bank of Cyprus – thereby causing a significant loss of value of certain bank deposits. The depositors affected by this measure brought an action for damages against the Commission and the ECB,[39] as well as an action for annulment of the MoU itself. As stated by the Advocate General in his Opinion, the main issue raised by the *Ledra* case is the role of the European Commission in the functioning of the ESM.[40] Both the General Court, and the Court of Justice in the appeal case, found the action for annulment of the MoU inadmissible: as the MoU was formally concluded by the ESM (a non-EU body), it could not form the object of an annulment action under Article 263 TFEU. However, the Court of Justice acknowledged the hybrid nature of the MoU in the parallel action for damages. It found the action for damages against the Commission admissible. Since one of the general tasks of the Commission, under Article 17 TEU, is to ensure observance with EU law, it must perform that task also *extra muros*, when participating in the negotiation and conclusion of the MoU. It would thus be liable for damages if that activity led to a violation of the right to property.[41] At the end, though, the Court rejected the claim on substance, by holding that the limitation of the right to property was justified by the public interest, choosing to give precedence to the overriding interest of maintaining the stability of the eurozone pursued by the MoU of 26 April 2013 over the right to property. We can thus see, in this judgment, how the hybrid nature of the financial assistance operations of the ESM implies that the 'shadow of EU law' applies to an agreement which is, formally speaking, one of international law. The Court's approach goes 'some way towards bringing collective Member State action within the constitutional space of the EU'.[42]

This very same MoU is also interesting for the developments it triggered at the international level, in the arbitration case *Marfin v Cyprus*.[43] In this case, the Marfin Investment Group argued that Cyprus's measures imposed to the Laïki Bank in the MoU violated the Cyprus-Greece bilateral investment treaty, as its stake in Laïki was diluted by those measures. Without going into the details of this case, it is nonetheless interesting in two respects. In general terms, it illustrates the question of the shared responsibility of the EU and its Member States when they interact in the context of international investment law.[44] More specifically, it is worth noting that the ICSID award assumes that the MoU was concluded by the 'Troika' (European Commission, ECB and IMF) whereas the ESM is not even mentioned.[45] This is a legal mistake, since it

[39] They claimed compensation for damage caused by a violation of Art 17 of the Charter of Fundamental Rights of the European Union, protecting the right to property.

[40] Opinion of Advocate General Wahl in the *Ledra* case, delivered on 21 April 2016, para 1.

[41] See, on this aspect of the judgment, A Poulou (n 8 above), at p1007 ff.

[42] T Tridimas, 'Constitutional Fluidity and the Problem of Authority in EU Law', in F Amtenbrink et al (eds), *The Internal Market and the Future of European Integration: Essays in Honour of Laurence W. Gormley*, (Cambridge University Press, 2019) 65–80, 77.

[43] *Marfin Investment Group Holdings SA, Alexandros Bakatselos and others v Republic of Cyprus*, ICSID Case No ARB/13/27.

[44] See on this question A Delgado Casteleiro, *The International Responsibility of the European Union. From Competence to Normative Control* (Cambridge University Press, 2016) 209–14.

[45] ICSID Case No ARB/13/27, op cit., particularly points 1252 to 1265. The terms used in this award show the absence of the ESM in the reasoning of the Tribunal. For example, it uses the terms 'the measures proposed by the Troika' (point 1263) to refer to the MoU of 26 April 2013.

is clear from the text of the ESM Treaty that MoUs that accompany financial assistance operations are signed by the Commission 'on behalf of the ESM',[46] so that the ESM is the real party to the agreement. This mistake illustrates the confusion that arises from the complex architecture of the ESM. The subtle hybridity creates a contrast between the formal legal situation (in which the ESM is the party to the agreement with the assisted state, as the Court of Justice confirmed in *Ledra*) and the political and media appearances, which put the Troika in the forefront and seem to make this into an action of the European Union.

These reflections about the litigation triggered by the ESM's assistance to Cyprus illustrate the sometimes blurred dividing line between the Union's legal order and the international legal order. They also lead us to consider the comparisons to be made between the intergovernmental mode of action chosen by the Member States within the framework of EMU governance, and other fields affected by this complex relationship between EU law and international law. In this regard, some parallels can be made between the field of EMU and that of mixed agreements.

IV. Reflections on the Mixed Nature of the Economic Governance of the EU: A Comparison with the Issues Arising in the Field of Mixed Agreements

In this section, we will seek to elaborate our point, made in the introduction, that the semi-intergovernmental path followed in the framework of EMU can be usefully compared with the legal regime of mixed agreements in external relations. Let us start, though, by repeating the obvious limit to that comparison: in the context of the conclusion of mixed agreements, the Member States and the Union act in concert to conclude one and the same legal instrument, whereas within the EMU context the measures adopted by the EU and by (some of) its Member States are formally separate but are joined together in a 'mixed' political domain.

The first reason that justifies the comparison is the fact that, in both cases, legal acts come into being through the joint action of the EU and its Member States. In the case of mixed agreements, their action coincides at the time of signature, but both before (during the negotiation) and afterwards (between signature and ratification), the EU and the Member States act separately. In the EMU cases described in this chapter, it is always either/or: legal acts or factual measures are undertaken either by the Union or by its Member States (or by an organisation created by them) – but a combination of them is needed for the legal operation to come to fruition. Without the work of the Commission, the ESM cannot conclude a MoU with an assisted country, and that crucial role of an EU institution is reflected by the fact that the Commission actually signs the MoU, albeit on behalf of the ESM. Similarly, for the SRM to function effectively, an EU legislative measure had to be complemented by an intergovernmental agreement,

[46] ESM Treaty, Art 13(4).

and future banking resolution measures under the backstop may similarly require the concurring acts of an EU agency (the SRB) and the ESM.

Secondly, both fields of joint action are marked by the existence of intertwined competences. In the external relations field, 'parts of the agreements fall under EU exclusive competence, while other provisions fall under the [Member States'] reserved competences that they share with the EU'.[47] In a similar way, the main justification for resorting to the intergovernmental method in the field of economic governance is the existence of shared competences. The distinction made in external relations law, between 'necessary' and 'facultative' mixity, is also a relevant one for economic governance: in some cases, action by means of an international agreement between the Member States seemed genuinely necessary (as was the case with the ESM treaty), whereas in other cases, 'going intergovernmental' was just an option which the Member States decided to use even though they might have acted through EU law instead (here, the agreement relating to the SRF is probably a good example). In other terms, both in the field of mixed agreements and in that of the EU economic governance, the hybrid or mixed action of the EU and its Member States is justified both by the limited scope of the EU's competences and by the fact that 'the involvement of the EU Member States is only legally precluded if every single matter comes under the EU's exclusive competences'.[48] The fundamentally shared nature of competences explains the joined action of the Member States and the EU in the case of mixed agreements and in the functioning of the EMU.

Thus, the significant role played by the Member States in these two fields are, to a large extent, the result of *political* choice rather than *legal* necessity. We know the political reasons[49] for choosing a mixed approach to the conclusion of international agreements.[50] The choice of the intergovernmental approach in the field of EMU responds to similar considerations, whereby the Member States (or at least some key players among them) want to 'keep control' on common action.

A final similarity is that both mixed agreements and hybrid action in economic governance raise difficult issues concerning the allocation of responsibility between the EU, the Member States and/or the ESM in case of breach of the applicable legal rules. While the allocation of responsibility in the field of mixed agreements has already given rise to a significant doctrine,[51] the issue of determining responsibility (between Member States and EU) for economic governance is less developed. In the context of

[47] E Neframi, 'Mixed Agreements as a Source of European Union Law', in E Cannizzaro, P Palchetti, R Wessel (eds), *International Law as Law of the European Union* (Martinus Nijhoff Publishers, 2011) 326.

[48] M Chamon, 'Constitutional Limits to the Political Choice for Mixity', in E Neframi, M Gatti (eds), *Constitutional Issues of EU External Relations Law* (Nomos, 2018) 139.

[49] See Ch Kaddous, « Les accords mixtes », *in* N Aloupi, C Flaesch-Mougin, Ch Kaddous, C Rapoport, *Les accords internationaux de l'Union européenne (Commentaire J. Mégret, 3e éd.)* (Bruxelles, Éditions de l'Université de Bruxelles, 2019); and Ch Hillion/P Koutrakos (ed), *Mixed Agreements Revisited* (Oxford, Hart Publishing, 2010).

[50] M Chamon, I Govaere (eds), *EU External Relations Post-Lisbon. The Law and Practice of Facultative Mixity* (Brill-Nijhof, 2020).

[51] See for example M Björklund, 'Responsibility in the EC for Mixed Agreements – Should Non-Member Parties Care?' (2001) *Nordic Journal of International Law* 373–402; M Cremona, 'External Relations of the EU and the Member States: Competence, Mixed Agreements, International Responsibility, and Effects of International Law', EUI Working Paper LAW No 2006/22; P Ruka, *International Responsibility in Mixed Agreements: The Case of the WTO Agreement* (Springer, 2017). See further the contribution by Andrés Delgado Casteleiro and Cristina Contartese in this book.

the functioning of the ESM, the *Pringle* jurisprudence tells us that it is up to the Member States to take responsibility for the acts that they produce. In reality, though, it is not clear that issues arising from the system of contributions to the SRF or from the financial assistance operations of the ESM should entirely be laid at the door of the participating Member States, since some of the EU institutions or bodies are closely involved with these operations.

V. Conclusion

It has been said that 'the boundaries between EU law and collective action by the Member States are porous in a way that serves to disguise the true source of authority'.[52] This porosity can be observed in several policy domains, ranging from development policy and external migration policy to patent law, but nowhere is it more striking than in the domain of EMU law.

We have tried, in this chapter, to show how important parts of the EU's Economic and Monetary Union are marked by the hybrid operation of the Union together with some or all its Member States, thereby drawing a parallel between the joint action that takes place around external agreements – particularly the mixed ones – and that which exists within the framework of the Union's economic policy. From these developments several interesting points of comparison have emerged, which lead us to focus, in a final consideration, on two main issues: one concerning the reasons for joint action by the Union and its Member States, and the other concerning the allocation of responsibility for such action.

The first question highlights the link between, on the one hand, the distribution of competences between the Union and its Member States and, on the other hand, the political need for joint action. In the field of the conclusion of external agreements, joint action by the Union and its Member States – the practice of mixed agreements – is quite common, and often for eminently political motives. As said above, considerations of a similar nature had justified some cases of joint action of the EU and its Member States in the field of economic policy: this is in fact the result of both the distribution of competences between the Union and Member States in the field of economic policy, which does not always allow for action by the EU alone, and the economic necessity and urgency justifying the mixed nature of the action.

The question of responsibility is the second issue we would like to highlight in the context of these conclusions. For each of the examples considered, the question of the allocation of responsibility between Member States and EU institutions or bodies has indeed arisen. The allocation of responsibility in the functioning of the ESM was already raised before the ECJ in the *Ledra* case of 2016.[53] In that case, it was made clear that the Court had no jurisdiction to award damages for the harm possibly caused by the ESM in the context of the implementation of an MoU (since the ESM is not an EU body or

[52] T Tridimas (n 42 above), p 71.
[53] *Ledra* judgment (n 37 above).

institution). However, the Court also said that the injured party may bring an action for damages against the Commission, as that EU institution keeps its role as guardian of the Treaties also in the functioning of the ESM. From that example, it seems to follow that *separate* action by the Member States outside the EU framework is subject only to the compliance instrument of the infringement action launched by the Commission (since the Member States remain subject to a duty to respect EU law even when acting together in concluding an international agreement). However, when the Member States prefer to construct a *hybrid* system, whereby the EU institutions are called to collaborate within an intergovernmental approach, they must accept that a broader set of EU accountability instruments (including the action for damages) will apply to that hybrid system.

7

Nomen est Omen?

The Relevance of 'EU Party' in International Law

SABRINA SCHAEFER AND JED ODERMATT

I. Introduction

Since the early 1960s, the European Union's (EU) external action has brought forward a bouquet of treaty practice and language accommodating the peculiarities of the EU and its legal order. A trademark has been the introduction of mixed agreements, that is, treaties co-concluded by the EU and its Member States with one or more third states.[1] Scholarly writing has covered the practice of mixed agreements extensively,[2] assessing it through different lenses – the international or European law perspective – and from different angles – regarding the external dimension or the internal EU-Member States relationship. While European lawyers have mainly focused on the intra-EU relationship, especially concerning the extent of the EU's external competences,[3] international lawyers concentrated mostly on the outer sphere, focusing on the relationship with the third state, often regarding questions such as responsibility.[4]

From an international law perspective, however, it can also be interesting to look at the intra-EU relationship in mixed agreements, descriptions of which range from 'one party'[5] to 'single contracting party'[6] and the 'EU Party'. Compared to other

[1] For the first mixed agreement, see the Association Agreement (AA) with Greece [1963] OJ L26/294.

[2] See generally D O'Keeffe and HG Schermers (eds), *Mixed Agreements* (Deventer, Kluwer, 1983); J Heliskoski, *Mixed Agreements as a Technique for Organizing the International Relations of the European Community and its Member States*, The Erik Castrén Institute Monographs on International Law and Human Rights 2 (Boston, Kluwer Law International, 2001); C Hillion and P Koutrakos (eds), *Mixed Agreements Revisited: The EU and its Member States in the World*, Modern Studies in European Law 21 (Oxford, Hart Publishing, 2010).

[3] See, eg M Cremona, 'External Relations and External Competence: The Emergence of an Integrated Policy' in PP Craig and G de Búrca (eds), *The Evolution of EU Law* (Oxford, Oxford University Press, 1999).

[4] Regarding international law issues of mixed agreements, see, eg J Odermatt, 'Facultative Mixity in the International Legal Order: Tolerating European Exceptionalism?' in M Chamon and I Govaere (eds), *EU External Relations Post-Lisbon: The Law and Practice of Facultative Mixity*, Studies in EU External Relations 16 (Boston, Brill Nijhoff, 2020). On responsibility, see the chapter by C Contartese and AD Casteleiro in this volume and C Tomuschat, 'Liability for Mixed Agreements' in D O'Keeffe and HG Schermers (eds) (n 2); PJ Kuijper, 'International Responsibility for EU Mixed Agreements' in C Hillion and P Koutrakos (eds) (n 2).

[5] G van der Loo and RA Wessel, 'The Non-Ratification of Mixed Agreements: Legal Consequences and Solutions' (2017) 54 *Common Market Law Review* 735, 736.

[6] Case C-53/96, *Hermès International v FHT Marketing Choice BV*, EU:C:1998:292, para 14.

denominations, the term 'EU Party' has even found its way into the text of so-called bilateral mixed agreements. Despite the number of parties, these mixed agreements are considered bilateral in structure, creating a relationship between the EU and its Member States, on the one hand, and the third state(s), on the other. While the prefixes vary from '*EC* Party' in the pre-Lisbon era to the '*EU* Party' since 2009 and '*Union* Party' in the Strategic Partnership Agreement (SPA) with Japan,[7] these descriptions all use an international treaty law concept: the 'Party'.

Quoting the Chinese philosopher Confucius, 'The beginning of wisdom is to call things by their proper name'.[8] What does the use of 'EU Party'[9] tell us about the relationship between the EU and its Member States in mixed agreements? Is it a merely linguistic simplification, or does it denote a collective (treaty party) status of the EU and its Member States? This could have practical consequences under international law. The parties to a treaty participate in and determine the 'life' of the agreement; they decide on issues such as accession[10] and denunciation.[11] But who enjoys these privileges? The 'EU Party' acting together, or the EU and its Member States individually?[12]

Aiming to answer these questions, this chapter analyses the EU's current bilateral mixed trade agreements for their use of the term 'EU Party' and the implications thereof.[13] In doing so, it first considers the EU and Member States' formal treaty status (section II), assessing the impact of their designation in the treaty texts on the extent to which they are individually bound by the agreements (section III). Secondly, the chapter explores patterns behind the use of the term 'EU Party' in the evaluated agreements (section IV) and examines typical treaty clauses concerning their statements on the party status of the EU and its Member States (section V). It concludes that while the EU and its Member States, respectively, are formally 'full' parties, the EU uses the possibilities of treaty law and language to create the perception of a single party (section VI). Although used sporadically and inconsistently, the term 'EU Party' underlines this perceived status.

II. The EU and its Member States as Treaty Parties – To Be or Not to Be!

When considering the status of a state or an international organisation (IO) in a treaty, the 1969 and 1986[14] Vienna Conventions on the Law of Treaties form the starting point.

[7] [2018] OJ L216/4.

[8] Analects of Confucius, Zi Lu, 3.

[9] Except for quotations, the term 'EU Party' will represent the different designations throughout the text.

[10] Vienna Convention on the Law of Treaties (VCLT) (adopted 23 May 1969, entered into force 27 January 1980) 1155 UNTS 331, Art 15(c).

[11] VCLT, Art 54(b).

[12] Reference to the 'EU Party' is also made in the context of Brexit, see, eg RG Volterra, 'The Impact of Brexit on the UK's Trade with the Non-EU Member States Under the EU's Mixed Free Trade Agreements' (*Oxford Business Law Blog*, 17 May 2017) www.law.ox.ac.uk/business-law-blog/blog/2017/05/brexit-negotiations-series-impact-brexit-uk%E2%80%99s-trade-non-eu-member.

[13] The selection is based on an overview provided by the European Commission, 'Negotiations and Agreements' www.ec.europa.eu/trade/policy/countries-and-regions/negotiations-and-agreements/.

[14] Vienna Convention on the Law of Treaties between States and International Organizations or between International Organizations (VCLT-IO) (adopted and opened for signature 21 March 1986) UN Doc A/CONF.129/15.

Drafting the 1969 VCLT, the International Law Commission (ILC) identified five different 'categories of State',[15] which describe the grade of involvement of a state with a treaty, depending on the degree of commitment and status of the treaty. To be a party, a state or IO must have consented to be bound, and the treaty must have entered into force, either definitely or with regard to the respective participant.[16] The very idea of mixity being co-conclusion, in the case of bilateral mixed trade agreements, the EU and all its Member States conduct their internal approval procedures and express their consent to be bound vis-à-vis their treaty partners.[17] Upon entry into force of the mixed agreements, the EU and its Member States, thus, become formal treaty parties – a status that the listing in the preamble, the testimonium (where included) and the signature blocks further visualise.[18]

At the same time, the EU's treaty practice has coined another definition of the 'Party'. Here, the term '(EU) Party' is defined as 'the European Union or its Member States or the European Union and its Member States within their respective areas of competence as derived from the Treaty on European Union and the Treaty on the Functioning of the European Union'.[19] While, at first sight, acknowledging the EU and its Member States' status as treaty parties, the extent of said status seems to depend on their internal division of competences – a view which the European Court of Justice (ECJ) appears to corroborate when referring to 'the provisions to which [the then European Economic Community] may possibly subscribe'.[20]

Externally, however, a division of competences between the EU and its Member States is generally irrelevant for third states, constituting a *res inter alios acta*.[21] Even where third states through the conclusion of *mixed* agreements recognise that competences are divided between the EU and its Member States,[22] whether a state or an IO 'may possibly subscribe' to (meaning: is competent to conclude) a treaty or certain parts of it does not as such limit the extent to which it becomes bound by a treaty.[23] Instead, a party's consent and, thereby, the extent to which it is bound in principle covers the entire treaty.[24]

[15] VCLT, Art 2 (1)(e)-(h). The fifth category, 'States entitled to become parties to the treaty', in the view of the Commission 'did not appear to require definition', see ILC, 'Report of the International Law Commission on the Work of its 34th Session'(3 May–23 July 1982) UN Doc A/37/10 190.

[16] VCLT, Art 2(1)(g); VCLT-IO, Art 2(1)(g).

[17] On the ratification clauses of bilateral mixed agreements, see below V.B.i. For problems caused by individual ratification, see van der Loo and Wessel (n 5).

[18] See, eg Comprehensive Economic Trade Agreement with Canada (CETA) [2017] OJ L11/23. For a more 'traditional' treaty, including a testimonium, see AA Turkey [1964] OJ L217/3687.

[19] CETA, Art 1.1.

[20] Opinion 1/78, *International Agreement on Natural Rubber*, EU:C:1979:224, para 5.

[21] A Bleckmann, 'The Mixed Agreements of the EEC in Public International Law' in D O'Keeffe and HG Schermers (eds) (n 2) 161.

[22] See, eg P Olson, 'Mixity from the Outside: The Perspective of a Treaty Partner' in C Hillion and P Koutrakos (eds) (n 2) 333.

[23] Rather, a lack of internal competence may lead to the treaty being voidable; something neither the EU nor the Member States has so far invoked, see, eg E Steinberger, 'The WTO Treaty as a Mixed Agreement: Problems with the EC's and the EC Member States' Membership of the WTO' (2006) 17 *European Journal of International Law* 837, 844ff.

[24] ILC, 'First Report on the Law of Treaties, by Sir Humphrey Waldock, Special Rapporteur' UN Doc A/CN.4/144 and Add 1 53; Draft Convention on the Law of Treaties (adopted 20 February 1928) (1935) 29 *American Journal of International Law* 657, Art 20.

Thus, the EU and its Member States are each formal parties to the mixed agreements, a status that the internal division of competences as such does not limit. Rather, the question addressed in the following part is whether they have actively limited their consent to avoid becoming party to sections of an agreement for which they are not competent. In that case, the 'EU Party' could be considered a composite party, consisting of the EU and its Member States as 'partial parties', each along the lines of their competences.

III. Joint Participation of the EU and its Member States – Being Part of a 'Party'?

If a state or IO wishes to become bound by only parts of a treaty, Article 17 VCLT provides a possibility for limiting its consent: where either the treaty so permits or the treaty partners agree. None of the examined mixed agreements includes provisions on partial consent.[25] Nevertheless, limited consent by the EU and its Member States could follow from how they are addressed in the treaty – either because treaty provisions refer to the EU or its Member States individually or because the term '(EU) Party' requires reading in light of the EU's internal division of competences.[26]

Thus, it is first necessary to assess what 'if the treaty so permits' means (section A) to decide whether through the designation of the parties the mixed agreements themselves allow for partial consent by the EU and the Member States (section B). Ultimately, however, the question arises whether partial consent – permitted by the treaty or agreed on by the parties – is compatible with the EU's dynamic division of competences (section C).

A. Partial Consent and Article 17 VCLT

According to one definition,[27] 'to permit' means 'to consent to expressly or formally',[28] a reading corroborated by the negotiating history in the ILC. The first considered draft article on partial consent read: 'Unless the treaty *expressly* contemplates that the participating States may elect to become bound by a part or parts only of the treaty, the instrument of ratification must apply to the whole treaty'.[29] Although 'expressly' was eventually dropped from the text, the ILC maintained its finding that '[s]ome treaties *expressly* authorize States to consent to a part or parts only of the treaty … and then, of course, partial ratification … is admissible'.[30]

[25] Regarding specific ratification clauses, see also below V.B.i.

[26] Cp KD Stein, *Der Gemischte Vertrag im Recht der Außenbeziehungen der Europäischen Wirtschaftsgemeinschaft*, Schriften zum Völkerrecht 84 (Berlin, Duncker and Humblot 1986) 95ff.

[27] See VCLT, Art 31(1) referring to the 'ordinary meaning'.

[28] 'Definition of Permit' (*Merriam-Webster Dictionary)* www.merriam-webster.com/dictionary/permit.

[29] ILC, 'Summary Records of its 14th Session' (24 April–29 June 1962) UN Doc A/CN.4/SR.647 111(emphasis added).

[30] ILC, 'Reports of the International Law Commission on the Work of its 18th Session'(4 May–19 July 1966) UN Doc A/CN.4/191 201–202 (emphasis added); see also ILC, 'First Report Law of Treaties' (n 24) 53. The drafting of Art 17 VCLT-IO is based on the drafting of Art 17 VCLT (ILC, 'Report 34th Session' (n 15) 32).

Judging from the treaty practice on which the ILC relied,[31] the notion of 'expressly' must be understood in a twofold manner. First, the treaty provisions considered made it very clear that they were dealing with the act of expressing consent. Mostly placed in the final provisions, the wording *explicitly* referred to the 'acceptance',[32] 'ratification'[33] or 'accession'[34] of a State that could 'extend'[35] to or 'exclude'[36] parts of the treaty. Secondly, the treaty's respective parts included or excluded from consent were *precisely* named, leaving no room for uncertainties.[37]

Thus, for the EU and its Member States to only be 'partial parties', the mixed agreements would have to include express permission in this regard, explicitly allowing a limitation of consent and precisely stating to which parts of the treaty.

B. Partial Consent of the EU and its Member States in Mixed Agreements

Few provisions in mixed agreements expressly address the competent party on the EU side by referring to either the EU or the Member States and attaching certain rights or obligations to the specified party.[38] Although such delimitation is undoubtedly precise, it is unconvincing to draw conclusions hereof for the parties' consent. Rights and obligations in treaties do not necessarily have to be reciprocal in the sense that all parties must perform the same obligations. Accordingly, not all treaty provisions will address all parties. In a treaty that obliges State A to pay money, State B to transfer land, and both to exchange information, clearly, Article 1 must address State A, Article 2 State B, and only Article 3 can refer to the 'Parties'. If State A were considered to have consented to be bound by Articles 1 and 3 only, partial consent would not be an exception but dilute the basic principle of *pacta sunt servanda*. Hence, although provisions may address only one or the other party, they nevertheless bind both.

The majority of provisions in mixed agreements refer to 'the Parties', 'a Party' – or the 'EU Party'. To establish the right addressee for the EU side, one must resort to the parties' definition: 'the Union or its Member States, or the Union and its Member States, in accordance with their respective competences'.[39] Regularly included in the final provisions (and thereby in close proximity to the ratification clause),[40] these definition

[31] See, eg ILC, 'Summary Records 1962' (n 29) 112.

[32] Convention concerning Labour Inspection in Industry and Commerce (Labour Inspection Convention) (adopted 11 July 1947, entered into force 7 April 1950) ILO C081, Art 25.

[33] Convention concerning Migration for Employment (Migration Convention) (adopted 1 July 1949, entered into force 22 January 1952) ILO C097, Art 14.

[34] Revised General Act for the Pacific Settlement of International Disputes (Pacific Dispute Settlement Act) (adopted 28 April 1949, entered into force 20 September 1950) 71 UNTS 101, Art 38.

[35] Pacific Dispute Settlement Act, Art 38.

[36] Labour Inspection Convention, Art 25; Migration Convention, Art 14.

[37] Pacific Dispute Settlement Act, Art 38; Labour Inspection Convention, Art 25; Migration Convention, Art 14.

[38] See Stein (n 26) 102, who points to the Second ACP-EEC Convention ([1980] OJ L347/2) as an example of a mixed agreement that in large parts adheres to the differentiation between the (then) EEC and its Member States.

[39] SPA Japan, Art 45.

[40] But see the definition at the beginning of the treaty text in CETA, Art 1.1.

clauses could be read as providing for partial consent by the EU and its Member States along the lines of their internal division of competences. Accordingly, some provisions would be binding on all, while to some provisions only the EU or only the Member States would have consented.

However, such a reading cannot be regarded as an express limitation of consent. First, the definition clauses usually begin with the phrase '[f]or the purpose of this Agreement, the term "the Parties" *means*'[41] and are headed with 'Definition of the Parties'. A definition can create a specific understanding for interpretative purposes but cannot be understood as explicitly limiting the consent of the EU and its Member States. Similarly, interpretative declarations provide a certain understanding of a treaty. In contrast to reservations, they do not, however, limit the party's consent.

Secondly, a reference to the internal division of competences is not a precise delimitation of the EU and its Member States' consent. While the EU's treaty partner may have acknowledged a division of competences, it is arguably impossible,[42] or at least unreasonable,[43] to expect a non-Member State to know the details. Thus, achieving the raison d'être of the 'express' condition would require a demarcation of mixed agreements along the lines of EU and Member State competences – a notion that in the context of multilateral treaty regimes sparked the idea of Declarations of Competence (DoC).[44] Initially, such DoCs 'ought to be sufficiently precise and informative so as to serve the interest of the other contracting parties in legal certainty and predictability'.[45] However, in practice, they often prove 'imprecise, incomplete and open-ended'[46] – and deliberately so. Even with advancing ECJ jurisprudence,[47] internal disputes over competences remain, making it impossible or, at least, undesirable for the EU to define the competences with regard to every mixed agreement clearly.

Thus, neither direct reference to the EU or its Member States nor the definition clauses can be interpreted as permitting partial consent. Both types of provisions do not explicitly refer to a limitation of the EU or Member States' consent. The definition clause, furthermore, is too imprecise to guarantee legal certainty to the treaty partners.

C. Partial Consent and the Dynamic Evolution of EU Competences

Ultimately, however, an application of Article 17 VCLT to mixed agreements would come down to whether partial consent can evolve in the same manner as the EU's

[41] See, eg SPA Japan, Art 45 (emphasis added).

[42] P Allot, 'Adherence to and Withdrawal from Mixed Agreements' in D O'Keeffe and HG Schermers (eds) (n 2) 105.

[43] Tomuschat (n 4) 130.

[44] See generally AD Casteleiro, 'EU Declarations of Competence to Multilateral Agreements: A Useful Reference Base?' (2012) 17(4) *European Foreign Affairs Review* 491; J Heliskoski, 'EU Declarations of Competence and International Responsibility' in MD Evans and P Koutrakos (eds), *The International Responsibility of the European Union: European and International Perspectives* (Oxford, Hart Publishing 2013).

[45] Heliskoski (n 44) 201.

[46] Ibid 202.

[47] For a more recent example, see Case 2/15, *FTA Singapore Opinion*, EU:C:2017:376.

division of competences. Even if it were possible – and the EU side willing to – clearly distinguish the 'EU parts' and the 'Member State parts' of a treaty at the time of conclusion, this division might potentially change in the future. To reflect the EU legal order dynamics, the consent of the EU and its Member States would have to expand to or withdraw from treaty parts for which the division of competences has changed. In other words: Is consent to be bound static, or can it evolve dynamically?

Treaty amendments generally require a renewed expression of consent by the parties.[48] If new consent is required to change a treaty, consent appears to be static. On the other hand, treaties can change over time – where a treaty allows amendments or contains generic terms 'whose content the Parties expected would change through time'.[49] These situations are, of course, different from a change in the competences of some of the parties. Treaty amendments and evolutive interpretation generally alter *how* treaties are applied, not by *whom*. However, they, too, create a situation where the treaty is applied differently from what the parties had initially consented to. Are amendment mechanisms and evolutionary interpretation, then, evidence of dynamic consent in treaty law?

Where a treaty allows amendments, it usually sets out limits and conditions for their adoption. As long as an amendment falls within these parameters, it is covered by the original consent. Similarly, if a state consents to a generic term, its consent begins at meaning X, the understanding at the time of conclusion, and ends at meaning Y, an understanding no longer covered by the ordinary meaning of the word. Any interpretation that evolves – be it X_1, X_5, or X_{10} – falls within the original consent range and is still (or already) covered by it. In both cases, the parties' consent encompasses potential new applications of the treaty. Thus, evolutive interpretation and amendment mechanisms are evidence of a dynamic application of the treaty, not dynamic consent. On the contrary, the consent remains static as it already covers the whole range of possible applications.

The very idea of partial consent would, however, be a limitation of the consent of the EU and its Member States to those parts of mixed agreements for which they are competent. Being static, such partial consent along the competence lines would 'freeze'[50] the division of competences externally: In a mixed agreement, the EU's consent would cover parts X_1, X_2, and X_3, the Member States' consent parts Y_1 and Y_2. If the EU now acquired the competence for part Y_2, this part would be outside the scope of its original consent, and renewed consent by (at least) the EU would be necessary. Thus, an internal shift of competences would result in the EU internally being competent for treaty provisions to which it is not bound. The Member States, in turn, would remain bound by parts of a treaty to which they have consented, but they are internally no longer competent – a situation that partial consent was thought to avoid.

Partial consent is thus not a reasonable concept for mixed agreements. Even with a precise delimitation of the EU and Member State competences, it cannot accommodate

[48] VCLT, Art 39.

[49] O Dörr, 'Article 31' in O Dörr and K Schmalenbach (eds), *Vienna Convention on the Law of Treaties: A Commentary*, 2nd edn (New York, Springer, 2018), para 25.

[50] JHH Weiler, 'The External Legal Relations of Non-Unitary Actors: Mixity and the Federal Principle' in JHH Weiler (ed), *The Constitution of Europe: 'Do the New Clothes have an Emperor?' and Other Essays on European Integration* (Cambridge, Cambridge University Press, 1999) 181.

the dynamics of the EU's division of competences. Hence, the EU and its Member States have each consented to each mixed agreement as a whole[51] and are also bound by those parts not falling within their competences.[52]

IV. The Term 'EU Party' in Mixed Agreements – *Nomen* or *Omen*?

The EU and its Member States becoming 'full parties' to the mixed agreements rebuts the idea of the 'EU Party' as a composite of 'partial parties'. Consequently, the next two parts of this chapter will move away from a formal approach and consider the effects of the 'EU Party' as a linguistic device used in mixed agreements. This part will begin by retracing the use of the term in the evaluated group of bilateral mixed trade agreements. Following an overview (section A), it will analyse possible patterns and their consistency (section B).

A. Preliminary Observations on the Use of the Term 'EU Party' in Mixed Agreements

The first and most frequent use of the 'EU Party' in the context of bilateral mixed trade agreements is the 2008 Economic Partnership Agreement (EPA) with the CARIFORUM States.[53] Since then, the use of 'EU Party' seems somewhat inconsistent at first sight. The EU and its Member States signed 18 additional mixed trade agreements, of which 14 referred to the 'EU Party',[54] and four made no use of the term.[55] Besides, the quantity of its application varies greatly – from 302 appearances of the 'EU Party' in the EPA CARIFORUM to one reference in the Annex of the Partnership and Cooperation Agreement (PCA) with Iraq.

[51] This finding is supported by the practice of national parliaments to consider the whole agreement during their national approval procedure, cp G van der Loo, 'Less is More?: The Role of National Parliaments in the Conclusion of Mixed (Trade) Agreements' [2018] CLEER Paper Series 1, 25–26. See, eg the German national approval act to the AA Ukraine which states that the agreement 'is approved' (own translation) without any reference to divided competences (Gesetz zu dem Assoziierungsabkommen vom 21 März 2014 und vom 27 Juni 2014 zwischen der Europäischen Union und der Europäischen Atomgemeinschaft und ihren Mitgliedstaaten einerseits und der Ukraine andererseits, BGBl 2015 II, 530).

[52] See also Weiler (n 50) 181–82 and Olson (n 22) fn 48 for the perspective of a treaty partner. For an analysis based on a multilateral mixed agreement, see Steinberger (n 23). For the implications with regard to Brexit, see the chapters by Christine Kaddous and Habib Touré and by Yuliya Kaspiarovich and Ramses A Wessel in the present volume.

[53] [2008] OJ L289/3.

[54] See the Interim Economic Partnership Agreements (Interim EPA) with the Pacific States [2009] OJ L272/2, Cameroon ('Central Africa Party') [2009] OJ L57/2 and the Eastern and Southern Africa (ESA) States [2012] OJ L111/2; the EPAs with the SADC EPA States [2016] OJ L250/3, the Ivory Coast [2009] OJ L59/3 and Ghana [2016] OJ L278/3; the Trade Agreement (TA) with Colombia and Peru [2012] OJ L354/3; the AAs with Central America [2012] OJ L346/3 and Ukraine [2014] OJ L161/3; the Free Trade Agreement (FTA) with Korea [2011] OJ L127/6; the Partnership and Cooperation Agreements (PCA) with Iraq [2012] OJ L204/20 and Armenia [2018] OJ L23/4; CETA and the SPA Japan.

[55] See the PCAs with Kazakhstan [2016] OJ L29/3 and Cuba [2016] OJ L337I/3 and the AAs with Moldova [2014] OJ L260/4 and Georgia [2014] OJ L261/4.

On closer inspection, however, some patterns seem to emerge. Since the EPA CARIFORUM, all seven mixed trade agreements signed with a group of third states use the term 'EU Party'.[56] The same applies to all mixed trade agreements signed with African, Caribbean, and Pacific States (ACP States). Overlapping with the first category, these include five agreements with a group of third states and the two EPAs with the Ivory Coast and Ghana. A majority of nine out of 15 treaties referring to the 'EU Party' are, therefore, concluded with a group of third states and/or with ACP States.

Compared to these nine treaties, the use of the term 'EU Party' in the remaining six agreements appears somewhat incidental. This group comprises different forms of trade agreements with countries worldwide,[57] lacking a common denominator such as the plurality or identity of treaty partners. Instead, four of these treaties seem to have more in common with the post-CARIFORUM agreements that do not make use of the 'EU Party'. While the PCAs with Iraq and Armenia and the Association Agreement (AA) with Ukraine refer to the 'EU Party', the PCAs with Kazakhstan and Cuba and the AAs with Moldova and Georgia do not.

Finally, the observations regarding the identity and number of treaty partners coincide with the frequency of the term 'EU Party'. In relation to the length of the treaty texts, the number of appearances of the term 'EU Party' in treaties concluded with a group of third states or an ACP State is, except for the AA Ukraine, considerably higher than in the remaining agreements.

The use of the term 'EU Party', thus, has not increased over the years. It seems to have rather focused on certain types of mixed agreements – either because of their structure or the treaty partner(s).

B. Analysis of the Use of the Term 'EU Party' in Mixed Agreements

Why does the 'EU Party' appear so extensively in some agreements and not (at all) in others? In analysing the mixed agreements with one third state, different applications of the term can be identified (section i). While the manner of application helps to explain the relevance of the identity (section ii) and the number of treaty partners (section iii) for the frequency of the use of 'EU Party', the overall practice, nevertheless, remains inconsistent (section iv).

i. The Use of 'EU Party' in Mixed Agreements Concluded with One Third State

The PCAs with Iraq and Armenia do not shed much light on the use of 'EU Party', all mentions of the term being in the Annexes. The SPA Japan refers to the 'Union Party'

[56] EPA CARIFORUM; Interim EPA Pacific States; Interim EPA ESA States; TA Colombia/Peru; AA Central America; EPA SADC EPA. The Interim EPA Central Africa has so far been signed only with Cameroon. Art 101, however, provides for the accession of further 'Central African States'.

[57] See, eg FTA Korea; CETA; SPA Japan.

three times in the treaty text, once in the preamble and twice in the entry into force clause. Article 47 provides that the agreement shall be 'approved or ratified by the Union Party', and the 'Union Party' shall provide Japan with a single instrument confirming the completion of internal procedures. Likewise, Article 15.10(5)(a) of the Free Trade Agreement (FTA) with Korea provides for two notifications on provisional application, one by 'the EU Party' and one by Korea. Besides entry into force and provisional application, the EPAs with the Ivory Coast and Ghana also use the term in the provisions on accession.[58]

The FTA Korea and CETA primarily use the 'EU Party' where definitions or the applicability of treaty sections differ between the EU and its Member States, on the one hand, and the third state, on the other. In CETA, for example, 'citizen' is defined 'for the EU Party'[59] and '[f]or the EU Party, Sections B and C do not apply'.[60] In the EPAs with Ghana and the Ivory Coast and the AA Ukraine, such application of the 'EU Party' considerably increases beyond definitions with references such as 'products originating in the EC Party',[61] the 'territory of the EU Party',[62] 'EU Party companies'[63] or 'EU Party legislation'.[64]

Substantively, the provisions of the FTA Korea and CETA mainly address 'the Parties'. In contrast, the provisions of the EPAs with Ghana and the Ivory Coast and the AA Ukraine regularly differentiate between the EU and its Member States and the treaty partner. Referring to Ghana, the Ivory Coast, or Ukraine, on the one side, the treaty provisions address the 'EU Party' on the other side. So, while 'each Party shall notify the other Party of its contact points', 'the EU Party shall inform Ukraine … of changes to the EU Party legislation'.[65] Such differentiation becomes necessary, where treaty rights and obligations are not strictly reciprocal and, therefore, cannot address 'the Parties' or 'a Party'.

Thus, in principle, three different uses of the 'EU Party' can be identified, all of which serve to linguistically differentiate between the EU and the third state side of the agreement. First, procedural provisions refer to the 'EU Party'. Here, treaty-related actions, such as notifications, are summarised vis-à-vis the third state. Secondly, the 'EU Party' is used as a descriptive term, distinguishing the geographical and institutional entity that the EU and its Member States form from the third state(s). Thirdly, where a provision provides for an obligation that is not mutually corresponding, the 'EU Party' is used functionally with treaty rights and obligations imposed on it. Thus, the more treaty obligations differentiate between the EU and the third state(s) side, the more frequent the functional use of 'EU Party'.

ii. The Relevance of the Identity of the Treaty Partner for the Use of 'EU Party'

One factor for greater differentiation and, consequently, a higher frequency of the use of 'EU Party' is the identity of the treaty partner(s) or, dependent hereon, the type of

[58] See, eg EPA Ghana, Art 77.
[59] Art 1.2.
[60] Art 8.2(3).
[61] EPA Ghana, Art 13.
[62] AA Ukraine, Art 62(15).
[63] AA Ukraine, Art 154(3).
[64] AA Ukraine, Art 67(3).
[65] AA Ukraine, Art 67.

mixed agreement concluded.[66] The more provisions are reciprocal, the less differentiation is needed – reference to 'the parties' suffices. The amount of reciprocity, in turn, is influenced by the character and aim of the treaty.

PCAs, for example, are 'agreements of a general nature',[67] where the 'concrete substantive scope … is limited'.[68] Accordingly, the PCA Cuba essentially contains provisions on mutual cooperation and, here, only four out of 89 articles do not (just) address 'the Parties' but refer to Cuba and/or the EU specifically. In contrast, the AA Ukraine displays a comparably high level of differentiation and use of the 'EU Party'. Since its objective is 'Ukraine's association with EU policies and participation in [EU] programmes and agencies' as well as its 'gradual integration in the EU Internal Market', this seems only logical.

Likewise, differences in the treaties' objectives explain a high use of 'EU Party' in the EPAs and scarce references in other trade agreements. Whereas the EPAs with ACP States aim to preserve the trade preferences under the ACP-EC-Partnership Agreement,[69] allowing largely customs-free EU market access to products originating in the ACP States but not vice versa,[70] the objective of the FTA Korea is to 'progressively and reciprocally liberalise trade in goods'.[71] Necessarily, such differing starting points create situations where differences in treatment will manifest themselves throughout the treaty.

A difference in development between the sides – the EU side and the non-Member State(s) – can, thus, work both ways: As in the case of the EPAs, it can result in less reciprocity and, accordingly, more frequent use of 'EU Party'. Regarding PCAs, it can also lead to less elaborate agreements where differentiation between the sides is, thus, scarce.

iii. The Relevance of the Number of Treaty Partners for the Use of 'EU Party'

A second reason for greater differentiation is the number of non-Member State treaty partners. Like any mixed trade agreement with one third state, the agreements concluded with a group of third states intend to create a bilateral relationship. In contrast to the first, however, this latter bilateral relationship is twofold: On the one hand, it exists between the EU and its Member States, acting collectively, and every single third state, creating in effect several bilateral agreements combined in one instrument. Title III of the Trade Agreement (TA) with Colombia and Peru, for example, governs the trade in goods between the EU side and Colombia and Peru, respectively, but explicitly does not apply 'to the trade and economic relations between individual signatory Andean Countries'.[72] On the other hand, some parts of the agreements envision bilateral cooperation between

[66] For a description of the different types of bilateral mixed agreements, see M Maresceau, 'A Typology of Mixed Bilateral Agreements' in C Hillion and P Koutrakos (eds) (n 2).
[67] Ibid 20.
[68] Ibid 21.
[69] [2000] OJ L317/3.
[70] See, eg EPA Ghana, preamble, recital 2, Arts 12, 13.
[71] Art 2.1.
[72] Art 7(1).

the EU and its Member States, on the one side, and the third states group, on the other. The Central American parties to the AA Central America, for example, 'commit to act collectively'[73] within the institutional framework set up by Title II of the agreement.

The result is that mixed agreements concluded with a group of third states not only have to distinguish between the two sides of the agreement but also regarding individual and joint obligations of the third state group. Thus, they must be formulated in a way that some provisions address the third states individually and some collectively while at the same time leaving their internal relations unaffected. The definitions of the parties reflect this. Most to the point, Article 233 EPA CARIFORUM provides:

> 3. For the purposes of this Agreement, the term 'Party' shall refer to the CARIFORUM States acting collectively or the EC Party as the case may be. The term 'Parties' shall refer to the CARIFORUM States acting collectively and the EC Party.
>
> 4. Where individual action is provided for or required to exercise the rights or comply with the obligations under this Agreement reference is made to the 'Signatory CARIFORUM States'.

Thus, although a treaty provision might be reciprocal, where it shall address the EU side and the CARIFORUM States acting individually, it still cannot refer to 'the Parties'. Instead, it must refer to the 'Signatory CARIFORUM States' and the EU or its Member States or the EU and its Member States – or, in short, 'the 'EU Party'. Accordingly, instead of addressing 'the Parties', Article 30 EPA CARIFORUM provides that 'the EC Party and the Signatory CARIFORUM States shall … exchange information concerning customs legislation and procedures'.

iv. The Use of 'EU Party' in Mixed Agreements – A Consistent Practice?

The EPAs suggest a certain consistency regarding the use of 'EU Party' – it frequently appears throughout the texts of all post-CARIFORUM EPAs, used respectively in a descriptive, functional and procedural manner. Yet, continuous use of 'EU Party' in the texts of these EPAs is unsurprising: All of them are provided for in the ACP-EC Partnership Agreement[74] and based on a single negotiating directive.[75] The preliminary observations and the analysis of other types of mixed agreements, however, show that beyond this context, the practice surrounding the 'EU Party' is far from settled. The AA Ukraine being the bilateral mixed trade agreement with the most mentions of the 'EU Party' beside the EPAs presents the perfect example.

First, although its consistent appearance in the EPAs suggests otherwise, reference to the 'EU Party' varies even among one type of mixed agreement. Since the AA with Greece, the treaties with Ukraine and Central America are the only AAs that use the term 'EU Party'. While one could argue that most associations were established before the term 'EU Party' was first introduced, the AAs with Moldova and Georgia were signed subsequent to the EPA CARIFORUM and include no reference to the 'EU Party'.

[73] Art 352(3).
[74] Art 36(1).
[75] Permanent Representatives Committee (EC) 9930/02, Recommendation authorising the Commission to negotiate Economic Partnership Agreements with the ACP countries and regions, Annex I.

This is not due to a lack of nonreciprocal provisions in the treaties. Rather, the drafters used other means of linguistic differentiation between the EU side and the associated states. Instead of using the 'EU Party', the AAs with Moldova and Georgia simply refer to 'the EU'[76] or 'the Union'.[77]

Secondly, even the mixed agreements that use the term 'EU Party' do not do so consistently. The AA Ukraine refers to 'Union' legislation in the preamble and 'EU Party legislation' in the substantive provisions.[78] While it functionally usually refers to the 'EU Party', in parts, it addresses the EU or its Member States individually.[79] Furthermore, not all provisions addressing the 'EU Party' in fact require differentiation. Throughout its treaty text, the AA Ukraine repeatedly refers to 'the EU Party and Ukraine',[80] thereby increasing the count of 'EU Party'. However, here, a simple reference to 'the Parties', expressly defined as Ukraine and the 'EU Party',[81] would have sufficed.

Thus, although some patterns and three general manners of application are distinguishable, the use of 'EU Party' is far from consistent – both regarding if and how it is applied in the different treaties. While the need for linguistic differentiation may explain why 'EU Party' is used more frequently in some agreements than others, it does not explain why the term is used in certain agreements at all. Instead of representing a settled concept evolved from treaty practice, the term 'EU Party' requires interpretation in its specific context.

V. International Law Effects of the 'EU Party' – Are We One or Are We Many?

While continuing the treaty text-based approach, this part will consider the use of the 'EU Party' in its specific context. Based on the three previously identified manners of application, it will attend to the use of the 'EU Party' in the context of the substantive (section A) and procedural provisions (section B) of the evaluated mixed agreements. It will analyse how the context of its application influences the interpretation of the term 'EU Party' and how this, in turn, affects the perception of the EU and its Member States – as individual parties or a joined 'EU Party'.

A. The Use of 'EU Party' in Substantive Provisions

In the substantive provisions of the bilateral mixed trade agreements, the term 'EU Party' is used in a descriptive and functional manner. In its descriptive use, reference to

[76] See, eg AA Moldova, Art 24 ('The EU and Moldova shall'), Art 27 ('EU rules').

[77] See, eg AA Moldova, Art 179(15) ('For the Union, the term "territory" or "country" means the territory of the Union'), Art 184(3) ('the Union shall inform the Republic of Moldova well in advance of changes to Union legislation'); AA Georgia, Art 77(h) ('natural persons of the Union').

[78] Art 67.

[79] See, eg Arts 452, 479(6); individual reference to Ukraine, the EU and the Member States is made in Art 7. For further examples in other treaties, see, eg CETA, Arts 1.3, 28.2 and FTA Korea, c 10, s B, subss B, C, D.

[80] See, eg Arts 193(1), 213(1).

[81] Art 482.

the 'EU Party' acknowledges the geographical and institutional entity that the EU and its Member States form. The 'EU Party' serves as a common denominator to define, distinguish and relate treaty objects or concepts to the EU and its Member States. Here, just like its alternatives, such as 'Community'[82] or 'Union',[83] the 'EU Party' shapes the content of the treaty provisions; it does not, however, have any added value as regards its international law implications for the EU and its Member States.

In its functional use, however, the 'EU Party' is the addressee of treaty provisions. Where, for example, previous AAs[84] had addressed 'the Community and Jordan',[85] 'the Community and its Member States'[86] or 'the Member States and Jordan',[87] the AA Ukraine avoids such direct reference by addressing the 'EU Party'. From an international law perspective, this is interesting for two reasons.

First, as the addressee of treaty provisions, the 'EU Party' assumes a function equivalent to a contracting party: to be the subject of treaty rights and obligations.[88] Does the 'EU Party', therefore, replace the EU and its Member States as individual parties? Although Article 26 VCLT requires the performance of the treaty, treaty law leaves it to the parties to decide how they do so. Similarly, in the EPAs, the third state groups fulfil some obligations collectively as the 'CARIFORUM States', without, however, thereby calling into question their respective status as individual parties.

Instead – and this is the second point – in the case of the EU and its Member States, it is precisely their status as individual, 'full' parties that enables the use of the 'EU Party' at all. Having consented to and being bound by the whole agreement, the term 'EU Party' is open to interpretation and a dynamic division of competences. Defined as 'the EU or its Member States or the EU and its Member States according to their respective competences', the term avoids direct reference, especially where competence is controversial, and provides for a joint or alternative performance of treaty obligations.[89]

B. The Use of 'EU Party' in the Final Provisions

The term 'EU Party' is, however, also used in some bilateral mixed agreements' final provisions. On the one hand, merging the EU and its Member States here seems to make sense. Where treaty obligations are performed jointly or alternatively, coordination regarding procedural issues seems advisable. In contrast to substantive obligations, however, procedural treaty-related action is generally associated with individual actions of the parties. This is especially so where treaty law envisages – or even presupposes – an individual expression of intent, such as in the case of ratification (section i), accessions

[82] See, eg Euro-Mediterranean AA with Jordan [2002] OJ L129/3, Art 7 ('products originating in the Community'), Art 30(2) ('Community companies') and Art 32 ('territory of the Community').
[83] See, eg AA Moldova, Art 179(15), Art 184(3).
[84] See the Euro-Mediterranean AAs and the Western Balkan Stabilisation and Association Agreements, eg AA Jordan and the SAA with Montenegro [2010] OJ L108/3.
[85] AA Jordan, Art 6.
[86] AA Jordan, Art 30(1).
[87] AA Jordan, Art 54.
[88] See VCLT, Art 26.
[89] On joint and alternative treaty performance, cp in detail Heliskoski (n 2), ch 4.

(section ii), and denunciation (section iii). What role do the EU and its Member States play here individually, and how does the 'EU Party' impact it?

i. Consent to be Bound and Entry into Force of Mixed Agreements

Provisions on entry into force generally set out the procedure with which states or IOs can express their consent to be bound and the treaty's subsequent date of entry into force. While bilateral treaties usually require an exchange of instruments of approval, it is common for a depository to receive and register the notifications necessary for the entry into force of a multilateral treaty.[90] Although formally multilateral treaties, most mixed agreements resort to a typically bilateral procedure, providing for reciprocal exchanges of instruments or notifications.[91] Even where mixed agreements resort to a depository, such as the Secretary-General of the Council of the EU,[92] the wording regularly adapts these procedures, diminishing the multilateral impression. Thus, some mixed agreements combine the bilateral phrasing of reciprocal notification with the duty to send these notifications to a depositary.[93] Others provide for two depositaries: the EU Council and a designated ministry or institution of the third state(s).[94]

In addition, while multilateral treaties regularly provide for entry into force between some parties, pending ratification by others, all assessed mixed agreements provide for entry into force only once the EU and all Member States have completed their internal procedures. In mixed agreements concluded with one third state, this creates a typically bilateral situation, where entry into force logically depends on the approval by both parties – or, in the case of bilateral mixed agreements, both sides. While the TA Colombia/Peru allows for partial entry into force, this only underlines the EU and its Member States' relatedness. Only once the EU side has completed its internal procedures, the TA can enter into force between 'the EU Party and each signatory Andean Country'.[95]

With such a level of bilateralisation, the use of the 'EU Party' linguistically underlines this two-sided approach. At the same time, even approval and exchange of instruments by the 'Union Party'[96] or a depositary for 'the EU Party'[97] does not replace individual action by all parties – the EU, its Member States and the third state(s). For the agreements to be mixed, consent to be bound by the EU and its Member States is mandatory. The term 'EU Party', where used, may, therefore, streamline the process for the EU and its Member States. However, it must necessarily be read as the EU *and* its Member States.

[90] VCLT, Art 78.

[91] See ILC, 'Provisional Application of Treaties, Memorandum by the Secretariat' UN Doc A/CN.4/707 para 5: 'While mixed agreements are typically registered as bilateral treaties, they require the ratification, approval or acceptance of the European Union and each of its Member States. Accordingly, mixed agreements share certain structural characteristics with bilateral and multilateral treaties, particularly those multilateral treaties with limited membership.'

[92] EPA SADC EPA, Art 113(1), (2), (7).

[93] EPA CARIFORUM, Art 243(2), (3).

[94] CETA, Art 30.7(2), (4).

[95] TA Colombia/Peru, Art 330(2).

[96] SPA Japan, Art 47(1).

[97] AA Central America, Art 353(3).

ii. Accession to Mixed Agreements

Regarding accession to mixed agreements, two different constellations can be distinguished: the accession of a third state and that of a new EU Member State. The first has only occurred once,[98] although the mixed trade agreements concluded with a regional group of states contain accession provisions. In contrast, accession by the new Member States has occurred far more often. While most of the examined mixed agreements have, thus, experienced EU enlargement, only some include explicit accession clauses for the new Member States.[99]

The third state accession clauses are mostly framed bilaterally, their wording being reminiscent of the ratification clauses.[100] Frequent reference to the 'EU Party' is made in the context of pre-accession action, such as negotiations and mutual information, but also as regards the actual approval. Thus, in the EPA ESA States, consent by all parties is bilateralised into the 'legal procedures of the EC Party and the ESA States',[101] and the EPA CARIFORUM provides for both negotiations and approval by 'the EC Party'.[102] Regarding negotiation or mutual information, in the only case of third state accession, the EU conducted the talks with Ecuador for 'the EU Party'.[103] In the context of consent, however, the use of 'EU Party', just as in the original process of ratification, must necessarily be understood to read the EU *and* its Member States.

In the absence of accession provisions,[104] previous EU enlargements generally involved the conclusion of accession protocols. Although being mixed agreements themselves, the ratification clauses of these accession protocols deviate significantly from those of the original mixed agreements. While the preamble lists all Member States, the protocols are not signed by their 27 individual plenipotentiaries but 'for the Member States'[105] by an EU Council representative. Thus, where all original mixed agreements explicitly recognise the Member States' individual participation – the approval by all parties – the accession protocols 'shall be approved by the Community [and] by the Council of the European Union on behalf of the Member States'.[106] This does not mean that the Member States have not individually consented to the accession of the new Member States to the existing mixed agreements. In obliging the new Member State to accede to these treaties in the EU Act of Accession,[107] they have arguably expressed

[98] See the accession of Ecuador to the TA Colombia/Peru, [2016] OJ L356/3.

[99] Such explicit provisions on new EU Member State accessions are included in some, but not all, more recent bilateral mixed trade agreements, see below.

[100] For exceptions, see Interim EPA Central Africa and EPA SADC EPA.

[101] Art 66.

[102] Art 248.

[103] TA Colombia/Peru/Ecuador, preamble, recital 7.

[104] Some mixed agreements mention the possibility of further EU accessions in the context of agreements on customs unions or free trade areas, see, eg SAA Bosnia and Herzegovina [2015] OJ L164/2, Art 37(3).

[105] See, eg the Bulgarian and Romanian Accession Protocol to the AA Israel [2007] OJ L317/65, signature block.

[106] Accession Protocol AA Israel, Art 8.

[107] See, eg the Croatian Act of Accession to the EU [2012] L112/21, Art 6(2): 'the accession of Croatia to such [mixed] agreements shall be agreed by the conclusion of a protocol to such agreements between the Council, acting unanimously on behalf of the Member States, and the third country or countries or international organisation concerned'.

their consent to such accession – albeit not vis-à-vis their treaty partners in the mixed agreements.

The newly introduced EU accession clauses in the EPAs[108] and CETA make these additional protocols redundant, providing for an automatic accession of the new Member State(s) 'by means of a clause to that effect in the act of accession to the European Union' or – in the absence of such a clause – 'by depositing an act of accession'.[109] Thus, in the most recent case of EU accession, Croatia acceded to the EPA Ghana by depositing an instrument of accession, while necessary changes to the mixed agreement were agreed by the EPA Committee.[110]

Just like ratification, accession, in legal terms, boils down to the issue of consent by all parties – either to an additional accession agreement or a pre-determined accession procedure – and, thus, joint action by the EU *and* its Member States. In contrast to the original ratification, however, the visibility of the Member States' participation decreases, especially with regard to Member State accessions.

iii. Denunciation of Mixed Agreements

Denunciation differs from the previous final provisions. While it, too, requires an expression of intent, it does not presuppose action by *all* parties. Any party can withdraw from a treaty in line with the respective requirements of the VCLT.[111] Accordingly, Advocate-General Sharpston reasoned that '[w]here an international agreement is signed by both the European Union and its Member States, each Member State remains free under international law to terminate that agreement', seeing as '[t]he ability to act independently as an actor under international law reflects the continuing international competence of the Member State'.[112]

At the same time, the parties can draft denunciation clauses, determining not only the procedure, as in the case of ratification and accession, but, if they wish, also who may denounce the treaty. Most mixed agreements here, too, resort to bilateral treaty language, allowing 'either Party' or the third state and 'the EC Party'[113] denunciation 'by means of a written notification delivered to the other party'.[114] Regardless of the involvement of at least 29 treaty parties, the act of denunciation thus appears only two-sided. The question is, therefore, not whether the EU and its Member States remain capable under international law *generally* to terminate mixed agreements, but whether they can – as AG Sharpston asserted – individually do so 'in accordance with whatever is the appropriate termination procedure under the agreement'.[115]

[108] See, eg EPA CARIFORUM, Art 247.

[109] CETA, Art 30.10(5). Likewise, AA Central America, Art 359(5) allows for automatic accession of any Central American state joining the Central American integration process, if its joining act so provides.

[110] Decision No 1/2019 of the EPA Committee set up by the Stepping Stone Economic Partnership Agreement between Ghana, of the one Part, and the European Community and its Member States, of the other Part, regarding the Accession of the Republic of Croatia to the European Union [2019] OJ L33/154.

[111] VCLT, Arts 42(2), 54.

[112] Opinion 2/15 *FTA Singapore (*Opinion of the Advocate General) [2015] EU:C:2016:992, [77].

[113] Interim EPA ESA States, Art 62(7).

[114] CPA Armenia, Art 381(2).

[115] *FTA Singapore*, AG Sharpston (n 112) [77].

In case of ratification, a reading of the '(EU) Party' as the EU *and* its Member States is mandatory: not as a result of an interpretation along the division of competences, but because international law requires consent from the EU and its Member States if all 28 are to become parties. The same applies to accessions. Concerning denunciation, however, international law does not prescribe such an obligatory reading. According to the definition of the parties in the mixed agreements, recourse, thus, has to be taken to the EU's division of competences. Hence, denunciation in accordance with the treaty's termination procedure is not a question of ability under international law but the interpretation of competences under EU law.

Nevertheless, two observations regarding denunciation can be made under international law. These relate to the previous findings of this chapter and the use of bilateral treaty language such as the 'EU Party'. First, denunciation does not take place along the lines of competences. Had the EU and its Member States, in contrast to the findings above, only partially consented to the mixed agreements, one could consider a partial termination along the division of competences. The mixed agreement could be understood as one instrument encompassing two treaties – between the EU and the third state(s) and between the Member States and the third state(s) – which respectively and independently could be terminated. However, since the EU and its Member States remain 'full parties', denunciation by the EU or one of the Member States would necessarily relate to their consent to the whole agreement.

Secondly, the wording of the mixed agreements does not envisage an 'independent' possibility of denunciation for the EU or its Member States. This can best be seen when contrasting the 'EU Party' and a third state group regarding the wording and consequence of denunciation. The EPA CARIFORUM, for example, allows termination by 'either Party', being defined as the CARIFORUM States acting collectively or the 'EC Party',[116] or by a 'Signatory CARIFORUM State'[117] acting individually. Thus, while the CARIFORUM States can decide to act collectively or individually, any action by the EU and/or its Member States must – according to the parties' definition – be regarded as an action by the 'EU Party'. Additionally, denunciation by a participant on the EU side leads to the treaty's termination.[118] While mixed agreements concluded with a group of third states remain in force when a non-EU Member State withdraws, they are 'terminated in case of withdrawal by the EU Party'.[119]

In light of this, the assumption by AG Sharpston that, if a Member State were to terminate unilaterally, 'the effect of Article 216(2) TFEU will be that … it continues to be bound by the areas of the agreement concluded under EU competence'[120] does not accord with the termination procedures under the bilateral mixed agreements. Instead, were the EU or its Member States to denounce one of the assessed mixed agreements, it would not only terminate *its* treaty relationship but that of the *whole* 'EU Party' unilaterally.[121] While this creates a certain symmetry between ratification and

[116] Art 233(3).
[117] Art 244(2).
[118] An exception is AA Central America, Art 354.
[119] See, eg TA Colombia/Peru, Art 331(3).
[120] *FTA Singapore*, AG Sharpston (n 112) [77].
[121] For the special case of Brexit, see the chapters by H Touré and C Kaddous and by Y Kaspiarovich and RA Wessel in the present volume.

termination – the treaty is either in force for all participants on the EU side or none – termination differs in that action by a single party – under international law – suffices.[122]

VI. Conclusion – *Nomen* may be *Omen*

The very idea of mixity is that the EU and its Member States conclude an agreement jointly. In examining the status of the EU and its Member States in mixed agreements, this chapter, first, considered the formal aspect of the conclusion, before analysing how the treaty language – especially through the use of 'EU Party' – realises the element of *joint* participation.

The EU and its Member States are all parties to mixed agreements, their consent extending to the whole agreement, regardless of the division of competences. Such 'full' conclusion may, at first sight, speak against joint participation: Intuitively, two partial (instead of 'full') parties – the EU and its Member States – would form one 'EU Party'. Instead, this chapter has shown that conclusion of the whole agreement by the EU and its Member States, respectively, enables the translation of the dynamic division of competences onto the international level.

One of the effects is the use of the term 'EU Party' – defined as the EU or its Member States or the EU and its Member States according to their respective competences. While an evaluation of current mixed trade agreements shows that the use of 'EU Party' remains far from consistent, it is a practical linguistic device to create and maintain the bilateral character of the mixed agreements. Instead of addressing the EU or its Member States individually, treaty provisions can refer to the 'EU Party', accommodating internal shifts of competences.

More complex problems arise, however, when it comes to the final provisions of these agreements. Where the term 'EU Party' is used in the context of ratification and accession, international law requires a strict differentiation between mere procedural issues, such as negotiations or notifications, and the actual legal acts, such as ratification. While the first may be performed by the EU or its Member States for the 'EU Party', individual action by the EU *and* its Member States is mandatory in the latter. This raises interesting legal questions regarding termination where action by the EU *or* its Member States is theoretically possible under international but most likely inconceivable under EU law.

Hinting at the treaty law concept of a 'Party', the term 'EU Party' implies a new type of combined party status of the EU and its Member States. While not being one 'EU Party' in the formal sense (yet), there appears to be no reason why such a joint party status could not develop under international law.[123] As for now, the EU and its

[122] Under EU law, the concept of sincere cooperation in Art 4(3) TEU would, arguably, prevent the EU or individual Member States from acting individually.

[123] This would depend not only on the text of the agreements but also on the practice of the EU and third states in respect of these agreements, cp J Odermatt, 'The Development of Customary International Law by International Organizations' (2017) 66 *International & Comparative Law Quarterly* 491.

Member States have taken advantage of the (linguistic) possibilities already available under international treaty law to create the perception of a single party – with the 'EU Party' accommodating the EU's internal design to a point where international law requires a mandatory interpretation. In doing so, instead of allowing mixed agreements to 'rupture the [EU's] unity',[124] terms like the 'EU Party' create a unity that has been accepted by the EU's treaty partners.

[124] J Klabbers, *An Introduction to International Institutional Law*, 2nd edn (Cambridge, Cambridge University Press, 2009) 294.

8

Conformity of International Dispute Settlement Mechanisms with EU Law

Does the EU's Participation Really Matter?

BARTOSZ SOLOCH AND MAKANE MOÏSE MBENGUE

I. Introduction

This chapter aims to examine whether and to what extent the European Union's (EU) participation in international agreements is determinative for the conformity of dispute settlement mechanisms contained therein with EU law, as opposed to the participation of EU Member States only. Although many international treaties contain dispute settlement mechanisms to which the EU and/or its Member States are a party, there have been instances of the Court of Justice of the European Union (CJEU) ruling that international dispute settlement mechanisms are not in conformity with the principle of autonomy of EU law.[1] Given the complexity of scholarship dealing with the principle of autonomy, it is clear that its comprehensive analysis would go far beyond the scope of this chapter. Consequently, the authors have decided to concentrate only on one aspect. As shall be discussed in more detail below, the issue of interference of international dispute settlement mechanisms with the distribution of competences within the EU has featured prominently in the CJEU's case law. Thus, elucidating how the EU's participation in international dispute settlement mechanisms would influence their conformity with EU law should contribute to furthering our understanding of the autonomy principle.

[1] The topic of autonomy of EU law has been discussed extensively in the legal literature, see eg works such as Jan Willem van Rossen, 'Pushing Limits: The Principle of Autonomy in the External Relations Case Law of the European Court of Justice' in Mads Andenas et al (eds), *EU External Action in International Economic Law* (Springer, 2020), 35–68; Andreas Bergmann, *Zur Souverenitätskonzepzion des Europäischen Gerichtshofs* (Mohr-Siebeck, 2018); Jed Odermatt, 'The Principle of Autonomy: An Adolescent Disease of EU External Relations Law?' in Marise Cremona (ed), *Structural Principles in EU External Relations Law*, (Hart, 2018) 290–316; Daniel Halberstam, '"It's the Autonomy, Stupid!" A Modest Defense of Opinion 2/13 on EU Accession to the ECHR and the Way Forward' (2015) University of Michigan Law School, Public Law and Legal Theory Research Paper Series no 439, https://papers.ssrn.com/sol3/papers.cfm?abstract_id=2567591#; Gráinne de Búrca, 'The European Court of Justice and the International Legal Order After Kadi' (2010) *Harv Intl L J* 1–49; René Barents, *The Autonomy of Community Law* (Kluwer Law International, 2004).

It is something of a truism that recent years have seen a real proliferation of international dispute settlement mechanisms. This general development has serious implications for the EU's international relations law[2] as the EU is increasingly faced with the problem of submitting to the jurisdiction of external bodies. In fact, in certain areas, it is precisely the EU that advocates for the introduction of dispute settlement mechanisms, such as in the case of free trade agreements (FTAs). Prominent examples include the Comprehensive Economic and Trade Agreement (CETA[3]) between Canada and the European Union and its Member States and efforts to introduce the Multilateral Investment Court (MIC). In such circumstances, the issue of the EU submitting itself to dispute settlement bodies operating outside of the framework provided by the Treaties could be viewed even as determinative for the EU's ability to conduct the external action. Arguably, the case law of the CJEU does not provide satisfactory guidance in this regard, as analysed in more detail below.

Until recently, the CJEU's jurisprudence[4] seemingly suggested that the conformity of a given dispute settlement mechanism with EU law would largely depend on the EU's participation (or lack thereof). In fact, these were the mixed agreements (ie agreements concluded by the EU and its Member States) which the CJEU identified as problematic. Arguably, the CJEU's Opinion 2/13[5] concerning the EU's accession to the European Convention on Human Rights (ECHR; Convention)[6] would be a primary example of the approach emphasising the role of the EU's participation. It concerned a unique situation where all the EU Member States had been and remained bound by an agreement on many instances interfering with EU law, and only EU's accession to it was viewed as somewhat problematic. As shall be explained in more detail below, the CJEU concentrated on issues of apportionment of responsibility between the Member States and the EU, prior involvement of the CJEU in the proceedings before the ECtHR and providing a dispute settlement mechanism parallel to the framework foreseen in EU law. Given that most of the issues related to the ECHR's influence on the EU legal system covered by the CJEU in this opinion are independent of the EU's participation in the agreement, it is even more evident that it was the EU's participation that rendered the ECHR incompatible with EU law. It has to be stressed that, since the CJEU's Opinion concentrated on technical issues of interaction between different legal regimes rather than on the ECHR's character as a human rights treaty, the ECHR Opinion can be viewed as a representative example of the autonomy-related jurisprudence of the CJEU.[7]

[2] The term 'EU international relations law' shall be used to describe the law defining the relationship between EU law and international law. For its earlier use, see Panos Koutrakos, *EU International Relations Law* (Hart, 2015).

[3] Comprehensive Economic and Trade Agreement (CETA) between Canada, on the one part, and the European Union and its Member States, of the other part [2017] OJ L 11/23.

[4] Of course, one has to remember that the CJEU's jurisprudence is not fully representative of the treaty practice of the EU, with many dispute settlement mechanisms having never been scrutinised by the Court, mostly due to the possible conflicts having been resolved by negotiations between the Commission and the Member States concerned.

[5] Opinion 2/13, *European Convention on Human Rights*, EU:C:2014:2454.

[6] Convention for the Protection of Human Rights and Fundamental Freedoms, ETS No 005.

[7] See literature in (n 1) above.

As demonstrated below, however, this picture was soon deconstructed by the CJEU's later jurisprudence pertaining to international investment arbitration. In the CJEU's *Achmea* judgment,[8] it stated for the first time that a dispute settlement clause in an agreement concluded solely between the Member States in the intra-EU setting, without the EU's participation, can also violate the principle of autonomy of EU law. The shift from the focus on modalities of the EU's participation to the actual impact of an agreement on the EU legal system became even more apparent with the CJEU's later *CETA* Opinion.[9] In this case, it was arguably the EU's participation (along with the Member States) that contributed to introducing specific provisions allowing the accommodation of the autonomy-related problems and, thus, ensuring the dispute settlement mechanism's conformity with EU law. Consequently, as will be explained in more detail below, the CJEU's focus shifted from the EU's participation to the substantive impact of the agreements on the EU legal system, which leaves all the actors with less guidance as to the agreement's conformity with EU law.[10]

The chapter shall have the following structure. Firstly, it shall be explained that the CJEU 2/13 Opinion's focus was limited solely to the issues around the EU's participation in the ECHR. Further, it will be demonstrated that, in doing so, the CJEU turned a blind eye to the very similar structural problems in the relationship between the ECHR and EU law existing even in the absence of the EU's accession to the ECHR. This approach is then contrasted with the stance taken by the CJEU towards the investor-state dispute settlement mechanisms (ISDS) contained in bilateral investment treaties (BITs) concluded between the Member States. In that context, the EU's top court not only focused on substantive compatibility but, arguably, even created a situation where the EU's participation in the treaty contributed to the conformity of the dispute settlement mechanism with EU law.

II. Setting the Scene

It cannot be denied that, until recently, the bulk of the CJEU's jurisprudence referring to international dispute settlement mechanisms was limited to international treaties with the participation of the EU as a party, with the vast majority being mixed agreements[11] and one concluded solely by the Union.[12] Single judgments pertaining to international

[8] Case C-284/16, *Achmea*, EU:C:2018:158.

[9] Opinion 1/17, *CETA*, EU:C:2019:341.

[10] One could contemplate whether the principle of autonomy of EU law that has been recognised by the CJEU long since could not provide sufficient guidelines for such cases. This question should be answered in the negative – if the CJEU's jurisprudence on autonomy and the accompanying research on the topic thereof (examples of which are listed in n 1 above) show anything, it is that this principle is all but unambiguous. Unfortunately, given the constraints of this chapter, it is not possible to dedicate more space to this topic.

[11] Opinion 1/76, *Laying-up fund*, EU:C:1977:63; 19; Opinion 1/91, *European Economic Area*, EU:C:1991:490; Opinion 1/92, *European Free Trade Agreement*, EU:C:1992:189; Case C-459/03, *Commission v Ireland*, EU:C:2006:345; Opinion 1/09, *European Patent Court*, EU:C:2011:123; Opinion 2/13 (n 5). Here it deserves highlighting that in the case of Opinion 1/76, the CJEU declared the whole international framework incompatible with EU law due to it being parallel to EU law and dedicated relatively little attention to the issue of the court's status as such.

[12] Opinion 1/00, *European Common Aviation Area*, EU:C:2002:231.

dispute settlement mechanisms in agreements concluded between the Member States only confirm these bodies' eligibility to make a preliminary reference to CJEU.[13] Thus, the above jurisprudence would strongly suggest that the bulk of problems related to the EU's membership in international dispute settlement mechanisms would boil down to its participation in international agreements. This would be particularly true in the case of mixed agreements.

Even the CJEU itself, in its *European Aviation Area* opinion, seemed to have acknowledged that the lack of the Member States participation removes the problems related to the risk of an external body deciding on the issues of competence division within the EU or the Member States, featuring prominently in the 1/91 opinion.[14] This view would be hardly surprising in the context of the Court's jurisprudence: in all but one ruling concerning mixed agreements, it found a breach of EU law due to the mechanisms' interference with the distribution of competences within the EU. In Opinion 1/91,[15] the adjudicating bodies were said to have too much influence on the matters of distribution of powers within the EU. For example, in the *Mox Plant* case,[16] Ireland's use of dispute settlement mechanisms contained in UNCLOS was deemed to violate the intra-EU division of powers. In another example, the European Patent Court was declared incompatible with EU law largely because it applied and interpreted EU law outside of the EU's judicial system. And perhaps the most significant instance was reached in Opinion 2/13[17] where, as will be explained in more detail below, the EU's accession to the ECHR was found to violate EU law, while the participation of all the Member States in the mechanism did not give raise to any questions.

Arguably, the above conclusions would not be altered even if it were acknowledged that the CJEU jurisprudence does not fully reflect the practice in the field of EU's external relations law. All in all, it cannot be denied that the EU, along with its Member States, is a party to many treaties containing dispute settlement provisions that have never been scrutinised by the CJEU from the point of view of their conformity with EU law.[18] Nonetheless, the silence of the CJEU on the topic does not necessarily mean that these agreements would be declared compatible with EU law.

In light of the above, from CJEU's autonomy-related jurisprudence, one could infer that the bulk of autonomy-related issues where an external body decides on the division of competences between the EU and the Member States, the issue of EU's participation is of crucial importance. Consequently, as a matter of principle, both the EU's

[13] Case C-337/95, *Parfums Christian Dior*, EU:C:1997:517 concerning the Benelux Court and Case C-196/09, *Miles*, EU:C:2011:388 concerning European Schools Board.

[14] Opinion 1/00 (n 12) paras 16–17.

[15] Opinion 1/91 (n 11).

[16] C-459/03, *Commission v Ireland* (n 11).

[17] Opinion 2/13 (n 5).

[18] Examples include Covered Agreements of the World Trade Organization (WTO); UNCLOS or Aarhus Convention; see also Christina Eckes, 'EU Autonomy and Decisions of (Quasi-)Judicial Bodies. How Much Differentness is Needed?' (2011) Amsterdam Centre for European Law and Governance Working Paper Series 10/2011; Laurens Ankersmit, 'Judging International Dispute Settlement: From the Investment Court System to the Aarhus Convention's Compliance Committee' (2017) Amsterdam Centre for European Law and Governance Research Paper 5/2017, https://papers.ssrn.com/sol3/papers.cfm?abstract_id=3080988.

non-participation in a given agreement and its exclusive participation would serve as a strong indication of its conformity with EU law. On the other hand, it would seem that mixed participation in a given treaty would suggest the mechanism's lack of conformity with EU law.[19]

As shall be explained in more detail below, however, the CJEU's recent ISDS-related jurisprudence effectively turned the tables and made this somewhat simplistic understanding no longer tenable.

III. Opinion 2/13 on the ECHR Accession: The EU's Participation as the Troublemaker?

Emphasising the interplay between the EU's participation and the agreement's impact on the autonomy of EU law is best illustrated by considering Opinion 2/13 in more detail. Firstly, it is argued that all the autonomy-related problems identified by the CJEU were intrinsically connected to the EU's participation in the agreement (section A). Secondly, it will be demonstrated that this conclusion is corroborated by the fact that most of the problems identified by the CJEU already existed in the absence of the EU's accession due to the Member States' participation in the Convention (section B).

A. Opinion 2/13: EU's Participation as the Source of Troubles

Given that Opinion 2/13 has been thoroughly analysed many times,[20] the elements most relevant to the main topic of this chapter will be exclusively discussed. At this juncture, it suffices to say that the Draft Accession Agreement scrutinised by the CJEU was the result of a long evolution and changes introduced to the Treaty on European Union expressly mandating the EU to accede to the ECHR.[21] Eventually, a signed project of the Accession Agreement[22] was submitted to the CJEU for a legal opinion in accordance

[19] In this direction see Matthias Müller, *Das Rechtsprechungsmonopol des EuGH im Kontext völkerrechtlicher Verträge. Untersucht anhand der Rechtsprechung des Gerichthofs der Europäischen Union*, (Nomos, 2012) 59.

[20] See eg Przemysław Tacik, *Przystąpienie Unii Europejskiej do Europejskiej Konwencji Praw Człowieka* (IWEP 2017); Federico Fabbrini and Joris Larik, 'The Past, Present and Future of the Relation between the European Court of Justice and the European Court of Human Rights' (2016) *YEL* 1; Louise H Storgaard, 'EU Law Autonomy Versus European Fundamental Rights Protection – On Opinion 2/13 on EU Accession to the ECHR' (2015) *HRLR* 485; Tobias Lock, 'The Future of the European Union's Accession to the European Convention on Human Rights after Opinion 2/13: Is it Still Possible and is it Still Desirable?' (2015) 11 *ECLR* 239 or the Editorial Comment 'The EU's Accession to ECHR – a "NO" from the EJC!' (2015) 52 *CMLR* 1–16. Opinion 2/13 is also extensively analysed in the literature dedicated to the autonomy of EU law (see n 1).

[21] Treaty on European Union [2012] OJ C326/01. The introduction of these provisions was itself an effect of the earlier failed attempt at the ECHR accession, see Opinion 2/94, *Accession of the EC to the ECHR*, EU:C:1996:140.

[22] The Accession project itself was an effect of many years of rapprochement between EU law and the ECHR, which resulted in the need for their harmonisation to unify the protection of fundamental rights in Europe. Giuseppe Martinico and Oreste Pollicino, *The Interaction Between Europe's Legal Systems. Judicial Dialogue and the Creation of Supranational Laws* (Edward Elgar 2012) 138; Fabbrini, Larik (n 20) 5–7; Nina Półtorak, 'Przystąpienie Unii Europejskiej do Konwencji o Ochronie Praw Człowieka – Projekt u Mowy Akcesyjnej a Prawo UE' (2012) 9 *Europejski Przegląd Sądowy* 4.

with Article 218(11) of the Treaty on Functioning of the European Union (TFEU).[23] As is well known, despite the existence of certain provisions addressing the peculiarities of the EU's membership, the CJEU declared the agreement incompatible with the Treaties, much to the dismay of many legal scholars.[24] An analysis of these general critiques and lines of argument goes beyond the scope of this chapter.

i. The EU's Participation Makes a Difference

As highlighted above, unlike in its earlier Opinion 2/94, in Opinion 2/13 related to the ECHR, the CJEU concentrated on the actual conformity of the Accession Agreement with EU law instead of limiting itself to a simple competence analysis. Somewhat surprisingly, the Court's reasoning revolved around only legal issues related to modalities of EU's membership in ECHR.[25] Indeed, even a cursory analysis of Opinion 2/13 reveals that the EU's participation in the agreement and its modalities were a decisive factor for the CJEU. Consequently, the CJEU stressed that without the EU becoming a party to the Convention, the latter was not *formally incorporated into the legal order of the EU.*[26] Thus, the ECHR would have become binding upon the EU,[27] with the EU's institutions becoming subject to the control of ECHR[28] – also as a matter of international law[29] – only after the EU's accession. Building on this, the CJEU went further and explained that EU fundamental rights, including the Charter, should be interpreted in accordance with EU law,[30] thus reclaiming its responsibility for the application of fundamental rights across the EU.[31] Consequently, according to the CJEU, EU institutions would be bound by the ECHR and ECtHR decisions *in the exercise of their internal powers*[32] only with EU accession to the ECHR. The CJEU noted in this regard that, as a result of the EU becoming a party to the Convention, the ECtHR could negatively assess the CJEU's interpretation of EU law, primarily in respect of the EU Charter on Fundamental Rights,[33] with legal effects also within the EU.

[23] Treaty on Functioning of the European Union [2012] OJ C326/01.

[24] See the literature invoked in (n 20) above. Titles of contemporaneous expert blog posts would be even more telling: Sionaidh Douglas-Scott, 'Opinion 2/13 on EU Accession to the ECHR: A Christmas Bombshell from the European Court of Justice' (*Verfassungsblog* 24 December 2014), https://verfassungsblog.de/opinion-213-eu-accession-echr-christmas-bombshell-european-court-justice-2/ accessed 20 October 2020; Steve Peers, 'The CJEU and the EU's Accession to the ECHR: A Clear and Present Danger to Human Rights Protection' (*EU Law Analysis*, 18 December 2014) http://eulawanalysis.blogspot.com/2014/12/the-cjeu-and-eus-accession-to-echr.html accessed 20 October 2020.

[25] Allan Rosas, 'The EU and International Dispute Settlement' (2017) 1 *Europe and the World: A Law Review* 1, 10–12. Arguably, the issues related to the Common Foreign and Security Policy (CFSP) were analysed by the Court from a different angle (the possibility of submitting matters falling outside of CJEU's jurisdiction to external adjudicating bodies), though further analysis of this issue would go beyond the scope of this chapter.

[26] Opinion 2/13 (n 5), para 179.

[27] Ibid, para 180.

[28] Ibid, para 181.

[29] Ibid, para 185; see also Opinion of AG Kokott in Opinion 2/13, *European Convention on Human Rights*, EU:C:2014:2475, para 1.

[30] Opinion 2/13 (n 5), para 177.

[31] Ibid, paras 188–89.

[32] Ibid, para 184, see also Eckes (n 18) 17 while underscoring that only then would the CJEU be forced to assess the legal effect of the ECHR's decisions. This being said, it has to be stressed that the ECHR influences the EU legal order even in the absence of the EU's accession as a source of general principles of EU law and interpretative aid to the Charter of Fundamental Rights [2012] OJ C 326/01, see section III.B below.

[33] Opinion 2/13 (n 5), para 186.

Nonetheless, Section III.B will demonstrate that this assessment of the CJEU was disputable. Regardless of its accuracy, however, at least on the dogmatic level, the CJEU made it clear that its findings were related to the legal situation generated by the EU's accession and not to the problems related to the ECHR being an agreement concluded between the Member States (and external parties) and not the EU.

ii. No Alternative Dispute Settlement within EU

Having come to the above conclusions, the Court began analysing the ECHR provision allowing the ECHR Parties to bring interstate claims before the ECtHR.[34] Rather unsurprisingly, the CJEU concluded that this provision violated its exclusive jurisdiction with regard to interstate claims between EU Member States relating to EU law. The EU's participation seemingly played a decisive role in declaring this mechanism incompatible with EU law. This is because the CJEU observed that with ECHR becoming part of EU law as an international agreement, the ECtHR would become exclusively responsible for adjudicating Convention disputes between the Member States and the EU, and between the Member States themselves.[35]

Without ECHR provisions safeguarding the CJEU's jurisdiction in this respect, the ECtHR could decide upon disputes regarding the application of EU law to the exclusion of the CJEU.[36] The CJEU made it clear that this danger could be averted only by the express exclusion of the ECtHR's jurisdiction.[37] Importantly, the CJEU's argument was also extended to disputes between the Member States.[38]

These general findings were followed by the critique of the mechanism envisaged in Protocol 16 of the ECHR, allowing for preliminary references of national courts to the ECtHR.[39] This critique was somewhat spurious given that the EU was not to be a party to Protocol 16 and that mechanism.[40] The issues around Protocol 16 should have consisted solely in allowing national courts to choose preliminary references in matters related to the ECHR as part of EU law to the ECtHR instead of the CJEU, which has been the case since the Protocol's inception.[41] At first glance, it could be somewhat surprising that the CJEU, while analysing the Accession Agreement's conformity with EU law, referred to an instrument to which the EU was not to become a party and, thus, would not have been bound by. Regardless of the correctness of this reasoning,[42] it is

[34] Convention for the Protection of Human Rights and Fundamental Freedoms, ETS No 005, Art 33 (*Any High Contracting Party may refer to the Court any alleged breach of the provisions of the Convention and the protocols thereto by another High Contracting Party.*).

[35] Opinion 2/13 (n 5), para 204.

[36] Ibid, para 205.

[37] Ibid, para 213.

[38] See eg ibid, paras 212–13.

[39] Protocol No 16 to the Convention for the Protection of Human Rights and Fundamental Freedoms, CETS No 214. For the legal analysis of the Protocol, see Ada Paprocka, Michał Ziółkowski (2015) 'Advisory Opinions Under Protocol No 16 to the European Convention on Human Rights' (2015) 11 *Eur Const Law Rev* 274.

[40] Opinion 2/13 (n 5), para 197.

[41] Opinion 2/13 (n 5), para 198.

[42] AG Kokott rightly observed that the risk of making preliminary references to the ECtHR instead of the CJEU existed independently from the EU's participation in the agreement, Opinion of AG Kokott (n 29) para 140. The same concerns the art 33 interstate claims, see Halberstam (n 1) 18, 38. This is particularly

quite clear that the CJEU linked problems of the conformity of the EU's participation in the ECHR with the TFEU provisions on the CJEU's jurisdiction.

At this point, it should be noted that the CJEU supported its arguments by invoking the principle of mutual trust in paras 168, 191 and 194 of its Opinion. However, this argument was connected mainly to instruments of EU law within the area of security, freedom and justice, foreseeing automatic recognition of foreign judgments (paras 191, 194), rather than with fundamental principles of EU law, as in the later *CETA* Opinion.

iii. Determining the Right Party

Another problem with the EU's accession to the ECHR was intrinsically connected to the issue of selecting the right respondent. The EU's accession to the ECHR would create a situation where the ECtHR could be faced with an individual application and forced to determine whether a claim should be directed against the EU or rather individual Member States. It was proposed that this problem should be solved by creating the possibility of the ECtHR deciding on allowing the EU or the Member States to join the proceedings.

It is rather obvious that, by its very nature, this challenge was specific to mixed participation of both the EU and the Member States in a given agreement and could not have arisen outside of this context.[43] The problems related to selecting the right respondent were related mainly to the well-known issue that 'wrong' attribution or apportionment of responsibility for decisions would *interfere with the division of powers between the EU and its Member States.*[44] Furthermore, the CJEU was of the opinion that any such operation would necessarily require the external court to 'apply' or 'interpret' EU law – be it only in the form of *making an assessment of the rules of EU law.*[45] Again, even if criticisms of the CJEU for ignoring the existence of delimitation clauses applied in different international agreements while assessing the issue of selecting the proper respondent[46] was justified, it would not change the conclusion that this subset of problems was intrinsically linked to the modalities of the EU's participation in the mechanism.

iv. Prior Involvement

Similarly, the CJEU's critique of the prior involvement mechanism[47] is necessarily linked to the issue of the EU's participation. This issue would not arise if the EU were not involved.[48] The problem lies simply in the fact that the Accession Agreement did

evident in comparison with the relative leniency vis-à-vis other dispute settlement mechanisms such as UNCLOS or WTO, see Odermatt (n 1) 300. In any case, this problem could have been solved by unilateral declarations, see Opinion 2/13 of AG Kokott (n 29) para 120; Opinion 2/13 (n 5) para 213; Halberstam (n 1) 14–15.

[43] As AG Kokott observed, only in such a constellation the delimitation of competences would have been binding for the EU, see Opinion of AG Kokott (n 29) para 128.

[44] Opinion 2/13 (n 5) paras 225 and 231, see the autonomy-related case law discussed in chapter 2.

[45] Ibid, paras 224, 230; see also van Rossen (n 1) 45–46.

[46] As explained in the Opinion of AG Kokott (n 29), paras 48–50, the issue was not covered by the CJEU.

[47] Opinion 2/13 (n 5) paras 236–48.

[48] Opinion of AG Kokott (n 29) para 127.

foresee a situation in which the ECtHR would analyse a provision of EU law without the CJEU providing a definite interpretation thereof.[49] In fact, the CJEU's monopoly would be infringed already in case of ECtHR deciding whether there is a sufficiently definitive interpretation of EU law conducted by the CJEU and choosing by itself from possible interpretations of EU law.[50]

In any case, it must be highlighted that the CJEU concerned itself exclusively with the analysis of the relevant Accession Agreement provisions and did not consider whether the ECtHR's handling of the subsidiarity principle would not provide sufficient safeguards against bypassing the CJEU.[51] Nonetheless, the requirement of providing for an effective prior involvement procedure should be viewed as a necessary expression of the CJEU's more general competence to decide on the division of competences between the EU and its Member States,[52] again inextricably linked to the EU's participation in international agreements.

v. Common Foreign and Security Policy (CFSP)

Last but not least, the CJEU made it clear that the EU may not accept the jurisdiction of an external court over its own actions with regard to which the CJEU has no jurisdiction,[53] even if these actions would have been measured solely against the benchmark of the ECHR and not EU law.[54] Despite this issue not being directly linked to the problem of the form of the EU's participation but rather the exact content of the Treaties (ie TEU and TFEU), it is evident that this issue could only have been raised in connection with the EU's participation in the agreement.

B. Strengthening the Argument: Even without the EU, the ECHR is Problematic

The above analysis, however, cannot obfuscate the question as to whether all the problems covered by the CJEU were not limited to the situation of the EU's accession. In particular, the problem of bypassing the EU's legal framework for settling disputes seems to exist independently of the EU's participation. Indeed, there are compelling arguments that the ECtHR is already meddling with the autonomy of EU law even in the absence of the latter's accession, as shall be explained below. Paradoxically, however, this conclusion only corroborates the thesis in the CJEU's decision that the EU's participation in

[49] Opinion 2/13 (n 5) paras 238–39, 246.

[50] Cristina Contartese, *The Procedures of Prior Involvement and Referral to the CJEU as Means for Judicial Dialogue Between the CJEU and International Jurisdictions*, Geneva Jean Monnet Working Papers 27/2016, 14–15.

[51] This problem was observed by the AG Kokott, who indicated that in the case of the EU acting as the respondent, the problem would have been solved by the subsidiarity principle, Opinion of AG Kokott (n 29) para 128.

[52] Müller (n 19) 224.

[53] Opinion 2/13 (n 5) paras 252, 255–56. Critically of the veracity of this Opinion, Rosas (n 25) 12.

[54] Opinion 2/13 (n 5) para 255.

international agreements and its form should be viewed as a decisive factor in assessing their conformity with EU law.

Indeed, even upon cursory examination, it becomes evident that the problems highlighted by the CJEU remain relevant even in the absence of the EU's accession. To begin with, the ECHR is an international agreement binding on all EU Member States and enjoying a quasi-constitutional status, in certain respects similar to EU law.[55] It is by no means a coincidence that many commentators while awaiting the accession, treated it as *enhancing* rather than *revolutionising* the system of human rights protection in the EU, particularly given the abandonment of the *Bosphorus* doctrine and foreseeing deferential treatment of EU Member States actions implementing EU law by the ECtHR.[56] It is not surprising as the ECtHR had been competent to conduct *indirect* control of EU law by means of reviewing Member States' actions aimed at the implementation of EU law for many years. In any case, the ECtHR reviewed the implementation of EU law by the Member States on many occasions.[57] Additionally, it has to be stressed that, from the point of view of EU law, even if it became a mixed agreement in the aftermath of the EU's accession,[58] the Convention would still enjoy a rank in the hierarchy of legal norms below the primary law. This would most likely not elevate the Convention's rank beyond its special status as a source of principles of EU law already enjoyed on the basis of Article 6.3 TFEU and its role in interpreting interpreting the provision of the Charter of Fundamental Rights (Art 52.3, Art 53).[59]

Furthermore, it is very clear that, as it currently stands, the Member States are perfectly capable of initiating Article 33 ECHR proceedings against each other in all matters of the Convention, including matters covered by EU law. Besides, even in the absence of the EU's accession, the ECtHR would be *seized* with such a dispute, regardless of its relationship vis-à-vis EU law.[60]

Similarly, the ECtHR assesses the division of competences between the EU and its Member States on a regular basis while determining the responsibility of a Member State. This determination, though not binding for the EU, is binding as a matter of international law for its Member States. Furthermore, it seems that it was precisely the ECtHR jurisprudence related to their responsibility or conduct in the exercise of EU law that seemingly influenced the International Law Commission (ILC) decisively while

[55] Giuseppe Martinico, 'Is the European Convention Going to Be "Supreme"? A Comparative-Constitutional Overview of ECHR and EU Law before National Courts' (2012) 23 *EJIL* 401; Alec Stone Sweet, 'A Cosmopolitan Legal Order: Constitutional Pluralism and Rights Adjudication in Europe', (2012) 1 *Global Constitutionalism* 53–90, in particular 65–72 and App I.

[56] Halberstam (n 1) 31 ff Robert Uerpmann-Wittzack, 'Rechtsfragen und Rechtsfolgen des Beitritts der Europäischen Union zur EMRK' in W Obexer (ed) *Die Europäische Union im Völkerrecht* (Europarecht, Beiheft 2/2012)181; Tacik (n 20) 593 f.

[57] For a detailed analysis of ECtHR case law related to the enforcement of EU law, see Daniel Engel, *Der Beitritt der Europäischen Union zur EMRK*, (Mohr Siebeck, 2015), 42–67.

[58] Uerpmann-Wittzack (n 56) 183.

[59] Krystyna Kowalik-Bańczyk, 'Stosowanie Europejskiej Konwencji Praw Człowieka Jako Umowy UE' (2014) 1 *Europejski Przegląd Sądowy* 44.

[60] As the CJEU did not refer to the actual practice of the Convention, the fact that no such interstate proceedings were conducted as between the EU Member States was irrelevant, see list of Art 33 ECHR cases as of 20 October 2020 prepared by the CoE secretariat, www.echr.coe.int/Documents/InterState_applications_ENG.pdf.

drafting the rules on the responsibility of international organisations.[61] Consequently, it could even be argued that the ECHR jurisprudence on the division of competences – to the extent it became part of customary international law – might become *indirectly* binding on the EU as part of customary international law.[62] Needless to say, in the absence of EU membership, there has been no prior involvement procedure, and the EU could have influenced ECtHR decisions related to EU law through the medium of *amici curiae* at best.

Also, the possibility of referring cases pertaining to EU law to Strasbourg instead of Luxembourg on the basis of Protocol 16 is not hampered by the lack of the EU's accession to the Convention. In particular, there already exists the risk of certain Member State courts asking the Strasbourg Court to conduct an assessment of EU law from the viewpoint of the Convention, in lieu of making an Article 267 TFEU preliminary reference.

Last but not least, it has to be stressed that the ECHR has a particular potential to disrupt the uniform application of EU law due to 'cross-cutting through virtually all … areas of competence and policy', just like international investment treaties.[63] This is even more so given that the ECtHR's jurisprudence has not only diverged from that of the CJEU on many occasions but has even at times contradicted it. In fact, in some instances, the ECtHR's judgments prompted the CJEU to abandon its earlier jurisprudence. To give the most prominent examples, it was precisely due to the influence of the ECtHR that the CJEU changed its jurisprudence regarding issues such as the defendant's right to abstain from submitting self-incriminating materials in cartel proceedings.[64] More importantly, even without the EU being a party to the Convention, the ECtHR jurisprudence arguably led to a far-reaching transformation of the principle of mutual trust, which had been stringently defended by the CJEU, particularly in respect of asylum-seeking[65] and the European Arrest Warrant,[66] regulations. Even if certain limits were set to this transformative effect,[67] it could not be denied that the ECtHR had a

[61] Pieter Jan Kujiper and Eva Paasivirta, 'EU International Responsibility and Its Attribution: From the Inside Looking Out' in Malcolm Evans and Panos Koutrakos (eds), *The International Responsibility of the European Union. European and International Perspectives* (Hart, 2013) 66–67. See also chapter by Andrés Delgado Casteleiro and Cristina Contartese in this volume.

[62] For the EU's international status being largely determined by customary international law, see Carolin Damm, *Die Europäische Union im Universellen Völkergewohnheitsrecht* (Mohr Siebeck, 2016) 57, 68; Delano Verwey, *The European Community, the European Union and the International Law* (Asser Press, 2004) 157.

[63] Maciej Szpunar, *Is the Court of Justice Afraid of International Jurisdictions?* (2017) XXXVII *PYIL*, 141.

[64] Case 94/02, *Roquette Frères SA*, EU:C:2002:603 adopting the ECHR viewpoint on the issue; see also Półtorak (n 22) 4, 7.

[65] Case C-411/10, *NS*, EU:C:2011:865, see also Koen Lenaerts, 'La Vie Après L'Avis: Exploring the Principle of Mutual (Yet not Blind) Trust' (2017) 54 *CMLR*, 834.

[66] Case C-404/15, *Aranyosi and Căldăraru*, EU:C:2016:198, which starkly contrasts with AG Bot's opinion, recommending upholding earlier jurisprudence, AG Bot Opinion in Case C-404/15, *Aranyosi and Căldăraru*, EU:C:2016:140 see also Tomasz Ostropolski, 'Naruszenie Praw Podstawowych Jako Przesłanka Odmowy Wykonania ENA – Uwagi do Wyroku Trybunału Sprawiedliwości z 5.04.2016 r w Sprawach Połączonych C-404/15 Aranyosi i C-659/15 PPU Căldăraru' (2016) 11 *Europejski Przegląd Sądowy* 20. Whereby it could be argued that this judgment addressed mainly concerns voiced by the German Federal Constitutional Court, the CJEU supported its reasoning leading to a transformation of its earlier jurisprudence by numerous references to the case law of ECtHR rather than the German Court.

[67] Halberstam (n 1) 24 ff.

great deal of impact on the EU legal system and, particularly, the scope of the principle of mutual trust.

Consequently, given that the CJEU in its Opinion 2/13 or other jurisprudence did not consider the above matters, it may be safely assumed that it considered them problematic solely in the context of the EU's participation in the agreement. Thus, it may be inferred that only the EU's participation led the CJEU to identify incompatibilities with EU law.

IV. Turning the Tables: ISDS's Salvation Through EU's Participation

The above understanding of the close interrelation between the EU's participation was challenged by the CJEU's decisions concerning ISDS mechanisms in investment treaties. Firstly, in its *Achmea* judgment, the CJEU declared ISDS clauses in BITs concluded between EU Member States incompatible with EU law due to the violation of the principle of autonomy of EU law, even without the EU's participation. Later, in its *CETA* Opinion, the CJEU accepted similar ISDS mechanisms in FTAs concluded as mixed agreements between the EU and its Member States on the one hand and third states on the other. More importantly, it most likely did so because the EU's participation catalysed the introduction of certain mechanisms aimed at safeguarding the autonomy of EU law. Consequently, it turned out that not only does the EU's participation in an international agreement itself not have to be treated as a challenge to its conformity with EU law, but it may even serve as the saving factor. Consequently, together these CJEU decisions may be viewed as a kind of gamechanger.

A. CJEU *Achmea* Judgment: Violation without EU's Participation

Being foreseeable as to the substance,[68] the *Achmea* judgment, or rather the formulation of its justification could have been viewed as a forerunner of change in the CJEU's argumentation related to international dispute settlement mechanisms. After all, while not being the first CJEU judgment to assert the primacy of EU law over Member States' *inter se* agreements,[69] it was the first one to find a 'violation of the principle of autonomy' by a dispute settlement mechanism contained in an agreement concluded exclusively between two Member States.[70]

[68] Stephen Schill, 'Opinion 2/13 – The End for Dispute Settlement?' (2015) 16 *The Journal of World Investment & Trade*, 382; Cristina Contartese and Mads Andenas, 'EU Autonomy and Investor-State Dispute Settlement Under *inter se* Agreements Between EU Member States: *Achmea*' (2019) 56 *CMLR*, 159, 190.

[69] See eg Case 10/61, *Commission of the European Economic Community v Italian Republic*, EU:C:1962:2, 10.

[70] Interestingly, in its judgment of 5 May 2015, in Case C-146/13, *Spain v European Parliament and Commission*, EU:C:2015:298, the CJEU declared lack of jurisdiction to hear Spain's Art 263 TFEU annulment action targeting an international agreement between the Member States aimed at creating the United Patent Court by indicating that, *in an action brought under Article 263 TFEU, the Court does not have jurisdiction to rule on the lawfulness of an international agreement concluded by Member States* (para 101).

AG Wathelet's opinion,[71] containing a lengthy argument on the irrelevance of *inter se* Member State agreements with dispute settlement clauses in respect of EU law, is illustrative of the formalistic way of thinking. In part D of the opinion, much ink was spilt to explain why, even if not considered the Member States' Courts, investment arbitration tribunals would not infringe the autonomy of EU law in any way whatsoever. Firstly, it was observed that disputes between the Member States and individuals did not come within the remit of Article 344 TFEU.[72] More importantly, in the latter part of his opinion, he underscored that in the case of both the *Mox Plant* judgment and the *ECHR* Opinion, the CJEU was concerned with the accidental application of EU law by ITLOS and the ECtHR solely because of the EU being party to these agreements,[73] which would render the principles contained therein inapplicable to intra-EU BITs to which EU is not the party.[74] Lastly, AG Wathelet denied arbitral tribunals of interpreting EU law by underlining that EU law was not applied in the arbitration proceedings.[75] Despite admitting certain investment protection rules partially overlap with the TFEU, though without contradicting the Treaties,[76] he underscored that they were different enough to allow differentiation between the application of the TFEU and BITs.[77] Lastly, he explained that investment arbitration should be accepted from the point of view of the autonomy principle in a way analogous to commercial arbitration.[78] Consequently, it appears that AG Wathelet's opinion relied heavily on the strict distinction between agreements concluded with or without the EU's participation and the latter being of relevance to the autonomy of EU law.

There is one problem, however. The CJEU not only ignored AG Wathelet's opinion but also came to precisely the opposite conclusions.[79] After making it clear that arbitral tribunals are not part of the Member States' judicial system, the CJEU moved to the issue of ISDS' conformity with the autonomy of EU law. It focused, among others, on the possible application of EU law by the arbitral tribunals, coming to the conclusion that EU law could have been at least *taken into account* during the application of the BIT, either as part of international law or domestic law.[80] The CJEU continued by denying the ISDS tribunals the quality of Member States' Courts,[81] as well as pointing out the limitations of judicial control over arbitral awards.[82] The above findings were made in the context of the role ascribed to the principle of mutual trust. Interestingly, in contrast to Opinion 2/13, the principle was widely defined so as to encompass the basic

[71] Opinion of AG Wathelet of 19 September 2017 in Case C-284/16, *Achmea*, EU:C:2017:699.
[72] Ibid, paras 138–59, particularly para 150 differentiating the case at hand from opinions 1/91 and 1/09.
[73] Ibid, paras 163–64.
[74] Ibid, para 167.
[75] Ibid, paras 173–78.
[76] Ibid, para 210 ff.
[77] Ibid, para 228.
[78] Ibid, paras 229–72.
[79] Bartosz Soloch, 'CJEU Judgment in Case C-284/16 Achmea: Single Decision and Its Multi-Faceted Fallout', (2019) 18 *The Law & Practice of International Courts and Tribunals* 3, 10 with further references. AG Wathelet's opinion was also criticised in legal scholarship for its highly selective approach to the earlier CJEU's jurisprudence, see eg Contartese, Andenas (n 68) 157–92.
[80] C-284/16, *Achmea* (n 8) paras 39–42.
[81] Ibid, paras 43–49.
[82] Ibid, paras 50–55.

principles of EU law as binding between the Member States and EU,[83] rather than be limited to the context of mutual recognition of judgments. Lastly, while summarising its findings, the CJEU emphasised that the institutional arrangements regarding intra-EU BITs caused the ISDS mechanism to circumvent EU law and, thus, violated the principle of autonomy of EU law.[84]

Consequently, regardless of the details of the CJEU's reasoning and their assessment,[85] it is blatantly clear that, on the one hand, the EU's non-participation in the ISDS mechanism played no role in the CJEU's evaluation of its conformity with the principle of autonomy of EU law and, on the other, its outcome was dependent on the features of a particular mechanism, not the EU's participation and its form. This stood in striking contrast to the approach taken in Opinion 2/13, where, arguably, problems very similar to those covered in the *CETA* Opinion, such as interpretation of EU law by an external body, were linked directly to the EU's participation.

B. *CETA*: Salvation Through the EU's Participation

This detachment of the issue of dispute settlement mechanisms' conformity with EU law from the EU's participation became even more evident in light of the later *CETA* Opinion. Seen together with the *Achmea* decision, the *CETA* Opinion shows some remarkable features: it is the first time an international dispute settlement mechanism has been brought into conformity with EU law largely through the EU's participation in the form of a mixed agreement.[86]

This is particularly visible in the CJEU's declaration that, at least as a matter of principle, its jurisdiction does not take precedence before the jurisdiction of other international courts.[87] This relative benevolence by the CJEU could have been caused by the fact that, contrary to Member States' BITs, CETA should be viewed as a part of the foreign commercial policy of the EU and its Member States rather than as an instrument potentially threatening the balance of the Internal Market.[88] Further, CETA was the poster child of the Commission's 'ISDS reform' endeavours in international fora, particularly the UNCITRAL Working Group III.[89] Thus, the CJEU's decision regarding CETA

[83] Ibid, paras 33–34.

[84] Ibid, para 56.

[85] Arguably, while defining the autonomy principle, the CJEU was consistent with its earlier case law, see Steffen Hindelang, 'Conceptualisation and Application of the Principle of Autonomy of EU Law – The CJEU's Judgment in Achmea Put in Perspective' (2018), https://papers.ssrn.com/sol3/papers.cfm?abstract_id=3266123; Soloch (n 79) 3, 11.

[86] Nikos Lavranos, 'CJEU "Opinion 1/17": Keeping International Investment Law and EU Law Strictly Apart' (2019) 4 *European Investment Law and Arbitration Review* 240, 257.

[87] Opinion 1/17 (n 9), para 116. Notably, this declaration was accompanied by a visible change of tone on the part of the CJEU, see Panos Koutrakos, *The Anatomy of Autonomy: Themes and Perspectives on an Elusive Principle*, Building Bridges: Central Banking Law in an Interconnected World, ECB Legal Conference 2019, (European Central Bank, 2019) 96.

[88] This finds support in the EU's treatment of CETA as a model new generation agreement, see Joint statement Canada-EU Comprehensive Economic and Trade Agreement (CETA) of 29 February 2016. http://trade.ec.europa.eu/doclib/docs/2016/february/tradoc_154330.pdf, calling CETA *Gold Standard Agreement*; Luca Pantaleo, *The Participation of the EU in International Dispute Settlement. Lessons from EU Investment Agreements* (Springer the Hague, 2019) 96, 148.

[89] See submission of 12 December 2017 A/CN.9/WG.III/WP.145.

could be seen as decisive for the limits of EU capabilities to undertake external action.[90] This being said, however, one cannot forget that, even if serving the EU's external policy goals, a dispute settlement mechanism in CETA would still have to conform to EU law.

The analysis of the *CETA* Opinion will be focused on the CJEU's analysis of the dispute settlement mechanism's itself, rather than the parts referring to the agreement's conformity with the Charter of Fundamental Rights or the principle of non-discrimination.[91] It follows that the CJEU's analysis in this regard revolved around the issue of influencing the EU legal order by external adjudicating bodies, which is one of the traditional autonomy-related topics. The EU Court began by setting in unequivocal terms that a lack of powers to interpret EU law and having no impact on the internal powers of EU institutions is a precondition to submitting the EU to any international dispute settlement mechanism whatsoever.[92] Building upon these statements, the CJEU observed that Article 8.31.1 CETA limited the law to be applied by the CETA Tribunal to CETA and international law applicable between the parties (ie EU with its Member States on the one hand and Canada on the other). Article 8.31.2 expressly excludes the determination of the legality of measures taken by each of the parties under their domestic law, thus confining the CETA Tribunal's jurisdiction solely to the CETA Agreement.[93] In fact, it was Article 8.31.2, excluding the *de jure* interpretation of EU law, that was indicated as the main point that distinguished *CETA* from *Achmea.*[94] Nonetheless, ignoring the problem of de facto interpretation of EU law required adopting a formalistic perspective,[95] substantively narrower than in the earlier *Achmea* and *ECHR* decisions.

This exclusion of jurisdiction over EU law matters served as the CJEU's main argument to differentiate between the case at hand and Opinion 1/09[96] and, more importantly the *Achmea* judgment. In doing so, the CJEU seemingly relied on two arguments: firstly, it merely stated that, unlike the CETA Tribunal, BIT Tribunals could have given rulings in disputes that might have concerned the interpretation or application of EU law.[97] This rather cursory statement should be understood in the context of the

[90] See eg Magdalena Słok-Wódkowska, 'Opinia TSUE w Sprawie CETA – Status UE Jako Podmiotu Prawa Międzynarodowego Uratowany' [Eng 'CJEU *CETA* Opinion – EU's Status of Subject of International Law savoured'] (*Przegląd Prawa Międzynarodowego*, 30 April 2019), http://przegladpm.blogspot.com/2019/04/opinia-tsue-w-sprawie-ceta-status-ue.html.

[91] Similarly, Maria Fanou, 'The CETA ICS and the Autonomy of the EU Legal Order in Opinion 1/17 – A Compass for the Future' (2020) *CYELS* 14.

[92] Opinion 1/17 (n 9) para 118.

[93] Ibid, paras 121–22.

[94] François Biltgen, *The Concept of Autonomy of EU Law: From Opinion 2/13 Accession to the ECHR) to Achmea and Opinion 1/17*, Building Bridges: Central Banking Law in an Interconnected World, ECB Legal Conference 2019 (European Central Bank 2019) 87; see also Koutrakos, (n 87) 97, with the latter author recognising that the CJEU made a 'leap of faith' while taking the position that CETA Tribunal will not interpret EU law. See also Lavranos (n 86) 240, 243.

[95] Cristina Contartese, Achmea and Opinion 1/17: Why do intra and extra-EU bilateral investment treaties impact differently on the EU legal order?, in *The New Challenges Raised by Investment Arbitration for the EU Legal Order*, ECB Legal Working Paper Series 19/2019, 12. In contrast, Pantaleo (n 88) 152, who, while observing despite admitting the existence of potentially serious consequences of the de facto interpretation, eventually concludes that such a view would have excluded the EU's participation in any dispute settlement mechanism.

[96] Opinion 1/17 (n 9) paras 123–24.

[97] Ibid, para 126.

further parts of this section of the opinion where the CJEU emphasised the lack of the binding character of CETA Tribunals' interpretation vis-à-vis the parties[98] and the fact that the domestic law of the parties (including EU law) interpreted in accordance with the prevailing interpretation of the domestic organs would be taken into account solely as a matter of fact.[99] This would also apply to the CETA Appellate Tribunal, whereby the CJEU stated *expressis verbis* that examining manifest errors in appreciation of domestic law would not count as an *interpretation* of EU law.[100] Secondly, the CJEU indicated that the *Achmea* judgment was based upon the principle of mutual trust, applicable within the EU but not in the external relations (where it is replaced by the principle of reciprocity).[101] This, in turn, should be read in a broader context of the Court emphasising the 'reciprocal character' of the agreement,[102] with these features justifying the lack of mechanisms for interaction between the CJEU and CETA Tribunal.[103]

Despite this seemingly dogmatic attitude vis-à-vis CETA, the CJEU also addressed the issue of possibilities of influencing EU internal affairs by awards challenging EU policies through excessive compensations.[104] Fortunately for CETA, the CJEU stated that the agreement's material provisions safeguarding the parties' competence to follow regulatory measures pursuing public interest[105] or underlining their right to regulate[106] resulted in the tribunals not having jurisdiction to adjudicate upon these matters.[107] This removed the danger of imposing undue limitations on the EU's regulatory freedom. Consequently, it is clearly visible that the CJEU shifted its attention from the modalities of participation as in the *ECHR* Opinion towards an agreement's actual impact on the EU legal system.

Lastly, rather surprisingly, matters specific to EU participation, that is, the distribution of competences between the EU and the Member States were addressed very briefly. The CJEU observed that, contrary to Opinion 2/13, the CETA Tribunal would not be competent to decide on the proper respondent, which sufficed to insulate the EU legal order from unwanted external influence in this regard.[108]

C. Mistakes in the CJEU's Assessment?

Upon closer scrutiny, many assessments made by the CJEU in the *CETA* Opinion, when compared to the *Achmea* judgment, seem disputable. Indeed, even advocates of the

[98] Ibid, para 130.
[99] Ibid, para 131. Some commentators went so far as to declare that the obligation to follow the prevailing interpretation effectively eliminated the need to interpret EU law, see Biltgen (n 94) 87.
[100] Opinion 1/17 (n 9) para 133.
[101] Ibid, paras 127–28. Interestingly the Court expanded the principle so as to encompass certain basic features of the EU judicial system, such as the right to an effective remedy.
[102] Ibid, paras 109, 117.
[103] Koutrakos, (n 87) 96.
[104] Opinion 1/17 (n 9) paras 148–50.
[105] Ibid, paras 152–53.
[106] Ibid, paras 154–55.
[107] Ibid, paras 159–60.
[108] Ibid, para 132. On the lack of the tribunals powers to determine respondents, see Pantaleo (n 88) 108–09.

reconciliation of EU law with international investment arbitration highlight that this change of heart required 'considerable legal gymnastics'.[109]

To begin with, the distinction between the matters of law and matters of fact playing such a prominent role in the *CETA* Opinion does not seem to be too convincing. As rightly observed by Lang, it played little if any role in the CJEU's assessment in *Achmea* and was highly formalistic.[110] In any case, it cannot be excluded that the CETA Tribunal, while applying international law, would also apply principles common to both EU and international law, thus *applying* EU law according to these narrow, formalistic criteria.[111] The existence of provisions ordering the arbitral tribunals to follow the prevalent interpretation of EU law cannot obscure the fact that they would be empowered to choose by themselves the interpretation of EU law as they see fit, and would not make up for the lack of the CETA Tribunal's preliminary reference powers.[112] This problem would be even more visible in the context of the CETA Appeals Tribunal, which could assess the correctness of the interpretation of EU law conducted by the arbitral tribunals (although as a matter of *fact*),[113] while not being bound by the obligation to follow the prevailing interpretation.[114] In any case, the CJEU's analysis did not address seriously the issue of the CETA dispute settlement mechanism allowing the removal of certain disputes from the jurisdiction of EU courts.[115]

Further, while stating that the substantive provisions safeguarded the legislator's freedom, the CJEU overlooked the fact that not only is it disputable whether these provisions really introduced revolutionary standards or rather codified the existing investment jurisprudence,[116] but equally the Tribunal would necessarily have to balance the public interest against the investor's rights.[117] Trying to present the CETA Tribunal's rulings as non-binding seems to be equally misguided. After all, by virtue of being New York Convention awards (Art 8.41(5) CETA[118]), the payment orders will also bind EU institutions and be enforceable against them before municipal courts

[109] Lavranos (n 86) 240, 241.

[110] Andrej Lang, 'Die Autonomie des Unionsrechts und die Zukunft der Investor-Staat-Streitbeilegung in Europa nach "Achmea". Zugleich ein Beitrag zur Dogmatik des Art 351 AEUV', Beiträge zum Transnationalen Wirtschaftsrecht, (2018) 156, 17–18, 43; Joanna Lam and Paweł Marcisz, 'Dopuszczalność arbitrażu inwestycyjnego: między Achmeą a Cetą – glosa do orzeczenia Międzynarodowego Centrum Rozstrzygania Sporów Inwestycyjnych ARB/12/12, Vattenfall (w kwestii Achmei), (2019) 11 *Europejski Przegląd Sądowy* 38. see also Odermatt (n 1) 302 who rightly indicates that bypassing the autonomy problem by qualifying EU law as a simple fact was excluded already in the Opinion 2/13. But see Fanou (n 91) 18.

[111] Lavranos (n 86) 245.

[112] Leszek Bosek, Grzegorz Żmij, 'W sprawie zgodności CETA z prawem Unii Europejskiej i Konstytucją RP w świetle opinii 1/17 Trybunału Sprawiedliwości z 30.04.2019 r', (2020) 7 *Europejski Przegląd Sądowy* 4, 11–12. It has to be stressed that this competence to choose from among possible interpretations of EU law was deemed to encroach upon EU law's autonomy in its *ECHR* Opinion, see Opinion 2/13 (n 5) paras 224, 230.

[113] Ankersmit, (n 18) 23, Lavranos (n 86) 240, 241.

[114] Lavranos (n 86) 240, 247.

[115] Opinion 2/15, *EUSFTA*, para 292; see also Similarly Fanou (n 91) 20–21; Contartese, Andenas (n 68) 187.

[116] Christian Tietje and Kevin Crow, *The Reform of Investment Protection Rules in CETA, TTIP, and Other Recent EU FTAs: Convincing?* in Stefan Griller, Walter Obwexer and Erich Vranes (eds), *Mega-Regional Trade Agreements: CETA, TTIP, and TiSA: New Orientations for EU External Economic Relations* (OUP, 2017) 96–97.

[117] Lavranos (n 86) 240, 250–51.

[118] At this point, it may be noted that it cannot be excluded that certain external courts would not necessarily treat these awards as arbitral awards within the meaning of the New York Convention, see Pantaleo (n 88) 134.

in various jurisdictions.[119] Consequently, apparent analogies to the WTO system coming under the umbrella of 'reciprocity' seem to overlook fundamental features of the ISDS mechanism, its accessibility to individuals and binding character of judicial decisions.[120] Lastly, even if the CJEU's view that the CETA Tribunals could not interpret EU law and de facto influence EU legal order were accepted, one would still be left with a forum parallel to the EU judicial system and, thus, allow bypassing of the judicial structure foreseen in the treaties, as has been strongly defended by the CJEU.[121]

D. Assessment: EU's Internal Affairs over Participation

The abovementioned problems with the *CETA* Opinion, regardless of whether they are substantiated, do not alter the conclusion that, at least as a matter of law, the CJEU shifted its attention from analysing the form of the EU's participation in a given agreement to its actual impact on the EU legal system. This is illustrated particularly by the juxtaposition between the presence[122] of *mutual trust* between the Member States and the EU on the one hand and *reciprocity* in the relationships with the outside world on the other.[123] Given the context of both the *Achmea* and *CETA* decisions, it is clear that this division may not be conflated with the form of EU participation in the agreements (and, consequently, the distribution of competences between the EU and its Member States). In particular, in the *Achmea* case, the CJEU decisively rejected AG Wathelet's proposal relying heavily on the reading of Opinion 2/13 emphasising the primary importance of the EU's participation in international agreements in order to conclude that dispute settlement mechanisms in international agreements between the Member States were neutral vis-à-vis EU law.

V. Conclusions

In light of the CJEU's recent ISDS jurisprudence, it is clear that the conformity with EU law of international dispute settlement mechanisms does not depend on the EU's

[119] Ankersmit (n 18) 23. At this point, it could be questioned as to how far this may be reconciled with the CJEU's long-standing jurisprudence according to which the decisions of adjudicating bodies are applicable within the EU only insofar as their agreements, see Pantaleo (n 88) 136.

[120] Hindelang (n 85) 12; see also Eckes (n 18) 23, explaining why the ECHR demand different treatment than the WTO, but see Contartese, Andenas (n 68) 185. Interestingly, despite its reliance on the *reciprocity* concept, utilised earlier in the WTO jurisprudence, the CJEU made it clear that it is mindful of the differences between the enforcement of WTO and CETA awards, see Opinion 1/17 (n 9) para 146.

[121] Contartese, Achmea and Opinion 1/17 (n 95) 18; Ankersmit (n 18) 17; Hindelang (n 85) 15–16.

[122] Lavranos (n 86) 240, 245.

[123] Contartese, Achmea and Opinion 1/17 (n 95) 9. On the exclusion of the principle of *reciprocity* within the EU, Case 90/63, *Commission v Luxembourg*, EU:C:1964:80, Müller (n 19) 39; in similar vein Barents (n 1) 261. For the fundamental importance of the reciprocity principle for the CJEU's jurisprudence related to WTO, see Case C-149/96, *Portugal v Council*, EU:C:1999:574, paras 36, 42–47. Interestingly, it was only with the entry into force of the WTO agreement, marking the judicialisation of the GATT system, that the court shifted its argument for the inapplicability of WTO law within the EU from the alleged legal nature of the organisation to the need for reciprocity protection, see Matthias Kottmann, *Introvertierte Rechtsgemeinschaft* (Springer, 2014) 251.

participation therein or its form. Contrary to Opinion 2/13, while analysing the conformity of both intra-EU BITs and CETA's dispute settlement provisions with EU law, hardly any attention was paid to the issue of the modalities of EU participation. What counted was solely the mechanisms' possible impact on the functioning of the EU legal system. In fact, in certain situations, the EU's participation along with the Member States could help introduce institutional solutions safeguarding the mechanism's conformity with EU law by limiting the agreement's legal effects within the EU.

Arguably, this principle is caught by the *mutual trust/reciprocity* dichotomy, with the former concept representing the fundamental principles of the EU legal order and the way of arranging relations between the Member States and EU. While in Opinion 2/13, mutual trust was apparently invoked mainly in the context of the recognition of judgments, in a way parallel to the main argumentation regarding the EU's participation, in the *Achmea* judgment and *CETA* Opinion, its scope was substantially broadened. Furthermore, in the *ECHR* Opinion, the concept was not used to draw a line between the legal assessment of the intra- and extra-EU effects of dispute settlement mechanisms, which only happened in the *CETA* Opinion. Consequently, as a matter of principle, mechanisms designed to solve disputes within the sphere of *reciprocity* would not encroach upon the autonomy principle, whereby the mechanisms capable of meddling with *mutual trust* would most likely contradict EU law. This dichotomy seems to neatly reflect the CJEU's view on the autonomy of EU law vis-à-vis international law.

Interesting as it may seem, shifting the emphasis from the form of EU participation to the mechanism's actual impact on the EU legal system in the ISDS-related case law may have serious downsides. By its very nature, the assessment of the agreement's impact on the EU legal system involves a substantial degree of discretion and does not provide satisfactory levels of predictability to the stakeholders. The *CETA* Opinion may serve here as a very good example: as discussed above, the CJEU's conclusions as to CETA's conformity with EU law were by no means the only possible conclusions. Further, it is clear that rigorous observance of the substantive criteria set in ISDS jurisprudence could undermine the legality of practically any agreement containing a dispute settlement mechanism.

Most obviously, these developments seem to create further hurdles for the contemplated EU accession to the ECHR. If the substantive test were to be applied, a new Accession Agreement would necessarily have to not only address the issues indicated in Opinion 2/13 but, additionally, contain provisions minimising the impact of the Convention and ECtHR's jurisdiction on the EU legal system. The problem, however, goes deeper. If the conformity of the ECHR with EU law was to be measured by the same token as in the case of BITs or FTAs, one could even ask whether the EU Member States' participation in the Convention does not encroach upon the autonomy of EU law.

In any case, the ECHR would not be the only possible candidate. In fact, any earlier agreement containing a dispute settlement clause could be subject to similar treatment, such as the European Convention for the Peaceful Settlement of Disputes,[124] where the parties agreed to submit to the International Court of Justice (ICJ) all international legal

[124] European Convention for the Peaceful Settlement of Disputes opened to signature on 24 April 1957, ETS no 023.

disputes which may arise between them. The ICJ could become seized with disputes coming within the exclusive jurisdiction of the CJEU, as evidenced by Belgium bringing a case against Switzerland concerning the interpretation of the Lugano Convention concluded as a mixed agreement between the EU and its Member States, among others, Switzerland.[125]

Of course, the possibility of the CJEU eliminating all international agreements containing dispute settlement provisions does not seem to be very likely to materialise in the near future. Nonetheless, the above examples show that further guidance from the CJEU is needed in order to delineate the contours of the somewhat nebulous concept of the autonomy of EU law.

[125] Eventually, however, Belgium abandoned its claim, and the proceedings were discontinued, see *Jurisdiction and Enforcement of Judgments in Civil and Commercial Matters (Belgium v Switzerland)*, Order of 5 April 2011, ICJ Reports 2011, 5.

9

International Responsibility of the EU and/or its Member States in International Agreements

From Joint Participation to 'Participation'

ANDRÉS DELGADO CASTELEIRO AND CRISTINA CONTARTESE

I. Introduction

The EU and its Member States' participation in international agreements can be approached from two angles. A formal angle (participation *stricto sensu*) linked to the division of competences to conclude international agreements. The questions posed by participation *stricto sensu* are mostly related to mixed agreements and formal joint participation in international agreements. However, there is another angle from which to analyse the participation of the EU and its Member States in international agreements. From this angle (participation *lato sensu* or 'participation'), the EU and its Member States would jointly 'participate' in international agreements, even when they are not formally parties to the agreements. The EU Member States would 'participate' in EU-only international agreements when acting as the Council; for example, they establish the positions to be adopted on the Union's behalf in a body set up by that agreement. A Member State organ 'participates' in an EU-only international agreement when implementing an EU provision adopted to comply with the agreement. Likewise, an EU organ might 'participate' in an agreement that the EU Member States have concluded when it takes a decision that impacts the EU Member States' legal obligations stemming from the agreement. When speaking about a multilevel actor such as the EU, participation in an international agreement goes beyond formal participation.

The different ways in which the EU and its Member States can take part in the life cycle of an international agreement, both in terms of participation *stricto sensu* and 'participation', pose plenty of questions when it comes to their responsibility in the event of a breach of an international agreement. Is the EU responsible for breaches of an international agreement committed by a Member State organ when the latter is implementing EU law? Does the fact that competence to conclude an agreement does not necessarily entail the competence to implement it play a role in how responsibility should be attributed? Can the EU be responsible for a breach of an agreement to which only its Member States are parties to but the EU is exclusively competent under EU law? Does the fact that an agreement is mixed play a role in how we understand the apportionment of responsibility between the EU and its Member States? When it comes to the answer given in practice to these questions, formal participation plays a crucial role in establishing who is responsible. While this link between participation and responsibility is more than logical,[1] it is not exempt from problems, especially when it comes to the complex way in which the EU acts externally.

This contribution provides a taxonomy of the different problems that participation and 'participation' in an international agreement pose on the responsibility of the EU and/or its Member States in the event of a breach. More specifically, it focuses on the issues arising from a breach of an international agreement to which either the EU or both are parties.

The chapter is structured in four parts. First, we set out some general considerations on how to approach the issue of international responsibility of the EU. To understand the different interactions between EU participation and responsibility, we argue that it is necessary to focus on the EU's actual international practice (section II). Second, the chapter examines the classical question of responsibility under mixed agreements by recalling the main provisions and rules that have been codified or elaborated for such a purpose (section III). Third, we consider to what extent the division of competences within the EU plays a fundamental role in how participation in international agreements is structured and the practical problems it presents in EU-only agreements. This section shows how the theoretical problems that the division of competence presents *vis-à-vis* EU-only agreements have been dealt with satisfactorily at a practical level (section IV). The chapter finishes with some conclusions on how to better understand the link between participation, 'participation', and responsibility when it comes to the EU and its Member States' external relations (section V).

II. International Responsibility and the EU: Some General Considerations

A. A Factual Approach to the EU's Responsibility

There are two approaches in which the debates on the international responsibility of the EU can be articulated. The first approach focuses on whether the EU's responsibility exists altogether (existence of responsibility), whereas the second pertains to the scope of the responsibility. These two approaches resemble the traditional distinction within EU external relations law between the existence and the nature of EU external competences,[2] and are connected as both responsibility and the division of competences in the EU derive from the EU's international legal personality.

[1] It must not be forgotten that among the requisites for an internationally wrongful act to arise, it is necessary that the subject breaching an international obligation must be bound by it. See Art 2 Articles on State Responsibility and Art 4 of Articles on Responsibility of International Organizations (ARIO).

[2] Opinion 1/03, *Competence of the Community to Conclude the new Lugano Convention on Jurisdiction and the Recognition and Enforcement of Judgments in Civil and Commercial Matters*, EU:C:2006:81,

i. The Existence of the EU's Responsibility as a Corollary to its International Legal Personality

The EU's responsibility is inextricably linked to its international personality.[3] The possibility to be held responsible is one of the elements that inform the existence of the international personality of the EU.[4] Thus, regardless of how we understand the nature of the EU as an international actor, the question of whether the EU can be held responsible for breaches of its international obligations (existence of EU responsibility) can be seen as a corollary to its international personality.[5] Since the EU can assume international responsibility, it can be effectively regarded as an international person from an international law vantage point irrespective of what Article 47 TEU might explicitly provide. This discussion on the existence of the EU's responsibility has to a certain extent been put to rest by international practice since the EU has acted both bringing claims and being the respondent to multiple international disputes.[6]

ii. The Scope of the EU's Responsibility

More interesting for the purpose of this chapter is the second approach to the EU's international responsibility. The focus of this approach shifts from whether the EU can be held responsible to the scope of that responsibility. In other words, though the EU might have a legal personality, the extent to which the EU is internationally responsible is far from settled.[7]

Different theories have been advanced to define the scope of the EU's responsibility. The first set of theories consider that the EU, insofar as it is an international organisation bestowed with a set of functions and powers by its Member States, the latter remain responsible under international law for their obligations towards third parties.[8]

para 126. See Marise Cremona, 'External Relations and External Competence of the European Union: The Emergence of an Integrated Policy' in Paul Craig and Gráinne de Burca (eds), *The Evolution of EU Law*, 2nd edn (OUP, 2010) 221.

[3] Christian Tomuschat, 'The International Responsibility of the European Union' in Enzo Cannizazaro (ed), *The European Union as an Actor in International Relations* (Kluwer Law International, 2002) 183.

[4] Eric Stein, 'External Relations of the European Community: Structure and Process' 1 *Collected Courses of the Academy of European Law* 115, 131; Elisa Baroncini, Susanna Cafaro and Criseide Novi, *Le Relazioni Esterne dell'Unione Europea* (G Giappichelli Editore, 2012) 1.

[5] Daniel Müller, 'Union Européenne et Responsabilité International' in Myriam Benlolo-Carabot, Ukas Candas and Eglantine Cujo (eds), *Union Européenne et Droit International En L'Honneur de Patrick Dlaillier* (Pedone, 2012) 340; Jan Klabbers, *The European Union in International Law* (Pedone, 2012) 27. See also Commentary 2 to Art 64 ARIO.

[6] Christophe Hillion and Ramses A Wessel, 'The European Union and Dispute Settlement: Mapping Principles and Conditions' in Marise Cremona, Anne Thies and Ramses A Wessel (eds), *The European Union and Dispute Settlement* (Hart, 2017) 9. On the contribution of the EU to the development of International Dispute Settlement, see Danae Azaria, 'The European's Union Contribution to the Law on Standing and Jurisdiction in International Dispute Settlement' in ibid 55–81; Frank Hoffmeister, 'The Contribution of EU Practice to International Law' in Marise Cremona (ed), *Developments in EU External Relations* (OUP, 2008) 37–127.

[7] Andrés Delgado Casteleiro, *The International Responsibility of the EU: From Competence to Normative Control* (CUP, 2016) 14; José Manuel Cortés Martín, *Las Organizaciones Internacionales: Codificación y Desarrollo Progresivo de su Responsabilidad Internacional* (Instituto Andaluz de Administración Pública, 2008) 79.

[8] Emilija Leinarte, 'The Principle of Independent Responsibility of the European Union and its Member States in the International Economic Context' 21 *Journal of International Economic Law* 171, 191.

Therefore, any issue concerning the responsibility of the EU would lead to the joint and several responsibilities of the EU and its Member States.[9]

The second set of theories understand that the scope of the EU's international responsibility is linked to its powers. Thus, the EU's responsibility should take into account its division of competences in one way or another. This competence-based approach[10] has become the most prevalent view within the scholarship devoted to the EU's international responsibility,[11] though there might be some differences on the specifics on how competences play a role in establishing the EU's international responsibility.[12]

Regardless of the theory of responsibility that might be advanced, practice shows that the scope of the EU's responsibility follows to a certain extent the EU's division of competences in a broad sense.[13]

B. Modes of Participation of International Agreements and their Impact on the EU's Responsibility

While the link between competence and responsibility provides a path towards establishing when the EU and/or its Member States should be responsible, the picture becomes a little more complex due to the different EU modes of participation in international agreements. As mentioned in the introduction, participation can be

[9] André Nollkaemper, 'Joint Responsibility between the EU and Member States for Non-Performance of Obligations under Multilateral Environmental Agreements' in Elisa Morgera and Gracia Marín Durán (eds), *The EU and International Environmental Law* (CUP, 2012) 304. In more general terms, see André Nollkaemper and others, 'Guiding Principles on Shared Responsibility in International Law' 31 *European Journal of International Law* 15; Ian Brownlie, 'The Responsibility of State for the Acts of International Organizations' in Maurizzio Ragazzi (ed), *International Responsibility Today Essays in Memory of Oscar Schachter* (Martinus Nijhoff, 2005); Rosalyn Higgins, 'Report for Institute de Droit International, The Legal Consequences for Member States of the Non-fulfilment by International Organizations of their Obligations toward Third Parties' in Rosalyn Higgins (ed), *Themes and Theories: Selected Essays, Speeches, and Writings in International Law*, vol 2 (OUP, 2009).

[10] Cristina Contartese, 'Competence-Based Approach, Normative Control, and the International Responsibility of the EU and Its Member States' 17 *International Organizations Law Review* 418.

[11] Simone Vezzani, 'The International Responsibility of the European Union and of Its Member States for Breaches of Obligations Arising from Investment Agreements: Lex Specialis or European Exceptionalism?' in Mads Andenas and others (eds), *EU External Action in International Economic Law: Recent Trends and Developments* (TMC Asser Press, 2020) 300; Pieter Jan Kuijper and Esa Paasivirta, 'EU International Responsibility and its Attribution: From the Inside Looking Out' in Malcolm Evans and Panos Koutrakos (eds), *The International Responsibility of the European Union European and International Perspectives* (Hart, 2013); Frank Hoffmeister, 'Litigating against the European Union and its Member States – Who Responds Under the ILC's Draft Articles on International Responsibility of International Organizations?' 21 *European Journal of International Law* 723.

[12] For instance, Contartese (n 10) and Vezzani (n 11) contrast competence-based models to normative control as different models for understanding the EU's international responsibility, while Delgado Casteleiro (n 7) considers normative control to be a refined version of a competence-based model, which focuses on the exercise of the competence. Likewise, Gracia Marín Durán, 'Untangling the International Responsibility of the European Union and Its Member States in the World Trade Organization Post-Lisbon: A Competence/Remedy Model' 28 *European Journal of International Law* 697, 700, situates her competence/remedy model as a variant of the competence-based approach.

[13] See sections III and IV.

conceptualised in two different ways, which intersect between them: participation (or participation *stricto sensu*) and 'participation' (or participation *lato sensu).*

*i. Participation (*Stricto Sensu*)*

Participation (*stricto sensu*) relates to the principle of conferral and the division of competences. The EU responsibility is linked to the different modes of participation of the EU and/or its Member States in international agreements. The most basic taxonomy identifies three ways of participating based on whether the EU has the competence to enter into an international agreement: International agreements to which the EU is a party, but not its Member States (EU-only agreements), agreements to which both the EU and its Member States are parties to (mixed agreements) and agreements to which the EU Member States, but not the EU, are a party (Member States agreements).

In terms of responsibility, the first and the last category (EU-only agreements and Member States agreements), in principle, should not be problematic in a competence-based model of responsibility.[14] Insofar as the EU is the only party, it bears the responsibility for any breach of the international agreement. Since the EU had the competence to enter into the agreement alone, it also has the competence to bear the responsibility of any breach. Likewise, the Member States are responsible for those agreements they have entered.

To say that the question of responsibility under mixed agreements is more complicated would be an understatement.[15] Joint participation in mixed agreements blurs the line between the EU and Member States competences,[16] raising issues as to whether competence can solve the issue of responsibility. The CJEU has implicitly addressed this issue in a couple of cases.[17] The Court seems to understand that in the absence of an instrument apportioning the division of competences between the EU and its Member States in a mixed agreement, responsibility would be shared between the EU and its Member States.[18] However, recently the Court seems to be slightly shifting its position.[19]

*ii. Participation (*Lato Sensu*) or 'Participation'*

By participation '*lato sensu*' or 'participation', we mean those ways in which the EU and/or its Member States take part in an international agreement without formally being a party to it. The most obvious example would be that EU participation in an

[14] See section IV.

[15] In fact, it has been described as 'a mess'. Tomuschat (n 3); Leinarte (n 8) 171.

[16] Joseph HH Weiler, 'External Legal Relations of Non-Unitary Actors' in Joseph HH Weiler (ed), *The Constitution of Europe: Do The New Clothes Have an Emperor?* (CUP, 1999). See also in this edited book, the chapter by Yuliya Kaspiarovich and Ramses A Wessel.

[17] Case C-316/91, *Parliament v Council*, EU:C:1994:76; Case C-239/03, *Commission v France (Ètang de Berre)*, EU:C:2004:598.

[18] See section III. Pieter Jan Kuijper, 'International Responsibility for EU mixed agreements' in Christophe Hillion and Panos Koutrakos (eds), *Mixed Agreements Revisited The EU and Its Member States in the World* (Hart, 2010) 210.

[19] See section IV.

international agreement creates obligations for its Member States. Article 216 (2) TFEU provides that 'Agreements concluded by the Union are binding upon the institutions of the Union and on its Member States'. As a matter of EU law, the Member States must comply with those international agreements concluded by the EU.[20] On the one hand, this obligation stems from the constitutional architecture through which EU law is implemented, usually known as executive federalism.[21] As with EU law, international agreements concluded by the EU are most of the time implemented by the Member States organs. Thus, the Member States 'participate' in an international agreement when they are implementing it by virtue of Article 216(2) TFEU.

Finally, especially when it comes to international dispute settlement, the EU has also participated in investment disputes brought against one of the EU's Member States. This has become especially relevant as the EU has used its participation in those disputes to advance the competence-based model of responsibility.[22]

III. Joint Participation of the EU and its Member States in Mixed Agreements: Questions Left Unanswered within a Variety of Solutions

Under mixed agreements, several solutions have been laid down in order to deal with the international responsibility of the EU and its Member States. In an attempt to provide a picture of this complex subject matter, it is necessary to distinguish between those mixed agreements that are 'silent' on the allocation of responsibility between the EU and its Member States – that is, those agreements that do not foresee rules or mechanisms that regulate it – from those mixed agreements where ad hoc provisions were laid down, directly or indirectly, for that purpose.

A. Mixed Agreements with Ad Hoc Provisions: From Declarations of Competence to the Rule of Proceduralisation

When approaching the analysis of (bilateral and multilateral) mixed agreements that lay down some provisions that should guide, directly or indirectly, the attribution of international responsibility to the EU and/or its Member States, one obtains a puzzle of solutions. The most common instruments vary from declarations of competence attached to the agreement to the so-called rules of proceduralisation.[23]

[20] Case 181/73, *Haegeman*, EU:C:1974:41, para 5. For a general overview of the approach, see Panos Koutrakos, *EU International Relations Law* 2nd edn (Hart, 2015) 185; Stephen Hyett, 'The Duty of Cooperation: a Flexible Concept' in Allan Dashwood and Cristophe Hillion (eds), *The General Law od EC External Relations* (Sweet & Maxwell, 2000).

[21] On EU's executive federalism and its impact on international responsibility, see Delgado Casteleiro (n 7) 41.

[22] *Electrabel v Hungary* (ICSID Arbitral Tribunal, Case No ARB/07/19, 30 November 2012), para 3.18.

[23] Among other less common solutions, the joint responsibility rule can be listed, that is, an automatic allocation of responsibility to both the EU and its Member States in the case of mixed agreements without questioning the respective division of competences or any other relevant rule for that purpose. For an overview of this solution, see Cristina Contartese, Luca Pantaleo in Eleftheria Neframi and Mauro Gatti (eds), *Constitutional Issues of EU External Relations* (Nomos, 2018), 409–45, 418–20.

To start with, declarations of competence are the instrument through which the division of competences between the EU and its Member States becomes the key element for the attribution of international responsibility. Under a competence-based approach, in essence, there should be a direct relationship between possession of competence and international responsibility. However, this relationship is far from being straightforward. The instrument of declarations of competence has been applied differently. From the perspective of international practice, their role was disregarded in the legal reasoning of some international tribunals, whereas in the context of some decisions, the declarations of competence did not completely solve the question of the attribution of responsibility and were only one element of the analysis.[24] From an EU law perspective, the CJEU's case-law also appears inconsistent in this respect.[25] In sum, declarations of competence have been generally defined as unable to achieve the purpose for which they were laid down.[26]

Differently from the declarations of competence, the solution which was laid down in the recent (mixed) EU Investment Protection Agreements[27] (hereafter IPAs) leaves to the EU the identification of the proper respondent party in an investor-state dispute settlement (hereafter 'ISDS') proceeding against the EU and/or its Member State. This is referred to as a 'rule of proceduralisation'. Under the EU IPAs, which do not foresee provisions regulating the attribution of international responsibility to the EU and/or its Member States, the rule on the determination of the respondent party entitles the EU to identify who is the proper respondent by requiring that the investor delivers a notice requesting such a clarification.[28] Accordingly, the identification of the respondent remains, in essence, an 'internal' EU matter. From an EU perspective, this procedure does not raise concerns as the legal reasoning of the CJEU concludes in Opinion 1/17.[29]

B. 'Silent' Mixed Agreements

In the scenario of 'silent' mixed agreements, a further distinction needs to be drawn between bilateral and multilateral mixed agreements. As for 'silent' *bilateral* mixed

[24] For an analysis of the relevant cases (*MOX Plant* case *(Ireland v United Kingdom)* (Order No 3) (2003) 126 ILR 310); *Chile v European Union* (the *Swordfish* case) (*Case Concerning the Conservation and Sustainable Exploitation of Swordfish Stocks in the South-Eastern Pacific Ocean (Chile/European Union)* (Order of 16 December 2009) ITLOS Reports 2008/10); and the Request for an Advisory Opinion Submitted by the Sub-Regional Fisheries Commission (SRFC Advisory Opinion) (*Request for an Advisory Opinion Submitted by the Sub-Regional Fisheries Commission (SRFC)* (Advisory Opinion of 2 April 2015), see Delgado Casteleiro (n 7) Ch 5; Contartese (n 10) 355–68.

[25] Andrés Delgado Casteleiro, 'EU Declarations of Competence to Multilateral Agreements: A Useful Reference Base?' (2012) 17 *European Foreign Affairs Review* 503–07.

[26] On declarations of competence, see L Lijnzaad, 'Declarations of Competence in the Law of the Sea, a Very European Affair' in MW Lodge and MH Nordquist (eds), *Peaceful Order in the World's Oceans. Essays in Honor of Satya N. Nandan* (Leiden: Brill, 2014), 186–207; Joni Heliskoski, 'EU Declarations of Competence and International Responsibility' in Evans, Koutrakos (n 11) 189–212.

[27] For an example falling under this typology, see the European Commission's website, https://trade.ec.europa.eu/doclib/press/index.cfm?id=961.

[28] See, for instance, the *EU-Singapore Investment Protection Agreement*, Art 3.5 (Notice of Intent).

[29] In Opinion 1/17, *CETA*, EU:C:2019:341, the CJEU concluded that the EU-Canada Free Trade Agreement was compatible with EU law.

agreements, the CJEU's case-law[30] and legal scholars,[31] at least in the first stage of the debate, seemed to converge in supporting joint responsibility. This means that, initially, when the expression which refers to the contracting parties to the agreement was 'the Community and its Member States of the one part and the [third Party] of the other part',[32] the EU and its Member States are seen as constituting 'an undivided whole'[33] with regard to third parties. Accordingly, they are considered *jointly liable* to those latter states. It is important to emphasise that, at that stage of the debate, what seemed to matter was the interpretation of the *wording of the treaty* at stake, rather than the internal rules of the EU legal order as such. Today, in the light of the new wording indicating the EU and its Member States as Contracting Parties,[34] identifying the responsible party under mixed bilateral agreements is not an easy task.

A further complexity emerges when the analysis moves from 'silent' bilateral to 'silent' multilateral mixed agreements. Here, the EU and its Member States are certainly not perceived as indivisible but rather have legal obligations as *distinct* and *separate* contracting parties. The most well-known examples of 'silent' multilateral mixed agreements are the World Trade Organization (hereafter WTO), which will be discussed below,[35] and the Energy Charter Treaty (hereafter ECT).

The ECT lays down procedures for ISDS mechanism (under Article 26 ECT) and dispute settlement between Contracting Parties (under Article 27 ECT), without further foreseeing the criteria under which international responsibility should be attributed to the EU and/or its Member State.[36]

From an EU law perspective, the ISDS based on the ECT can be distinguished in two typologies: intra-EU disputes, that is, disagreements between an investor of an EU Member State and another EU Member State; and extra-EU disputes, where either the applicant or the respondent is not related to an EU Member State.

[30] *European Parliament v Council of the European Union* (n 17) para 29. In this case, the CJEU was dealing with the Fourth ACP-EEC Convention, whose art 1 reads as follows: 'The Community and its Member States, of the one part, and the ACP States, of the other part (hereinafter referred to as the 'Contracting Parties')'.

[31] Christian Tomuschat, 'Liability for Mixed Agreements' in David O'Keeffe and Henry G Schermers (eds), *Mixed Agreements* (Kluwer, 1983), 129–32.

[32] We have noted elsewhere (Contartese (n 10) 346–47) that, in some recent bilateral agreements, the expression, which refers to the contracting parties to the agreement, 'the Community and its Member States of the one part and the [third Party] of the other part' has been substituted with 'the Union, or its Member States, or the Union and its Member States, in accordance with their respective powers as derived from the Treaty on the Functioning of the European Union, of the one part, and [the third party] of the other part'.

[33] Giorgio Gaja, 'The European Community's Rights and Obligations under Mixed Agreements' in David O'Keeffe and Henry G Schermers (eds), *Mixed Agreements* (Kluwer, 1983) 137.

[34] On the different wording used to refer to the EU and its Member States as Contracting Parties under mixed agreements, see Sabrina Schaefer and Jed Odermatt, 'Nomen est Omen? The Relevance of 'EU Party' for International Law' in this volume.

[35] See section IV.

[36] For an argument according to which the ECT would acknowledge the allocation of competences between the EU and its Member States for the attribution of international responsibility, see Philipp Theodor Stegmann, *Responsibility of the EU and the Member States under EU International Investment Protection Agreements. Between Traditional Rules, Proceduralisation and Federalisation* (Springer, 2019) 122–28.

As for intra-EU disputes, after CJEU's *Achmea*,[37] this dimension of ISDS is no longer controversial under intra-EU BITs. The latter are to be terminated.[38] However, the case law before investment tribunals does not only concern the validity of these agreements under international law. It also displays further complexities where it has to be assessed whether the responsibility falls under the EU or/and its Member State.[39]

The well-known *Electrabel v Hungary* case is relevant in this respect since the Tribunal stressed that an EU Member State should not bear responsibility when it acts to comply with EU law.[40] From an EU law perspective, the approach under which the EU Member States should be exonerated from responsibility when implementing EU law[41] was codified in the EU Regulation on the apportionment of financial responsibility (between the EU and its Member States) rising from ISDS.[42] This Regulation, specifically, foresees a rule under which treatment that an EU Member State affords to the investor is required by EU law; the Union bears responsibility unless the controversial act aims at remedying a prior violation of EU law.[43] The reference to this Regulation was also expressly added

[37] C-284/16, *Achmea*, EU:C:2018:158. See Cristina Contartese and Mads Andenas, 'EU autonomy and investor-state dispute settlement under *inter se* agreements between EU Member States: *Achmea*', (2019) 56 *Common Market Law Review* 157–92.

[38] In Opinion 1/20, the CJEU will have to rule on the compatibility of the ECT with EU law, more specifically, on whether the draft modernised Energy Charter Treaty is compatible with Art 19 TEU and Art 344 TFEU; and whether Art 26 ECT or other ECT provisions allow for intra-EU disputes. See Matthew Happold, 'Belgium Asks European Court of Justice to Opine on Compatibility of Energy Charter Treaty's Investor-State Arbitration Provisions with EU Law', ejiltalk.org/belgium-asks-european-court-of-justice-to-opine-on-compatibility-of-energy-charter-treatys-investorstate-arbitration-provisions-with-eu-law/. See also the recent Opinion of Advocate General Saugmansgaard Øe in Joined Cases C-798/18 and C-799/18, *Federazione Nazionale delle Imprese Elettrotecniche ed Elettroniche (Anie) and Others* (C-798/18), *Athesia Energy Srl and Others*, (C-799/18) *v Ministero dello Sviluppo Economico, Gestore dei Servizi Energetici (GSE) SpA*, EU:C:2020:876), fn 55: 'In the light of [the *Achmea*] judgment, it seems that, inasmuch as *Article 26 of the Energy Charter*, which is headed 'Settlement of disputes between an investor and a Contracting Party', provides that arbitral tribunals may resolve such disputes, that provision *is not applicable to intra-Community disputes*. In my view, it may even be the case, having regard to the observations made by the Court in that judgment – especially in relation to the particular nature of the law established by the Treaties and the principle of mutual trust between the Member States – that the Energy Charter is entirely inapplicable to such disputes (emphasis added).

[39] See in this edited book, the ch by Bartosz Soloch and Makane Moïse Mbengue.

[40] The Tribunal concluded that 'Where Hungary is required to act in compliance with a legally binding decision of an EU institution, recognised as such under the *ECT*, it cannot (by itself) entail international responsibility for Hungary. Under international law, Hungary can be responsible only for its own wrongful acts. The Tribunal considers that it would be absurd if Hungary could be liable under the *ECT* for doing precisely that which it was ordered to do by a supranational authority whose decisions the *ECT* itself recognises as legally binding on Hungary', *Electrabel v Hungary* (n 22) para 6.72 (see also 4.167–4.172). For criticism of the *Electrabel* case also in the light of the *AES* case (*AES Summit Generation Limited and AES-Tisza Erbmii Kft v Republic of Hungary* (ICSID Case No ARB/07/22), see Tomoko Ishikawa, 'The Protection of Energy Investments under the ECT: An Extra-EU Country's Perspective', (2017) 2 *EILA REV* 277.

[41] See Vezzani (n 11) 293–333.

[42] Regulation EU (No) 912/2014 of the European Parliament and the Council of 23 July 2014 establishing a framework for managing financial responsibility linked to investor-to-state dispute settlement tribunals established by international agreements to which the European Union is party, [2014] OJ L 257/121.

[43] Ibid, Art 3.

in the EU Statement to the ECT in 2019.[44] This new Statement[45] lays down the following procedure (following the pattern of the rule of proceduralisation):[46] when either the Commission or an EU Member State receive notice by a claimant who wishes to initiate arbitration proceedings, the Commission and the Member State concerned will decide who is the proper respondent pursuant to the principles foreseen under the Regulation. After identifying the proper respondent, the EU will have to inform the claimant within 60 days from the date of the claimant's notice.[47]

However, the approach of the *Electrabel* Tribunal, exonerating the EU Member States from their international responsibility when implementing EU law, remains an exception since most of the current cases being heard before such arbitral tribunals do not concern the implementation of EU law. Instead, the debate mainly focuses on the objection to the competence of tribunals jurisdiction and identification of the applicable law, rather than the allocation of responsibility to the EU and/or its Member States. While the EU has intervened through *amicus curiae* in most of them, the applicants are not asking for joint responsibility in any of them. In the explosion of cases in the ECT, the respondent is either a EU Member State or the EU.[48] This latter is currently involved in two cases: in the first one, *Nord Stream 2 AG v European Union*, where the applicant is a Swiss investor, the arbitral tribunal has already been constituted;[49] in the second one, which has not been formally lodged, the EU is sued jointly with Latvia by AS PNB Banka, a company incorporated in the Republic of Latvia, whose investors are nationals of the United Kingdom.[50]

C. A Possible Way Forward?

What emerges from the (still limited) practice considered above is that focusing on the typology of participation in international agreements – in this case, joint participation – is not at all sufficient to lead to a consistent pattern in the attribution of international

[44] Statement submitted to the Energy Charter Treaty (ECT) Secretariat pursuant to Art 26(3)(b)(ii) of the ECT replacing the statement made on 17 November 1997 on behalf of the European Communities ([2019] OJ L 115/1–2).

[45] The 2019 Statement substituted the previous 1994 Statement. This latter, Statement submitted by the European Communities to the Secretariat of the Energy Charter Treaty pursuant to Art 26, para 3, b, ii, of the Energy Charter Treaty ([1994] OJ L 336/115), laid down that: 'The Communities and the Member States will, *if necessary*, determine among them who is the respondent party to arbitration proceedings initiated by an Investor of another Contracting Party. In such case, upon the request of the Investor, the Communities and the Member States concerned will make such determination within a period of 30 days'. The footnote to the declaration specifies that the determination made by the EU and its Member States 'is *without prejudice to the right of the investor* to initiate proceedings against both the Communities and their member states' (emphasis added).

[46] See above section III.A.

[47] Art 3 B and C Statement submitted to the ECT Secretariat pursuant to Art 26(3)(b)(ii) of the ECT replacing the statement made on 17 November 1997 on behalf of the European Communities ([2019] OJ L 115/1–2).

[48] For the list of cases currently pending under the ECT, see the official website: www.energychartertreaty.org/cases/list-of-cases/.

[49] See the ECT's official website, www.energychartertreaty.org/details/article/nord-stream-2-ag-v-european-union-uncitral/.

[50] For the two cases currently involving the EU under the ECT, see the European Commission's official website: https://ec.europa.eu/trade/policy/accessing-markets/dispute-settlement/investment-disputes/#_cases.

responsibility to the EU and/or its Member States. It is rather the opposite: one can observe a multitude of solutions that vary from case to case. From this perspective, the role of 'participation' should not be disregarded when assessing to what extent an EU Member State breached an international obligation while implementing EU law, as in the *Electrabel* case. In the light of this erratic legal scenario, 'internalising' rather than 'externalising' the complex relationship between the EU and its Member States appears a 'safe' solution. As long as neither the EU nor its Member States evades their responsibility, laying down procedural rules provides a proper approach. In this sense, the 2019 EU Statement to the ECT is an important development, however, a formal amendment to the ECT foreseeing a *binding* procedural rule to 'internalise' the identification of the proper respondent between EU and its Member State could be a more transparent solution.[51]

IV. 'Participation' and EU Responsibility

The conundrum that joint participation creates in terms of responsibility has been at the centre of the traditional approaches to the EU's international responsibility. However, 'participation' also poses challenges to the EU's responsibility. Special attention should be paid to two specific aspects. First, EU-only agreements seem, in theory, to solve the responsibility conundrum by establishing a clear link between participation and responsibility, but what about the practice? If we consider that in those agreements, participation equals competence, would agreements that fall entirely within EU competence entail the EU's exclusive responsibility? Second, if we assume that responsibility follows competence, how does EU law ensure that 'participation' does not affect its responsibility in such a way that it diminishes its international personality?

A. EU Responsibility and Agreements Falling Exclusively within EU Competence.

Multilateral agreements were mostly mixed, and traditionally, only multilateral agreements contained dispute settlement provisions. Thus, mixed agreements were where most of the practice on the EU's responsibility could be found. Until recently, bilateral agreements concluded by the EU, like association agreements or bilateral fisheries agreements, did not contain dispute settlement provisions.[52] Instead, within the bodies set up under these agreements, consensus and political compromises negotiations were how disputes were settled.

[51] The present authors have reached this conclusion elsewhere, see Andrés Delgado Casteleiro, 'Disconnecting from the Energy Charter Treaty: Disconnection Clauses and Normative Conflicts Between European Union Law and the Energy Charter in Treaty' in Angelos Dimopoulos (ed), *The EU and Investment Arbitration Under the Energy Charter Treaty* (CUP), forthcoming; Contartese, Pantaleo (n 23) 409–45, spec 444–45.

[52] Esa Paasivirta, 'The European Union and Dispute Settlement: Managing Proliferation and Fragmentation' in Marise Cremona, Anne Thies and Ramses A Wessel (eds), *The European Union and Dispute Settlement* (Hart, 2017) 51.

However, the new Association Agreements and Free Trade Agreements (hereafter FTAs) include dispute settlement provisions. Moreover, in the aftermath of *Opinion 2/15*, the EU institutions decided to split the new FTAs into EU-only FTAs, which entirely fall within the scope of the Common Commercial Policy (hereafter CCP) and mixed investment agreements. This decision paves the way for issues of responsibility to arise in the new Union FTAs eventually. In fact, within the remaining mixed FTAs (those concluded before *Opinion 2/15*),[53] the dispute settlement provisions have already been triggered, albeit by the EU against its counterpart.[54] However, it cannot be excluded that the third party might eventually bring a case against the EU.[55] More importantly, these third countries could even bring cases against the EU over Member States actions not falling within an EU exclusive competence.[56]

In those agreements where the EU would be the only party besides the third country, the Union would bear international responsibility for any breach of the FTA regardless of whether committed by the EU, a Member State or stemming from an EU exclusive competence or a Member State one. Moreover, the CJEU could be seized to make sure that Member States comply with an eventual award regardless of whether internally the subject matter falls outside EU competence.[57] In the EU-only FTAs, it could be argued that participation *stricto sensu* would make the EU responsible for any issue that 'participation' could create.

Another interesting situation regarding 'participation' and the EU responsibility would be the EU's responsibility in the WTO after the entry into force of the Lisbon Treaty, and the reconfiguration of the scope of the CCP carried out in Opinion 2/15.[58] On the one hand, the WTO is now covered by the CCP competence.[59] On the other hand, the practice in the WTO reflects, to a certain extent, how the WTO agreements have become false mixed agreements.[60] Thus the Member States' joint participation in the WTO would appear to be a formal affair rather than one where the Member States continue to have some competence.[61]

[53] Free trade Agreement between the European Union and its Member States, of the one part, and the Republic of Korea, of the other part, [2011] OJ L 127/6; Association Agreement between the European Union and the European Atomic Energy Community and their Member States, of the one part, and the Republic of Moldova, of the other part, [2014] OJ L 260/4; Association Agreement between the European Union and its Member States, of the one part, and Ukraine, of the other part, [2014] OJ L 161/3; Comprehensive Economic and Trade Agreement (CETA) between Canada, of the one part, and the European Union and its Member States, of the other part, [2017] OJ L 11/23.

[54] See https://ec.europa.eu/trade/policy/accessing-markets/dispute-settlement/bilateral-disputes/.

[55] Including a dispute settlement procedure in an agreement makes it more likely that disputes will arise. See Jan Klabbers, 'Continent in Crisis' (2016) 27 *European Journal of Int'l Law* 555.

[56] See Gracia Marín Durán, 'Sustainable Development Chapters in EU Free Trade Agreements: Emerging Compliance Issues' (2020) 57 *Common Market Law Review* 1031.

[57] Case C-66/18, *Commission v Hungary (Central European University)*, EU:C:2020:792 paras 85–93. For a detailed discussion of the case, see Andrés Delgado Casteleiro and Cristina Contartese, 'Case C-66/18 *Commission v Hungary (Central European University)*' (N° 54, 2021) Revista General de Derecho Europeo 196–215. Also, see section IV.B of this chapter.

[58] *Opinion 2/15, EU-Singapore Free Trade Agreement*, EU:C:2017:376.

[59] Ibid paras 36 and 54.

[60] Allan Rosas, 'The European Union and Mixed Agreements' in Dashwood and Hillion (n 20).

[61] See Case C-66/18 *Commission v Hungary (Central European University)* (n 57), Opinion 2/15, *EU-Singapore Free Trade Agreement* (n 58).

However, since the entry into force of the Lisbon Treaty, there has been an increase in complaints brought against the EU and a Member State that would cast doubts over the falseness of the mixed nature of the WTO.[62] Yet, while the other WTO parties might have increased the joint targeting of the EU and its Member States, no panel has established the joint responsibility of the EU and its Member States,[63] with one notable exception.[64] None of this new set of WTO disputes has led to the constitution of a panel. For instance, *European Union and a Member State – Seizure of Generic Drugs in Transit* continues to be formally in consultations since 2010.[65] Likewise, in *European Union and a Member State – Certain Measures Concerning the Importation of Biodiesel*, Argentina requested the establishment of a panel in 2012, but the Dispute Settlement Body deferred it.[66] Essentially, it would appear that WTO contracting parties are jointly targeting the EU and its Member States as part of a litigation strategy similar to the 'divide and rule' strategy used by the US in the LAN dispute.[67]

In summary, reading the WTO example in light of both the recent CJEU case-law and recent WTO disputes, it can be argued that insofar as competence covers the whole agreement, there is no joint participation in terms of responsibility.

B. 'Participation', Responsibility and the Reality of the Implementation of International Agreements in the EU

When it comes to the EU's international responsibility, it has been commonly assumed that the EU-only agreements do not present many problems. Since only the EU had the competence to participate in the agreement, it made sense for the EU to bear the sole responsibility for its implementation.[68] More specifically, two aspects of the EU's 'participation' make the issue of a competence-based responsibility more complicated than just following a straight line between competence and responsibility. The first aspect is the complex nature of the EU's multilevel architecture through which EU law is implemented (executive federalism). The second aspect is the lack of parallelism between EU external and internal competences.

Under the EU's executive federalism,[69] even when the Member States are not parties to a Union agreement, they still 'participate' in it. As per Article 216(2) TFEU, international agreements concluded by the EU form an integral part of the EU legal order

[62] Marín Durán (n 12).

[63] WT/DS443/1, *European Union and a Member State – Certain Measures Concerning the Importation of Biodiesels;* WT/DS409/1, *Request for the Establishment of a Panel. European Union and a Member State – Seizure of Generic Drugs in Transit. Request for Consultations by Brazil*; WT/DS452/1, *European Union and Certain Member States – Certain Measures Affecting the Renewable Energy Generation Sector – Request for Consultations by China*; WT/DS600/1, *European Union and Certain Member States – Certain Measures Concerning Palm Oil and Oil Palm Crop-Based Biofuels – Request for Consultations by Malaysia.*

[64] WT/DS346/R, *European Communities and Certain Member States – Measures Affecting Trade in Large Civil Aircraft – Report of the Panel.* On a critical appraisal of the decision, see Delgado Casteleiro (n 7) 188.

[65] See www.wto.org/english/tratop_e/dispu_e/cases_e/ds409_e.htm.

[66] See www.wto.org/english/tratop_e/dispu_e/cases_e/ds443_e.htm.

[67] Kuijper (n 18), Leinarte (n 8).

[68] See, for instance, the third recital of Regulation (EU) No 912/2014 (n 42).

[69] See section II.B.ii.

and the Member States have to implement them as a matter of EU law. The logical consequence of this approach is that if a Member State were to breach an international obligation binding on the EU, they would also be breaching an EU law obligation.[70] More importantly for our analysis, it is how the EU's international responsibility motivates the need to ensure that its Member States do not breach Union agreements. In *Kupferberg*, the CJEU established its jurisdiction to interpret an EU-only agreement on the basis that 'In ensuring respect for commitments arising from an agreement concluded by the Community institutions the member states fulfil, within the community system, an obligation in relation to the community, which has assumed responsibility for the due performance of the agreement'.[71]

From *Kupferberg* onwards, the CJEU developed competence-based reasoning to assert its jurisdiction to implement both Union and mixed agreements.[72] In those cases where the EU has concluded an international agreement and exercised its internal competences over a subject matter covered by that agreement,[73] the Member States have an EU law obligation to implement not making the EU incur into international responsibility.[74]

Yet, what happens when the EU has not exercised internal competence? Do the EU Member States have an EU law obligation to implement Union agreements when the EU has an external competence but has no internal competence, which would trigger the implementation of the international obligation through executive federalism? The interplay between the lack of parallelism in the division of competences and the obligations assumed by the EU in Union agreements makes it more complicated.

Opinion 2/15[75] brought this issue to the forefront in a very clear fashion. The CJEU expanded the scope of the EU's CCP to include both social and environmental protection.[76] These two subject areas are not only shared competence internally,[77] but also the EU has not exercised its competence in such intensity to trigger an external parallel exclusive competence. This lack of parallelism linked to the competence-based model on which the CJEU has developed its jurisdiction would create problems for the EU's international responsibility under EU-only agreements.[78] Since the EU would not legally be able to ensure that its Member States would, within their sphere of competence, comply with an EU-only agreement, there would be a case for some alternative

[70] Case C-66/18, *Commission v Hungary (Central European University)* (n 57) para 69; Opinion 1/17, *CETA* (n 29) para 117; Case C-366/10, *Air Transport Association of America and Others*, EU:C:2011864.

[71] Case 104/81, *Kupferberg*, EU:C:1982:362, para 9.

[72] Koutrakos (n 20) 239.

[73] This is especially relevant when it comes to mixed agreements, see Panos Koutrakos, 'Intepretation of Mixed Agreements' in Hillion and Koutrakos (n 18); Eleftheria Neframi, 'Mixed Agreements as a Source of European Union Law' in Enzo Cannizazaro, Paolo Palcehtti and Ramses A Wessel (eds), *International Law as Law of the European Union* (Martinus Nijhoff, 2012); Marise Cremona, 'Defending the Community Interest: The Duties of Cooperation and Compliance' in Marise Cremona and Bruno De Witte (eds), *EU Foreign Relations Law Constitutional Fundamentals* (Hart, 2008).

[74] Case 12/86, *Demirel*, EU:C:1987:400, para 11. See JHH Weiler, 'Thou Shalt Not Oppress a Stranger: On the Judicial Protection of the Human Rights of Non-EC Nationals – A Critique' 3 *European Journal of International Law* 65, 75.

[75] Opinion 2/15, *EU-Singapore Free Trade Agreement* (n 58).

[76] Ibid para 164.

[77] Art 4 (2) TFEU.

[78] Marín Durán (n 56) 1031.

model to the competence model for the EU's international responsibility designed to provide a remedy more than to abide by the division of competences.[79]

However, this vision does not acknowledge that the CJEU's jurisdiction, though competence-based, relies on the risk that the EU might be internationally responsible because of an action by one of its Member States.[80] In the *Central European University* case, Hungary argued that since higher education did not fall within an EU competence, the CJEU lacked jurisdiction, and it was for the Member States to bear the responsibility under international law.

The Court's response was to extend its jurisdiction over enforcement action to cover areas that are internally shared competence at best.[81] The Court extended how it understands the exercise of competence when it comes to its jurisdiction. As mentioned before, the Court's jurisdiction relied on the fact that some competence had to have been exercised internally.[82] While the case law had taken a loose approach to what counted as an exercise of competence,[83] it nevertheless based its reasoning on the existence of Union legislation that would support a Union interest for the EU Member States to comply with an international agreement. Yet, the Court understood that since the GATS (formally a mixed agreement) fell within the CCP,[84] every commitment enshrined in GATS, even those that internally are not EU competence, fall within the exclusive competence of the Union.[85] The CJEU did not refer to any piece of EU legislation to show that it had jurisdiction. It is enough for the EU to have exercised its external competence over an agreement for the CJEU to have jurisdiction to control any infringement connected to it.

To sum up, the EU's international responsibility plays an important role in the CJEU's reasoning to assert its jurisdiction over infringement actions against the Member States regardless of whether an internal competence has been exercised. The broad scope of the CJEU's jurisdiction characterised by a cryptic line of reasoning and incremental nature[86] ensures that the Member States comply with the EU's international obligations even when they 'participate' in international agreements within their sphere of competence. The case for competence model of responsibility focused not so much on the exercise of EU competence internally but on whether the EU concluded the agreement that would be supported by the role that the CJEU plays internally in ensuring that the Member States comply with the EU-only agreements.

V. Conclusions

This chapter tackled the question of whether the forms of participation and 'participation' of the EU and its Member States in international agreements exert an impact on the

[79] Marín Durán (n 12).
[80] Piet Eeckhout, *EU External Relations Law* 2nd edn (OUP, 2011) 282.
[81] C-66/18, *Commission v Hungary* (*Central European University*) (n 57) para 59.
[82] Case C-13/00, *Ireland v Commission (Berne Convention)* [2002] ECRI-2943; *Commission v France* (*Étang de Berre*) (n 17).
[83] Eeckhout (n 80) 282.
[84] Opinion 2/15, *EU-Singapore Free Trade Agreement* (n 58) para 54.
[85] C-66/18, *Commission v Hungary* (*Central European University*) (n 57) para 74.
[86] Koutrakos (n 20) 242.

attribution of international responsibility and, if so, to what extent. What emerged is that assessing whether the EU participates in international agreements alone (EU-only agreements) or with its Member States (mixed agreement) is only the very first stage of the analysis. The complex relationship between the EU legal order and its Member States requires investigating other questions: How does the division of competence impact the regime of international responsibility? To what extent should the notion of 'executive federalism' be a key element of the analysis? What are the international agreements' provisions regulating, directly or indirectly, international responsibility between the EU and its Member States? Are these satisfactory?

As for the international responsibility of the EU and its Member States in mixed agreements, at (very) first glance, one may be tempted to conclude that joint responsibility is the proper answer to joint participation, and to a certain extent, it is also a quick fix solution. This is, however, not the case. The structure of the EU legal order is, in fact, much more complex. The WTO is the most significant example in this sense since, inter alia, EU competence, in that policy field, underwent an evolution from shared to exclusive. May the division of competence, therefore, be the key answer? At first sight, it would appear that competence is no longer the key. Since the entry into force of the Lisbon Treaty, there has been an increase of WTO disputes where the EU and some Member States were jointly targeted. However, none of those cases moved to the panel stage. Finally, it was observed that, whereas there is no uncontroversial principle or set of criteria under which international responsibility could be attributed consistently throughout the different scenarios of the composite EU/Member States relationship, 'internalising' this issue seems a proper approach.

In those cases where the EU ratifies an international agreement without its Member States, two aspects mentioned above re-emerge: firstly, the role of EU's executive federalism; secondly, the potential lack of parallelism between EU external and internal competences. The CJEU, aware of these scenarios, expanded its jurisdiction over infringement actions against the Member States even in those circumstances where an internal competence has not yet been exercised. The rationale behind the CJEU's legal reasoning seems to be the willingness to ensure, *internally*, that Member States comply with the EU's international obligations even when they 'participate' in international agreements within their sphere of competence. The role of the CJEU is central to any approach to the EU's responsibility based on competence. There is an argument for the EU to bear responsibility internationally only to the extent that the CJEU effectively controls how Member States participate and 'participate' in international agreements concluded by the EU.

PART III

The EU and its Member States' Parallel Participation in International Agreements

10

The Future of the Istanbul Convention before the CJEU

PANOS KOUTRAKOS AND VIKTORIJA SOŅECA*

I. Introduction

The Council of Europe Convention on preventing and combating violence against women and domestic violence (Istanbul Convention) is only the second international human rights treaty that the European Union (Union) has signed. The first was the United Nations Convention on the Rights of Persons with Disabilities (UNCRPD).[1] This is by no means the only respect in which it is significant, as the Istanbul Convention is also the first gender-focused and binding instrument on violence against women.[2] In terms of its substantive contribution, in the words of the Venice Commission,

> [t]he added value of the Istanbul Convention … is that it is the first European instrument to deal with violence against women and domestic violence in a comprehensive manner. It introduces new provisions requiring a specific institutional setup … and foresees concrete prevention measures …; protection measures … and – under substantive law – civil, administrative and criminal law measures, as well as procedural safeguards for victims. It is also the first European instrument that links these phenomena expressly to harmful gender stereotypes.[3]

* All views expressed in this chapter are solely those of the author and may not be attributed to the institution that employs her.

[1] Council Decision 2010/48 concerning the conclusion, by the European Community, of the United Nations Convention on the Rights of Persons with Disabilities [2010] OJ L 23/35. On the process of negotiation, see G de Búrca, 'The European Union in the Negotiation of the UN Disability Convention' (2010) 35 *EL Rev* 174. On its application, see D Ferri, 'The Unorthodox Relationship Between the EU Charter of Fundamental Rights, the UN Convention on the Rights of Persons with Disabilities and Secondary Rights in the Courts in the Court of Justice Case Law on Disability Discrimination' (2020) 16 *European Constitutional Law Review* 275.

[2] S Preschal, 'The European Union's Accession to the Istanbul Convention' in K Lenaerts et al (eds), *An Ever-Changing Union? Perspectives on the future of EU Law in Honour of Allan Rosas* (Hart Publishing, 2019) 279.

[3] Venice Commission Opinion 961/2019 'Opinion on the constitutional implications of the ratification of the Council of Europe Convention on Preventing and Combating Violence against Women and Domestic Violence (Istanbul Convention) (Armenia)', Council of Europe doc CDLAD (2019)018 (14 October 2019), www.venice.coe.int/webforms/documents/?pdf=CDL-AD(2019)018-e. See also L Grans, 'The Istanbul Convention and the Positive Obligation to Prevent Violence' (2018) 18 *Human Rights Law Review* 133.

Accession to the Istanbul Convention has provided the backdrop for considerable tension in both the Member States and the Union. On the one hand, the participation of the former has been characterised by divergent approaches, tensions and controversies. On the other hand, there has been inter-institutional conflict about the signature and conclusion of the Istanbul Convention on behalf of the Union. This dispute is about everything a Union external relations lawyer would like to talk about, namely competences, procedure and political disagreement.

The unfolding episode of the signature and conclusion of the Istanbul Convention and the way it plays out before the Court of Justice in Opinion 1/19,[4] is, therefore, more than a dispute about this important human rights instrument. It provides a snapshot of the difficulties that the Union and the Member States face in their effort to coexist within the framework of an international legal order organised in a manner that does not reflect the constitutional idiosyncrasies of the Union legal order. In fact, Opinion 1/19 follows a body of recent case law on the negotiation, conclusion and application of international agreements, which highlighted the continuing tensions raised by the Union's international action. It is in that context that Advocate Hogan pointed out that 'the relationship between the Member States and the Union in respect of the conclusion of international agreements which bind both parties is apt to present some of the most difficult and complex questions of Union law'.[5]

Viewed from this angle, the way the Union and the Member States have approached the signature and conclusion of the Istanbul Convention raises fundamental questions about the role and management of mixed agreements under Union law. The aim of this chapter is threefold: first, to provide a critical analysis of the issues raised in the Parliament's request for an Opinion and explore their implications for mixed agreements in general and the Istanbul Convention in particular; second, to argue that the choice of legal basis has become neither less complex nor less controversial despite the existence of a solid body of case law on the matter and the long engagement of the EU's institutions in the treaty-making process; third, drawing on the pending procedure before the Court of Justice, to reflect on the continuous ambiguity that permeates the coexistence of the Union and the Member States in the context of mixed agreements.

II. The Istanbul Convention: An Overview

The text of the Istanbul Convention was negotiated by an expert group, the Ad Hoc Committee on Preventing and Combating Violence against Women and Domestic Violence (CAHVIO).[6] CAHVIO met nine times and finalised the draft text in December 2010. The Istanbul Convention entered into force on 1 August 2014. In addition to the text of the Istanbul Convention, CAHVIO has produced an Explanatory Report.[7] It should be emphasised that the CAHVIO reports show that the Commission sent

[4] At the time of writing, the Court has not yet ruled on the matter. AG Hogan handed down his Opinion on 11 March 2021: Opinion in Opinion 1/19, EU:C:2021:198.

[5] Ibid, para 1.

[6] Documents on the negotiations are available at www.coe.int/en/web/istanbul-convention/cahvio.

[7] Explanatory Report to the Council of Europe Convention on Preventing and Combating Violence Against Women and Domestic Violence Istanbul of 11 May 2011, https://rm.coe.int/16800d383a.

representatives to the Committee,[8] and the Commission itself stated that the 'Union participated, alongside Member States, as an observer in these meetings'.[9]

The purpose of the Istanbul Convention is to protect women against all forms of violence and prevent, prosecute and eliminate violence against women. It applies to, among others, domestic violence, which affects women disproportionately. The purposes of the Istanbul Convention are set out in Article 1 as follows:

> The purposes of this Convention are to:
>
> a. protect women against all forms of violence, and prevent, prosecute and eliminate violence against women and domestic violence;
> b. contribute to the elimination of all forms of discrimination against women and promote substantive equality between women and men, including by empowering women;
> c. design a comprehensive framework, policies and measures for the protection of and assistance to all victims of violence against women and domestic violence;
> d. promote international co-operation with a view to eliminating violence against women and domestic violence;
> e. provide support and assistance to organisations and law enforcement agencies to effectively co-operate in order to adopt an integrated approach to eliminating violence against women and domestic violence.

In order to achieve its purposes, the Istanbul Convention provides a wide range of measures that straddle various fields, such as data protection, awareness-raising, education and training, protection and support, civil remedies and the criminalisation of various forms of violence. It includes a specific chapter on asylum and immigration (chapter VII) and requires, among others, that the parties 'take the necessary legislative or other measures to ensure that gender-based violence against women may be recognised as a form of persecution' within the meaning of the Refugees Convention 'and as a form of serious harm giving rise to complementary/subsidiary protection'.[10] It establishes, moreover, a monitoring mechanism operated through, on the one hand, an independent group of experts (GREVIO) and, on the other hand, the Committee of the Parties, composed of the representatives of the parties to the Convention and responsible for issuing recommendations to the individual parties.

While it rules out reservations in principle,[11] the Istanbul Convention provides that any Union Member States may, at the time of signature or when depositing its instrument of ratification, acceptance, approval or accession, submit reservations for two specific purposes: not to apply or to apply only in specific cases or conditions certain provisions;[12] and to provide for non-criminal sanctions, instead of criminal sanctions,

[8] COM(2016) 109 final, *Proposal for a Council Decision on the Conclusion, by the European Union, of the Council of Europe Convention on Preventing and Combating Violence Against Women and Domestic Violence*, www.europarl.europa.eu/cmsdata/115844/council-decision.pdf.

[9] COM(2016) 111 final, *Proposal for a Council Decision on the Signing, on Behalf of the European Union, of the Council of Europe Convention on Preventing and Combating Violence Against Women and Domestic Violence*, 2. Available at https://data.consilium.europa.eu/doc/document/ST-6695-2016-INIT/en/pdf.

[10] Art 60(1) Istanbul Convention, which refer to Art 1.A(2) of the 1951 Convention relating to the Status of Refugees.

[11] Art 78(1) Istanbul Convention. On reservations, see Art 2 (1)(d) of the Vienna Convention on the Law of Treaties.

[12] Art 78(2)(1) refers to Art 30, para 2; Art 44, paras 1.e, 3 and 4; Art 55, para 1 in respect of Art 35 regarding minor offences; Art 58 in respect of Arts 37, 38 and 39; Art 59.

for psychological violence and stalking.[13] Such reservations are valid for five years from the day of the entry into force in respect of the party concerned.

There are currently 34 signatories to the Istanbul Convention,[14] 22 of which have made reservations or declarations.[15] While the Union and its Member States are all signatories, there is considerable divergence in the approach of the latter. Six Member States have not yet ratified the Istanbul Convention (Bulgaria, the Czech Republic, Hungary, Latvia, Lithuania and the Slovak Republic), while Poland has announced, controversially, its intention to withdraw from it.[16] Most of the Member States, moreover, have made reservations/declarations concerning part of the Istanbul Convention's provisions (Latvia, Lithuania, Croatia, Cyprus, the Czech Republic, Denmark, Finland, France, Germany, Greece, Ireland, Malta, Netherlands, Poland, Romania, the Slovak Republic, Spain and Sweden). Reservations are narrow in scope. For example, Latvia's reservation is about the right not to apply Article 55 (1) in respect of Article 35 regarding minor offences, whereas Ireland has reserved the right not to apply the provisions of the Istanbul Convention laid down in Articles 30 (2) and 44 (3). There are also declarations of a broad nature: Latvia, Lithuania and Poland, for instance, have declared that they would apply the Istanbul Convention in conformity with the principles and provisions of their Constitution.

In addition to the above divergence of approaches, there have been express disagreements between the Member States about their respective positions. A case in point is Austria's formal objection to the Polish Declaration mentioned above as incompatible with the object and purpose of the Istanbul Convention. Given its general and indeterminate scope, the Declaration is viewed as not clearly defining the extent to which Poland has accepted the obligations laid down in the Convention. Netherlands, Sweden and Finland have also objected to the Declaration made by Poland on similar grounds and suggest that it casts doubt as to the commitment of Poland to fulfil its obligations under the Convention. Finland, in particular, has also suggested that the Polish Declaration is incompatible with the general principle that a party may not invoke the provisions of its domestic law as justification for a failure to perform its treaty obligations and, therefore, with Article 19 of the Vienna Convention on the Law of the Treaties.[17]

A clear sense of discord, therefore, emerges from the approach of the Member States to the conclusion of the Istanbul Convention. This is in stark contrast to the UNCRPD,

[13] Art 78(3) Istanbul Convention, which refers to Arts 33 and 34, respectively.

[14] Albania, Andorra, Austria, Belgium, Bosnia and Herzegovina, Croatia, Cyprus, Denmark, Estonia, Finland, France, Georgia, Germany, Greece, Iceland, Ireland, Italy, Luxembourg, Malta, Monaco, Montenegro, Netherlands, North Macedonia, Norway, Poland, Portugal, Romania, San Marino, Serbia, Slovenia, Spain, Sweden, Switzerland and Turkey. Comprehensive information, www.coe.int/en/web/conventions/full-list/-/conventions/treaty/210/signatures.

[15] Serbia, Romania, Poland, North Macedonia, Monaco, Malta, Latvia, Ireland, Andorra Armenia, Sweden, Switzerland, Slovenia Finland, France, Georgia, Germany, Greece, Croatia, Cyprus, Czech Republic, Denmark. Comprehensive information available at www.coe.int/en/web/conventions/full-list/-/conventions/treaty/210/signatures.

[16] Poland Announces Withdrawal from 'Harmful' Istanbul Convention. 28 July 2020, https://exit.al/en/2020/07/28/poland-announces-withdrawal-from-harmful-istanbul-convention/. See also www.euronews.com/2020/07/27/istanbul-convention-poland-s-plan-to-quit-domestic-violence-treaty-causes-concern.

[17] On Art 19 VCLT, see O Corten and P Klein (eds), *The Vienna Conventions on the Law of Treaties. A Commentary* (OUP, 2011), 443–45.

where no Union Member State had made a declaration or a reservation. This state of affairs implies uncertainty about the process of the conclusion of the Convention on behalf of the Union as well as the effective application of its provisions. It also reflects a widening gap between the Union Member States in the context of human rights. This gap has emerged with striking force and been developing with increasing intensity on the internal plane in relation to the organisation of the judiciary. There is now a solid body of case law against Poland[18] and voluminous literature on the rule of law issues in that country and Hungary.[19] The unfolding episode of the conclusion of the Istanbul Convention provides another manifestation of the divergence of views on fundamental issues between the Member States.[20] The spokesperson of the Council of Europe referred to the non-ratification of the Convention as 'an anti-European, and an anti-Union gesture' and the ensuing discord as involving 'traditionalists against progressives in Europe'.[21] Therefore, we see an external context within which internal divisions between the Member States manifest themselves. From this angle, this case is not just about the technicalities of a legal formula that has tested the ingenuity of Union policymakers and baffled external partners.[22] While it does throw the modalities of mixity into sharp relief, it also touches upon the underlying differences between the Member States, which the international context of this legal dispute amplifies further.

III. The Background to and the Subject-Matter of the Request for an Opinion

It is settled case law that 'the rules regarding the manner in which the Union institutions arrive at their decisions are laid down in the Treaties and are not at the disposal of the Member States or of the institutions themselves'.[23] The general procedure for

[18] See, for instance, Case 192/18, *Commission v Poland*, EU:C:2019:924; Joined Cases C-585/18, C-624/18 and C-625/18, *AK and Others*, EU:C:2019:982; Joined Cases C-558/18, Case C-619/18, *Commission v Poland*, EU:C:2019:531; C-563/18, Miasto Łowicz and Prokurator Generalny, EU:C:2020:234; C-272/19, *Land Hessen*, EU:C:2020:535; C-256/19, *Maler*, EU:C:2020:523; and ongoing C-487/19, *WŻ* (AG Tanchev Opinion) EU:C:2021:289 and C-518/19, *MF v JM* (AG Tanchev Opinion) EU:C:2021:290. See also, in the case of Romania, Joined Cases C-83/19, C-127/19, C-195/19, C-291/19, C-355/19, C-397/19, Asociația *Forumul Judecătorilor Din România* et al, EU:C:2021:393.

[19] See, for instance, P Bogdanowicz et al, 'Guest Editorial: A Potential Constitutional Moment for the European Rule of Law – The Importance of Red Lines', (2018) 55 *CMLRev* 983, L Pech, 'Protecting Polish Judges from Poland's Disciplinary "Star Chamber"' (2021) 58 *CMLRev* 137, Pech, L and Kelemen, DR, 'The Uses and Abuses of Constitutional Pluralism: Undermining the Rule of Law in the Name of Constitutional Identity in Hungary and Poland' (2019) 21 *CYELS* 59, S Platon, 'Court of Justice, Preliminary References and Rule of Law: Another Case of mixed signals from the Court of Justice regarding the independence of national courts: *Miasto Lowicz*', (2020) 57 *CMLRev* 1843, A Ploszka, 'Shrinking Space for Civil Society: A Case Study of Poland' (2020) 26 *EPL* 941, K Scheppele and R Kelemen, 'Defending Democracy in EU Member States: Beyond Article 7 TEU' in F Bignami (ed), *EU Law in Populist Times: Crises and Prospects* (CUP, 2020) 413.

[20] That is not to say that the discord is confined to the EU Member States: Turkey, for instance, annulled its ratification of the Convention in March 2021.

[21] Daniel Höltgen, quoted in M De Law Baume, 'How the Istanbul Convention Became a Symbol of Europe's Cultural Wars' [12 April 2021), www.politico.eu/article/istanbul-convention-europe-violence-against-women/.

[22] See P Olson, 'Mixity from the Outside: the Perspective of a Treaty Partner' in C Hillion and P Koutrakos (eds), *Mixed Agreements Revisited – The EU and its Member States in the World* (Hart, 2010) 331.

[23] Case C-28/12, *Commission v Council*, EU:C:2015:282, para 42 and case law cited.

negotiation, signature and ratification of international agreements is set out in Article 218 TFEU. The legal dispute in Opinion 1/19 is about the decision to sign and conclude the Istanbul Convention. In accordance with Articles 218(5) and (6) TFEU, it is for the Council, following a proposal by the Commission, to adopt the decisions authorising the signing and concluding the agreement, respectively. The Council does so, in principle, by a qualified majority pursuant to Article 218 (8) TFEU subparagraph 1 TFEU.[24]

The Commission had not submitted a recommendation that the Council should decide to open negotiations, nominate the Commission to negotiate on behalf of the Union and allow it to participate in the negotiations. On 4 March 2016, it adopted two proposals for Council Decisions on the signing[25] and conclusion[26] of the Istanbul Convention on behalf of the Union. The former cited Article 218(5) TFEU and the latter Article 218(6)(a) TFEU as the procedural legal basis. As for the substantive legal bases, the Commission relied upon the judicial cooperation in criminal matters Chapter of the TFEU (Title V, chapter 4) and cited Articles 82(2) and 84 TFEU. The former provision is about 'facilitat[ing] the mutual recognition of judgments and judicial decisions and police and judicial cooperation in criminal matters having a cross-border dimension', whereas the latter is about 'establish[ing] measures to promote and support the action of the Member States in the field of crime prevention, excluding any harmonisation of the laws and regulations of the Member States'.

The Council departed from the Commission's proposal in two respects. First, on 11 May 2017, it adopted two, rather than one, separate decisions on the signing of the Convention on behalf of the Union.[27] Second, the legal basis of these measures differed from those proposed by the Commission: Decision 2017/856 is based on Articles 82(2) and 83(1) TFEU, the latter providing for 'establish[ing] minimum rules concerning the definition of criminal offences and sanctions in the areas of particularly serious crime with a cross-border dimension resulting from the nature or impact of such offences or

[24] Under Art 218(8) subpara 2 TFEU, unanimity is required for agreements covering a field for which unanimity is required for the adoption of a Union act, for association agreements, for the agreements referred to in Art 212 TFEU with the States which are candidates for accession, and for the Union's accession to the European Convention for the Protection of Human Rights and Fundamental Freedoms. For an analysis of these procedures, see A Dashwood in A Dashwood et al, *Wyatt and Dashwood's European Union Law* 6th edn (2011) 936 et seq and P Koutrakos, *EU International Relations Law* 2nd edn (2015) Ch 4.

[25] COM(2016) 111 final, (n 9 above), 9–10.

[26] COM(2016) 109 final, (n 8 above).

[27] Council Decision (EU) 2017/865 of 11 May 2017 on the signing, on behalf of the European Union, of the Council of Europe Convention on preventing and combating violence against women and domestic violence with regard to matters related to judicial cooperation in criminal matters [2017] OJ L 131/11; Council Decision (EU) 2017/866 of 11 May 2017 on the signing, on behalf of the European Union, of the Council of Europe Convention on preventing and combating violence against women and domestic violence with regard to asylum and non-refoulement [2017] OJ L 131/13. This practice has also been followed in relation to the UN Smuggling of Migrants Protocol: Council Decision 2006/616/ EC on the conclusion, on behalf of the European Community, of the Protocol Against the Smuggling of Migrants by Land, Sea and Air, supplementing the United Nations Convention Against Transnational Organised Crime concerning the provisions of the Protocol, in so far as the provisions of this Protocol fall within the scope of Articles 179 and 181a of the Treaty establishing the European Community [2006] OJ L 262/24 and 2006/617/EC: Council Decision 2006/617/EC on the conclusion, on behalf of the European Community, of the Protocol Against the Smuggling of Migrants by Land, Sea and Air, supplementing the United Nations Convention Against Transnational Organised Crime concerning the provisions of the Protocol, in so far as the provisions of the Protocol fall within the scope of Part III, Title IV of the Treaty establishing the European Community [2006] OJ L 2262/344.

from a special need to combat them on a common basis'; Decision 2017/866 is based on Article 78(2) TFEU which provides for the adoption of measures for a common European asylum system.

The Istanbul Convention was signed on behalf of the Union on 13 June 2017 but has not yet been ratified. It was in the light of the Council's approach, however, that the Parliament applied for an Opinion under Article 218(11) TFEU and raised two issues. The first is about the substantive legal basis: should the Union conclude the Istanbul Convention under Articles 82(2) and 84 TFEU (as proposed by the Commission) or Articles 78(2), 82(2) and 83(1) TFEU (as decided by the Council)? The Parliament also asked whether it was necessary or possible to separate the decisions concerning the signature and the conclusion of the convention as a consequence of that choice of legal basis. The second issue is about the adoption of the Council Decision to conclude the Istanbul Convention on behalf of the Union: is it compatible with Article 218(6), given the absence of mutual agreement between all the Member States regarding their consent to be bound by that Convention? These will be examined in turn.

IV. The Issue of Legal Basis

The choice of legal basis and the division of competence between the EU and the Member States are questions that are 'closely linked'.[28] As highlighted in other contributions to this book, the division of competence between the Union and the Member States is based on the principle of conferral (Article 5(2) TEU) and the assumption that competences not conferred upon the Union remain with the Member States (Articles 5(2) and 4(1) TEU). In the context of the Istanbul Convention, the issue was not whether the Union had exclusive competence over the entirety of the Istanbul Convention. In fact, the Commission had acknowledged in its proposal that the Member States 'remain competent for substantial parts of the Convention, and particularly for most of the provisions on substantive criminal law and other provisions in Chapter V to the extent that they are ancillary'.[29] It was, instead, the implications of its position that was contentious, namely that the Union has competence 'for a considerable part of the provisions of the Convention'[30] or, as it put it in the preamble to the proposed decision, for 'most of the provisions of the Istanbul Convention'.[31]

It is settled case law that the choice of legal basis is a matter of constitutional significance[32] and must be made on objective factors that are amenable to judicial review, including the aim and the content of the measure.[33] It is also settled case law that,

> if an examination of a European Union measure reveals that it pursues a twofold purpose or that it comprises two components and if one of these is identifiable as the main or predominant purpose or component, whereas the other is merely incidental, the act must be based on

[28] Opinion 1/08, *GATS*, EU:C:2009:739, para 111.
[29] COM(2016) 111 final, (n 9 above), 7.
[30] Ibid.
[31] Ibid, 11–12, para 5.
[32] Opinion 2/00, *Cartagena Protocol on Biodiversity*, EU:C:2001:664, para 5.
[33] Case C-263/14, *European Parliament v Council (EU-Tanzania Transfer Agreement)*, EU:C:2016:43, para 43.

> a single legal basis, namely that required by the main or predominant purpose or component. Exceptionally, if it is established, however, that the act simultaneously pursues a number of objectives, or has several components, which are inextricably linked without one being incidental to the other, such that various provisions of the Treaty are applicable, such a measure will have to be founded on the various legal bases corresponding to those components.[34]

While the choice of legal basis may be a complex exercise at the best times,[35] the wide-ranging scope of the Istanbul Convention makes it even more so. It is further complicated by the different types of the Union competence that cover different provisions of the Istanbul Convention, namely exclusive, shared and supporting, coordinating or supplementary.

In its proposal, the Commission referred to various Treaty provisions that pertain to areas covered by the Istanbul Convention: Article 16 TFEU (data protection), Article 19(1) TFEU (sex discrimination), Article 23 TFEU (consular protection for citizens of another Member State), Articles 18, 21, 46, 50 TFEU (free movement of citizens, free movement of workers and freedom of establishment), Article 78 TFEU (asylum and subsidiary and temporary protection), Article 79 TFEU (immigration), Article 81 TFEU (judicial cooperation in civil matters), Article 82 TFEU (judicial cooperation in criminal matters), Article 83 TFEU (definition of the Union-wide criminal offences and sanctions for particularly serious crimes with a cross-border dimension), Article 84 TFEU (non-harmonising measures for crime prevention), and Article 157 TFEU (equal opportunities and equal treatment of men and women in areas of employment and occupation). However, the main thrust of the Commission's position is that the predominant purpose of the Convention 'lies in the prevention of violent crimes against women, including domestic violence, and the protection of victims of such crimes'.[36] For this reason, it proposed Article 84 TFEU as a legal basis (along with Article 82(2) TFEU, which was uncontroversial).

In some ways, the Commission's approach is somewhat narrow. It is striking, for instance, that non-discrimination should not be considered a main component of the Istanbul Convention and that it does not rely upon Article 19 TFEU.[37] This is all the more so, given the prominent place of non-discrimination in the Istanbul Convention itself.[38] In this vein, it is interesting that, back in 2015, the Commission itself would have stressed the contribution of the ratification of the Istanbul Convention to its commitment to gender equality and the Union's commitments in the context of the UNCRPD,[39]

[34] Ibid, para 44.

[35] See, for instance, P Koutrakos, 'Legal Basis and Delimitation of Competence in EU External Relations' in M Cremona and B De Witte (eds), *EU Foreign Relations Law – Constitutional Fundamentals* (Hart Publishing, 2008) 171.

[36] Ibid, 9.

[37] See also Preschal, (n 2 above), at 283 and De Vido, 'The Ratification of the Council of Europe Istanbul Convention: A Step Forward for the Protection of Women from Violence in the European Legal System' (2017) 9 *European Journal of Legal Studies* 69, 85–86.

[38] See, for instance, the prominent position in the preamble to the Convention of the '[r]ecogni[tion] that the realisation of *de jure* and *de facto* equality between women and men is a key element in the prevention of violence against women'.

[39] EU Commission, Roadmap A (possible) EU accession to the CoE Convention on preventing and combating violence against women and domestic violence (October 2015, 2015/JUST/010 and EU Commission) 1, https://ec.europa.eu/smart-regulation/roadmaps/docs/2015_just_010_istanbul_convention_en.pdf.

the latter having also been concluded under Article 13 EC (now Article 19 TFEU).[40] From this angle, the Commission's proposal is somewhat sweeping in its assumption that the matters not covered by its proposed legal bases are ancillary in nature.

While narrow in its choice of legal basis, the Commission's proposal is broad in terms of the scope of the Union's competence. In fact, its approach is based on the assumption that the Union may exercise its competences 'over the entirety of the Convention and excluding elements over which it would have no competence'.[41] The broad accession of the Union in the Istanbul Convention has also been supported by the Parliament.[42]

Another aspect of the Commission's proposal is the exclusive nature of the Union's competence. The Commission argues that there is 'abundant legislation in most' of the areas of the Istanbul Convention covered by the Union competence[43] and that the latter is exclusive to the extent that the Istanbul Convention might affect those rules or alter their scope in the meaning of Article 3(2) TFEU.[44] It is recalled that, in order to ascertain whether the Union's competence is exclusive, 'a comprehensive and detailed analysis of the relationship between the envisaged international agreement and the Union law in force' is required which 'must take into account the areas covered by the Union rules and by the provisions of the agreement envisaged, their foreseeable future development and the nature and content of those rules and those provisions in order to determine whether the agreement is capable of undermining the uniform and consistent application of the Union rules and the proper functioning of the system which they establish'.[45] For this assessment to be carried out, it is not necessary for the Union rules and the provisions of the agreement in question to coincide fully.[46] Instead, they need to be covered to a large extent.[47]

A detailed analysis of the extent to which each provision of the Istanbul Convention corresponds to Union competence is beyond the scope of this chapter.[48] At this juncture, suffice it to point out that the broad scope of the Istanbul Convention and the varying intensity of the duties it imposes makes this exercise quite complex. Take, for instance, the issue of minimum standards. Article 73 of the Istanbul Convention allows the parties to introduce more favourable rights. In this vein, a number of measures mentioned in the Commission's proposal, such as the Victim's Rights Directive[49]

[40] Along with Art 95 EC (now Art 114 TFEU): Council Decision 2010/48 [2010] OJ L 23/35.

[41] COM(2016) 111 final (n 9 above), 9–10.

[42] European Parliament Resolution of 14 March 2017 on equality between women and men in the European Union in 2014–15 (2016/2249(INI)), para 33.

[43] Ibid, 7.

[44] Art 3(2) TFEU reads as follows: 'The Union shall also have exclusive competence for the conclusion of an international agreement when its conclusion is provided for in a legislative act of the Union or is necessary to enable the Union to exercise its internal competence, or in so far as its conclusion may affect common rules or alter their scope'.

[45] Opinion 1/13, *Hague Convention*, EU:C:2014:2303 at para 74, as well as Opinion 1/03, *Lugano Convention*, EU:C:2006:81 at paras 126, 128 and 133, and Case C-114/12, *Commission v Council (Neighbouring Rights)*, EU:C:2014:2151 para 74.

[46] Opinion 1/13, *Hague Convention*, ibid, para 72.

[47] Opinion 1/03, *Lugano Convention*, (n 45 above), para 126, and Case C-114/12, *Commission v Council (Neighbouring Rights)*, (n 45 above), para 70.

[48] See K Nousiainen and C Chinkin (eds), *Legal Implications of EU Accession to the Istanbul Convention* (European Network of Legal Experts in Gender Equality and Non-Discrimination, 2015).

[49] Directive 2012/29/EU of the European Parliament and the Council of 25 October 2012 establishing minimum standards on the rights, support and protection of victims of crime, and replacing Council Framework Decision 2001/220/JHA [2012] OJ L 315/57.

and Directive 2011/93/EU on combating the sexual abuse and sexual exploitation of children,[50] state expressly that they set minimum standards and allow the Member States to adopt higher standards. The Commission does not deal with this issue in any detail: in its proposal, it argues that '[e]ven if many of the existing provisions referred to above are minimal rules, it cannot be ruled out that, in the light of recent case law, some of them may also be affected or their scope altered'.[51] And yet, the Court has held that an agreement allowing its parties to introduce stricter requirements would not affect the Union common rules in the meaning of what is now Article 3(2) TFEU.[52]

At the other end of the spectrum, the Council's approach to the issue of legal basis reflects a narrow understanding of the exercise of the Union's competence. It provides for the signing of the Istanbul Convention only with regard to matters related to judicial cooperation in criminal matters[53] and asylum and non-refoulement.[54] The Council's view is based on the premise that the Union should accede to the Istanbul Convention 'as regards matters falling within the competence of the Union insofar as the Convention may affect common rules or alter their scope'.[55] This statement is not accompanied by a reference to either Article 3(2) TFEU on the exclusivity of the Union competence or Article 216(1) on the existence of the Union competence (the wording of these two provisions is almost identical).[56] The approach adopted in the two Council Decisions in question also deviates from the prevailing practice that decisions by the Council on the signature or conclusion of international agreements on behalf of the Union do not, in principle, refer expressly to the provisions of the agreements in relation to which the Union exercises its competence.[57]

This narrow reading of the Union's competence raises questions. First, it illustrates a one-dimensional understanding of the exercise of the Union's competence in the context of mixed agreements. While it may be underpinned by a concern that the powers of the Member States in the areas covered by the Convention might be impinged upon, this view appears to ignore the different guises of mixity which aim to facilitate the coexistence of the Union and the Member States on the international scene. Second, the Council's approach is difficult to reconcile with the acknowledgement that the Union competences and the powers of the Member States in the context of the Convention are 'interlinked'.[58] Third, it may undermine effective application further, all the more

[50] Directive 2011/93/EU of the European Parliament and the Council of 13 December 2011 on combating the sexual abuse and sexual exploitation of children and child pornography, and replacing Council Framework Decision 2004/68/JHA [2011] OJ L 335/1.

[51] COM(2016) 111 final, (n 9 above) p 9, where no reference to case law is included, https://data.consilium.europa.eu/doc/document/ST-6695-2016-INIT/en/pdf.

[52] Opinion 2/91, ILO *Convention n 170*, EU:C:1993:106 as clarified in Case C-114/12, *Commission v Council*, (n 45 above), para 91.

[53] Art 1 Council December 2017/865.

[54] Art 1 Council December 2017/866.

[55] Recital 6 of the preamble to Council December 2017/865 and December 2017/866.

[56] On the conceptual difficulties raised by the formulation of Arts 3(2) and 216(1) TFEU, see G de Baere, *Constitutional Principles of EU External Relations* (OUP, 2008) 70 and P Koutrakos, (n 24 above), 126–30.

[57] There are exceptions: for instance, Council Decision 94/69/EC of 15 December 1993 on the conclusion on behalf of the Union of the United Nations Framework Convention on Climate Change [1994] OJ L 33/11, Council Decision 94/800/EC of 22 December 1994 on the conclusion of the Agreement establishing the World Trade Organization [1994] OJ L 336/1.

[58] Recital 8 of the preambles to Council December 2017/865 and December 2017/866.

so given that the Council itself refers to the coherent exercise of rights and fulfilment of obligations laid down in the Convention.[59] In this vein, it is worth noting that that narrow construction of the exercise of the Union's competence entails a territorial limitation on the application of the Convention by the Union, given the AFSJ (area of freedom, security and justice) context of the Union's accession.

The divergence between the Union's institutions that emerge from the above is significant because it tells us about the choice of legal basis for this Convention in particular and the overall of what process of the choice of the appropriate legal basis. The cornerstone of the process is its objective nature. However, over the years, neither the Union's institutions have found it easier to apply it, nor has the volume of ensuing legal disputes decreased. The analysis in this section provided a snapshot of institutional attitudes that have allowed this state of affairs to persist, namely the somewhat vague and sweeping manner in which the Commission substantiated its proposal and the Council's narrow approach. In addition, the strong disagreement among the Member States about different aspects of the Istanbul Convention and its application sets out a politically charged context within which this legal dispute unfolds.

The choice of legal basis emerges, therefore, as neither less complex nor less controversial than it has always been. This is noteworthy not only because the Union is positively mature in age but also, perhaps more importantly, given the emphasis in the Lisbon Treaty on clarifying competence and developing a solid body of case law purported to introduce clarity in the area. In his Opinion in Opinion 1/19, Advocate General Hogan put forward yet another approach to the choice of legal basis. He suggested that the latter be determined on the basis of the objectives and components not of the Istanbul Convention itself but, instead, of the Council's decision authorising the conclusion of the Convention.[60] The corollary of this argument is that the Council may choose which shared competences pertaining to the Convention would be exercised by the Union. This position appears difficult to reconcile with prior case law on the legal basis of Union measures concluding international agreements, which is about the content, objectives and overall balance of the latter.[61] It also entails considerable discretion for the Council, the exercise of which may end up marginalising certain shared competences and potentially reducing the scope of treaty obligations that the Union is prepared to assume. Ultimately, the argument put forward by Advocate General Hogan would not only politicise further the practice and management of mixed agreements but might also increase the complexity of mixity.

Articulating a set of workable principles that would enable the Union to conclude international agreements in a predictable manner without wasting considerable energy and time on legal basis disputes is no mean feat. One of the authors of this chapter wrote quite some ago that, while 'the choice of the appropriate legal basis becomes even more complex and the need for clarity more compelling[,] … a degree of realism is necessary: complete clarity and predictability are simply not possible as the politically

[59] Ibid.
[60] (n 4 above), paras 73 et seq.
[61] See, for instance, Opinion 2/00, (n 32 above), para 25.

charged character of this process, its constitutional repercussions and the political and economic realities of international relations render a degree of uncertainty inevitable'.[62] This combination of legal principle and realism is necessary not only in the context of the choice of legal basis but also in the coexistence of the Union and the Member States in the process of the conclusion of mixed agreements. The following section will focus on the latter issue.

V. The Issue of Mutual Agreement

As the analysis in section II illustrated, the process of the accession of the Member States to the Convention has been far from smooth. There has been considerable divergence about the scope of the obligations the Member States are prepared to assume, legal objections to the practice of certain Member States, and even a Member State that has expressed its intention to withdraw. It is against this background that the second question raised by the Parliament before the Court needs to be understood. In particular, how may the absence of mutual agreement among the Member States about their consent to be bound by the Istanbul Convention be reconciled with the qualified majority voting requirement required under Article 218(6) TFEU?[63]

The starting point for our analysis is the procedure laid down in Article 218(6) TFEU. Described as 'the procedural code' of the Union's treaty-making,[64] Article 218 TFEU has been viewed by the Court to 'constitute …, as regards the conclusion of treaties, an autonomous general provision, in that it confers specific powers on the [Union] institutions … [w]ith a view to establishing a balance between those institutions …'.[65] This provision is silent on the timing of the Council's decision to conclude an international agreement. Drawing on this lacuna, Advocate General Hogan argued that not only does the Council enjoy considerable discretion as to when to conclude the Istanbul Convention but that there are also 'strong practical reasons' for the Council to wait until all Member States have concluded it.[66]

While the political context within which mixed agreements are approached by the Union institutions is never far from the practice of mixity, the Court has not been sympathetic to legal formulas that deviate from the procedural rules set out in Article 218 TFEU. This was illustrated clearly in the case of hybrid decisions, that is, decisions adopted by the Council and Representatives of the Governments of the Member States meeting within the Council dealing with issues of both Union and national competence. In Case C-28/12 *Commission v Council*, the Court held that such measures should not be adopted for the signature and provisional application of mixed agreements as they

[62] Koutrakos, (n 35 above), 197.
[63] The unanimity requirement provided for in Art 218(6) TFEU does not apply to the Conclusion of the Istanbul Convention.
[64] A Dashwood in A Dashwood et al, *Wyatt and Dashwood's European Union Law* 6th edn (2011) at 936.
[65] Case C-327/91, *France v Commission*, EU:C:1994:305, para 28.
[66] AG Hogan, (n 4 above), para 218.

violate Article 218(2), (5) and (8) TFEU (and, therefore, Article 13(2) TEU).[67] It was the conflation of different procedures and the ensuing deviation from that required under Article 218 TFEU that was found objectionable.[68] In this view, to render mutual agreement between Member States about the consent to be bound by a mixed agreement a requirement for the conclusion of that agreement by the Union under Article 218(6) TFEU would be tantamount to altering the procedure for the conclusion of the latter. In addition to interfering with the constitutional nature of the procedural code of EU external relations, this formula may also prevent the Union from exercising even its exclusive competences.

While this may be the position as a matter of principle, its practical implications may be difficult to manage. A case in point is the effect of the Istanbul Convention in light of the failure of certain Member States to ratify it. Would the latter be bound by it as a matter of Union law so far as the Convention covers areas of Union competence but not in so far as it covers areas of national powers?[69] If so, how would this work, given the interlinked nature of the Union and national competences pertaining to the Istanbul Convention and the wide-ranging scope of the provisions of the latter? If not, would the absence of mutual agreement not impede the fulfilment of the Union's obligations under the Istanbul Convention, in which case the further question of compatibility with Article 27 of the Vienna Convention on the Law of Treaties might be raised?[70] The dynamic nature of the Union's competence raises an inherent difficulty in approaching the question of the Union's ratification of an agreement in the absence of national ratification. As the division of competence under a mixed agreement is subject to constant redefinition, the ratification by the Union only may amount gradually to the imposition of duties on the non-ratifying Member States not covered by the provisions ratified originally by the Union.

The implications of the joint participation of the Member States and the failure of some to ratify the Convention create a legal knot of considerable complexity. To what extent may the duty of cooperation help approach it?[71] It is settled case law that, in the

[67] Case C-28/12, *Commission v Council*, (n 23 above).

[68] See the analysis in Joni Heliskoski, 'The Procedural Law of International Agreements: A Thematic Journey Through Article 218 TFEU' (2020) 57 *CML Rev* 113, 90–94 and P Koutrakos, 'Institutional Balance and Sincere Cooperation in Treaty-Making under EU Law' (2019) 68 *ICLQ* 13–16.

[69] See G Van der Loo and R Wessel, 'The Non-Ratification of Mixed Agreements: Legal Consequences and Solutions' (2017) 54 *CML Rev* 735.

[70] In a different context, this issue was raised in *LaCrand (Germany v United States of America)* ICJ Reports 2001, 466.

[71] From the voluminous literature on the duty of cooperation, see F Casolari, 'Like a Bridge over Troubled Water: the 2/15 Opinion Through the Lens of EU Loyalty' in I Bosse-Platière and C Rapoport (eds), *The Conclusion and Implementation of EU Free Trade Agreements – Constitutional Challenges* (Cheltenham: E Elgar Publishing, 2019) 85; M Clamert, *The Principle of Loyalty in EU Law* (OUP, 2014), M Cremona, 'Defending the Community Interest: The Duties of Cooperation and Compliance' in M Cremona and B De Witte (eds), *EU Foreign Relations Law: Constitutional Fundamentals* (Oxford: Hart Publishing, 2008) 125; C Hillion, 'Mixity and Coherence in EU External Relations: The Significance of the Duty of Cooperation' in Hillion and Koutrakos (eds), (n 22 above), 87; J Larik and A Delgado Casteleiro, 'The Duty to Remain Silent: Limitless Loyalty in Eu External Relations', (2011) 36 *ELRev* 524, P Van Elsuwege, 'The Duty of Sincere Cooperation and Its Implications for Autonomous Member State Action in the Field of External Relations' in M Varju (ed), *Between Compliance and Particularism – Member State Interests and European Union Law* (Springer, 2019) 283, E Neframi, 'The Duty of Loyalty: Rethinking Its Scope through Its Application in the Field of EU External Relations' (2010) 47 *CML Rev* 323.

case of mixed agreements, the Union institutions and the Member States are under a duty to ensure close cooperation in the process of negotiation, conclusion and application of these agreements.[72] How far, however, does this duty take us when it comes to the ratification of international treaties? Article 51 of the Vienna Convention on the Law of Treaties attaches great importance to the independent decision of Member States to ratify international agreements, and the Venice Commission points out that 'the ratification of a treaty is a sovereign act of the State, which means that the State is entirely free in its choice of whether or not to ratify a treaty and, as a result, be bound by its obligations. It is also a sovereign act of the State to choose the type of relationship it would like to establish between its domestic and the international legal order, that is what status a treaty will have within the domestic legal order, once it is ratified'.[73] Viewed from this angle, extending the scope of the duty of cooperation to cover the ratification of an international agreement would interfere with a fundamental right of the Member States as sovereign subjects of international law in so far as this concerns provisions of the Convention that fall within their competence.[74]

The non-ratification of the Convention by certain Member States may have implications for the relationship of the latter not only with the Union but also with the Member States that have ratified it. May it be argued that the refusal to ratify would amount to a change of the Convention, distinguishing it from that to which the latter Member States assumed their ratification referred? This question becomes all the more relevant in the light of the strong responses by certain Member States to declarations submitted by the other Member States that limited the scope of application of the Convention considerably. There are, therefore, policy implications for the Member States. In legal terms, however, while pertinent to international agreements with a strong element of reciprocity (such as the Energy Charter Treaty or the World Trade Organisation Agreements), this point becomes less convincing in the context of an agreement such as the Istanbul Convention, which is not a package deal and the *raison d'être* of which does not depend on the establishment of reciprocal arrangements.

The process of accepting the Istanbul Convention in the domestic legal order of the Member States has been far from smooth. The recent Latvian experience is indicative. On 3 August 2020, the Constitutional Court of the Republic of Latvia started proceedings[75] on an application by 21 members of the Latvian Parliament (Saeima). The applicants argue that Article 12(1) of the Istanbul Convention,[76] along with the general obligation

[72] Opinion 1/94, EU:C:1994:384, para 108, Opinion 2/00, *Cartagena Protocol*, (n 32 above), para 18, Case C-246/07, *Commission v Sweden*, EU:C:2010:203, para 73, Case C-28/12, *Commission v Council*, (n 23 above), para 54.

[73] Venice Commission Opinion 961/2019 'Opinion on the constitutional implications of the ratification of the Council of Europe Convention on Preventing and Combating Violence against Women and Domestic Violence (Istanbul Convention) (Armenia)', Council of Europe doc CDLAD(2019)018, 3.

[74] This is also the position taken by AG Hogan in his Opinion in Opinion 1/19, (n 4 above), paras 203–04. See also N Levrat and Y Kaspiarovich, 'Are EU Member States Still States Under International Law?', *GSI Working Paper Prof PhDc LAW 2019/02*.

[75] Decision of the Constitutional Court of 3 August 2020 in the case No 2020-39-02, www.satv.tiesa.gov.lv/web/viewer.html?file=/wp-content/uploads/2020/08/2020-39-02_Lemums_par_ierosinasanu-3.pdf#search=.

[76] Art 12(1) reads as follows: 'Parties shall take the necessary measures to promote changes in the social and cultural patterns of behaviour of women and men with a view to eradicating prejudices, customs, traditions and all other practices which are based on the idea of the inferiority of women or on stereotyped roles for women and men'.

of Article 4(3),[77] require the state to take the necessary measures to promote changes in the mentality and attitude of society and would not allow discrimination with respect to persons who do not self-identify with their biological sex but self-identify with another sex (gender). The applicants argue that the contested provisions are incompatible with the family and Christian values that form the constitutional identity of the State of Latvia and are included in the Latvian Constitution, the right to freedom of thought and conscience,[78] as well as protection for the traditional family.[79] The applicants also point out the potential incompatibility between Article 4(4) of the Istanbul Convention with the constitutional prohibition on discrimination, as the special measures for prevention of violence could cause differential treatment on the basis of sex. Also, that Article 14 of the Istanbul Convention requires the state to include in its education curriculum issues pertaining to persons who do not self-identify with their biological sex and argue that this would be incompatible with the constitutionally protected right of the child's parent to ensure the compatibility of their children education with their religious convictions and philosophical views.

Finally, another layer in this episode is about the enforcement of the Convention and issues of responsibility. As mentioned above, the Istanbul Convention provides for the establishment of a specific independent monitoring body (GREVIO), tasked with ensuring effective implementation of its provisions by the Contracting Parties. This monitoring body's functions and powers are set out in detail in Chapter IX of the Istanbul Convention. The Contracting Parties must submit detailed reports on legislative and other measures giving effect to the Convention, which would then be evaluated by GREVIO. The latter would define a monitoring procedure and may execute country visits during which its members enjoy the privileges and immunities set out in the Appendix to the Istanbul Convention. The GREVIO will draw up a report and conclusions, which must be rendered public as soon as they are adopted, together with any comments by the Contracting Party. The GREVIO's report and conclusions may form the basis for the Committee of the Parties' recommendations to the Contracting Party, which may also be required to report on the implementation of the recommendations by a certain date. The GREVIO may conduct urgent enquiries, the results of which are to be submitted to the Contracting Party, the Committee of the Parties and the Committee of Ministers of the Council of Europe.

The Union, like any other party to the Convention, will become subject to the above procedure upon accession and all Union institutions, bodies, offices and agencies will be subject to this control/monitoring mechanism.[80] As the Union could not exempt

[77] Art 4(3) reads as follows: 'The implementation of the provisions of this Convention by the Parties, in particular measures to protect the rights of victims, shall be secured without discrimination on any ground such as sex, gender, race, colour, language, religion, political or other opinion, national or social origin, association with a national minority, property, birth, sexual orientation, gender identity, age, state of health, disability, marital status, migrant or refugee status, or other status'.

[78] Protected under Art 99 Latvian Constitution.

[79] Protected under Art 110 Latvian Constitution.

[80] See recital 7 to the preambles to Council Decision (EU) 2017/865 and Council Decision (EU) 2017/866. This in itself is not controversial, as the EU submits to monitoring mechanisms established under agreements to which it accedes. It is also accepted, in principle, that a treaty setting up a judicial body with jurisdiction binding on the institutions of the parties, including the EU's judiciary, may be compatible with the EU's primary rules (Opinion 1/91 (EEA) EU:C:1991:490, paras 39–40). In practice, the Court has been far from

these spheres from the scope of the Istanbul Convention's obligations, it is curious that the Commission's proposals should have overlooked this aspect of accession. This is all the more so given that the question of the obligations that the Union would incur for its own institutions and public administration had been raised in the context of the UNCRPD, which is the only other human rights convention to which the Union has acceded. The declaration of competence eventually made by the Union in regard to the UNCRPD explicitly mentions the matter of the Union's own obligations under that Convention for the Union's institutions and public administration.[81] It is interesting that the first monitoring report that the Union received under the UNCRPD should have been critical of its institutions and required that the Union address the perceived shortcomings and report back.[82] The responsibility, therefore, that the Union might incur for its own institutions and public administration under the Istanbul Convention is worth considering.

VI. Conclusion

The process of the Union's accession to the Istanbul Convention and the pending proceedings before the Court provide an intriguing glimpse of the challenges that the conclusion of mixed agreements may raise for both the Union and its Member States. Not only does it raise a range of issues, both substantive and procedural, that are central to mixity, but it brings them into sharp relief. The stark manner in which these issues have emerged may be explained by the timing and the current state of Union integration. The prevailing climate in the Union is characterised by the emergence of a small but vocal number of the Member States whose views of how to organise society differ considerably from the liberal mainstream EU norm. In such a climate, the aims and methods of the Convention have attracted greater attention, and objections to them have found fertile ground.

There is also the issue of mixity itself. The questions raised by the ratification of the Istanbul Convention are so central to mixity that it is surprising that they should not have been addressed so far. This is even more so given the long life of the principle and its gradual evolution shaped by the Court's case law and treaty-making practice. It is a testament to the pragmatism of the Union's institutions and the Member States as well as the dynamism of the Union legal order that mixity should have become central to the Union's international presence, even though fundamental principles about its function and implications have been ambiguous at best.

enthusiastic about this prospect and its case law (eg Case C-459/03 *Commission v Ireland (re: Mox Plant)* EU:C:2006:345, *Opinion 1/09* EU:C:2011:123, *Opinion 2/13* EU:C:2014:2454) has given rise to an intense debate and voluminous literature on the autonomy of EU legal order (for a snapshot, see, for instance, Jan Klabbers and Panos Koutrakos (eds), 'Special Issue: An Anatomy of Autonomy' (2019) 88 *Nord J Int'l L* 1 et seq and K Lenaerts and Jos A Gutierrez-Fons and Stanislas Adam, 'Exploring the Autonomy of the European Union Legal Order' (2021) 81 *ZaRV* 47.

[81] Annex II to the Council Decision of 26 November 2009 concerning the conclusion, by the European Community, of the United Nations Convention on the Rights of Persons with Disabilities, [2010] OJ L 23/35.

[82] Information regarding United Nations Convention on the Rights of Persons with Disabilities, https://ec.europa.eu/social/main.jsp?langId=en&catId=1138.

In the light of the above, and given the wide membership of the Union and diversity among the Member States, it was only a matter of time before the very limits of this formula would be tested. After all, the dispute about the conclusion of the Istanbul Convention on behalf of the Union touches upon the very function of mixity as a pragmatic solution to the coexistence of Union competence and national powers in the context of a given agreement. There is, therefore, a strong policy dimension against which this episode may be viewed. This was not lost to the Commission, for instance: in its 2015 Roadmap to the accession to the Istanbul Convention, it argued as follows:

> Provided that the Union would accede, alongside Member States, to the full extent of its competences, ratification of the Istanbul Convention would put the Union in a strong position as regards monitoring of enforcement of the Istanbul Convention also beyond the Union and would send a firm political message. At the same time, the Union would become internationally accountable for the implementation of those parts of the Istanbul Convention. Union accession would also answer the calls from the European Parliament and stakeholders for binding measures at Union level.[83]

The ambition underpinning this statement sits uneasily with the discord between the institutions about how to exercise the Union's competence. It is undermined by the fundamental divergence of views between the Member States about the ratification of the Convention and the effectiveness of its provisions within their legal order. Addressing these issues while taking into account the constitutionally significant procedure in Article 218 TFEU will be no mean feat.

[83] Roadmap to the accession to the Istanbul Convention, www.europarl.europa.eu/legislative-train/theme-area-of-justice-and-fundamental-rights/file-eu-accession-to-the-istanbul-convention.

11

The New Review Mechanism of the UN Smuggling of Migrants Protocol

Challenges in Measuring the EU's and its Member States' Compliance

TAMÁS MOLNÁR* AND CHLOÉ BRIÈRE

I. Introduction

> The question of divided [EU and Member State] competences remains a matter of some concern from the perspective of the coherence of treaty rights and obligations – including the responsibility for any breach that may occur.[1]
>
> UN International Law Commission in 2006.

All the European Union (EU) Member States except Ireland ratified the 2000 United Nations (UN) Protocol against Migrant Smuggling by Land, Sea and Air[2] ('Smuggling of Migrants Protocol' or 'SoM Protocol'), which supplements the UN Convention against Transnational Organized Crime (UNTOC)[3] and must be interpreted together with it.[4] The EU became a party to the Protocol in 2006,[5] and annexed a declaration to

*The views expressed in this chapter are solely those of the author and do not necessarily represent the views or the position of the European Union Agency for Fundamental Rights.

[1] ILC (2006), *Fragmentation of International Law: Difficulties Arising from the Diversification and Expansion of International Law*, A/CN.4/L.682.

[2] Protocol against the Smuggling of Migrants by Land, Sea and Air, supplementing the United Nations Convention against Transnational Organized Crime, New York, 15 November 2000, entered into force 28 January 2004 (UNTS Vol 2241, 507).

[3] United Nations Convention against Transnational Organized Crime, New York, 15 November 2000, entered into force 29 September 2003 (UNTS Vol 2225, 209). For a comprehensive analysis of the SoM Protocol, see AT Gallagher and F David, *The International Law of Migrant Smuggling* (CUP, 2014); and D McClean, *Transnational Organized Crime. A Commentary on the UN Convention and its Protocols* (OUP, 2007) Part 3.

[4] SoM Protocol, Art 1(2).

[5] Council Decision of 24 July 2006 (2006/617/EC) [2006] OJ L262/34 and Council Decision of 24 July 2006 (2006/616/EC) [2006] OJ L262/24.

the Protocol delineating in vague terms the EU's competences in the matters covered by it.[6] Remarkably, compliance with the undertaken obligations by contracting parties has not really been measured since the entry into force of the SoM Protocol in 2004, as no oversight or monitoring mechanism has been established under neither the UNTOC nor the SoM Protocol.

In October 2018, this was remedied by the establishment of a Mechanism for the Review of the Implementation of the UNTOC and the Protocols thereto, with a view to strengthening, inter alia, the implementation of the SoM Protocol.[7] This peer-review process started at the end of 2020 with the drawing of lots to do the pairing of contracting parties for the review process[8] and covering all contracting parties. Together with its Member States, the EU itself shall be subject to such Review Mechanism,[9] but the modalities of its participation are yet to be finalised.

Based on the rules and modalities of the Review Mechanism, this chapter seeks to examine how its drafters addressed the specificities of the mixity stemming from both the EU's and its Member States' participation in the SoM Protocol; and the implications of this mixity in future practice. Within the multilateral 'mixed agreements', third parties typically want to know beforehand who is voting (to avoid the double exercise of rights), who is implementing (to ensure compliance) and who is responsible for the infringements of the agreement (even before an internationally wrongful act is actually committed).[10] The same applies to who should respond to the external review of the implementation of undertaken international obligations, and this exercise was not carried out in advance for the SoM Protocol.

From the oversight perspective, this chapter thus analyses a concrete example of an international agreement with joint participation of the EU and its Member States. It analyses the roots of mixity (section II), then a concrete example of this mixity in the implementation of the SoM Protocol (section III) and its new refractions under the Review Mechanism (section IV); then formulates some concluding remarks and presents an outlook for the future (section V).

II. The EU as Party to the Smuggling of Migrants Protocol: The Roots of Mixity

To answer this multifaceted phenomenon called 'migrant smuggling', the SoM Protocol relies on a variety of measures to fight criminals involved in the smuggling of people, but

[6] Declaration submitted to the UN Secretariat available at https://treaties.un.org/Pages/ParticipationStatus.aspx?clang=_en (accessed 1 February 2021), under Ch XVIII, 12b (s 'Declarations and Reservations').

[7] Conference of the Parties to the UNTOC, Resolution 9/1 (2018), Establishment of the Mechanism for the Review of the Implementation of the UNTOC and the Protocols thereto.

[8] Result of drawing lots available at https://www.unodc.org/documents/organized-crime/Drawing_of_Lots/Final_-_Output.pdf (accessed 1 February 2021). During the review phase (until October 2030), the UNTOC Secretariat (practically the UNODC) will work with states to support and assist the desk reviews and prepare the report on trends and patterns.

[9] The EU will be reviewed in the second year of the process by Austria and Saint Kitts and Nevis.

[10] P-J Kuijper, *Of 'Mixity' and 'Double-hatting'. EU External Relations Law Explained* (Amsterdam University Press, 2008) 12; A Delgado Casteleiro, 'EU Declarations of Competence to Multilateral Agreements: A Useful Reference Base?' (2012) 17 *European Foreign Affairs Review* 4, 492.

also to ensure the respect of migrants' rights and effective border controls. Whereas the EU Member States remain sovereign in managing migration, they have conferred certain competences to the EU, including those aiming to prevent and combat migrant smuggling. These competences, which expanded over time, encompass the development of a common migration policy (Article 79 TFEU) or the approximation of certain criminal offences (Article 83 TFEU). This section seeks to succinctly present the core elements of the SoM Protocol and the reasons why the EU became party to it, alongside its Member States.

A. Overview of the SoM Protocol: The Content

The purpose of the SoM Protocol is to prevent and punish migrant smuggling and to promote cooperation among states on this matter (Article 2) while protecting the rights of smuggled migrants and preventing the worst forms of their exploitation, which often characterise the smuggling process ('prevent – punish – protect').

The Protocol is the first international instrument of universal character which defines 'smuggling of migrants' (Article 3). This means 'the procurement, in order to obtain, directly or indirectly, a financial or other material benefit, of the illegal entry of a person into a State Party of which the person is not a national or a permanent resident'. The offences must be 'transnational in nature' and involve an 'organized criminal group' as defined in the UNTOC, since the provisions of the UNTOC apply, in principle, to the Protocol (Article 1(2)).[11] The definition of 'smuggling of migrants' thus covers intentional acts driven by some form of material gain[12] and connects smuggling with organised crime.[13] The formulation of the definition implies the non-criminalisation of humanitarian assistance provided to people on the move, as confirmed by the Interpretative Notes to the Protocol.[14] States have to adopt legislation criminalising those smuggling others for a profit – but not those who facilitate the entry and stay of others for humanitarian reasons, nor those who have been smuggled (Article 6).[15]

The SoM Protocol also sets out measures against smuggling of migrants by sea, accompanied by fundamental rights safeguards (Articles 7–9); the duty to exchange information to further prevention and international cooperation (Article 10); obligations to strengthen border controls (Article 11) and enhance document security (Articles 12–13); as well to engage in training and technical cooperation (Article 14); alongside taking other preventive measures (Article 15). A number of protection and assistance measures are laid down in Article 16 (eg the obligation to protect the rights of smuggled migrants under international law, which include the right to life and the right

[11] Organised crime is not a constitutive element required to prosecute the smuggling of migrants in national law, but this element triggers the application of the SoM Protocol.

[12] United Nations Office of Drugs and Crime, *Issue Paper: The Concept of 'Financial or Other Material Benefit' in the Smuggling of Migrants Protocol* (New York, UN, 2017).

[13] V Mitsilegas, 'The Normative Foundations of the Criminalization of Human Smuggling: Exploring the Fault Lines Between European and International Law' (2019) 10 *New Journal of European Criminal Law* 1, 70.

[14] Interpretative notes for the official records (*travaux préparatoires*) of the negotiation of the UNTOC and the Protocols thereto, A/55/383/Add 1 (3 November 2000) para 92.

[15] Nevertheless, the SoM Protocol does not prevent the parties from adopting broader definitions of migrant smuggling under their national law, in light of Art 34(3) of the UNTOC (Gallagher and David, above, 362 and below section III).

not to be subjected to torture or other forms of ill-treatment, and the right to consular assistance). A self-standing provision is devoted to the return of smuggled migrants (Article 18), which has to be carried out 'in an orderly manner and with due regard for the safety and dignity of the person'. The Protocol also includes a specific saving clause: none of its provisions can impact existing rights and obligations, including those related to human rights, international humanitarian law and refugee law (Article 19).

The SoM Protocol thus covers a variety of issues equally falling under Member States' and EU's powers, and calls for the EU's participation, a possibility explicitly foreseen in the Protocol.[16]

B. The EU's Accession to the SoM Protocol and the Delimitation of Competences: The 'Original Sin'

The EU has been the first – and so far, only – international organisation to ratify the UNTOC and its Protocols. However, a problem arose in the delimitation of the competences of the EU and the Member States in the context of the ratification and then implementation of the SoM Protocol. Under the pre-Lisbon version of EU Treaties, in force at the time of the adoption of the Protocol, the then European Community (EC) and the EU already acquired competences to adopt measures concerning the fight against organised crime and irregular migration, as well as border management.[17]

Regarding migration, the above-mentioned fields of action fell into EC competence, transferred to the Community (ex-first pillar) by the 1997 Amsterdam Treaty. Additionally, the EU acquired limited competences in criminal matters, notably preventing and combating (organised) crime.[18] These areas of action fall under the 'area of freedom, security and justice' (AFSJ) and are considered as being, by default, an area of shared competence between the EU and its Member States.[19] The AFSJ also presents certain specificities under which the Member States may retain their competences to act (either due to a derogatory regime or through an explicit provision in the EU Treaties). As both the EU and the Member States are thus competent to implement the Protocol, tensions in the delimitation of their respective competences arose since the very beginning of the negotiations of the SoM Protocol.

Negotiations started in January 1999, with the EC being an observer and the Member States coordinating their positions.[20] In July 1999, the EC tabled a recommendation for a Council Decision authorising it to negotiate all the elements of the UNTOC and its Protocols that are subject to EU competence.[21] The Council authorised

[16] SoM Protocol Art 21(2) referring to 'regional economic integration organizations'.

[17] Ex-Art 62(2) of the then Treaty establishing the European Community (TEC) ([2002] OJ C325/33), ex-Art 63(3) TEC and ex-Art 29 of the Treaty on European Union (TEU) ([2002] OJ C325/5), introduced by the Treaty of Amsterdam ([1997] OJ C340/1), which entered into force on 1 May 1999.

[18] Ex-Art 29 TEU.

[19] Art 4(2)(j) TFEU.

[20] A Delgado Casteleiro, 'The International Responsibility of the European Union – The EU Perspective: Between Pragmatism and Proceduralisation' (2017) 15 *Cambridge Yearbook of European Legal Studies* 574, and the references therein.

[21] This is recapped in EC, 'Proposal for a Council Decision on the signing, on behalf of the European Community, of the UNTOC and its Protocols on combating trafficking in persons, especially women and

the Commission – in separate decisions, adopted under ex-Article 300(2) TEC (now Article 218(2) TFEU) – to negotiate the draft UNTOC[22] and, inter alia, the draft SoM Protocol.[23] However, this did not completely resume the tensions on the delimitation of competences, with the Member States stressing, for instance, the limited mandate of the Commission.[24] Once the negotiations were completed, the Council authorised the signing of the UNTOC and its Protocols on behalf of the EC.[25]

Following the signing of the SoM Protocol by the EC in December 2000, the Commission drafted a proposal in 2003 for a decision authorising the conclusion by the EC of the SoM Protocol, in which it developed a lengthy argument[26] justifying the Community's participation therein.[27] The Commission, invoking Articles 62(2) and 63(3) TEC[28] as substantive legal bases, referred to Protocol provisions falling under Community competence, such as those providing for measures to be taken at borders or concerning travel documents. According to the Commission, such measures fell within the scope of the *acquis communautaire*, namely the Convention implementing the Schengen Agreement[29] and supplementing secondary EU legislation,[30] as well as EU Regulations on visas.[31] However, the Council did not share this view and did not take further action in the following years, mainly due to the delimitation of competences. This power struggle is well evidenced by a 2005 Commission Communication concerning the fight against trafficking in human beings, regretting that the Council did not adopt the decision on the conclusion of the SoM Protocol due to disagreement on the extent of Community competence.[32]

The Commission finally tabled an amended proposal in October 2005 for a Council Decision approving the Protocol on behalf of the EC.[33] The revised version reflects notably the evolution and adoption of new pieces of secondary EU law related to migration

children, and the smuggling of migrants by land, air and sea' COM (2000) 760 final. See also 'Proposal for a Council Decision on the conclusion, on behalf of the European Community, of the UNTOC', COM (2003)512 final.

[22] Council Decision of 2 May 2000 (not published).

[23] Council Decision of 14 February 2000 (not published).

[24] Ad Hoc Committee on the Elaboration of a Convention against Transnational Organized Crime, ninth session, Vienna, 5–16 June 2000, A/AC.254/28, para 15, quoted in Delgado Casteleiro (2017) above.

[25] Council Decision of 8 December 2000 (2001/87/EC) on the signing, on behalf of the EC, of the UNTOC and its Protocols on combating trafficking in persons, especially women and children, and the smuggling of migrants by land, air and sea [2001] OJ L30/44.

[26] J Monar, 'The EU as an International Actor in the Domain of Justice and Home Affairs' (2004) 9 *European Foreign Affairs Review* 3, 407–08.

[27] Proposal for the conclusion of the UNTOC, above.

[28] Art 62 TEC governed measures at external borders, whereas Art 63(3) TEC concerned measures on immigration policy, including illegal immigration and illegal residence and repatriation of illegal residents.

[29] Arts 26 and 27(1) of the Convention implementing the Schengen Agreement of 14 June 1985 between the Governments of the States of the Benelux Economic Union, the Federal Republic of Germany and the French Republic on the gradual abolition of checks at their common borders [2000] OJ L239/19.

[30] Council Directive 2001/51/EC of 28 June 2001 supplementing Art 26 of the Convention implementing the Schengen Agreement of 14 June 1985 [2001] OJ L187/45.

[31] Council Regulation (EC) No 1683/95 of 29 May 1995 laying down a uniform format for visas [1995] OJ L164/1, amended by Regulation (EC) No 334/2002 [2002] OJ L53/7.

[32] EC, 'Fighting Trafficking in Human Beings: An Integrated Approach and Proposals for an Action Plan' (Communication COM(2005)514 final) 6.

[33] EC, 'Amended proposal for a Council Decision on the conclusion, on behalf of the European Community, of the Protocol against the Smuggling of Migrants by Land, Sea and Air, supplementing the UNTOC' COM(2005) 503 final.

and borders between 2003 and 2005. All of these subsequently adopted EU instruments led to a redefinition of the scope of Community competences regarding the conclusion of the SoM Protocol and implicated the inclusion of new legal bases in the draft decision, such as Article 66 TEC (administrative cooperation between the Member States' authorities), Article 179 TEC (development cooperation) and Article 181a TEC (economic, financial and technical cooperation with third countries).

After some back and forth, in July 2006, the Council finally gave its authorisation, in two separate decisions because of different legal bases, to conclude the SoM Protocol by the Community. One was adopted on legal bases relating to development cooperation and economic, financial and technical cooperation with third countries[34] and another on the basis of primary EU law provisions relating to immigration and external borders.[35] The decisions have been paired with a declaration on the extent of the EC's competence,[36] an obligation for 'regional economic integration organizations' under the Protocol (Article 21(3)). This declaration does not contain substantial differences from the declaration annexed to the Commission's amended Proposal. It has been categorised as a rather general and vague declaration of competence, without any reference to specific provisions of the SoM Protocol for which the EC (now: the EU) would be competent, or indicating which entity exercises which rights and implements which obligations.[37] This contrasts, for instance, with the declaration of competence deposited to the UNTOC, which includes references to specific provisions of the Convention relating to EU competence.[38]

The subject matters covered and the actions envisaged by the SoM Protocol, which fall under EU competence, typically belong to AFSJ shared competences, under which the EU is competent to adopt measures relating to irregular migration and crime prevention. Other minor aspects of the Protocol fall under the EU's competence in development cooperation, another area of shared competence under Article 4(4) TFEU. Consequently, as in multiple other occasions, the content of the SoM Protocol required its conclusion as a 'mixed agreement' as used in the EU jargon.[39]

The declaration of competence, deposited along with the EU's ratification instrument, reproduced partially below, reflects the above complexity:

> The Community points out that it has competence with regard to crossing of external borders of the Member States, regulating standards and procedures when carrying out checks on persons at such borders and rules on visas for intended stays of no more than three months. The Community is also competent for measures on immigration policy regarding conditions of

[34] Council Decision of 24 July 2006 (2006/616/EC), above.

[35] Council Decision of 24 July 2006 (2006/617/EC), above.

[36] Annex II of Council Decisions 2006/616/EC and 2006/617/EC, attached to the EU's ratification instrument.

[37] Delgado Casteleiro (2017) above, 509.

[38] Council Decision of 29 April 2004 (2004/579/EC) on the conclusion, on behalf of the EC, of the UNTOC [2004] OJ L261/69.

[39] On the mixed agreements in general, see eg C Kaddous, 'Les Accords Mixtes' in N Aloupi et al (eds), *Les Accords Internationaux de l'Union Européenne (Commentaire J Mégret)* (Editions de l'Université de Bruxelles, 2019, 3rd edn) 301–43; C Hillion and P Koutrakos (eds), *Mixed Agreements Revisited: The EU and its Member States in the World* (Hart Publishing, 2010); J Heliskoski, *Mixed Agreements as a Technique for Organizing the International Relations of the European Community and its Member States* (Kluwer Law International, 2001); NA Neuwahl, 'Joint Participation in International Treaties and the Exercise of Power by the EEC and Its Member States: Mixed Agreements' (1991) 28 *Common Market Law Review* 717.

> entry and residence and measures to counter illegal immigration and illegal residence, including repatriation of illegal residents. Relevant Community legislation is comprised in the Schengen acquis on external borders and on travel and identity documents, as integrated into the framework of the European Community, and its further development. Hence in these fields it is for the Community to adopt the relevant rules and regulations and, within its competence, to enter into external undertakings with third States or competent international organisations.
>
> In addition, Community policy in the sphere of development cooperation complements policies pursued by Member States and includes provisions to prevent and combat smuggling of migrants.

In addition, the competences conferred to the EU have evolved over time. This happens when an area of shared competence becomes exclusive EU competence by way of pre-emption;[40] and when amendments to the founding treaties redraw the boundaries of the EU and Member State powers by conferring further competences – either shared or exclusive – to the Union. This impacted the EU's delimitation of competences for the implementation of the SoM Protocol, even though some aspects of the Protocol remain covered by EU legal instruments adopted in the early 2000s. The below table (table 11.1) gives an overview of the key provisions of the SoM Protocol pertaining to either the EU or Member State competences (or both) as regards the subject matters covered, based on the current powers of the EU under the post-Lisbon TFEU.

Table 11.1 Tentative Attribution of EU and Member State Competences with Regard to the SoM Protocol

<table>
<tr><th colspan="2">Provisions of/Issues Covered by the Protocol</th></tr>
<tr><th>EU competence</th><th>Member State competence</th></tr>
<tr><td colspan="2">Definition of 'smuggling' and 'illegal entry'* (Art 3(a)–(b) of the Protocol)
➔ Requires legislation defining these concepts both at EU and national levels</td></tr>
<tr><td>Criminalisation of 'smuggling' and related acts (Art 6 of the Protocol)
➔ see Arts 79(2)(c) TFEU – combating illegal immigration and unauthorised residence, including removal and repatriation of persons residing without authorisation
➔ see Art 83(2) TFEU – adopting directives providing minimum rules on the approximation of criminal offences[41]
➔ secondary EU law = Facilitators' Package; composed of Directive 2002/90/EC defining the offence and Framework Decision 2002/946/JHA strengthening the penal framework to prevent facilitation</td><td>Measures against the smuggling of migrants by sea, including boarding and searching the vessel (Arts 8–9 of the Protocol)</td></tr>
</table>

(continued)

[40] A Arena, 'The Doctrine of Union Pre-emption in the EU Internal Market: Between Sein and Sollen' (2010–2011) 17 *Columbia Journal of European Law*, 477; A Arena, 'Exercise of EU Competences and Pre-emption of Member States' Powers in the Internal and the External Sphere: Towards "Grand Unification"?' (2016) 35 *Yearbook of European Law* 28.

[41] The CJEU had previously recognised the competence of adopting criminal legislation essential to ensure the effective implementation of a Union policy in an area subject to harmonisation measures (eg Case C-68/88 *Commission v Greece* [1989] EU:C:1989:339). Art 83(1) TFEU also lists the crimes for which the EU possesses an express competence to adopt criminal legislation, but migrant smuggling is not included in that list.

Table 11.1 ***(Continued)***

Provisions of/Issues Covered by the Protocol	
EU competence	***Member State competence***
Border measures (Art 11(1)–(2) and (5)–(6) of the Protocol) ➔ see Art 77(1)(b)–(c) TFEU – carrying out checks on persons and efficient monitoring of the crossing of external borders; the gradual introduction of an integrated management system for external borders ➔ secondary EU law: – Schengen Borders Code [Reg (EU) 2016/399] – European Border and Coast Guard (EBCG) Regulation (EU) 2019/1896 – Sea Borders Regulation [Reg (EU) 656/2014]	Verifying the legitimacy and validity of travel and identity documents (Art 13 of the Protocol)
Border measures – carrier obligations and carrier sanctions (Art 11(3)–(4) of the Protocol) ➔ see Art 77(1)(b)–(c) TFEU – carrying out checks on persons and efficient monitoring of the crossing of external border ➔ secondary EU law: – Carrier Sanctions Directive (2011/51/EC) – Advanced Passenger Information Directive (2004/82/EC) – Convention Implementing the Schengen Agreement, Art 26	
Security and control of travel and identity documents (Art 12 of the Protocol) ➔ see Arts 21(2) and 77(3) TFEU – facilitating the exercise of EU citizens' rights; measures concerning passports, identity cards, residence permits or any other such document ➔ secondary EU law: – Security Features and Biometrics in Passports Regulation (EU) No 2252/2004 – Security of Identity Cards and Residence Documents Regulation (EU) 2019/1157	
No criminal liability of migrants for the fact of having been the object of smuggling* (Art 5 of the Protocol)	
Cooperation to prevent and suppress the smuggling of migrants by sea* (Art 7 of the Protocol) ➔ *For the EU, see Art 77(1)(b)–(c) TFEU and the Sea Borders Regulation*	
Information exchange amongst Contracting Parties* (Art 10 of the Protocol) ➔ *For the EU, see Framework Decision 2002/946/JHA*	

(continued)

Table 11.1 ***(Continued)***

<table>
<tr><th colspan="2">Provisions of/Issues Covered by the Protocol</th></tr>
<tr><th>EU competence</th><th>Member State competence</th></tr>
<tr><td colspan="2">Training and technical cooperation, including on the prevention of smuggling of migrants and the humane treatment of migrants* (Art 14 of the Protocol)
➔ For the EU, see CEPOL Regulation [Reg (EU) 2015/2219]</td></tr>
<tr><td colspan="2">Protection and assistance measures* (Art 16 of the Protocol)
➔ For the EU, see Directive 2004/81/EC on residence permit for victims of trafficking and aggravated forms of migrant smuggling and various pieces of the EU asylum acquis</td></tr>
<tr><td colspan="2">Bilateral agreements and operational arrangements* (Art 17 of the Protocol)
➔ For the EU, see Arts 3(2) and 79(3) TFEU (readmission agreements); agreements and arrangements concluded by EU agencies (Europol, Eurojust, Frontex) in areas covered by the SoM, and diverse policy instruments developed with other regional organisations and third countries (eg mobility partnerships)</td></tr>
<tr><td>Return of smuggled migrants (Art 18 of the Protocol)
➔ see Art 79(2)(d) and (3) TFEU – combating illegal immigration and unauthorised residence, including removal and repatriation of persons residing without authorisation; concluding readmission agreements
➔ secondary EU law:
- Return Directive (2008/115/EC)
- Joint Return Flights Decision 2004/573/EC
- Directive 2003/110/EC on assistance in cases of transit for the purposes of removal by air</td><td></td></tr>
<tr><td colspan="2">Human rights saving clause* (Art 19 of the Protocol)
➔ For the EU, see the Charter of Fundamental Rights of the EU and various fundamental rights clauses in the Facilitators' Package, the Schengen Borders Code, the Sea Borders Regulation, the Return Directive, the EBCG Regulation etc.</td></tr>
</table>

Notes: * = matter of prima facie shared competence between the EU and its Member States.

Source: authors' compilation, based on pieces of EU acquis and areas of state sovereignty/domestic jurisdiction not touched by EU law.

As Table 11.1 displays, since the EU ratified the SoM Protocol, the competences conferred to the Union have drastically evolved. Most of the elements of the Protocol are regulated under EU law, framing the exercise of the Member States' operational and implementation powers in controlling the EU's external borders. Similar considerations apply to the more criminal justice-oriented measures of the SoM Protocol. The above complexity and evolving nature of the EU competences, as well as the prolific EU law-making since the accession to the SoM Protocol, point to the insufficiency and vagueness of the EU's declaration of competence, which gives little guidance to third partners about the exact width and depth of EU competences in the matters covered by the Protocol.

Seen from a broader international law perspective, the general rules of international responsibility as they currently stand do not specifically address the question of how to determine the respective obligations of an international organisation and its members in cases where both are parties to a treaty.[42] In this respect, the EC argued in its submissions on the draft Articles on the Responsibility of International Organizations (ARIO) to the International Law Commission (ILC) that the question of apportionment of international obligations should be 'entirely determined by the rules of the organisation, since these rules define the tasks and powers of the organisation which possesses its own international legal personality, vis-à-vis those of the member States'.[43] In addition, the EU takes the view that apportionment of obligations 'is really the primary question' and should be clearly distinguished from the secondary question of attribution of conduct.[44] This echoes the typically one-sided, EU-law centred approach, not endorsing the viewpoint of public international law under which attribution comes first and 'apportioning' of obligations is only an intra-EU matter which does not affect responsibility in the eyes of third partners.

C. The Need to Update the EU Declaration of Competences to the SoM Protocol

The delineation of the respective competences of the EU and its Member States under the SoM Protocol remains a complex issue. Not only was this exercise imperfect when the EC became a party to the SoM Protocol, but the EU failed to address this gap at a later stage. The declaration of competence attached to the SoM Protocol indeed suffers from an significant flaw: it has not been updated to reflect the important evolutions in EU constitutional and substantive law, such as the recognition of a legal personality to the EU, the abolition of 'pillars' and the development of new Union instruments in fields covered by the SoM Protocol.

Zooming in on one example from Table 11.1, the European Border and Coast Guard Agency (Frontex) has received increasing powers conferred to them in the assistance of national border guards for controlling the EU's external borders. Frontex is tasked with assisting and coordinating national border guards and creating a standing corps of 10,000 staff, with executive powers to effectively support on the ground Member States in their efforts to protect the external borders and fight cross-border crime.[45] Although the revamped Frontex Regulation indicates that it does not affect the division

[42] For more on this issue, J Heliskoski, 'EU Declarations of Competence and International Responsibility' in M Evans and P Koutrakos (eds), *The International Responsibility of the European Union. European and International Perspectives* (Hart Publishing, 2013) 189–212.

[43] ILC, *Responsibility of International Organisations: Comments and Observations Received from International Organisations*, Doc A/CN.4/545 (25 July 2004) 26 (para 2). See also the view taken by Advocate General Mischo in Case C-13/00, *Commission v Ireland*, EU:C:2001:643, para 30.

[44] ILC, *Responsibility of International Organisations: Comments and Observations Received from International Organisations*, Doc A/CN.4/545 (25 July 2004) 26 (para 3), quoted by G Marín Durán, 'Untangling the International Responsibility of the EU and Its Member States in the World Trade Organization Post-Lisbon: A Competence/Remedy Model' (2017) 28 *European Journal of International Law* 702.

[45] Regulation (EU) 2019/1896 of the European Parliament and of the Council of 13 November 2019 on the European Border and Coast Guard and repealing Regulations (EU) No 1052/2013 and (EU) 2016/1624 [2019] OJ L295/1, Art 54.

of competence between the Union and the Member States, nor the obligations of the Member States under international law, including the SoM Protocol,[46] it can be argued that the agency exercises functions sufficient to establish its responsibility for violations of human rights,[47] and it has been criticised for its role in contested operations.[48] Moreover, EU competences in the fields of development cooperation and migration are also well-established and intertwined, as recognised by the Court of Justice of the EU.[49] As per the EU's competence in criminal matters, the EU has in the previous decade signed or ratified international instruments using criminal law legal basis, such as Council of Europe's conventions on the prevention of terrorism[50] and the prevention of violence against women respectively,[51] establishing its competence to enter into international obligations in the field of criminal justice.

Despite these evolutions, the declaration of competences remains unchanged, a flaw shared by most of the declarations of competence made by the EU when ratifying multilateral treaties.[52] They often include a standard sentence pinpointing the dynamic nature of the scope and exercise of the EU's competences and referring to the instrument's provision providing for a duty to update declarations.[53] However, neither the Commission nor the EEAS is monitoring the need to update declarations of competences. This may be explained by the amount of work it would represent and the sensitive nature of such exercise. For instance, the precise scope or the nature of the EU's competence could be a controversial issue, with the Member States' views diverging from those of EU institutions. Consequently, declarations of competence are rarely updated,[54] even though a recent example can be found with the one attached to the UN Convention against Corruption (UNCAC) linked to the forthcoming review of the EU's implementation of the text.[55] This precedent pleads for a crucial preliminary step prior to the EU's actual participation in the Review Mechanism: the submission of an up-to-date declaration of competences regarding the SoM Protocol. To that end, a thorough

[46] Ibid, recital (20).

[47] M Fink, *Frontex and Human Rights, Responsibility in 'Multi-Actor Situations' under the ECHR and EU Public Liability Law* (OUP, 2018).

[48] Human Rights Watch, *EU: Probe Frontex Complicity in Border Abuses*, 9 November 2020, www.hrw.org/news/2020/11/09/eu-probe-frontex-complicity-border-abuses.

[49] Case C-377/12, *Commission v Council*, EU:C:2014:1903, paras 49–55.

[50] Council Decision (EU) 2018/889 [2018] OJ L159/1 based on Art 83(1) TFEU.

[51] Council Decision (EU) 2017/865 [2017] OJ L131/11. It was accompanied by a second Council Decision (EU) 2017/866 [2017] OJ L131/13, based on Art 78(2) TFEU with respect to issues on asylum and *non-refoulement*.

[52] C Contartese and L Pantaleo, 'Division of Competences, EU Autonomy and the Determination of the Respondent Party: Proceduralisation as a Possible Way-Out?' in E Neframi and M Gatti (eds), *Constitutional Issues of EU External Relations Law* (Nomos, 2018) 414.

[53] Declaration of competence attached to the SoM Protocol, para 5 referring to Art 21(3) of the Protocol. For another example, Council Decision of 26 November 2009 concerning the conclusion, by the European Community, of the United Nations Convention on the Rights of Persons with Disabilities [2010] OJ L23/35, Declaration of competence, para 6, referring to Art 44(1) of the Convention.

[54] For example, the EU declaration of competence attached to the UNCLOS, which has never been updated since 1982, G Marín Durán, 'EU External Environmental Policy', in RA Wessels and J Larik (eds), *EU External Relations Law* (Hart Publishing, 2020) 378.

[55] EC, 'Review of the EU under the Implementation Review Mechanism of the UNCAC' (Communication COM(2020) 793 final).

and meticulous analysis of how the obligations undertaken in the Protocol were implemented is necessary, notably to precisely identify the contours of areas in which the EU has competence.

The acquis adopted since the early 2000s in the fields covered by the Protocol constitutes a basis to precisely identify the areas in which the EU has competence and the nature of its competence, as well as the areas in which the Member States have kept their competence or retain a margin of discretion. From the perspective of apportioning international responsibility, Hoffmeister introduced the category of 'normative control' exercised by the EU to help determine the EU's shared or ancillary responsibility. He suggests two conditions for determining such 'normative control' of the Union: 1) EU law governs the substantive legality of the Member State action, and 2) the EU judiciary ultimately controls this.[56] One might argue that these conditions are met in a number of policy areas falling under the purview of the SoM Protocol, especially when it comes to controls at external borders, carrier sanctions and criminalisation of smuggling and related acts. The next section looks more closely at the legal issues stemming from this mixity in the implementation of the Protocol.

III. Mixity in the SoM Protocol and its Implementation: The Case of Criminalisation of Migrant Smuggling and Related Acts

Further to the conclusion of the SoM Protocol as a mixed agreement, accompanied by a declaration of competence with respect to the EU's participation, the ensuing analysis focuses on examining the ramifications of mixity in the implementation of the Protocol. It will delve into the criminalisation of migrant smuggling as an illustration of such mixity.

The importance and added value of the SoM Protocol are in the internationally agreed definition provided for the act of 'smuggling of migrants' and the complementary obligation for parties to criminalise this behaviour (Articles 3(a) and 6). This represents a major step in favour of international cooperation in criminal matters since the existence of a common definition of the offence facilitates compliance with the requirement of dual criminality, found in many extraditions and mutual assistance treaties. Of particular importance is the requirement of a 'financial or other material benefit' as one of the constitutive elements of the offence, allowing to distinguish criminals from bona fide rescuers and humanitarian helpers.

The 'implementation' of such obligation in the EU intervened in a specific pre-existing legal framework. At the time of the negotiations of the SoM Protocol, the first 'European' definitions of smuggling of migrants were included in diverse instruments, namely the CISA[57] and the Convention establishing Europol,[58] both requiring

[56] F Hoffmeister, 'Litigating against the EU and Its Member States: Who Responds under the ILC's Draft Articles on International Responsibility of International Organizations?' (2010) 21 *European Journal of International Law* 3, 734.

[57] CISA, Art 27(1), covering assistance to enter or reside within the territory of a Schengen participating state.

[58] Council Act of 26 July 1995 drawing up the Convention based on Art K.3 of the Treaty on European Union, on the establishment of a European Police Office [1995] OJ C316/1.

a 'financial gain', and coexisting within the EU legal order. Additionally, a 1997 Joint Action on combating trafficking in human beings defined trafficking for sexual exploitation as including the facilitation of entry into, transit through, residence in or exit from a Member State, thus adding to the confusion between the offences of trafficking and smuggling.[59]

In the early 2000s, the EU Member States stressed the importance of tackling the criminal networks making a profit from the trafficking in human beings, conflating again trafficking and smuggling. The negotiations of the UNTOC and its Protocols on Migrant Smuggling and Trafficking in Persons were clearly among the factors in favour of reinforcing the legal framework applicable to combat such behaviours. A 'specialisation movement' was noticeable with the adoption of separate EU instruments distinguishing between the crimes of trafficking in human beings, child pornography and assistance to irregular migration.

Although the Framework Decision on human trafficking explicitly referred to the new international instruments,[60] EU legislation addressing migrant smuggling results from a slightly different context. The proposal for reforming existing EU instruments was tabled by France in reaction to the '*drame de Douvres*', a tragic case of 58 migrants dying of asphyxia in a truck in the course of their migratory journey.[61] Relying on the right of initiative open at the time to the Member States, France proposed a single instrument,[62] and the proposal was later divided into two separate proposals: a proposal for a Directive and a proposal for a Framework Decision. This led to the adoption of two instruments known as the Facilitators' Package composed of a Council Directive defining the facilitation of unauthorised entry, transit and residence[63] and a Framework Decision on strengthening the penal framework to prevent the facilitation of unauthorised entry, transit and residence.[64] The Directive requires the Member States to criminalise the 'facilitation of unauthorised entry, transit and residence' (Article 1(1)), whereas the Framework Decision imposes on the Member States to make it punishable by effective, proportionate and dissuasive criminal penalties which may entail extradition (Article 1(1)). Such a complex legal architecture reflects the division of competences between the then Community, competent to adopt 'first pillar' instruments relating to migration, and the then Union, competent to adopt 'third pillar' instruments approximating national criminal legislations.

The Facilitation Directive contains the definition of migrant smuggling applicable within the EU legal order, which can be considered the transposition of the corresponding definition in the SoM Protocol. However, the EU legislator chose a different

[59] 97/154/JHA Joint Action of 24 February 1997 concerning action to combat trafficking in human beings and sexual exploitation of children [1997] OJ L63/2, Title I A (i) and B (b) (d).

[60] Council Framework Decision of 19 July 2002 (2002/629/JHA) on combating trafficking in human beings [2002] OJ L203/1, recital (4).

[61] S Claisse and J-S Jamart, 'La Lutte Contre L'Immigration Irrégulière au sein de l'Union Européenne: Enjeux et Perspectives de L'Harmonisation Pénale' (2002) 82 *Revue de Droit Pénal et de Criminologie* 1, 36.

[62] Council Doc 9892/00, 30 June 2000.

[63] Council Directive 2002/90/EC of 28 November 2002 defining the facilitation of unauthorised entry, transit and residence [2002] OJ L328/17.

[64] Council Framework Decision of 28 November 2002 (2002/946/JHA) on strengthening the penal framework to prevent the facilitation of unauthorised entry, transit and residence [2002] OJ L328/1.

terminology ('facilitation') and made its own definition of the constitutive elements of the offence. The requirement of a 'financial gain' only applies to persons who intentionally assist irregular *residence* within the territory of a Member State and does not apply to persons who intentionally assist irregular *entry in or transit across* the territory of a Member State. This differentiation results from a compromise between the Member States, divided between those in favour of retaining the financial gain test for all forms of assistance, and those willing to abolish it,[65] notably to facilitate the prosecution of offenders.[66]

This contrasts with the definition provided for in the SoM Protocol, which targets organised groups who smuggle migrants for financial or other material benefits.[67] This requirement is identified as essential in the *travaux préparatoires*,[68] later referred to in the Legislative Guides accompanying the Protocol, and in the Model Law against Migrant Smuggling. The distance of the EU's approach from the SoM Protocol is somehow tempered by the definition in the Framework Decision of aggravating circumstances, requiring the Member States to punish irregular entry and transit of a maximum sentence of not less than eight years when committed for financial gain (Article 2(3)).

Nevertheless, the EU's divergence from the SoM Protocol is not remedied by a clear exemption for those providing assistance to migrants without a financial motive and acting out of humanitarian considerations. The Facilitation Directive refers to the *possibility* for the Member States not to impose sanctions where the aim of the behaviour is to provide humanitarian assistance to the person concerned (Article 1(2)). This exemption is left at the discretion of the Member States[69] and thus fails to afford sufficient clarity and legal certainty to those who provide humanitarian assistance, something that an explicit reference to 'material gain' would have achieved.[70] Several sources account for the diversity of the national choices, including reports of the EU Fundamental Rights Agency,[71] a UNODC issue paper[72] and a study from the Council of Europe's European Committee on Crime Problems.[73]

Recent policy developments further failed to address this gap between the SoM Protocol and EU standards.[74] After an extensive evaluation, the Commission rejected the idea of revising the Facilitators' Package, arguing that their effective implementation and the reinforced exchange of knowledge and good practices could contribute to

[65] On such opposition, see N Rogers and S Peers, *EU Immigration and Asylum Law, Text and Commentary* (Martinus Nijhoff Publishers, 2006) 830–31.

[66] A Weyembergh, *Le Rapprochement des Législations: Condition de L'Espace Pénal Européen et Révélateur de ses Tensions* (Université Libre de Bruxelles, 2004), vol II, 258.

[67] UNODC, *Legislative Guides: UNTOC* (Vienna 2004) 340 (paras 28 and 32).

[68] Interpretative Notes, A/55/383/Add 1, 3 November 2000, para 88.

[69] S Carrera et al, 'Countering Migrant Smuggling: The EU's Policy Approach' in *Policing Humanitarianism: EU Policies Against Human Smuggling and their Impact on Civil Society* (Hart Publishing, 2019) 18.

[70] Claisse and Jamart, above 45.

[71] FRA, *Criminalisation of Migrants in an Irregular Situation and of Persons Engaging with Them* (Publications Office of the EU, 2014); FRA, *Fundamental Rights Report 2018* (Publications Office of the EU, 2018) s 6.3.3; and FRA, *Fundamental Rights Report 2019* (Publications Office of the EU, 2019) s 6.1.5.

[72] UNODC, *The Profit Element in the Smuggling of Migrants Protocol* (2017) 124.

[73] ECCP, *National Laws Relating to Smuggling of Migrants in Council of Europe Member States* (working document), 70th Plenary Session, Strasbourg, 27–30 June 2016.

[74] Mitsilegas, above, 169, fn 114.

avoiding the criminalisation of genuine humanitarian assistance.[75] This became a source of tension with the European Parliament, which called for the Member States to transpose, in line with the SoM Protocol, the humanitarian exemption provided for in the Directive.[76] The adoption, in September 2020, of Commission guidance on the implementation of EU rules on 'facilitation' as part of its New Pact on Migration and Asylum[77] does not remedy the situation either. Even though the soft law document clarifies that the criminalisation of those providing humanitarian assistance is not allowed under EU law, it only addresses a general policy recommendation to the Member States, inviting those who have not done so to make use of the exemption clause in the Facilitation Directive.[78] This raises further doubts regarding the correct implementation, within the EU legal order, of the obligation to criminalise migrant smuggling. Making use of the margin of discretion provided for in EU law, many Member States, like a number of other states parties to the SoM Protocol,[79] have not included a 'financial or other material benefit' element in their domestic definition of migrant smuggling. This results in a situation where they might comply with their obligations under EU law and not with those stemming from the SoM Protocol.

In that regard, the Commission's preference for soft law instruments over a revision of the EU instruments casts doubts on the capacity of the EU to trigger the amendment of the most contentious national legislations. Moreover, the non-compulsory nature of the exemption prevents the possibility for the Commission to initiate infringement proceedings against those Member States, which criminalise smuggling too broadly. In such context, could the EU be in breach of its obligations stemming from the SoM Protocol? This might be answered negatively, as the SoM Protocol read together with the UNTOC, only provides for minimum standards, leaving parties to adopt stricter measures than those provided for therein.[80] Furthermore, the EU's competence in defining criminal offences remains, even under the Lisbon Treaty, limited to the establishment of minimum rules, and its competence in exempting from criminal liability certain behaviours is even more limited with the only existing precedent providing for an invitation addressed to national authorities rather than for a fully harmonised and legally binding exemption.[81] States thus retain a wide discretion to criminalise both under the SoM Protocol and EU law, and the implementation of the obligation to criminalise under the SoM Protocol illustrates the challenges of doing so in fields of shared competences.

[75] EC, *REFIT Evaluation of the EU Legal Framework Against Facilitation of Unauthorised Entry, Transit and Residence*, SWD(2017) 117 final, 35.

[76] European Parliament, Resolution of 5 July 2018 on guidelines for the Member States to prevent humanitarian assistance from being criminalised, P8TA(2018)0314, paras 3 and 6.

[77] EC, *Guidance on the Implementation of EU Rules on Definition and Prevention of the Facilitation of Unauthorised Entry, Transit and Residence* (Communication C(2020)6470 final).

[78] Ibid, 7–8, analysed in A Marletta, 'The Commission "Guidance" on Facilitation and Humanitarian Assistance to Migrants' *EU Law Analysis Blog* (29 September 2020).

[79] UNODC, Working Group on Smuggling of Migrants, *Background Paper – Examination of the 'Financial or Material Benefit' Aspect of the Definition of Smuggling of Migrants*, CTOC/COP/WG.7/2017/4, para 26.

[80] UNTOC, Art 34(3).

[81] Directive 2011/36/EU of 5 April 2011 on preventing and combating trafficking in human beings and protecting its victims [2011] OJ L101/1, Art 8.

IV. The Review Mechanism and the SoM Protocol: Issues of Mixity in New Refractions

The compliance with the undertaken obligations, both by the EU and its Member States, in the SoM Protocol has not been measured since it entered into force, as no oversight or monitoring mechanism has been set up in the context of the Palermo instruments of transnational criminal law.

The issue regained attention in recent years with the October 2018 decision within the Conference of Parties (CoP) of the UNTOC and its Protocols to elaborate a Review Mechanism – after almost ten years of intergovernmental talks. This is a key development in parallel to the efforts for achieving universal ratification of the Protocols.[82] This section first addresses the content and future functioning of the Review Mechanism elaborated for assessing the implementation of the UNTOC and its Protocols (section IV.A), and then it moves on to a prospective analysis of the legal issues and challenges to be solved prior to the actual review of the EU's implementation of the SoM Protocol (section IV.B).

A. A Brief Overview of the Review Mechanism

The SoM Protocol – akin to its 'mother instrument', the UNTOC – has not been endowed a mechanism overseeing or monitoring its implementation. Article 32(4) of the UNTOC left the setting up of a Review Mechanism to the discretion of the CoP, without further accompanying guidance given by the Interpretative Notes.[83] For a while, the CoP itself reviewed the implementation of the Convention and its Protocols. However, its efforts to gather information on contracting parties' compliance with the undertaken obligations have not been successful, mainly due to a general 'reporting fatigue' of states, given their numerous reporting obligations under multiple treaties in other fields of international law,[84] which resulted in a low response rate to the questionnaire used for evaluation.[85] When the CoP changed its focus towards the elaboration of a formal review process in the late 2000s, long years of diplomatic struggles followed with a number of states disagreeing on the desirability of such a mechanism, the involvement of non-governmental organizations (NGOs) and its financial modalities.[86]

Nevertheless, the idea proved successful, and the CoP established in October 2018 a 'Mechanism for the Review of the Implementation of the UNTOC and the

[82] Number of ratifications available at https://treaties.un.org/Pages/ParticipationStatus.aspx?clang=_en, under Chapter XVIII [Penal Matters] (accessed 1 February 2021).

[83] UNODC, *Travaux Préparatoires of the Negotiations for the Elaboration of the UNTOC and the Protocols Thereto*, UN Publication Sales No E.06.V.5 (2006) 277.

[84] Conference of the Parties to the UNTOC, Report of the OSCE-UNODC Workshop on the 'Information-Gathering Mechanism to Support and Facilitate the Work of the Conference of the Parties to the UNTOC', CTOC/COP/2006/CRP.1 (14 August 2006) para 31.

[85] Conference of the Parties to the UNTOC, Relaunching the Conference of the Parties: Note by the Executive Director, CTOC/COP/2006/10 (4 October 2006) paras 8–12.

[86] C Rose, 'The Creation of a Review Mechanism for the UN Convention against Transnational Organized Crime and its Protocols' (2020) 114 *American Journal of International Law* 1, 51–52.

Protocols thereto', with a view to strengthening the implementation of the UNTOC and its Protocols.[87] This peer-review process covers all contracting parties, including the EU Member States and the EU itself. This intergovernmental process is meant to be 'transparent, efficient, non-intrusive, inclusive and impartial'[88] and at the same time, 'non-adversarial and non-punitive and promote universal adherence to the Convention and its Protocols'.[89]

The provisions of the SoM Protocol subject to review are grouped in clusters.[90] A flagrant missing provision from this list is Article 19, which serves as the fundamental rights saving clause. The four thematic clusters are as follows: 1) criminalisation and jurisdiction; 2) prevention, technical assistance, protection measures and other measures; 3) law enforcement and the judicial system; and 4) international cooperation, mutual legal assistance and confiscation.

The procedure is centred on country reviews, conducted through desk reviews, without the benefit of a country visit (based on self-assessment questionnaires). The country review will be conducted by two other states selected by drawing lots (one state from the same regional group as the country under review and the second from another regional group). In principle, the total number of reviewing states for all instruments may not exceed four. The reviewing states will produce a country review report within six months from receipt of the completed questionnaires to be submitted to the CoP's thematic working groups. The outcome of the country review will be a 'list of observations' to be finalised upon agreement between the reviewing states and the state under review. It will not necessarily be public. As a follow-up, working groups are to prepare recommendations for the CoP and states are 'encouraged to share … information on progress achieved in connection with the lists [of observations] and on any measures planned or undertaken'.[91]

Despite the added value of establishing a Review Mechanism for the UNTOC and its Protocols – which represents a general move within the UN system towards improved monitoring of the compliance with international obligations – it appears, according to commentators, to be weaker[92] than the Review Mechanism established under the 2003 UNCAC (eg no country visits will take place).[93]

Self-assessment questionnaires (for all four clusters of articles in each instrument), guidelines for conducting the country reviews, as well as a blueprint for the lists of observations and the summaries were adopted by the CoP in October 2020 to finalise

[87] Resolution 9/1 (2018), above.

[88] Ibid, Annex – Procedures and rules for the functioning of the Mechanism for the Review of the Implementation of the UNTOC and the Protocols thereto, para 4(a).

[89] Ibid, para 4(f).

[90] Resolution 9/1 (2018), above, Appendix, Table 1 Clusters of articles of the Convention and the Protocols thereto for the purpose of the review of implementation.

[91] Procedures and rules for the functioning of the UNTOC Review Mechanism, above, para 46.

[92] Rose, above, 60; M Shaw et al, 'What to Make of the New UNTOC Review Mechanism?' *Global Initiative against Transnational Organized Crime* (2 November 2018).

[93] United Nations Convention against Corruption (UNCAC), New York, 31 October 2003, entered into force 14 December 2005 (UNTS Vol 2349, 41). Review mechanism set up by Resolution 3/1 (2009) of the Conference of the Parties to the UNCAC.

the setting up of the process.[94] The CoP ultimately agreed on a 12-year programme of review for all contracting parties, covering all four instruments over the course of four phases.[95]

B. Legal Issues of the EU's and its Member States' Participation in the Review Mechanism

At this stage, it is already possible to highlight some of the limits and key elements that the EU and its Member States can and cannot do when they are under review for their implementation of the SoM Protocol. Both substantive and procedural legal issues are worth being subject to thorough inquiry, even though at present the Review Mechanism remains in a very early stage of its rollout, making our analysis a prospective one subject to potential revisions.

As a caveat, it is worth noting that the review of 'implementation' focuses – with a view to ensuring compliance – on contracting parties' existing laws and policies, and to some extent rulings of domestic courts, but not on actual 'enforcement' by various authorities.[96] This implementation review does not cover enforcement actions, that is, ongoing operations or investigations, as well as other individual acts of law enforcement, border and immigration authorities carried out within the scope of the Protocol. This approach is evidenced by the phrasing of the self-assessment questionnaire that the parties to the SoM Protocol will have to fill in. It focuses on compiling information about national legislations and measures adopted and identifying the needs for technical assistance.[97] Consequently, and owing to the shared competences of the EU and the Member States in designing and implementing such legislations and policies, both should be subject to review.

Moreover, the EU's and its Member States 'internal' implementations of the Protocol are interconnected, due to the EU's legal standards (see the Facilitators' Package and beyond) as well as EU's peculiar monitoring and enforcement mechanisms vis-à-vis Member State actions (consider eg the EU Pilot mechanism, the infringement proceedings, the preliminary ruling procedures, and the Schengen evaluations, etc). Although the EU and its Member States are parties to the SoM Protocol on an equal footing, the Member States' implementation techniques cannot be seen in isolation from the EU legal order in matters falling under Union competence and in which the EU has actually exercised its competence; while the Union is not allowed to deviate

[94] Conference of the Parties to the UNTOC, Launch of the review process of the Mechanism for the Review of the Implementation of the UNTOC and the Protocols thereto, Resolution 10/1 (2020), CTOC/COP/2020/L.4/Rev2, para 2. Guidelines are set out in Annex I to this Resolution, the Blueprints in Annex II, and the Self-assessment questionnaires in Annex III. On their adoption, see I Tennant, 'The 10th UN Conference of Parties to the UN Convention Against Transnational Organized Crime: What Happened and What Comes Next?' *Global Initiative against Transnational Organized Crime* (23 October 2020).

[95] Procedures and rules for the functioning of the UNTOC Review Mechanism, above, para 9.

[96] Rose, above, 54.

[97] UNODC, Draft harmonised self-assessment questionnaire for the Protocol against the Smuggling of Migrants by Land, Sea and Air, supplementing the UNTOC, CTOC/COP/WG.10/2020/CRP 4, July 2020. Questionnaire later adopted on the 10th session of the CoP in October 2020.

from the SoM Protocol's spirit and letter either. On this point, after the limits of the current EU instruments on the facilitation of irregular migration addressed above, the next sub-sections address additional substantive and procedural legal issues that arise from the consideration of the EU and its Member States as subjects of international law bound by obligations deriving from the SoM Protocol.

i. Substantive (International) Legal Issues

From an international law vantage point, the starting point of the conformity assessment is that the EU 'may not invoke the rules of the organization as justification for its failure to perform the treaty' (Article 27 of the 1986 Vienna Convention on the Law of Treaties), which obligation is arguably part of customary law. This means that the Union cannot invoke secondary EU legislation adopted in the matters covered by the SoM Protocol to shield the non-compliant performance of its treaty obligations.

Another consideration is that the relations between an international organisation and its members may allow the organisation to influence the conduct of its members. It is especially so for those who have the power to take decisions binding their members, such as the European Union. Pursuant to the ARIO,[98] the EU's international responsibility would be triggered if it circumvents an international obligation through binding decisions addressed to the Member States (Article 17 ARIO).[99] The responsibility of the EU is engaged whether or not the act in question (eg a piece of secondary EU legislation addressing migrant smuggling) is internationally wrongful for the Member States to which the decision is addressed (Article 17(3) ARIO). The commentaries to the ARIO add that such an ancillary form of responsibility implies 'an intention on the part of the international organisation to take advantage of [its] separate legal personality',[100] criticised in academia as unnecessarily restricting the scope of responsibility.[101] As was aptly noted by Austria while discussing the draft ARIO, 'an international organization should not be allowed to escape responsibility by "outsourcing" its actors'.[102] True, an EU Member State may be given discretion with regard to the implementation of a given piece of EU law,[103] bringing it closer to the category of an 'authorisation' under Article 17(2) ARIO.[104] This is the case of Article 1 of the Facilitation Directive, which – next to setting out the duty to criminalise migrant smuggling irrespective of financial or any other material benefit – allows the Member States to be exempt from criminalisation 'behaviour' qualifying as the provision of humanitarian assistance to the person

[98] International Law Commission, *Articles on the Responsibility of International Organizations*, annexed to UNGA Res 66/100 (2011) UN Doc A/Res/66/100 (27 February 2012).

[99] On this form of shared, derivative or ancillary responsibility, V Lanovoy, *Complicity and its Limits in the Law of International Responsibility* (Hart Publishing, 2016) 144–46, and N Voulgaris, *Allocating Responsibility Between Member States and International Organisations* (Hart Publishing, 2019) 128–142.

[100] Commentary to Art 17 ARIO, para 4, https://legal.un.org/ilc/texts/instruments/english/commentaries/9_11_2011.pdf (accessed 1 February 2021).

[101] A Nollkaemper and N Nedeski, 'Responsibility of International Organizations "in Connection with Acts of States"' (2012) 9 *International Organizations Law Review* 1, 48; Lanovoy, above 145.

[102] Official Records of the General Assembly, Fifty-ninth Session, Sixth Committee, 22nd meeting (A/C.6/59/SR.22) para 24.

[103] ECtHR, *Bosphorus Hava Yollari Turizm ve Ticaret Anonim Şirketi v Ireland*, Application No 45036/98, Judgment of 30 June 2005, Reports of Judgments and Decisions 2005-VI, 107.

[104] Voulgaris, above 129.

concerned. However, even in this scenario, some form of shared responsibility of the EU and its Member States can be established, notably, if a Member State has not employed this more favourable 'may clause' and thus 'circumvention actually occurs'.[105]

An analogous – or rather converse – situation may occur the other way around under Article 61 ARIO: A state's international responsibility incurs 'if, by taking advantage of the fact that the organization has competence in relation to the subject matter of one of the State's international obligations, it circumvents that obligation by causing the organization to commit an act that, if committed by the State, would have constituted a breach of the obligation'. This provision does not require the act to be internationally wrongful for the international organisation concerned. Zooming in on the EU, nothing prevents the scenario that more states could proceed with such an act by concerted action, that is, adopting a legal act via the EU institutions in a field where certain competences have been transferred to the EU (eg the Facilitation Directive, initiated by France) to circumvent the treaty obligations, namely those stemming from the SoM Protocol. In this regard, the ECtHR already held that a state could not free itself from its obligations by transferring functions to the EU.[106]

The above line of argument might be challenged, though. Alternatively, it can also be argued that Articles 17 and 61 ARIO have not been crafted to apply to situations where *both* the international organisation and its members are bound by the *same international obligation* – in casu, the SoM Protocol, which is binding on both the EU and its Member States. Still, this does not mean the EU – or its members – would escape from their international responsibility, but different – self-standing – forms of it kick in. In case of Union legislation not complying with the Protocol, this infringement entails the EU's responsibility under the *general rules of ARIO* (Articles 3–4). At the same time, and in parallel to this, the Member States aligning with such EU legislative measures can find themselves in breach of the Protocol, which incurs their responsibility under the *general rules of the Articles on the Responsibility of States for Internationally Wrongful Acts* (ARSIWA)[107] (Articles 1–2). One might argue, however, that to the extent the competences are divided between the EU and its Member States in this subject matter, they are bound by the same instrument (ie the SoM Protocol) but not by the same obligations. This approach might seem strange from an international law perspective, but not from an EU law perspective. All in all, these uncertainties support that Articles 17 and 61 ARIO might not fit or work in case of multilateral mixed agreements with the EU's and its Member States' participation – as timidly and implicitly foreseen by the *lex specialis* clause of ARIO (Article 64).

Be it as it may, the co-existence of EU-level and national-level implementation measures are amenable to create awkward situations for the Member States, who are at the end of this logical chain. One scenario is when a Member State complies with EU legislation adopted to implement the obligations undertaken in the SoM Protocol (eg the Facilitators' Package) while at the same time breaching international treaty

[105] Commentary to Art 17 ARIO, para 7.

[106] ECtHR, *Bosphorus*, above, para 154. Also Lanovoy, above 147; A Nollkaemper et al, 'Guiding Principles on Shared Responsibility in International Law' (2020) 31 *European Journal of International Law* 1, 15, commentaries to Principle 7 [Shared responsibility in situations of concerted action] para 10.

[107] International Law Commission, *Articles on Responsibility of States for Internationally Wrongful Acts*, annexed to UNGA Res 56/83 (2011) UN Doc A/RES/56/83 (12 December 2001).

obligations given the non-compliant nature of EU law with the latter (eg permitting the criminalisation of those providing humanitarian assistance). In this case, the international responsibility of both the EU and its Member State arises in view of the ARIO and the ARSIWA, whereas the Member State in question acts in conformity with EU law.

Another opposite scenario concerns the situation when a Member State's laws and policies do not follow such EU implementing legislation with the aim to comply fully with the SoM Protocol. In this case, the Member State acts in accordance with international law and is at the same time infringing its obligations under EU law, while the EU's international responsibility is engaged (Articles 3–4 ARIO) owing to its legislation which goes at variance with the SoM Protocol.[108] It remains to be seen how the Review Mechanism will navigate through these unchartered waters of joint, several, or shared responsibility of the EU and its Member States when their compliance with the SoM Protocol will be under scrutiny.[109]

ii. Procedural Challenges

Salient features of the procedure also come up. These include, among others, the following:

- how to ensure in the drawing of lots that Member States do not evaluate the EU itself (which was not avoided as Austria will be one of its first reviewers);
- how and whom to fill in the SoM Questionnaire for the EU – or maybe drawing up a separate, special one for the EU – and the detailed modalities of conducting the EU's review;[110]
- the ways of cooperation between the EU and the Member States during the review process – also in light of the principle of sincere cooperation set out in Article 4(3) TEU; and
- the application of the declaration of competence in practice in terms of apportioning the responsibilities of the EU and its Member States under the SoM Protocol in a given moment of the development of EU law/competences.

In these matters, some insights can be drawn from the EU's and its Member States' participation in the Review Mechanism of the UNCAC. As stated earlier, the UNCAC, to which the EU is also a party alongside its Member States, is accompanied by a Review Mechanism, which served as a source of inspiration when designing the UNTOC Review Mechanism. Two cycles of the UNCAC Review Mechanism, carried out in 2010 and 2015, covered different chapters of the Anti-corruption Convention. Most of the EU

[108] International Law Commission, *Draft Articles on the Responsibility of International Organizations, with Commentaries* (Yearbook of the International Law Commission, 2011, Vol II, Part Two), commentaries to draft Art 17, para 5.

[109] Regarding situations where the issue of the shared or joint international responsibility of the EU and its Member States is brought before an international dispute settlement body, see eg Contartese and Pantaleo, above.

[110] In this regard, it might also be necessary to adapt the questionnaire to take into account the specificities of the competences attributed to the EU. This would duplicate the work carried out under the country review for the individual EU Member States and contradict some of the objectives assigned to the Review Mechanism.

Member States have already completed their assessment, although they did not always allow the publication of the country report adopted at the end of the process.

A sampled analysis of the reports on the EU Member States publicly available reveals that their membership in the EU is expressly mentioned, together with their participation in other international and regional organisations active in countering corruption (OECD, Council of Europe, etc). Interestingly, EU Member States refer to the implementation of EU instruments as proof of their compliance with their obligations under the UNCAC. This was, for instance, the case regarding their obligation to exchange information on criminal records (Article 41 UNCAC), for which Belgium and France[111] referred to their participation in the European Criminal Records Information System.[112] Another example can be found in the reference to the European Arrest Warrant[113] by Bulgaria[114] as part of the implementation of its obligation to provide for the extradition of suspected or convicted offenders (Article 44 UNCAC). These practices are not isolated and have been used in other settings, such as before bodies monitoring the implementation of Council of Europe's conventions.[115]

The EU itself has not been yet subject to review – even though it possesses an exclusive competence regarding the prevention of corruption with respect to its administration, inside the EU institutions, agencies and other bodies.[116] The external pressure had been increasing to change this situation. The EU representatives firstly underscored the Union's commitment to the Review Mechanism and noted that the EU sought ways to be reviewed.[117] They later indicated that discussions had started with the UNODC on how the future review of the EU's implementation of the UNCAC could be organised.[118] The Commission recently noted, 'the unique position of the EU as the only regional economic integration organisation that is a party to the Convention adds some complexity as regards the modalities of the EU's participation in the exercise'.[119]

Without a doubt, the EU's review under the UNCAC will be of great interest to understand how it may participate in the future Review Mechanism concerning the SoM Protocol and the complexities and salient legal issues to address in practice. The EU's review under the UNCAC might have a cross-fertilisation effect and could also trigger updating the declaration of competence attached to the SoM Protocol.[120] The EU's

[111] Consider eg, UNODC, Country Review Report of Belgium (2017) 7, or UNODC, Country Review Report of France (2012) 95.

[112] Council Decision 2009/316/JHA of 6 April 2009 on the establishment of the European Criminal Records Information System (ECRIS) in the application of Art 11 of Framework Decision 2009/315/JHA [2009] OJ L93/33.

[113] Council Framework Decision of 13 June 2002 (2002/584/JHA) on the European arrest warrant and the surrender procedures between Member States [2002] OJ L190/1.

[114] UNODC, Country Review Report of Bulgaria (2012) 112.

[115] For example, GRETA, Report concerning the implementation of the Council of Europe Convention on Action against Trafficking in Human Beings by France, GRETA(2012) 16, paras 16 and 55.

[116] Council Decision of 25 September 2008 (2008/801/EC) on the conclusion, on behalf of the European Community, of the UNCAC [2008] OJ L287/1, Annex II – Declaration concerning the competence of the European Community.

[117] CoP UNCAC, Report of the Implementation Review Group on its ninth session, held in Vienna from 4 to 6 June 2018, CAC/COSP/IRG/2018/8, para 6.

[118] CoP UNCAC, Report of the Implementation Review Group on its tenth session, held in Vienna from 27 to 29 May 2019, CAC/COSP/IRG/2019/9, para 6.9.

[119] EC, Review of the EU under the Implementation Review Mechanism of the UNCAC, above, 2.

[120] Ibid, 3–4.

future review under the SoM Protocol will most likely focus on relevant EU instruments falling in areas covered by the Protocol, excluding their implementation by the Member States. Even though the substance of the review will probably be limited to EU legislation alone, it remains to be seen how the EU will deal with the most contentious issues, such as the broad criminalisation of smuggling and related acts under the Facilitators' Package.

V. Conclusions

The setting up of the Review Mechanism for the UNTOC and its SoM Protocol appears as a particularly noteworthy development, especially to foster the actual implementation of the Protocol, which remains incomplete more than 20 years after its adoption.[121] From the perspective of the EU and its Member States, their joint participation in the Protocol raises specific questions regarding the review of their implementation.

Mixity is necessarily present in the SoM Protocol, as many of its provisions fall under sensitive areas of shared competences. Unlike other criminal justice international agreements, such as those tackling corruption or money laundering, the smuggling of migrants calls for a response linked to both crime prevention and migration management. In such fields, the competences at the disposal of the EU are often limited to the adoption of minimum rules and the Member States attempt to retain a margin of discretion. Regardless, the EU's participation in the SoM Protocol's Review Mechanism will be an opportunity to provide a much-needed update to the declaration of competences to finally reflect the various consequences of the entry into force of the Lisbon Treaty and the evolution of the EU's *acquis* in areas covered by the Protocol. This would, for instance, allow to determine whether or not the EU's competence has, in certain areas, become exclusive by exercise (via pre-emption).

The review of the implementation of the SoM Protocol may also lead to interesting developments not only regarding the EU institution responsible for steering this process and ensuring the external representation of the EU but also concerning the intensity of such review. It is probable that similar to the review process under the UNCAC, the Commission would place itself as the focal point. Relying on Article 17 TEU, it has previously claimed coordinating, executive and management functions in implementing international agreements to which the Union is a party, and thus responsibilities for steering the EU's review process.[122] However, the Commission may, especially in areas of shared competence, consider its role limited to describing acts adopted by the EU, without entering into their implementation by the Member States, an element that can consider being covered by their own individual country review process.[123] As a consequence, there is a risk that the review of the EU's implementation may be limited to a simple check-listing exercise of the relevant instruments adopted at the EU level.

[121] A Schloenhardt and H MacDonald, 'Barriers to Ratification of the UN Protocol Against the Smuggling of Migrants' (2017) 7 *Asian Journal of International Law* 1, 14.
[122] EC, Review of the EU under the UNCAC Implementation Review Mechanism of the UNCAC, above, 2.
[123] Ibid, 5.

These limits may partially be traced back to the design of the Review Mechanism itself, centred around the compilation of information about legislations and measures and identifying needs of technical assistance. Unfortunately, this process, if applied, seems to fail again to clarify which entity – that is, the EU or its Member States, or both – may be considered responsible under international law for the implementation of the obligations flowing from the SoM Protocol.

12

The EU Accession to the ECHR and the Responsibility Question

*Between a Rock and a Hard Place**

VASSILIS PERGANTIS AND STIAN ØBY JOHANSEN

I. Introduction

The relaunch of the negotiations on EU accession to the ECHR elicits an inescapable feeling of *dejà-vu*, in that the EU's negotiation directives are replete with references to the conditions of accession laid down in Article 6§2 TEU and Protocol No 8 to the Lisbon Treaty, as well as to the additional issues raised in Opinion 2/13 by the CJEU.[1] It is worth recalling those terms, since they illustrate the near-impossible task facing the negotiators. Specifically, any adjustments to the ECHR regime in order to accommodate the Union's accession thereto must be limited to what is strictly necessary,[2] while respecting as much as possible the equality between the ECHR High Contracting Parties (the principle of equal footing).[3] Moreover, the draft accession agreement (DAA) should preserve the specific characteristics of the Union, addressing applications to the correct respondent, as well as not affect EU competences or EU institutions' powers. In other words, it must protect the autonomy of the EU legal order.[4]

* The text takes into account developments until December 2020. The authors acknowledge the editing assistance of Christos Zois.

[1] See Presidency of EU Council, 'Accession of the European Union to the European Convention for the Protection of Human Rights and Fundamental Freedoms (ECHR)' (20 September 2019) EU Council Doc 12349/19, para 1, referring to the previous negotiation directives (Council of EU, 'Council Decision authorising the Commission to negotiate the Accession Agreement of the European Union to the European Convention for the protection of Human Rights and Fundamental Freedoms (ECHR)' (8 June 2010) EU Council Doc 10817/10 declassified on 10 June 2015), Annex II, para 1), which mentioned the above documents, and to the CJEU Opinion 2/13 (paras 3ff).

[2] Ibid, EU Council Doc 12349/19, para 3.

[3] Presidency of EU Council, 'Accession of the European Union to the European Convention for the Protection of Human Rights and Fundamental Freedoms (ECHR) – State of Play' (2 October 2015) EU Council Doc 12528/15, para 17, https://db.eurocrim.org/db/en/doc/2379.pdf, last accessed 4 September 2021.

[4] Whereas autonomy has been placed at the heart of the CJEU's negative opinion on EU accession to the ECHR, it has been argued that autonomy's scope should be circumscribed in the case at hand because

These autonomy troubles are a direct consequence of the fact that, post-accession, the Union will become party to the ECHR alongside its Member States – effectively transforming the ECHR into a mixed agreement that strings together areas of exclusive or shared (coexistent and concurrent) competences, as well as parallel ones.[5] That said, even pre-accession the ECHR constitutes an example of indirect joint participation because EU decisions may impact Member States' ECHR obligations.[6] Nevertheless, the questions of autonomy and competence division will be raised with urgency post-accession since the ECtHR may then be called on to decide cases where both the Union and (one or more) Member States are co-respondents.

This contribution will explore the effects of the principle of autonomy on accession, focusing particularly on its interaction with the DAA's responsibility allocation provisions. Initially, we explain the cause of the CJEU's 2014 negative opinion, as far as it concerns issues of responsibility. To do so, we first outline the contours of the EU law principle of autonomy as applied to international dispute settlement mechanisms in treaties where the Union participates jointly with its Member States (section II). We then attempt to untangle the rather convoluted provisions on the attribution of conduct and shared responsibility in the 2013 DAA[7] and explain why the CJEU found them to be a threat to the autonomy of the EU legal order (section III).[8] We argue that any allocation of responsibility by the ECtHR between the Union and its Member States will necessarily imply an assessment of competence allocation between them. Consequently, the only obvious option for avoiding this appears to be the further simplification of these rules, so that they can be applied more or less automatically.

EU primary law *via* Art 6 para 2 TEU imposes upon the Union a duty to accede to the Convention. See B de Witte and S Imamović, 'Opinion 2/13 on Accession to the ECHR: Defending the EU Legal Order against a Foreign Human Rights Court' (2015) 40 *EL Rev* 683, 696; T Lock, 'Walking on a Tightrope: The Draft ECHR Accession Agreement and the Autonomy of the EU Legal Order' (2011) 48 *CML Rev* 1025, 1033. Nevertheless, it must be borne in mind that the obligation in the said Article is an imperfect one since its fulfilment does not depend on the Union and its Member States alone (see A Łazowski and RA Wessel, 'When Caveats Turn into Locks: Opinion 2/13 on Accession of the European Union to the ECHR' (2015) 16 *German Law Journal* 179, 183) or, alternatively, it is an obligation of means, not one of result, meaning that if the Union and its Member States make every effort possible to accede, the obligation is not breached in case of an outcome of non-accession, provided an even theoretical option of accession remains on the table (L Besselink et al, 'A Constitutional Moment: Acceding to the ECHR (or not)' (2015) 11 *European Constitutional Law Review* 2, 3; R Baratta, 'Accession of the EU to the ECHR: The Rationale for the ECJ's Prior Involvement Mechanism' (2013) 50 *CML Rev* 1305, 1305).

[5] For this classification, see A Rosas, 'Mixity Past, Present and Future: Some Observations' in M Chamon and I Govaere (eds), *EU External Relations Post-Lisbon: The Law and Practice of Facultative Mixity* (Leiden, Koninklijke Brill NV, 2020) 8.

[6] See the chapter by Casteleiro and Contartese in this volume, section I.

[7] 'Draft revised agreement on the accession of the European Union to the Convention for the Protection of Human Rights and Fundamental Freedoms', reproduced in CDDH 47+1 Ad Hoc Negotiation Group, 'Final Report to the CDDH' (5 April 2013) CoE Doc 47+1(2013)008 rev2, App I (hereinafter *2013 DAA*). Any reference to the 2013 DAA indicates this version, while the acronym DAA is employed as a generic term and as a reference to pre- and past-2013 DAA versions.

[8] We use the term 'shared responsibility' as an umbrella term, in accordance with how it is defined in Principles 2 and 3 in A Nollkaemper et al, 'Guiding Principles of Shared Responsibility in International Law' (2020) 31 *EJIL* 15.

This will, in turn, shift any requisite regulation of the responsibility allocation question and the consequences of wrongfulness to EU internal rules. Having explained how such a simplified system may operate, we will then evaluate whether it would sufficiently preserve the idea of the EU acceding to the Convention on equal footing (section IV). We conclude that such a simplified system has its own set of problems, which cannot be fully mitigated. The DAA negotiators are thus stuck in no man's land, with no obvious way out. The principle of autonomy thus serves to hinder the joint participation of the Union and its Member States in treaties that confer rights on individuals and give them access to judicial dispute settlement mechanisms.

II. The Contours of the Principle of Autonomy vis-à-vis International Dispute Settlement Mechanisms

The principle of autonomy of the EU legal order has attracted much attention over the last few years, becoming a cornerstone of EU external relations law. In a series of cases, the CJEU has, by elaborating this principle, effectively shaped the relationship between the Union's legal order and the international legal order.

In particular, autonomy has played a crucial role in determining the compatibility of international dispute settlement mechanisms with EU law. On the one hand, the Court has repeatedly declared that an international agreement providing for a judicial system of dispute settlement is not *in principle* contrary to the autonomy of the EU legal order, since the competence to conclude international agreements 'necessarily entails the power to submit to the decisions of a court which is created or designated by such an agreement as regards interpretation and application of its provisions'.[9] On the other hand, it has gone to great lengths to preserve the nature of the EU legal order and the scope of its authority to interpret and apply EU law.

Three main aspects of the CJEU's autonomy jurisprudence are directly relevant to mixed agreements containing dispute settlement mechanisms – which is what the ECHR will become post-accession.[10]

Firstly, the CJEU insists that no external dispute settlement mechanism can be granted the power to bind the EU and its Member States to a particular interpretation of Union law included in an external agreement, either through direct *renvoi* or in the form of provisions with a wording identical to Union law. In the case of the Agreement on the European Economic Area, the Court of Justice found it unacceptable that the EEA Court would have had the power to interpret *core provisions* of Community law incorporated virtually *verbatim* in the EEA Agreement. That would have endangered

[9] Opinion 1/91 *(EEA Court)* [1991] ECR I-06079, paras 40 and 70 [Opinion 1/91]; Opinion 1/09 *(Patent Court)* [2011] ECR I-01137, paras 74–76 [Opinion 1/09]; Opinion 1/17 *(CETA)* [2019] OJ C 369, para 106 [Opinion 1/17]; Opinion 2/13 *(EU accession to the ECHR)* [2015] OJ C 65/2, paras 182–83 [Opinion 2/13].

[10] T Lock, 'EU Accession to the ECHR: Implications for the Judicial Review in Strasbourg' (2010) 35 *EL Rev* 777, 796.

the interpretational uniformity of Union law, prejudicing the CJEU's exclusive and definitive interpretational authority in relation to corresponding Community rules.[11]

This requirement was recently revisited by the CJEU in *Opinion 1/17*. In confirming the compatibility of the CETA and its Tribunal with Union law, the CJEU stressed that the said Tribunal only has the power to interpret the CETA and cannot determine 'the legality of a measure … under the domestic law of a party'. This domestic law (and reflectively Union law) can be considered only as a matter of fact by the Tribunal when assessing the consistency of a measure with the CETA (Article 8.31.2 CETA).[12] Accordingly, the CETA does not impinge upon the autonomy of the Union legal order since 'any meaning given to domestic law by the Tribunal shall not be binding upon the courts or authorities of that Party' (and reflectively upon the CJEU).[13]

To what extent are these findings applicable to the case of the EU accession to the ECHR is yet unclear. The ECtHR, in its long-established case-law, avoids interpreting (and is obviously precluded from invalidating) domestic law.[14] Yet, the ECtHR does assess whether the interpretation offered by domestic authorities is consistent with the ECHR, and, at times, it might review that interpretation by offering its own.[15] The latter may also occur post-accession vis-à-vis Union law. Even in those cases, however, its judgments would not 'have the effect of binding the [Union] and its institutions, in the exercise of their internal powers, to a particular interpretation of the rules of [Union] law', which is the litmus test applied by the CJEU when reviewing the compatibility of mixed agreements with the EU legal system.[16] In other words, they will bind the Union only *externally*, as an international legal person. How far will the EU and its Court be bound *within* the Union's internal legal order to follow ECtHR judgments is strictly speaking an issue of EU law, over which the CJEU is the final arbiter. We will, therefore, revert to this issue in section IV when discussing whether further internalising the responsibility question is the way forward.

Secondly, the principle of autonomy requires that international agreements providing for the establishment of a dispute settlement mechanism do not change the essential powers of EU institutions. Thus, for instance, if a clause is inserted in an agreement limiting the function of the CJEU within that agreement to that of an advisory body, this could violate EU law.[17] EU accession to the ECHR does not appear to cause issues in this regard. While the so-called 'prior involvement procedure' would, in practice, give the CJEU a new power – to give preliminary rulings to the ECtHR – it is not an inherent threat to autonomy. Hence, the CJEU in Opinion 2/13 found fault with this

[11] Opinion 1/91, para 29; B de Witte, 'A Selfish Court? The Court of Justice and the Design of International Dispute Settlement Beyond the European Union' in M Cremona and A Thies (eds), *The European Court of Justice and External Relations Law: Constitutional Implications* (Oxford, Hart Publishing, 2014) 33, 37.

[12] Opinion 1/17, paras 123 and 130.

[13] Ibid, para 131.

[14] F Benoît-Rohmer, 'L'adhésion à la Convention européenne des Droits de l'Homme, un travail de Pénélope?' (2015) 51 *Revue Trimestrielle de Droit Européen* 593, 604.

[15] *Nejdet Şahin and Perihan Şahin v Turkey* App no 13279/05 (GC, 20 October 2011), para 49, with further references.

[16] Opinion 1/00 *Proposed Agreement Between the European Community and Non-Member States on the Establishment of a European Common Aviation Area* [2002] ECR I-03493, para 15.

[17] Opinion 1/91, paras 61–65.

procedure only in relation to an ambiguity that had crept into the Explanatory Report to the 2013 DAA.[18]

Then there is a third, and for our purposes, most crucial, aspect of the principle of autonomy: The international agreement cannot confer upon the external dispute settlement mechanism the jurisdiction to rule on the competence allocation between the Union and its Member States. The CJEU has clearly said so when confronted with the EEA Agreement, which stipulated that the EEA Court would settle disputes between Contracting Parties (Article 96(1)(a) EEA), which translated into a power to decide whether 'Contracting Party' meant the Union and the Member States jointly, or each one separately. This stipulation, the CJEU held, granted the EEA Court the power to determine the division of competences between the EU and the Member States, thus undermining the exclusive jurisdiction of the CJEU over such matters.[19] Since the judgments of such an external dispute settlement mechanism may bind the Union and its Member States, the principle of autonomy requires that the CJEU remain the exclusive arbiter with regard to competence allocation.[20]

The CJEU has revisited this requirement on multiple occasions, most recently in *Opinion 1/17*. There, the CJEU ruled that CETA Article 8.21, which stipulates that it is up to the Union to determine in a binding fashion who will be the respondent in an application by an investor before the CETA Tribunal, is compatible with Union law since it preserves the autonomy of the Union legal order and the exclusive jurisdiction of the CJEU in matters of competence allocation and responsibility determination.[21]

Post-accession, the ECtHR would have the final say on allocating responsibility between the Union and its Member States unless the DAA provides otherwise. In fact, even at present (pre-accession), where the EU is not a Contracting Party to the ECHR, the ECtHR must occasionally assess the existence and scope of the EU Member State discretion under Union law. That is because a key requirement for applying the ECtHR's famous 'equivalent protection doctrine' to a case is that the respondent state acted in compliance with strict legal obligations flowing from Union law.[22] This seems problematic in light of the existing CJEU case-law on the principle of autonomy.[23]

[18] According to the text of the relevant paragraph, the CJEU was only to rule on the 'validity' of secondary law; see Draft Explanatory Report to the 2013 DAA, para 66, annexed to *Final Report* (n 7) [hereinafter *Draft Explanatory Report*]. The CJEU read this as narrowly as possible, so as to exclude interpretation of secondary law; see Opinion 2/13, paras 242–48. Renewed negotiations from 2020 onwards are in the process of remedying this inadvertent omission; see CDDH 47+1 Ad Hoc Negotiation Group, 'Report of the Seventh Negotiation Meeting' (26 November 2020), §11.

[19] Opinion 1/91, paras 34–35.

[20] I Govaere, 'Beware of the Trojan Horse: Dispute Settlement in (Mixed) Agreements and the Autonomy of the EU Legal Order' in C Hillion and P Koutrakos (eds), *Mixed Agreements Revisited: The EU and its Member States in the World* (Oxford, Hart Publishing, 2010) 187, 193.

[21] Opinion 1/17, para 132; see also P Koutrakos, 'The Anatomy of Autonomy: Themes and Perspectives on an Elusive Principle' in ECB, *Building Bridges: Central Banking Law in an Interconnected World* (ECB Legal Conference, 2019) 90, 97.

[22] *Bosphorus Airways v Ireland* [GC], no 45036/98 (2005) paras 154–55; *MSS v Belgium and Greece* [GC], no 30696/09 (2011) para 338.

[23] This insistence by the CJEU on being final arbiter over the responsibility allocation between the Union and its Member States under international agreements has been fiercely criticised, notably for 'confus[ing] attribution of international responsibility with the EU law division of powers'; see P Eeckhout, 'Opinion 2/13

This need to preserve the autonomy of the EU legal order with regard to responsibility allocation was also at the forefront of the negotiators' minds in 2013. Indeed, the joint participation of the Union and its Member States in international agreements with judicial dispute resolution procedures is bound to challenge the CJEU's strict notion of autonomy. In the next section, we will analyse how the 2013 DAA attempted to preserve the autonomy of Union law and explain why the CJEU rejected that attempt.

III. The 2013 DAA: Preserving Autonomy with a Light Touch on the Responsibility Question

Drafting provisions on responsibility allocation in the 2013 DAA was no easy task. That is because the strict conditions concerning responsibility allocation that the CJEU has set for Union participation in international agreements providing for external judicial control of Union actions are exacerbated by two specific traits of the EU legal order. First, the delineation of competences between the Union and its Member States constantly evolves on the basis of the successive amendments of EU treaties, the ever-expanding exercise of powers by the EU in areas of shared competences, and the prolific case-law of the CJEU. The complexity is reflected in the Union's external relations, where the tool of mixed agreements is favoured in case of disputes between the Union and the Member States concerning the division of competences.[24] However, mixity simply shifts intra-EU competence allocation wrangling to the field of external relations, where the Union's treaty partners – and, as the case may be, individuals to whom the treaty confers rights – are confronted with increased legal uncertainty over who will be implementing the agreement and who will be responsible in the case of a breach of the agreement.[25]

Second, this uncertain state of affairs is compounded by the so-called 'executive federalism' that imbues the implementation of Union policies.[26] What distinguishes the EU from other international organisations is that while the Union exercises regulatory powers to an unprecedented extent, much of the implementation thereof is undertaken by Member State authorities. As a result, it is not always clear whether the Union, who adopted the act under consideration, or the Member States that have implemented it, should be responsible for a consequent violation of an international obligation.

This entanglement was evident in the EU's comments to the Draft Articles on the Responsibility of International Organizations (DARIO) of the International Law

on EU Accession to the ECHR and Judicial Dialogue: Autonomy or Autarky' (2015) 38 *Fordham International Law Journal* 955, 981–85. While this view has its merits, we assume, for the purposes of this paper, that the CJEU will follow its own case law.

[24] E Paasivirta and PJ Kuijper, 'Does One Size Fit All? The European Community and the Responsibility of International Organizations' (2005) 36 *Netherlands Yearbook of International Law* 169, 177–78.

[25] A Delgado Casteleiro, 'The International Responsibility of the European Union – The EU Perspective: Between Pragmatism and Proceduralisation' (2013) 15 *Cambridge Yearbook of European Legal Studies* 563, 573; M Chamon and I Govaere, 'Introduction: Facultative Mixity, More than Just a Childhood Disease of EU Law?' in Chamon and Govaere (n 5) 1, 6.

[26] See Casteleiro and Contartese (n 6) s 2.2 b).

Commission (ILC).[27] There, while the ILC opted for 'an organic model' on the attribution of conduct, reflected in Articles 6 and 7 DARIO, the latter supplemented by a factual criterion of 'effective control',[28] the EU argued that on the basis of the Union's particular traits responsibility should lie where the competence is according to the internal rules of the organisation.[29]

However, competence allocation may be irrelevant for purposes of attribution. This is most obvious in the case of ultra vires acts, which are attributable as long as they are performed by an organ of the state or organisation in question.[30] This follows from the fact that the attribution rules concern the link between certain *conduct* (acts and omissions) and (one or more) *international legal persons*.[31] What matters for attribution is who performed the conduct in question and on whose behalf. Competence allocation is, of course, a relevant factor when determining to whom to attribute a course of conduct, but it is not alone decisive. It simply does not tell the full story. Furthermore, in certain sub-fields of international law, various criteria have been suggested for determining the Union's responsibility, such as the existence of EU norms governing the subject-matter at hand;[32] the degree of normative control exercised by the EU over the Member States and the consequent degree of discretion enjoyed by the latter;[33] or the division of competences as declared to the other contracting parties, which might eventually diverge from the actual competence allocation within the EU legal order.[34] Still, attribution is determined factually in reliance on the act and/or the provision at the origin of the breach.[35]

It is on such a factual basis that Article 1 2013 DAA is apparently construed. The first sentence of Article 1(3) stipulates that 'acts, measures or omissions of [EU] institutions, bodies, offices or agencies, or of persons acting on their behalf' shall raise the Union's responsibility. Conversely, the first sentence of Article 1(4) states that 'acts, measures

[27] 'Report of the International Law Commission on the Work of its Sixty-third Session (26 April–3 June and 4 July–12 August 2011)' [2011] ILCYb II/2, Ch 5 (DARIO).

[28] F Salerno, 'International Responsibility for the Conduct of "Blue Helmets": Exploring the Organic Link' in M Ragazzi (ed), *Responsibility of International Organizations: Essays in Memory of Sir Ian Brownlie* (Leiden, Martinus Nijhoff, 2013) 415, 423.

[29] 'Documents of the Fifty-sixth Session' [2004] ILCYb vol II/1, 26, paras 1–5. See also PJ Kuijper and E Paasivirta, 'EU International Responsibility and its Attribution: From the Inside Looking Out' in M Evans and P Koutrakos (eds), *The International Responsibility of the European Union: European and International Perspectives* (Oxford, Hart Publishing, 2013) 35, 54–55.

[30] S Talmon, 'Responsibility of International Organizations: Does the European Community Require Special Treatment?' in M Ragazzi (ed), *International Responsibility Today: Essays in Memory of Oscar Schachter* (Leiden, Koninklijke Brill NV, 2005) 405, 409.

[31] SØ Johansen, 'Dual Attribution of Conduct to Both an International Organisation and a Member State' (2019) 6 *Oslo Law Review* 178, 181–82.

[32] C Contartese, 'Competence-Based Approach, Normative Control, and the International Responsibility of the EU and its Member States: What Does Recent Practice Add to the Debate?' (2019) 16 *International Organizations Law Review* 339, 351.

[33] T Lock, 'Accession of the EU to the ECHR: Who Would be Responsible in Strasbourg' in D Ashiagbor, N Countouris and I Lianos (eds), *The European Union after the Lisbon Treaty* (Cambridge, CUP, 2012) 109, 117.

[34] Talmon (n 30) 418.

[35] G Gaja, 'The "Co-Respondent Mechanisms" According to the Draft Agreement for the Accession of the EU to the ECHR' (2013) 2 *ESIL Reflections* para 6. For a comprehensive presentation of this question, see Casteleiro and Contartese (n 6) *passim*.

or omissions of organs of an [EU] member state or of persons acting on its behalf shall be attributed to that state', even if the latter merely implements EU legislation. Hence, post-accession, any application should continue to be directed against the party that has proceeded to the contested act, measure or omission.[36] Such assessments allow the ECtHR to decide on a mere factual basis to whom conduct should be attributed,[37] that is, without reviewing or affecting the competences or powers of the institutions.[38]

The just-quoted first sentence of Article 1(4) restates a foundational part of *Bosphorus*, where the ECtHR held that

> a Contracting Party is responsible under Article 1 of the Convention for all acts and omissions of its organs regardless of whether the act or omission in question was a consequence of domestic law or of the necessity to comply with international legal obligations.[39]

That the first sentence of Article 1(4) was intended as a mere restatement of this line of case-law is confirmed by the provision's rather complex negotiating history. The provision's origin is found in the aftermath of the first rounds of accession negotiations when several of the EU Member States had reservations about the original drafts drawn up by an expert group.[40] France, in particular, was worried about the ECtHR having jurisdiction over the Common Foreign and Security Policy (CFSP).[41] After internal negotiations between the EU Member States, the Union eventually suggested a detailed, two-part provision on attribution as a 'solution' to this CFSP issue.[42] The first part is virtually identical to what is today Article 1(4), minus the explicit reference to decisions under the TEU and TFEU.[43] The second part read as follows:

> acts or measures shall be attributable only to the member States of the European Union where they have been performed or adopted in the context of the provisions of the Treaty on European Union on the common foreign and security policy of the European Union, except in cases where attributability to the European Union on the basis of European Union law has been established within the legal order of the European Union.[44]

This latter part, which essentially provided that conduct in the implementation of CFSP acts, was attributed exclusively to the EU Member States except where Union law provides otherwise, received a lukewarm reception from the non-EU High Contracting

[36] Benoît-Rohmer (n 36) 596.

[37] E Wennesträm, 'EU Accession to the European Convention on Human Rights – the Creation of a European Legal Space for Human Rights?' in J Nergelius and E Kristoffersson (eds), *Human Rights in Contemporary European Law* (Oxford, Hart Publishing, 2015) 91, 95.

[38] Fifth Negotiation Meeting between the CDDH ad hoc Negotiation Group and the European Commission on the Accession of the European Union to the European Convention on Human Rights, 'Final Report of the CDDH' 47+1(2013)008 rev 2, para 22 (Final Report to CDDH).

[39] *Bosphorus Airways v Ireland* [GC], no 45036/98 (2005) para 152. This also followed implicitly from earlier case law, see eg European Commission on Human Rights, *M & Co v Germany (dec)*, no 13258/87 (1990).

[40] Presidency of the EU Council, 'Accession of the EU to the ECHR – State of Play' (8 November 2011) Council Doc 16385/11 at 1–2, a leaked copy of which can be obtained at https://www.statewatch.org/media/documents/news/2011/nov/eu-council-echr-accession-16385-11.pdf, last accessed 4 September 2021.

[41] Ibid, at 2.

[42] See suggested amendment 'c1' in CDDH 47+1 Ad Hoc Negotiation Group, 'Report of the Third Negotiation Meeting' (11 March 2012) CoE Doc 47+1(2012)R03 at 14 (fn 1).

[43] Ibid, suggested amendment 'c1 (aa)'.

[44] Ibid, suggested amendment 'c1 (bb)'.

Parties to the ECHR.[45] And, after further consideration, most of the non-EU parties circulated a common paper entirely rejecting the idea of establishing an exclusive attribution rule for the CFSP.[46] After this forceful rejection, this second part was dropped at the next negotiation meeting.[47] At the same meeting, the reference to decisions under the TFEU and TEU was added to the remaining (first) part – likely to further underline that violations arising out of the CFSP were to be treated in the same manner as other violations.[48]

This negotiation history demonstrates that the impetus for a provision on attribution was an attempt by the EU side to establish *lex specialis* rules on attribution for the CFSP. When drafting such a rule, it made sense also to restate the general rules on attribution. When the CFSP-specific attribution rule was rejected, however, the remaining part of Article 1(4) served no purpose other than to restate the obvious. The negotiators should, therefore, have taken up the suggestion by one delegation to delete Article 1(4), since it was unnecessary.[49]

Whether these rules on attribution of conduct would have been sufficient in a post-accession *Bosphorus*-like scenario is difficult to say.

On the one hand, the DAA attribution rules may be interpreted as being quite open to the idea of shared responsibility, thus recognising the complex and intertwined relationship between the Union and its Member States. Applied to the *Bosphorus* scenario, post-accession, this view would entail attributing the conduct of the Irish officials (the impounding of the aircraft) to Ireland under an organic link, according to Article 1(4).[50] If both the Union and Ireland were respondents in the case, the next question for the ECtHR would be whether the Union is *also* responsible. That shared responsibility is possible follows from the second sentence of Article 1(4), which provides that the first sentence 'shall not preclude the European Union from being responsible … for a violation resulting from [a member state] act, measure or omission'.

In the *Bosphorus* case, Ireland was acting on a direct instruction – in the form of Regulation 990/93 – that is clearly attributable to the Union.[51] The Regulation and the actual impoundment of the aircraft may be seen as cumulative contributions to the same (alleged) injury. Shared responsibility would thus arise due to there being two distinct courses of conduct leading to a single indivisible injury.[52] Alternatively, shared responsibility could arise due to the normative act of the Regulation being a form of control over, or aid and assistance to, the physical act of the impoundment. While the 2013 DAA does not include explicit rules on these forms of derived responsibility, that gap can be filled by drawing on the general international law laid down in DARS/DARIO. In both

[45] Ibid, para 7.

[46] Fourteen non-EU parties to the ECHR, 'Common Paper on Major Concerns Regarding the Draft Revised Agreement on the Accession of the EU to the ECHR' (11 March 2013) CoE Doc 47+1(2013)003 para 9.

[47] CDDH 47+1 Ad Hoc Negotiation Group, 'Report of the Fourth Negotiation Meeting' (23 January 2013) CoE Doc 47+1(2013)R04 para 8.

[48] Ibid, paras 8–9 and Annex IV.

[49] Ibid, para 8.

[50] DARS Art 4.

[51] DAA Art 1(3) – which mirrors Art 1(4), and thus also merely restates general international law.

[52] Principle 2(1) in A Nollkaemper et al (n 8) 15.

scenarios, and on the basis of the co-respondent mechanism, the EU and its Member State(s) would have been found jointly responsible under Article 3(7) 2013 DAA.

On the other hand, the above reconstruction of the *Bosphorus* case outcome using the 2013 DAA rules might be objected to on several grounds. First, the enactment of the Regulation is not per se wrongful conduct, and the Union cannot be found responsible for merely enacting the Regulation or for obliging its Member State to act accordingly. Second, while the aircraft's wrongful impounding is attributed to a Member State, the responsibility for it should be attributed exclusively to the EU. Any other solution piercing the Union's institutional veil would increase the risk of the Member States disobeying Union law under the pretence that they might be held responsible even if they blindly implement strict Union obligations.

In other words, in the case of strict obligations, such as the ones under consideration in the *Bosphorus* case, only the EU should be held responsible for the wrongful conduct of the Member State (even if the acts are factually attributed to the latter). This outcome is, however, not supported by the current phrasing of Article 1(3)–(4), which does not accommodate an attribution of responsibility scenario and cannot be supplemented by general international law rules to that effect, since Article 1(3)–(4) does not recognise the possibility of such rules filling the relevant gaps of the 2013 DAA.[53] Consequently, a basic scenario of indirect EU responsibility is left unregulated.[54]

Moreover, the last sentence of Article 1(4) together with Article 3(7), to which it refers, cannot serve as a separate and sufficient basis for attribution because Article 3(7) is *not* a rule on attribution but merely establishes a presumption of joint responsibility in case the Union or the Member State assent to be co-respondent(s) (Article 3(5)). This mechanism being voluntary, cannot prescribe a derivative responsibility rule that could fill the above gap.[55] Ultimately, the only leeway left to the Court according to the 2013 DAA in order to hold responsible the correct respondent can be found in the last sentence of Article 3(7) – provided the co-respondent mechanism is activated.

In any case, whether one follows a more positive assessment on the attribution rules encompassed in the 2013 DAA Article or a more critical one, there is no doubt that the ECtHR will be called to examine the degree of control exercised by the Union upon its Member States and whether the latter implement strict Union obligations. Yet, according to the CJEU's reasoning in *Opinion 2/13*, such assessment is likely to impinge upon the division of competences between the Union and its Member States.

[53] See, implicitly, A Delgado Casteleiro, 'United We Stand: The EU and its Member States in the Strasbourg Court' in V Kosta, N Skoutaris and V Tzevelekos (eds), *The EU Accession to the ECHR* (Oxford, Hart Publishing, 2014) 105, 112.

[54] PJ Kuijper, 'Attribution-Responsibility-Remedy: Some Comments on the EU in Different International *Regimes*' (2013) 46 *Revue Belge de Droit International* 57, 72. For further examples that might remain unregulated by the 2013 DAA, see J d'Aspremont, 'A European Law of International Responsibility? The Articles on the Responsibility of International Organisations and the EU' in Kosta, Skoutaris and Tzevelekos, ibid, 75, 77; E Cannizzaro, 'Beyond the Either/Or: Dual Attribution to the European Union and to the Member State for Breach of the ECHR' in Evans and Koutrakos (n 29) 295, 306–07; GI Hernández, 'Beyond the Control Paradigm? International Responsibility and the European Union' (2013) 15 *Cambridge Yearbook of European Legal Studies* 648, 651.

[55] T Lock, 'End of an Epic? The Draft Agreement on the EU' Accession to the ECHR' (2012) 31 *Yearbook of European Law* 162, 173. See, however, the Union's Draft Declaration annexed in the 2013 DAA (n 7) Appendix II, where it promises that it will request to become a co-respondent if the conditions are met. Even so, it is submitted that the clause of Art 3(5) remains a self-judging one.

In that perspective, it is clearly preferable that the CJEU rules on the division of competences before the ECtHR proceeds to its assessment, since the formal division of competences is relevant for the factual assessments that the ECtHR makes. That is why the 2013 DAA supplements the rules on attribution in Article 1 with the co-respondent mechanism so as to fully take into account the requirement of Protocol 8 to the Lisbon Treaty, according to which any application to the ECtHR after accession must be addressed to the correct respondent. Put differently, the co-respondent mechanism aims at taking into account the complex reality of the Union legal order as exemplified above.

Article 3(2) 2013 DAA allows the EU to become a co-respondent in proceedings before the ECtHR when applications addressed only towards the Member States raise issues of compatibility of an EU law provision with the ECHR, 'notably where that violation could have been avoided only by disregarding an obligation under EU law'. Moreover, Article 3(3) allows the Member States to become co-respondents in proceedings against the EU before the ECtHR when a provision of EU primary law seems to be the one producing the violation of the ECHR.[56] If the co-respondent mechanism is employed and a violation of the ECHR is established, the respondent and the co-respondent will be jointly responsible unless the Court decides otherwise (Article 3(7)). Ultimately, the co-respondent mechanism seeks to ensure that joint responsibility is the rule of thumb in cases involving both the Union and (one or more) Member States.[57]

Under the 2013 DAA, the ECtHR would have the final say on whether it is 'plausible' that the conditions in Articles 3(2) and 3(3) are met. The CJEU strongly objected to this in Opinion 2/13, asserting that the ECtHR would thus 'be required to assess the rules of EU law governing the division of powers between the EU and its Member States'.[58] This would be 'liable to interfere with the division of powers' and was, therefore, found incompatible with the principle of autonomy.[59] It follows that, as the CJEU views it, the allocation of responsibility is inextricably linked to an assessment of the division of competences within the European Union. While this is not entirely correct, as we demonstrate above, it is true that one cannot fully separate the division of competences from the allocation of responsibility.

Some examples may further illustrate the Court's position while addressing some common counter-arguments.

First, it has been argued that Article 3 2013 DAA cannot impinge upon the autonomy of the Union legal order because responsibility allocation by the ECtHR will not require an assessment of the competence division between the EU and its Member

[56] The rationale being that the Member States are responsible for the contents of the EU Treaties since they have 'freely entered into' them; see *Matthews v UK* [GC], no 24833/94 (1999) para 33.

[57] Opinion 2/13, Opinion of AG Kokott, para 216: 'Put simply, the respondent in each case will therefore be the party to which the impugned act, measure or omission is to be attributed, whereas the role of the co-respondent falls to the party which has the power, if necessary, to bring about an amendment of the provisions of EU law relating to that act, measure or omission'.

[58] Opinion 2/13, para 224.

[59] Opinion 2/13, para 225. For a critique of the Court's reasoning on this point, in the sense that the plausibility review would not be binding upon the EU and its Member States, see P Gragl, 'The Reasonableness of Jealousy: Opinion 2/13 and EU Accession to the ECHR' (2015) *European Yearbook on Human Rights* 27, 43. Yet, as has been pertinently observed, if during the plausibility assessment the ECtHR rejected the request for co-respondentship, this would constitute a de facto determination of the competence distribution; see Benoît-Rohmer (n 36) 597.

States but only an interpretation of EU law. As Piet Eeckhout observes, '[a]t most, it would need to determine whether the Member State was compelled by EU law … to adopt these measures'.[60] In practice, though, the existence of a margin of discretion is one of the factors that determine and enrich the division of competences, particularly the aspect of how those competences are exercised.[61] For instance, reviewing the margin of discretion in a *Bosphorus*-type case would necessarily involve a determination of whether the respondent Member State is implementing strict obligations under Union law, that is, whether it still retains a competence in the relevant field of activity by virtue of Union law.[62]

A second complication on avoiding competence assessment while apportioning responsibility relates to the question of attribution of omissions. The ECHR contains a large array of positive obligations that may give rise to responsibility for failure to legislate.[63] Such a failure is attributable to the entity that holds the legislative competence in the framework of the Union legal order – thus making it impossible to determine the responsibility question without assessing competences.[64] Additionally, as already alluded to, the expansion of Union competences will often render it difficult to disentangle whether the EU or its Member States have the competence to legislate in order to remedy violations of such positive human rights obligations.[65] Consequently, in this case too, who is competent and capable of remedying the violation must be determined with reference to competence allocation.[66] For instance, focusing on the entity that can remedy a breach through the modification of relevant legislation falls within this type of assessment.

These examples illustrate the impossible task of completely separating the responsibility question from a review of the division of competences between the EU and its Member States.[67] Apportioning responsibility and determining what measures should be taken in order to remedy the violation and by whom is part of the ECtHR's judicial function. Yet, those very functions risk undermining the autonomy of the Union legal order since they presuppose the Court's power to assess competence allocation.[68] Indeed, the joint participation of the Union and its Member States in a mixed agreement with judicial dispute settlement procedures will inevitably affect the autonomy of the Union legal order.

Having those parameters in mind, the negotiators drafted Article 3 2013 DAA so as to prevent as far as possible the ECtHR from impinging upon the autonomy of the EU legal order. Accordingly, the ECtHR was given the power to invite (but not order)

[60] Eeckhout (n 23) 983.

[61] Contartese (n 32) 374–76.

[62] JM Cortés-Martín, 'Sur l'adhésion à la CEDH et la sauvegarde de l'autonomie de l'ordre juridique de l'Union dans l'identification du défendeur pertinent: le mécanisme du codéfendeur' (2011) *Revue du Droit de l'Union Européenne* 615, 628.

[63] For an introduction, see J Gerards, *General Principles of the European Convention on Human Rights* (CUP 2019) 108–35.

[64] Lock, 'Accession of the EU' (n 33) 131–33.

[65] Cortés-Martín (n 62) 639.

[66] É Dubout, 'Une question de confiance: nature juridique de l'Union européenne et adhésion à la Convention européenne des Droits de l'Homme' (2015) 51 *Cahiers de Droit Européen* 73, 88–89.

[67] Opinion 2/13, Opinion of AG Kokott, paras 231–32, where she admits that allowing the ECtHR to decide on who should be responsible undermines the principle of autonomy.

[68] Cortés-Martín (n 62) 652–53.

a High Contracting Party to become co-respondent or decide upon the latter's request after assessing in this case whether the conditions of paragraphs 2 or 3 of the said Article were fulfilled (Article 3(5)). Moreover, if a violation were established while employing the co-respondent mechanism, the respondent and the co-respondent would be jointly responsible 'unless the Court, on the basis of the reasons given by the respondent and the co-respondent, and having sought the views of the applicant, decides that only one of them be held responsible' (Article 3(7)).

All in all, the co-respondent mechanism, in opting for a general rule of joint responsibility, was explicitly construed with the intention to ensure that the ECtHR would only rarely and to a limited extent rule on competence allocation between the Union and its Member States.[69] However, this was not sufficient to please the CJEU. That an exception to joint responsibility existed and it was up to the ECtHR to consider whether the conditions were met led the CJEU to find the co-respondent mechanism in the 2013 DAA incompatible with the principle of autonomy.[70] In doing so, the CJEU has placed the DAA negotiators in no man's land.

In the end, despite being rather simplistic and introducing a logic of automaticity (especially with regard to the joint responsibility clause in case of co-respondentship), the 2013 DAA scheme was found incompatible with the principle of autonomy by the CJEU. It is worth noting that the provisions in the agreement that granted certain flexibility to the ECtHR were most criticised by the Court.

IV. Further Simplifying and Internalising the Responsibility Question as a Way Forward?

The CJEU's negative opinion has led the negotiating parties back to the drawing board. Some scholars have argued for merely minimal changes in the co-respondent mechanism and the collateral attribution scheme, claiming that it is feasible for the ECtHR to limit itself to a determination that an act, measure or omission that is 'generally determined by EU law' violates the ECHR and to an automatic application of the joint attribution rule, without offering detailed reasoning on responsibility allocation, thus respecting the principle of autonomy.[71] Yet, as is readily admitted, the lack of responsibility allocation by the ECtHR increases the risk that the ruling will be implemented inadequately.[72]

[69] Final Report of the CDDH, App V, para 62; X Groussot, T Lock and L Pech, 'EU Accession to the European Convention on Human Rights: A Legal Assessment of the Draft Accession Agreement of 14th October 2011' (Foundation Robert Schumann Policy Paper, European Issues 218, 2011) 10 and 13.

[70] Opinion 2/13, paras 229–34. For a positive review of the Court's opinion on this particular point, see Łazowski and Wessel (n 4) 198. For a proposal that follows the CJEU's line of reasoning towards effacing the exception from Art 3 para 7 DAA, thus retaining only the rule of automatic joint responsibility, see X Groussot and E Stavefeldt, 'Accession of the EU to the ECHR: A Legally Complex Situation' in Nergelius and Kristoffersson (n 37) 7, 23; JP Jacqué, 'The Accession of the European Union to the European Convention on Human Rights and Fundamental Freedoms' (2011) 48 *CML Rev* 995, 1015.

[71] P Tacik, 'The Contribution of the EU Accession to the ECHR to Shared Responsibility in International Law' (ESIL Annual Conference, Riga, 7-9 September 2016) 24–25, https://euglobal.files.wordpress.com/2016/09/tacik_the_contribution_of_the_eu_accession_to_the_european_convention_on_human_rights_to_shared_responsibility_in_international_law.pdf, last accessed 4 September 2021.

[72] Ibid.

There are also two further obstacles. First, even this limited assessment over EU law might be considered incompatible with the principle of autonomy by the CJEU, as we have already highlighted. Second, it is doubtful if the CJEU will find acceptable a mechanism that relies on the ECtHR's good faith to limit itself when reviewing applications concerning EU law.

Consequently, an increasing number of scholars and actors involved in the negotiation have turned towards a different solution. More particularly, the further simplification and automaticity of the responsibility provisions through the further circumscription of Article 3(5) ECtHR's determination and the deletion of Article 3(7) 2013 DAA exception has been proposed.[73] This appears to be the only option for the negotiators after the CJEU's rejection of the 2013 DAA. However, such a strategy unavoidably translates into a more elaborate set of internal EU law rules on responsibility allocation, including arrangements determining who should implement ECtHR judgments.[74]

The need for EU internal rules to complement the co-respondent mechanism was highlighted by the EU during the previous round of negotiations,[75] and various scholars have paid considerable attention thereto.[76] Such rules are viewed as an additional safeguard (beyond the co-respondent mechanism) for preventing the ECtHR from undermining the autonomy of the Union legal order. Accordingly, they would supposedly resolve questions about how the Union reaches a decision on the activation and the implementation of the co-respondent mechanism.[77] Moreover, they would facilitate any inquiries about 'the origin of the violation and the precise share of responsibility' between the EU and its Member States on the basis of the internal allocation of competences,[78] clarifying who should be obliged to pay just satisfaction, as awarded by the ECtHR, or how much of it is incumbent upon each party, as well as who should adopt any normative measures ordered by the Court.[79] An additional internal mechanism to settle disputes between the Union and its Member States regarding the above elements might be necessary.[80] Such a mechanism could even provide for a special fund

[73] See CDDH 47+1 Ad Hoc Negotiation Group, 'Report of the Sixth Negotiation Meeting' (22 October 2020), §§13–14; Seventh Negotiation Meeting (n 18) §9.

[74] Common Statement of the Informal Group of Non-European Union Member States, Sixth Negotiation Meeting, ibid, Appendix III, §3; Seventh Negotiation Meeting, ibid, §6.

[75] Council of EU, 'Council Decision Authorising the Commission to Negotiate the Accession Agreement of the European Union to the European Convention for the Protection of Human Rights and Fundamental Freedoms (ECHR)' (8 June 2010) EU Council Doc 10817/10 (declassified on 10 June 2015) Annex III.

[76] See, indicatively, K Raba, 'Closing the Gaps in the Protection of Fundamental Rights in Europe: Accession of the EU to the ECHR' in S Morano-Foadi and L Vickers (eds), *Fundamental Rights in the EU: A Matter for Two Courts* (Oxford, Hart Publishing, 2015) 21, 40–41.

[77] P Gragl, 'A Giant Leap for European Human Rights? The Final Agreement on the European Union's Accession to the European Convention on Human Rights' (2014) 51 *CML Rev* 13, 39.

[78] S Lambrecht, 'The Sting is in the Tail: CJEU Opinion 2/13 Objects to Draft Agreement on accession of the EU to the European Convention on Human Rights' (2015) 1 *European Human Rights Law Review* 185, 192.

[79] JP Jacqué, 'Encore un effort camarades … l'adhésion de l'Union à la Convention européenne des Droits de l'Homme est toujours à votre portée' (2020) 1 *Europe des Droits & Libertés* 27, 35; LH Storgaard, 'EU Law Autonomy versus European Fundamental Rights Protection – On Opinion 2/13 on EU Accession to the ECHR' (2015) 15 *Human Rights Law Review* 485, 501.

[80] T Lock, 'The EU Before the European Court of Human Rights after Accession' in S Douglas-Scott and N. Hatzis (eds), *Research Handbook on EU Law and Human Rights* (Cheltenham, Edward Elgar Publishing, 2017) 226, 238.

under the control of the Commission that will ensure the prompt and effective compensation of the applicant.[81]

If the ECtHR's role is further limited to an automatic declaration of joint responsibility (ie if the last sentence of Article 3(7) is deleted), internal rules will become even more crucial, determining, for instance, the scope of obligations undertaken by each contracting party on the basis of the ECHR or to whom the wrongful conduct should be attributed in the first place.[82] Thus, the black box of the Union's composite nature will become completely inaccessible for the ECtHR and, reflectively, for the applicant.

In our view, such a strategy of shifting the details of responsibility to the EU internal rules is fraught with serious risks for the effective protection of human rights (section IV.B). Before delving into this issue, the nature of those rules according to general international law ought to be examined (section IV.A).

A. The Legal Nature of EU Internal Rules: Are they an Admissible *Lex Specialis*?

Internal arrangements are not automatically binding upon third states that are High Contracting Parties to the ECHR by virtue of the law of treaties.[83] The same conclusion can be reached through the application of the *lex specialis* principle, which requires that the special rule have the same status as the general rule and be applicable between the same parties.[84] This is not the case with the internal rules of an organisation, which are not concluded between an organisation and its Member States on the one side and third parties on the other side.[85]

Nevertheless, the wording of Article 64 DARIO on *lex specialis* seems to cover purely internal rules of the organisation.[86] This conclusion is, however, mitigated by the commentary to Article 64, which explicitly states[87] that it is modelled on Article 55 ASR, the latter insisting that the special rule is only applicable between the parties to the agreement that contains that rule.[88] More fundamentally, Christiane Ahlborn has argued that internal rules of an international organisation should not be treated as

[81] M den Heijer and A Nollkaemper, 'A New Framework for Allocating International Responsibility: the EU Accession to the European Convention on Human Rights' (SHARES Briefing Paper, Amsterdam Centre of International Law 2014) 17, www.sharesproject.nl/wp-content/uploads/2014/01/Binder11.pdf, last accessed 4 September 2021.

[82] Ibid, 9; Tacik (n 71) 22.

[83] 1969 Vienna Convention on the Law of Treaties, 1155 UNTS 331, Art 34; see also, regarding EU internal arrangements, I Govaere, '"Facultative" and "Functional" Mixity Consonant with the Principle of Partial and Imperfect Conferral' in Chamon and Govaere (n 5) 21, 25; Talmon (n 30) 416.

[84] P Bodeau-Livinec, 'Les faux semblants de la *lex specialis*: l'exemple de la Résolution 52/247 de l'Assemblée générale des Nations unies sur les limitations temporelles et financières de la responsabilité de l'ONU' (2013) 46 *Revue Belge de Droit International* 117, 122–23.

[85] JM Cortés-Martín, 'European Exceptionalism in International Law? The European Union and the System of International Responsibility' in M Ragazzi (ed), *Responsibility of International Organizations* (n 28) 189, 197–98.

[86] 'Such special rules of international law may be contained in the rules of the organization applicable to the relations between an IO and its members'.

[87] DARIO, Commentary to Art 64, para 7. See also, ibid, Commentary to Art 5, para 3.

[88] 'Draft Articles on Responsibility of States for Internationally Wrongful Acts [2001] ILCYb, vol II/2', Commentary to Art 55, paras 1–2. See also Hernández (n 54) 653–54.

lex specialis because they are not rules of the same legal order as those of general international law. Any other conclusion, she pertinently observes, 'may convey the false impression that Member States and international organizations could avoid compliance with their international obligations towards third parties by means of special internal "rules of the organization"'.[89]

The question, thus, is how such rules could become compulsory for third states. It has been argued, for instance, that third parties' consent to conclude a mixed agreement with the EU and/or its Member States (or to transform a pre-existing treaty into a mixed agreement) to some extent mutates those internal rules into international ones.[90] In our view, such an outcome would be possible only if the relevant EU internal rules are reproduced, or incorporated by reference, in the mixed agreement.[91] Yet, this option risks subjecting EU internal rules to the review powers of the competent international dispute settlement body, namely the ECtHR, in the case at hand.[92]

Moreover, even if the above arrangements make those rules an admissible *lex specialis* (ie internationalise them), its scope of application cannot be automatically extended to individual applicants, whether they are nationals of a High Contracting party to the ECHR or of a third state. States can indeed bestow rights on individuals and subject them to obligations without their consent.[93] But human rights treaties grant individuals procedural and substantive rights directly, and any restrictions beyond those provided by the treaty itself should not impinge upon the very essence of those rights.[94] Consequently, any internal rules regulating the responsibility question in the case of the EU accession to the ECHR should not adversely affect the essence of the applicant's procedural rights under the Convention. This perspective has been highlighted by the CJEU in *Opinion 1/17*, where it confirmed that international dispute settlement mechanisms contained in mixed agreements must respect the Charter of Fundamental Rights and, more specifically, the *very essence* of Article 47 CFR.[95] However, any incorporation in the DAA of provisions that relegate specific steps of the judicial process to EU internal rules might violate the procedural rights to a fair trial and an effective remedy enjoyed by the applicant before the ECtHR, as we will explain in the following section.

[89] C Ahlborn, 'The Rules of International Organizations and the Law of International Responsibility' (2011) 8 *International Organizations Law Review* 397, 437–38.

[90] See the eloquent analysis by J Odermatt, 'Facultative Mixity in the International Legal Order: Tolerating European Exceptionalism?' in Chamon and Govaere (n 5) 291, 295.

[91] S Vezzani, 'The International Responsibility of the European Union and of Its Member States for Breaches of Obligations Arising from Investment Agreements: *Lex Specialis* or European Exceptionalism?' in M Andenas et al (eds), *EU External Action in International Economic Law: Recent Trends and Developments* (The Hague, TMC Asser Press, 2020) 281, 312–13.

[92] Besides, incorporation by reference has the further drawback of depriving third states of any leverage if the rules are modified internally, their initial consent covering equally those amendments; see V Pergantis, *The Paradigm of State Consent in the Law of Treaties* (Cheltenham, Elgar, 2017) 139–41.

[93] M Waibel, 'The Principle of Privity' in M Bowman and D Kritsiotis (eds), *Conceptual and Contextual Perspectives on the Modern Law of Treaties* (Cambridge, CUP, 2018) 201, 208.

[94] For the term, see S van Drooghenbroeck and C Rizcallah, 'The ECHR and the Essence of Fundamental Rights: Searching for Sugar in Hot Milk' (2019) 20 *German Law Journal* 904.

[95] *Opinion 1/17*, paras 167, 190 and 201. See also *Waite and Kennedy Germany* [GC], no 26083/94 (1999) paras 59 and 73.

B. How May the Shift to EU Internal Rules Undermine the Effectiveness of the ECHR and the Procedural Rights of the Applicant?

Depriving the ECtHR of the opportunity to interpret Union law, allocate responsibility, and determine remedies for the execution of its judgments undermines the external control that it is meant to exercise. It thus challenges 'the very idea of the Strasbourg system',[96] by transforming the concept of external control into an empty shell.[97] Additionally, any conditioning of the ECtHR's judicial function on EU internal rules – such as in the case at hand, where the CJEU subsequent to an ECtHR judgment would exclusively determine who is ultimately responsible – undermines the very premise of the ECtHR's judicial independence.[98] By awarding to the EU and its internal rules such a prominent role, the CJEU becomes the sole interpreter of such internal arrangements, thus overriding the authority of the ECtHR and predetermining the outcome of the case and its execution.[99]

More worryingly, internalising the issue of responsibility allocation might also work at the expense of the applicant.[100] For instance, if the ECtHR distributes responsibility, the applicant will be better informed about where to address a claim of redress in the form of 'just satisfaction' or adoption of individual and general measures.[101] If the allocation of responsibility is instead left in the hands of the Union, the applicant might, at the subsequent stage of internal EU arrangements, remain uncertain about which entity should undertake remedial action.[102] Moreover, any internalisation of the responsibility allocation and execution processes might force the applicant 'to bring further actions (and possibly being sent from pillar to post)' for its injury to be properly remedied, thus putting him/her in a disadvantageous position in relation to applicants in other cases.[103]

To be fair, it is possible to mitigate some of these consequences. There are at least two possibilities. First, responsibility allocation could be conditioned on the consent of the applicant.[104] This solution, however, leaves the applicant vulnerable to pressures from a powerful respondent, notably the EU. Second, the applicant could be automatically

[96] Łazowski and Wessel (n 4) 199.

[97] Gaja (n 35) para 6; C Hillion and RA Wessel, 'The European Union and International Dispute Settlement: Mapping Principles and Conditions' in M Cremona, A Thies and RA Wessel (eds), *The European Union and International Dispute Settlement* (Oxford, Hart Publishing, 2017) 7, 18.

[98] Cortés-Martín, 'Sur l'adhésion à la CEDH' (n 62) 653.

[99] Lambrecht (n 78) 191–92. See also Seventh Negotiation Meeting (n 18) §10.

[100] See, generally, C Tomuschat, 'The International Responsibility of the European Union' in E Cannizzaro (ed), *The European Union as an Actor in International Relations* (The Hague, Kluwer, 2002) 177, 183. *Contra* T Lock, 'The Future of the European Union's Accession to the European Convention on Human Rights after Opinion 2/13: Is it Still Possible and is it Still Desirable? (2015) 11 *European Constitutional Law Review* 239, 269, who argues that in any case, the principle of joint responsibility translates into increased protection for the applicant.

[101] C Krenn, 'Autonomy and Effectiveness as Common Concerns: A Path to ECHR Accession after Opinion 2/13' (2015) 16 *German Law Journal* 147, 152.

[102] Lock, 'The Future' (n 100) 249.

[103] Den Heijer and Nollkaemper (n 81) 17.

[104] See *mutatis mutandis* D Halbestram, '"It's the Autonomy, Stupid!": A Modest Defense of Opinion 2/13 on EU Accession to the ECHR, and the Way Forward' (2015) 16 *German Law Journal* 105, 137, who proposes that such allocation be done by the ECtHR.

awarded compensation by an EU fund, leaving the question of responsibility apportionment between the Union and its Member States to be decided *inter se* at a later stage.[105] While attractive in its simplicity, this proposal does not consider Convention violations that can only be remedied through positive action, such as failures to legislate or restitution. In such cases, it will be impossible to execute the judgment automatically, and any later responsibility allocation between the EU and its Member State might delay (or create further roadblocks to) the cessation of the wrongful act and the adoption of the proper remedy.

Whereas some mitigation is thus possible, it remains that a shift to EU internal arrangements might disproportionately restrict the right to an effective remedy enjoyed by applicants before the ECtHR and create insurmountable obstacles for ensuring the Court's judicial independence and the enforcement of its judgments. It might also open up an opportunity for abuse if the Union and/or its Member States engage in a 'blame game'. Consequently, the Union and its Member States would no longer be on an equal footing with the other High Contracting Parties to the ECHR – which contradicts one of the most fundamental principles of the accession negotiations.[106]

V. Conclusion

Ultimately, any attempt to accommodate EU autonomy and the ECtHR's prerogative to allocate responsibility finds itself between a rock and a hard place. If the negotiators attempt to establish a mechanism for addressing the applications to the correct respondent, as the 2013 DAA attempts, the ECtHR will inescapably be called to assess the distribution of competences in order to allocate responsibility between respondents (the Union and/or its Member States). This is contrary to the Union's autonomy, as demonstrated by the CJEU's reaction to the current draft.

Conversely, if the new draft opts for a light touch with regard to responsibility allocation, for example, by establishing a (near-)automatic rule of shared responsibility in cases involving the Union, the effectiveness of the ECHR system is threatened. That is because solutions along these lines will invariably entail shifting the issue of determining who should implement ECtHR judgments to the EU internal sphere. Such a shift will also raise difficult issues with regard to whether these rules can be opposable to applicants before the ECtHR, especially if they are nationals of states that are not members of the CoE.

There is no obvious compromise position between these two extremes. Indeed, the 2013 DAA was an attempt at such a compromise, which went quite far in the direction of preserving the CJEU's precious principle of autonomy, but was rejected. We, therefore, do not envy the negotiators currently tasked with working out this part of the DAA after the resumption of the negotiations. Unless the CJEU changes course, we could thus be headed in the direction of another impasse, either because the parties

[105] Den Heijer and Nollkaemper (n 81) 17. But this does not resolve the problem of who will execute an individual or general measure ordered by the ECtHR as a remedy.

[106] Draft Explanatory Report (n 18) para 7.

simply will not agree, or the CJEU will again reject an attempt at compromise, or because the ECtHR will rebuff a simplified system shifting responsibility allocation to the EU internal sphere.[107]

In any event, these difficulties are not particular to the ECHR. In the case of joint participation of the Union alongside its Member States in a mixed agreement with dispute settlement procedures, the autonomy of the Union legal will invariably be threatened. Often, the threat to autonomy can be mitigated, for example, by simplifying and internalising the responsibility question. As demonstrated, that solution is unsatisfactory for treaties like the ECHR, which bestow individuals with substantive rights and access to judicial dispute resolution. In these cases, the principle of autonomy constitutes a serious hindrance to joint participation – and thus a hindrance to ensuring the Union's external human rights accountability.

[107] The latter risk is clearly present this time around, as the negotiators are considering asking the ECtHR for an opinion on the DAA once it is (re)negotiated; see 'Report of the sixth meeting of the CDDH ad hoc negotiation Group ("47+1") on the Accession of the European Union to the European Convention on Human Rights' (22 October 2020) CoE Doc 47+1(2020)R6, para 43.

PART IV

EU International Agreements in Uncertain Times

13

Social and Legal Relevance of Sincere Cooperation in EU External Relations Law in an Era of Expanding Trade

*The Belt and Road Initiative in Context**

ELAINE FAHEY AND JULIJA BRSAKOSKA BAZERKOSKA

I. Introduction

The complexity of the EU in the international legal order entails that arriving at an EU position does not arise from happenstance. Proof of a failure of unity, a lack of cooperation, a lack of participation and so on does not necessarily arise easily. The Court of Justice has provided for a notoriously broad definition of sincere cooperation to dominate the core and periphery of EU action across the board.[1] This 'lightly' legalised understanding of conduct increasingly takes place against extraordinarily backdrops – departing Member States or increased negotiation of agreements with third countries using soft law only.[2] It is commonly considered that joint participation[3] and the many legal principles surrounding Member State action are in fact heavily legalised or simply just *legal* concepts, rules and ideas and their attendance proof, evidence and causality.[4] They are framed as contestation or isolated disputes. In reality, there is a

* Thanks to Ivanka Karaivanova for her research assistance.

[1] Case C-433/03, *Commission v Germany*, EU:C:2005:462; Case C-246/07, *Commission v Sweden*, EU:C:2010:203; Case C-355/04, *Segi and Others v Council*, EU:C:2007:116.

[2] Ramses A Wessel, 'Normative Transformations in EU External Relations: the Phenomenon of "Soft" International Agreements' (2020) 44 *West European Politics* 72.

[3] In cases when the EU and its Member States are jointly participating in negotiations, or as members of international agreements or international organisations, the duty of sincere cooperation mainly represents the Member States obligation to remain silent in order not to undermine the EU position. In other cases, when the EU cannot be represented on the international arena, it is the duty of the Member States to sincerely cooperate and to represent actively the EU position internationally.

[4] See Andres Delgado Casteleiro, 'No More Mr. Nice Guy: the Evolution of the Duty of Sincere Cooperation in EU External Relations Law', in Javier Diez-Hochleitner and others (eds), *Recent trends in the case-law of*

distinctly law-light dimension to sincere cooperation where rules, if they are that, are often more regarded in their breach. The chapter will examine how much EU Member States increasingly disrespect the duty of cooperation within trade and at its margins by focussing upon its most complex international opponent and potential partner, China and its Belt and Road Initiative (BRI).

The Belt and Road Initiative (BRI) of China is understood to constitute a law-light, institution-light, treaty-light 'top-down' non-institutionalised form of globalisation, differing from the EU's globalisation through institutionalisation in 'bottom-up' structures at the core of the EU's deep and comprehensive post-Lisbon trade agreements.[5] It has thrived upon soft law instruments and a lack of 'hard' treaty power and institutional structure.[6] Instead, it relies on processes *outside* of traditional frameworks for the protection and promotion of investments, eg heavily conditional loans and adopts approaches which are a-legal such as disregarding local labour and environmental laws.[7] As a result, it might be said that any EU Member State engagement with the BRI is on its face contrary to EU commitments to good global governance and the commitments to upholding international law in Article 21 TEU. EU Member State engagement with the Belt and Road Initiative (BRI) of China is, as a result, highly significant, particularly in the wake of EU-China agreement in principle on investment[8] in late 2020. It is also a key study of joint participation, sincere cooperation and the ostensible irrelevance of EU action. The BRI is *not* an international organisation yet in its scale, span and

the Court of Justice of the European Union (La Ley, 2012); Joris Larik, '*Pars Pro Toto:* The Member States' Obligations of Sincere Cooperation, Solidarity and Unity' in Marise Cremona (ed), *Structural Principles in EU External Relations Law* (Hart Publishing, 2018); Marise Cremona, 'EU Treaty-Making after the Lisbon Treaty – A Test Case for Mutual Sincere Cooperation?' in Jeno Czuczai and Frederik Naert (eds), *The EU as a Global Actor, Bridging Legal Theory and Practice, Liber Amicorum in Honour of Ricardo Gosalbo Bono* (Brill Nijhoff, 2017); Peter Van Elsuwege, 'The Duty of Sincere Cooperation and Its Implications for Autonomous Member State Action in the Field of External Relations' in Marton Varju (ed), *Between Compliance and Particularism* (Springer, 2019).

[5] Julien Chaisse and Jamieson Kirkwood, 'Chinese Puzzle: Anatomy of the (Invisible) Belt and Road Investment Treaty' (2020) 23 *Journal of International Economic Law* 245; Benedict Kingsbury, 'Infrastructure and InfraReg: on Rousing the International Law 'Wizards of Is' (2019) 8 *Cambridge International Law Journal* 171; Mark Wu, 'Digital Trade-Related Provisions in Regional Trade Agreements: Existing Models and Lessons for the Multilateral Trade System' (2017) RTA Exchange International Centre for Trade and Sustainable Development and Inter-American Development Bank, https://perma.cc/KHM9-33U; Julien Chaisse and Jędrzej Górski, *The Belt and Road Initiative: Law, Economics and Politics* (Koninklinjke Brill, 2018); Chi He, 'The Belt and Road Initiative as Global Public Good: Implications for International Law', in Wenhua Shan, Kimmo Nuotio and Kangle Zhang (eds), *Normative Readings of the Belt and Road Initiative* (Springer, 2018); Giuseppe Martinico, 'Comparative Law Reflections on the Use of Soft Law in the Belt and Road Initiative' in Giuseppe Martinico and Xueyan Wu, *A Legal Analysis of the Belt and Road Initiative: Towards a New Silk Road?* (Palgrave Macmillan, 2020); Sten Idris Verhoeven, 'EU Legal Obstacles to the Belt and Road Initiative: Towards a China-EU Framework on the Belt and Road Initiative' in Francisco José B S Leandro and Paulo Afonso B Duarte (eds), *The Belt and Road Initiative* (Palgrave Macmillan, 2020). Although see Mingjiang Li, 'The Belt and Road Initiative: Geo-economics and Indo-Pacific Security Competition' (2020) 96 *International Affairs* 169 on the role of Chinese officials.

[6] Chaisse and Kirkwood (n 5); Martinico (n 5).

[7] Matthew Steven Erie, 'Chinese Law and Development' (2020) 61 *Harvard International Law Journal*, forthcoming; Sonia Rolland and David Trubek, *Emerging Powers in the International Economic Order* (CUP, 2019) 196; Fleur Johns, *Non-legality in International Law: Unruly Law*, (CUP, 2013).

[8] European Commission, 'EU and China Reach Agreement in Principle on Investment' (30 December 2020), https://ec.europa.eu/commission/presscorner/detail/en/ip_20_2541?mc_cid=51ec175ba0&mc_eid=d59f683373.

ambitions increasingly is impacting upon global and EU understandings of international law, regions and nation states vis-à-vis China and so it has a heightened relevance for the study of joint participation as a result.

This chapter explores the ironies, margins and outer limits of joint participation between the EU and the Member States in the context of the BRI. Joint participation is argued here to be chronically under-enforced and creates unnecessary power imbalances. Its case law favours repeat players or erratically tracks core competences; the EU is disincentivised from litigating; and informally also irrationally.[9] Case law on enforcement of joint participation is largely centred around 'repeat players', is rarely enforced and only where it bears upon more integrated competences or extraordinary levels of conflict. There is a severe lack of case law, which hampers serious analytical work upon the subject as an ordinary area of EU law. Where such case law exists, its precedential status is perhaps questionable. For instances, the decision of the Grand Chamber in *Germany v Council (OIV)* grants considerable powers to the EU to 'develop' itself in international organisations and act so as to protect its *acquis* where the EU has no formal status and not all Member States are members – yet where EU law still prevails.[10] This is despite the lack of legal basis in the treaties for joining international organisations and internationalisation. This legalisation of a de facto delegalised space has developed the intellectual threshold of sincere cooperation there arguably beyond its deserved station.

Critical approaches to EU international relations law are few and far between, a subject of a highly court-centric nature focusing upon the role of the Court. The chapter explores how it is bound up with an extraordinary array of principles from effectiveness, coherence and consistency. The absence of treaty rules on the seemingly grey areas surrounding the boundaries of EU action appears readily deployed by the EU itself. Joint participation state of the art does not capture how trade is increasingly embedded in legal and political ironies as evidenced by the BRI. The BRI is a useful template for critical analysis of the contours of trade with security, investment and development. The broader parameters of EU international relations law are also important to pinpoint – EU international relations are increasingly subject to degrees of informalisation, where soft law or non-binding instruments are used in key EU international relations contexts of controversy, evading scrutiny, judicial review, institutional analysis, and removing citizen scrutiny.[11] It is arguably no surprise to see the erosion of the contours of sincere cooperation as a serious legal principle. These informalisation developments take place principally in areas of shared competences, such as migration. However, they pose important challenges to the firmness of judicial control in areas of exclusive competence.

In this regard, the relationship between the Belt and Road Initiative (BRI) and Europe is an important one in the broader scheme of reflecting upon soft law and sincere cooperation in the context of joint participation. China is acknowledged by many as seeking regional influence but lacking experience, deep capital markets, soft power and legitimacy. It has as a result sought to expand its influence through instruments other than

[9] Eg Case C-399/12, *Germany v Council*, EU:C:2014:2258, because of agriculture; Case C-459/03, *Commission v Ireland*, EU:C:2006:345, nuclear.

[10] *Germany v Council* (n 9).

[11] Wessel (n 2); Manon Damestoy and Nicolas Levrat's chapter in this edited volume.

formal international law, principally the Belt and Road Initiative (BRI).[12] The BRI has a strong foothold in Europe and has managed arguably to divide the EU bilaterally and 'carve up' the Member States in ways in which no other global power has so managed. The BRI is ultimately a set of domestic policies and economic instruments supported by Chinese domestic institutions and law but devoid of multilateral or bilateral agreements, seemingly contrary to key EU principles of external action. The BRI activities are increasingly harmful, operating to threaten EU unity on human rights activities or thwarting EU negotiations with China.

The chapter will analyse the case of EU Member States joining in the BRI and will further explore whether EU itself should or is likely become a part of the BRI within the framework of joint participation or whether it is in breach of sincere cooperation. It will also argue, that the duty of sincere cooperation should be extended as an example to the future EU Member States from the Western Balkan region and explore these countries behaviour in connection with the BRI.

Section II explores the core of sincere cooperation, section III considers the BRI of China in Europe, section IV assesses the example set by the EU and the Members States engagement with the BRI for the new enlargement in the Western Balkans, while section V focuses on the analysis of the BRI and EU MS breach of sincere cooperation, followed by Conclusions.

II. EU External Representation: On Disintegration

The duty of sincere cooperation as defined in Article 4(3) TEU, as a mutual legal obligation for the EU and its Member States 'to assist each other in carrying out the tasks which flow from the Treaties', is especially important in relation to the Union representation in the international arena. This duty is important in those cases where the Member States and the Union have shared competences on the issues that arise in the EU's external relations. It is essential both for the Union and third parties in international relations to have security in terms of certainty who is the partner on the other side. The obligation of close cooperation in fulfilling the commitments between the Union and the Member States was established by the CJEU. It was developed primarily in Opinion 2/91[13] that was connected with the ILO and furthermore accomplished in Opinion 1/94.[14] Opinion 1/94 concerning the implementation of the WTO agreements, to which the Community was an original party alongside its Member States, provided that close cooperation between the Member States and Community institutions is essential both in the process of negotiating and concluding the agreements, and in the fulfilment of the commitments entered into.[15] The Court stated that the 'obligation to

[12] Rolland and Trubek (n 7).

[13] Opinion 2/91 of the Court of 19 March 1993, EU:C:1993:106.

[14] Opinion 1/94 of the Court 15 November 1994, EU:C:1994:384.

[15] See further: Stephen Hyett, 'The Duty of Cooperation: A Flexible Concept' in Alan Dashwood and Christophe Hillion (eds), *The General Law of EC External Relations* (Sweet and Maxwell, 2000); Marcus Klammert, *The Principle of Loyalty in EU Law* (OUP, 2014); Christophe Hillion, 'Mixity and Coherence in EU External Relations: The Significance of the Duty of Cooperation' (2009) CLEER Working Papers 2009/2;

cooperate flows from the requirement of unity in the international representation of the Community'.[16]

The duty of cooperation refers to all stages of external action, starting from negotiation; conclusion and execution of the international obligations either by concluding international treaties or agreeing to decisions of organs of international organisations. When negotiating with another international organisation, the Member States' positions should be coordinated and the coordination between the position of the Member States and the Union needs to be ensured in order to have stronger position. In case the coordination fails and a common position is not achieved, there will be no participation in the negotiations. The requirement of unity in the international representation of the Union is incompatible with individual behaviour of the Member States. When the shared competences are linked and complex, Member States acting alone would usurp Union powers. It might commit the Union under international law, by agreeing to international commitments in Union areas. Therefore, the logical conclusion is that there should be either coordinated action or no action at all.[17] Although it is very important to consider the EU position that is reached in due coordination, the Member States are mainly cautious in this area. Moreover, the Commission does not have any tool to force the Member States to enter into informal inter-institutional arrangements that are aimed at improving the process of coordination. The duty of sincere cooperation in the EU's external relations happens in the complex mix of exclusive, shared, parallel, and sui generis competences in this area. It has been developed in the broader context of the EU continuous support for multilateralism in trade issues and for those reasons it has been challenged in the case of the BRI, which is not an international organisation and rests upon the soft law instruments, and unlike the EU's multilateral approach to international trade, it uses bilateral and state-centric agreements.

A. The CCP 'Core' of Sincere Cooperation

The EU Common Commercial Policy (CCP) has always been the core of its external relations. By negotiating trade agreements with a wide range of partners and by providing unilateral trade preferences, the EU has been promoting its strategic interests, standards, values, as well as its development objectives. The EU is a strong proponent of multilateral trade cooperation in the WTO, but also it has been negotiating bilateral and regional trade agreements. In the past several years it has increasingly linked its trade policy to the pursuit of non-trade external policy goals and values established in the Lisbon Treaty. This was especially reflected in conditioning the preferential access to the EU market with respect for human rights and fundamental freedoms. When the WTO was created back in 1995, soon after the Maastricht treaty entered into force, the CCP

Peter Van Elsuwege, 'The Duty of Sincere Cooperation and Its Implications for Autonomous Member State Action in the Field of External Relations' in Marton Varju (ed), *Between Compliance and Particularism* (Springer, 2019).

[16] Opinion 1/94 (n 14) para 108.

[17] See further: Christiaan Timmermans, 'Organizing Joint Participation of EC and Member States' in Dashwood and Hillion (n 15).

was in the shared competence of both the Community and the Member States. In these complex times, at the beginning of EU's membership in the WTO, there were numerous cases that were raised before the CJEU which questioned the boundaries of the CCP.[18] During that period, these circumstances made sincere cooperation in the area of the CCP more important. However, since the entry into force of the Lisbon Treaty, the CCP falls within the exclusive competence of the EU as a whole. According to Article 2(1) TFEU in cases of exclusive Union competence 'only the Union may legislate and adopt legally binding acts, the Member States being able to do so themselves only if so empowered by the Union or for the implementation of Union acts'. With the Lisbon Treaty, the CCP was redefined and its competences include also trade in services, trade-related aspects of intellectual property, and foreign direct investment as integral components.[19]

According to Larik,[20] although the CCP is under the EU's exclusive competence, it again underlines the future importance of the principle of sincere cooperation in the CCP, especially in the context of the Member States using their right to be part of the WTO on their own, together with the EU. According to the Lisbon judgment of 2009 from the German Federal Constitutional Court, 'there is no need to address whether and to what extent the membership of the Member States of the European Union in the World Trade Organization would no longer exist at the substantive level but only at the institutional and formal level', because 'the Treaty of Lisbon may at any rate not force the Member States to waive their member status'.[21] According to the German Federal Constitutional Court, 'this particularly applies to the negotiations on multilateral trade relations within the meaning of Article III.2 of the WTO Agreement whose possible future content is not determined by the law of the European Union, and for which a competence of the Member States may therefore emerge in the future, depending on the course of future trade rounds.'[22]

At this point in time, there are numerous major challenges in adjusting the global trade to rapid technological changes and the growth of the digital economy; also to adapt it to global problems such as climate change, and at the same time to try and address the universal values on human rights. In this rapidly evolving and uncertain context, both the EU and the WTO need to reposition themselves. The WTO was not designed to address the trade issues in a world of a digital economy. It was intended to be the global forum where countries agree on rules of the game for trade policies and resolve trade disputes. It seems that it failed that task too and that there has been an ongoing crisis of the WTO, with one blow adding to another. Just in the past year, the organisation has been faced with the demise of the Appellate Body, with trade

[18] Case C-53/96, *Hermès International v FHT Marketing Choice*, EU:C:1998:292; Joined Cases C-300/98 and C-392/98, *Dior and Others*, EU:C:2000:688; Case C-431/05, *Merck Genéricos Produtos Farmacêuticos*, EU:C:2007:496; Opinion 1/08 of the Court (Grand Chamber) of 30 November 2009, EU:C:2009:739.

[19] Consolidated Version of the Treaty of Functioning of the European Union (TFEU) [2012] OJ C326/47, art 207(1) TFEU.

[20] Joris Larik, 'Sincere Cooperation in the Common Commercial Policy: Lisbon, a "Joined-Up" Union, and "Brexit"' in *European Yearbook of International Economic Law* (Springer, 2017).

[21] Judgment of the German Federal Constitutional Court (Second Senate) of 30 June 2009, 2 BvE 2/08, para 375.

[22] Ibid.

disputes and with the COVID crisis. The WTO is most visible with the dispute resolution mechanism, which cannot function because the Trump administration refused to renew the judges after 11 December 2019 when the terms of two of the remaining three members of the World Trade Organization's Appellate Body came to an end. With only one member left, the Appellate Body can no longer meet the three-member quorum required to review appeals. This development brings the WTO's dispute resolution mechanism to a standstill, but challenges the rules-based trading system as well. It also raises questions regarding the relevance of multilateral institutions in the current geopolitical environment.[23]

The role of the EU in this case, as a long-standing proponent of multilateralism, is to provide leadership to strengthening the existing alliances and building new ones which will contribute to defending the rules-based trading system. This includes an active support for WTO reform and addressing the stalemate in dispute settlement processes. Moreover, it needs to include a range of critical issues, such as addressing the negative spillover effects of subsidies and the behaviour of state-owned enterprises, climate change in line with the Paris Agreement, digitalisation and artificial intelligence.[24] The new EU Commission has declared its aims to become a role model for the digital economy, support developing economies in going digital, develop digital standards and promote them internationally.[25]

Sincere cooperation by the Member States has always been undermined by the geopolitical interests of individual states and the global powers' influence in Europe. The EU has traditionally been a close ally to the US, but after the Trump challenge to global trade and the decision by the Trump administration to revert to 'aggressive unilateralism' and pursue a more protectionist trade policy, this position has been challenged. In this context, trade has become a much higher-profile policy area for the EU. Trade policy is as well a core dimension of the rising concern in the EU regarding the competitive implications of China's industrial policies. While EU's approach in international trade is through multilateralism, it seems that the BRI projects which are financed and carried out by Chinese companies continues to be based on flexible legal instruments that tend to *avoid* multilateral BRI treaties and institutions. As will be outlined below, China's BRI projects are often based on informal, bilateral and state-centred practices.[26] Even though the BRI is an inclusive project, its ambiguous institutional and constitutional design creates rule of law gaps to the disadvantage of international trade.[27] The Union

[23] More on this issue in: Petros C Mavroidis and others, 'WTO Dispute Settlement and the Appellate Body: Insider perceptions and Members' revealed preferences' (2020) 54 *Journal of World Trade 667* and Bernard M Hoekman and Petros C Mavroidis, 'Burning Down the House? The Appellate Body in the Centre of the WTO Crisis' (2019) EUI Working Paper RSCAS 2019/56.

[24] San Bilal and Bernard M Hoekman (eds), *Perspectives on the Soft Power of EU Trade Policy* (CEPR Publishing, 2019).

[25] The Data Strategy and the White Paper on Artificial Intelligence are the first pillars of the new digital strategy of the Commission. The European strategy for data aims at creating a single market for data that will ensure Europe's global competitiveness and data sovereignty. Communication from the Commission to the European Parliament, the Council, the European Economic and Social Committee and the Committee of the Regions, 'A European strategy for data', 19.2.2020 COM(2020) 66 final; 'White Paper on Artificial Intelligence – A European approach to excellence and trust', 19.2.2020 COM(2020) 65 final.

[26] More on this in: Giuseppe Martinico and Xueyan Wu, *A Legal Analysis of the Belt and Road Initiative: Towards a New Silk Road?* (Palgrave Macmillan, 2020).

[27] Martinico (n 5).

needs to design appropriate responses to international trade conflicts and tensions, a task which is further complicated by the increasing complexity of the trade and external policy agenda given that these policies increasingly include dimensions of security. These issues are exacerbated by the BRI investments, as this account will consider below.

The following section examines the BRI in more detail, prior to considering its operation in the EU Member States.

III. The Belt and Road Initiative (BRI) of China

A. Overview

The BRI may have its effect of bringing Europe and Asia together, less through institutions but more through investments and structural developments. The BRI is not an international organisation, but it has managed through a highly complex network of agreements to influence EU–China relations in a very intricate manner. The emerging gap between EU and Chinese approaches to globalisation poses an important series of questions. As Menon pithily observes, as to China there is no single EU foreign policy: the EU is the 28th foreign policy in addition to those of each Member State.[28] One of the greatest challenges in engaging with China is that there is no agreed understanding in law of the meaning of the Chinese state and its reach with respect to global governance.[29] China is one of the other most unusual powers in the world today, and poses considerable challenges in international economic law for the definition of a market economy and state capitalism. In fact, what is at stake, as Lang eloquently argues, is the existence of the capacity and opportunity to innovate institutionally, its direction and its distribution between different states within the global economic system.[30] Tensions caused by institutional diversity have for the most part been resolved by gradual institutional convergence around Western market models.[31] Unsurprisingly, EU country reports on China, issued in accordance with its new trade defence rules, identify a huge array of sources of state disruption in the Chinese economy.[32] Although China has become a very prolific advocate of soft law, it is a particular feature

[28] Evidence from Malcolm Chalmers and Anand Menon to the Lords EU Sub-Committee on Foreign Affairs, Defence and Development inquiry into European security and EU military capabilities (10 November 2011). Steven Erlanger, 'E.U. Failure to Impose Sanctions on Belarus Lays Bare Its Weakness' *New York Times* (24 September 2020), www.nytimes.com/2020/09/24/world/europe/europe-sanctions-belarus-cyprus.html.

[29] See Mark Wu, 'The "China, Inc." Challenge to Global Trade Governance' (2016) 57 *Harvard International Law Journal* 261.

[30] Andrew Lang, 'Heterodox Markets and 'Market Distortions' in the Global Trading System' (2019) 22 *Journal of International Economic Law* 677, 681.

[31] Ibid 682.

[32] These range in a staggeringly long list, from state and party involvement in corporate management, the basic legal structure of socialist market economy, the risk assessment practices of financial firms, preferential government procurement practices, mechanisms for allocating land, investment screening systems, divergence of Chinese labour laws and practices from fundamental international labour standards as well as a wide range of sector specific policies, from research and development subsidies, preferential loads to favoured

of financial law and global governance and sources such as declarations, recommendations, guidelines, resolutions, codes of conduct, opinions, MoUs and memoranda of guidance dominate the BRI as much as the Chinese approach to internationalism. Adopting a steadfastly conventional view of international economic law as to BRI matters tends to skew the place of development in its construction of law, as to the BRI but also more broadly, which may be seen to be more of a globalisation study.[33]

Some contend that the BRI consists of primary agreements that can be regarded as a form of soft law, but those that repurpose soft law characteristics for project development rather than rule development. While they may have characteristics with respect to minimal legalisation, project-based activities that are coordinated and hub and spoke network structures, they are argued to display an increasing incongruence with existing soft law classifications.[34] This law-light approach to external relations sits perhaps at a notable turning point or juncture in Chinese legal culture, where in 2020 a civil code was adopted to come into force in 2021, after half a century of codification efforts.[35]

The EU and China launched negotiations on the Comprehensive Agreement on Investment (CAI) in 2014 and by summer 2020, 33 rounds of negotiations had taken place. The negotiations cover level playing field disciplines (state-owned enterprises, transparency rules for subsidies and rules tackling forced technology transfers) and sustainable development. In 2016, the EU and China agreed on the scope of the future agreement, that it would go beyond a traditional investment protection agreement to cover market access for investment and a number of important disciplines. It would also include provisions on sustainable development and dispute resolution. In July 2020, the first significant bilateral trade agreement was signed between the EU and China. Recently, the European Council has adopted decisions on the signature of the agreement between the EU and the government of China on geographical indications (GIs).[36] The agreement also includes a mechanism to add more GIs after that period in four years' time.[37] It constitutes a highly significant development between the two legal orders.

enterprises, export restrictions and incentives, tax incentives, land use cost relief, employment stabilisation plans and more: European Commission, 'Staff Working Document on Significant Distortions in the Economy of the People's Republic Of China for the Purposes of Trade Defence Investigations' SWD (2017) 483 final/2, considering factors including: the market in question being served to a significant extent by enterprises which operate under the ownership, control or policy supervision or guidance of the authorities of the exporting country; state presence in firms allowing the state to interfere with respect to prices or costs; public policies or measures discriminating in favour of domestic suppliers or otherwise influencing free market forces; the lack, discriminatory application or inadequate enforcement of bankruptcy, corporate or property laws; wage costs being distorted; access to finance granted by institutions which implement public policy objectives or otherwise not acting independently of the state.

[33] Erie (n 7); Heng Wang, 'The Belt and Road Initiative Agreements: Characteristics, Rationale and Challenges' (2021) 20 *World Trade Review*, forthcoming; Heng Wang, 'China's Approach to the Belt and Road Initiative' (2019) 22 *Journal of International Economic Law* 29.

[34] Wang, 'China's Approach to the Belt and Road Initiative' (n 33).

[35] Hao Jiang, 'The Making of a Civil Code in China: Promises and Perils of a New Civil Law' (2020) *Tulane Law Review*, forthcoming, also noting the major problem of applying contract law to state-owned enterprises (SOEs), with the lack of competitiveness of market conditions in which SOEs operate.

[36] Agreement between the European Union and the Government of the People's Republic of China on cooperation on, and protection of, geographical indications, Council of the European Union [2020] OJ L 408I/3.

[37] Ibid.

It follows in the wake of multiple EU-China Strategies increasingly lengthening-out, increasingly legalising and converging on a vast array of issues but in particular investment, development and trade more broadly.[38] In very late December 2020, agreement in principle on an investment agreement was finally reached.[39] This decision provoked a wide diversity of reactions and controversies as to Chinese human rights standards and conflicts between EU institutional actors and EU diplomats as to Chinese developments, but also a transatlantic divide.[40] Doubts about the deal were raised when in March 2021, the EU imposed sanctions against China for its treatment of the Uyghur Muslim minority in the Xinjiang region. These were the first human rights sanctions against China since the 1989 Tiananmen Square massacre. In response to these sanctions, Beijing announced counter-sanctions against members of the European Parliament and other officials. This move led to suspension of the ratification process on the EU side. Nevertheless, reaching the deal supports the view that significant development is taking place in EU-China relations across a brand range of areas, increasingly backed up by successful and 'law-heavy' negotiations, with binding agreements as outcomes.

B. The Member States Engaging with the BRI: On Depth and Breadth

i. Direct Engagement

The first countries in Europe with whom China signed memorandums of understanding to join the BRI were Central, Eastern and South Eastern European countries, with Hungary being the first European country to sign a BRI-related memorandum of understanding with China in 2015, a clear and direct form of engagement, politically at least.[41] By 2019, a further 22 European countries had signed BRI cooperation instruments – although the tally appears very complex on account of the lack of transparency of the operation of the BRI legally. Ties between China and Europe continue to grow with the latest European countries to sign BRI cooperation instruments being Luxembourg and Italy in March 2019. Three Member States in particular have particularly interesting

[38] EU-China Strategic Agenda for Cooperation (2020), https://eeas.europa.eu/archives/docs/china/docs/eu-china_2020_strategic_agenda_en.pdf.

[39] 'EU and China Reach Agreement in Principle on Investment' (n 8); See Jack Ewing and Steven Lee Myers, 'China and E.U. Leaders Strike Investment Deal, but Political Hurdles Await' *New York Times* (30 December 2020), www.nytimes.com/2020/12/30/business/china-eu-investment-deal.html; Alexandra Brzozowski, 'EU seeks to rebalance China ties with controversial investment agreement' (*Euractive*, 30 December 2020), www.euractiv.com/section/eu-china/news/eu-seeks-to-rebalance-china-ties-with-controversial-investment-agreement/; Theresa Fallon, 'The Strategic Implications of the China-EU Investment Deal' *The Diplomat* (4 January 2021), https://thediplomat.com/2021/01/the-strategic-implications-of-the-china-eu-investment-deal/; Sofia Baruzzi, 'EU, China Reach Agreement on Investments in Principle: What Does it Mean for Businesses' (*China Briefing*, 14 January 2021), www.china-briefing.com/news/eu-china-reach-agreement-on-investments-in-principle-what-does-it-mean-for-businesses/; Annabelle Timsit, 'Was the investment deal Europe signed with China worth it?' (*Quartz*, 15 January 2021), https://qz.com/1956673/the-eu-china-investment-deal-broken-down/.

[40] Noah Barkin, 'Watching China in Europe- January 2021' (2021), https://sites-gmf.vuturevx.com/61/6509/january-2021/january-2021(1).asp?sid=504eaec4-a13f-4a0b-bd39-56dbbc033363.

[41] Anastas Vangel, 'China's Engagement with the Sixteen Countries of Central, East and Southeast Europe under the Belt and Road Initiative' (2017) 25 *China & World Economy* 101.

relations with the BRI: the Netherlands, Italy and Austria.[42] As the largest of the EU Member States with a memorandum of understanding, though not the only EU Member State engaging in such negotiations, many raise the question as to the compatibility of the Italian position, as a non-binding statement of intent.[43] Austria, on the other hand, has been engaged as part of a third-party market cooperation agreement, which is aimed at using China's production capacity together with Austria's advanced technology to explore the markets of developing countries – and this is especially important in the context of Austrian ties with the CESEE countries, which seem to have great strategic importance for China.[44] Some Member States such as the Netherlands explicitly identify tensions in EU approaches to the future of EU-China relations as warranting coherence, unity and compromise as the key concepts.[45] Yet here the span of exclusive external compromise becomes complex. There is a delicate balance between negotiating individual relationships tainted by their lack of legal infrastructure/legality and the EU investment negotiations. The areas of Italy's MoU cooperation with China relate to unimpeded trade and investment and promoting market cooperation between Italy and China. It is an extremely lengthy and detailed document, signed in April 2019.[46] Ironically, the EU Council met on 22 March 2019 to discuss a common EU strategy toward China, to serve as a basis for the EU-China Summit to be held on 9 April 2019.[47] Extraordinarily, the next day the Italian government signed a memorandum of understanding (MOU) with Beijing to officially become a member of the BRI.[48] Trade remains first and foremost the successful and far-reaching exclusive competence of EU law, entailing that the EU alone can act internationally. It seems apparent that Member States such as Italy have been content to utilise the non-binding nature of BRI MoUs. Instead, here the scope of the MoU indicates a broadening of the significance of the trade relations being undertaken and increasingly puts the contours of the EU actions into doubt.

[42] Enrico Fardella and Giorgio Prodi, 'The Belt and Road Initiative Impact on Europe: An Italian Perspective' (2017) 25 *China & World Economy* 125; Steven Langendonk, 'Discourse Power as a Means to 'Struggle for Position': a Critical Case Study of the Belt and Road Narrative's Effects on Foreign Policy Formulation in the Netherlands' (2020) 25 *Journal of Chinese Political Science* 241; Alexandra Bykova and others, 'Economic Policy Implications of the Belt and Road Initiative for CESEE and Austria' (2018) *Policy Notes and Reports* No 23, The Vienna Institute for International Economic Studies; Federiga Bindi, 'Why Did Italy Embrace the Belt and Road Initiative?' (*Carnegie Endowment for International Peace*, 20 May 2019), https://carnegieendowment.org/2019/05/20/why-did-italy-embrace-belt-and-road-initiative-pub-79149; Femke van der Eijk and Angela Pandita Gunavardana, 'The Road that divided the EU: Italy joins China's Belt and Road Initiative' (*European Law Blog*, 25 June 2019), https://europeanlawblog.eu/2019/06/25/the-road-that-divided-the-eu-italy-joins-chinas-belt-and-road-initiative/.

[43] Bindi (n 42).

[44] Wang, 'The Belt and Road Initiative Agreements: Characteristics, Rationale and Challenges' (n 33); Bykova and others (n 42).

[45] Steven Langendonk, 'Discourse Power as a Means to 'Struggle for Position': a Critical Case Study of the Belt and Road Narrative's Effects on Foreign Policy Formulation in the Netherlands' (2020) 25 *Journal of Chinese Political Science* 241; 'Engaging but not Endorsing China's Belt and Road Initiative' (2019) Clingendael Policy Brief, www.clingendael.org/sites/default/files/2019-05/PB_China_Belt_and_Road_Initiative_May_2019.pdf.

[46] See Martinico (n 5).

[47] European Council, Conclusions March 21-22 2019 EUCO 1/19, p 4.

[48] Memorandum of Understanding between the Government of the Italian Republic and the Government of the People's Republic of China on Cooperation within the Framework of the Silk Road Economic Belt and the 21st Century Maritime Silk Road Initiative (2019), www.governo.it/sites/governo.it/files/Memorandum_Italia-Cina_EN.pdf.

ii. Indirect Engagements

One indirect aspect of EU Member States unilaterally becoming part of the BRI is the fact that it strengthens Chinese economic and political influence and contributes towards undermining the EU position on the international arena. One particular case is the Greek blocking of the European Union statement at the United Nations in June 2017, criticising China's human rights record.[49] The Greek decision undermined efforts to confront Beijing's crackdown on activists and dissidents and furthermore it also undermined EU effort to engage strongly within UN. This move has been seen as a sign that China has gained political sway with its Greek port purchase. As part of China's 21st Century Maritime Silk Road, which aims to better connect the country to commercial hubs in Africa, Asia, Europe and Oceania, buying Greece's Piraeus port was one of the cornerstones for further infiltration by China of the EU market. Since the purchase of Piraeus port by COSCO company in August 2016,[50] Greece has become a major stopover along the new Silk Roads. However, it was not until August 2018 that Greece formally joined the BRI. With the signing of the memorandum of understanding regarding cooperation within the framework of the 'Belt and Road Initiative' during a meeting in Beijing,[51] Greece deepened its relations with China, positioning itself as the main Mediterranean gateway to the new Silk Roads in Europe. The question is whether this investment in Piraeus port will bring the same developments as in connection with Chinese investments in the ports of Djibouti, Sri Lanka and Pakistan, which have been followed by Chinese naval deployments. Even though there are no public plans up until this point to turn European ports into Beijing's military bases, Chinese warships have already paid a 'friendly' visit to Greece's Piraeus port.[52]

We next consider the broader impact of BRI investment upon EU Enlargement members and the example being set for them.

IV. An Example to New Enlargement Members? On the Western Balkans and China

The issue of sincere cooperation goes beyond the borders of the European Union and has a spillover effect to the countries that want to become EU members in the future. The example given by the Member States in terms of how sincere their cooperation is in the external relations at this period of time will affect the future relationship of the candidate countries with the EU. It cannot be argued that the duty of sincere cooperation should be followed by the candidate countries for EU membership, since there is no such obligation in the Stabilisation and Association Agreements, but there is a

[49] 'Greece Blocks EU Statement on China Human Rights at UN' (*Euroactive*, 19 June 2017), www.euractiv.com/section/china/news/greece-blocks-eu-statement-on-china-human-rights-at-un/.

[50] George Georgiopoulos, 'China's Cosco Acquires 51 Pct Stake in Greece's Piraeus Port' (*Reuters*, 10 August 2016), www.reuters.com/article/greece-privatisation-port/chinas-cosco-acquires-51-pct-stake-in-greeces-piraeus-port-idUSL8N1AR252.

[51] Ibid.

[52] 'Chinese Naval Fleet Arrives in Greece for Friendly Visit' (*Ekathimerini*, 24 July 2017), www.ekathimerini.com/220324/article/ekathimerini/news/chinese-naval-fleet-arrives-in-greece-for-friendly-visit.

strong argument that the EU standards and the requirements of the Stabilisation and Association Agreements should be respected in both internal and external policies of the candidate countries. The period of association to the EU is supposed to be a period of time in which the potential member state should implement the EU *acquis*, but also incorporate the EU values in its policies. This section will focus on the Western Balkans–China relationship in the context of EU enlargement and respect of EU standards.

The enlargement context in the Western Balkans has changed, mainly because the region is characterised by legacies of war and a political climate that enabled the flourishing of organised crime, corruption and illegal migration. The EU first had to stabilise the region after the dissolution of Socialist Federal Republic of Yugoslavia and then associate the newly emerged countries. The Stabilisation and Association Process was launched in 1999 and granted the countries from the Western Balkans the status of potential candidate countries. In 2003, the Thessaloniki Agenda promoted political dialogue and cooperation in the area of the Common Foreign and Security Policy (CFSP), the strengthening of parliamentary cooperation and institution-building.[53] Therefore, the EU conditionality policy in the Balkans was designed as a multi-dimensional instrument directed towards reconciliation, reconstruction and reform. In addition to the 1993 Copenhagen criteria, the Western Balkans countries are expected to meet other criteria that are country-specific. The six Western Balkan countries that are moving towards EU membership are all at different stage of integration. Serbia and Montenegro have already opened negotiations with the Union, in 2014 and 2012 respectively, while the draft negotiating framework was presented to Macedonia and Albania in July 2020 following the decision of the Council in March 2020. Bosnia and Herzegovina and Kosovo are at the very early stages of their Euro integration path as potential candidates –the Stabilisation and Association Agreements having entered into force only in 2015 and 2016 respectively.

A. The Western Balkans and China: A Key Strategic Region for Investment

The Western Balkans is one of the key strategic regions for investment for China and is crucial for the Belt and Road Initiative. The region is important as a focal point in China's logistical and economic access to the EU. Even though, China's foreign direct investment remaining fairly low in the region their economic presence is strong due to loans, not investments.[54] All the Western Balkan countries except for Kosovo (since it is not recognised by China) are members of the '16+1' (now known as 17+1) framework. The Western Balkans' importance for China has become evident with the purchase of the Greek port of Piraeus, transforming it into the second largest port

[53] Council of the European Union, 'The Thessaloniki Agenda for the Western Balkans – Moving towards European integration' (2003) 10369/03 (Presse 166).

[54] Valbona Zeneli, 'The Western Balkans: Low Hanging Fruit for China?' *The Diplomat* (24 February 2020), https://thediplomat.com/2020/02/the-western-balkans-low-hanging-fruit-for-china/.

in the Mediterranean. With this purchase, China brings into life its plans to improve infrastructure in the Western Balkans which would further contribute to transport of goods being shipped from Piraeus through the Western Balkans and into the EU. Very often, China's investments in the Western Balkans are seen as a way to gain economic positions in the countries which may impact their potential accession in the EU.[55] Serbia is geopolitically the most important country in the region, where China's economic presence is illustrated with the investment financing and loans of $5.62 billion, whereas the ongoing Chinese infrastructure investments are almost 5 billion euros.[56] Perhaps the most worrying aspect of the Chinese investments in Serbia is Huawei's surveillance system of facial and licence-plate recognition which has been implemented in Serbia, while police officers have taken part in joint exercises with their Chinese counterparts.[57]

One of the most vulnerable countries in the Western Balkans region is Montenegro. China's influence through its so-called debt trap diplomacy[58] can be seen in the Bar–Belgrade highway project. The first phase of the China's highway project that is designed to connect the Montenegrin port city of Bar with Belgrade, the capital of Serbia has cost Montenegro approximately 1.3 billion euros, which is equivalent to a quarter of its 2018 GDP.[59] The loan that Montenegro took out with the Export-Import Bank of China has caused its GDP-to-debt ratio to increase to just over 80%. Montenegro is a candidate country for EU membership and opened negotiations back in June 2012, but these developments may endanger its EU future. Additionally, it makes Montenegro's economy highly vulnerable and its debt situation very prone to Chinese dependencies.[60] Furthermore, BRI also causes concerns over corruption risks. China was embroiled in a corruption scandal when leaked tapes suggested collusion between local politicians and Chinese state-owned companies and massive inflation of highway construction costs in North Macedonia. Sinohydro, a Chinese state-owned firm was contracted to build two highways in the country, and wiretaps in 2015 unveiled that the former Prime Minister and Transportation Minister were going to award the contract to Sinohydro at least in part because Sinohydro was willing to pay a bribe of around 25 million euros.[61] As for Bosnia and Herzegovina, another Western Balkan country where Chinese economic influence is significant, the issues of Chinese investments undermining the Energy Community Treaty (ECT), to which all the Western Balkan countries are parties, are growing. The ECT is designed to bring the environmental policies and pollution standards of these countries in line with those of the EU. Despite the EU's standards, there are cases of Western Balkan countries contracting Chinese state-owned firms to build

[55] Austin Doehler, 'How China Challenges the EU in the Western Balkans' *The Diplomat* (25 September 2019), https://thediplomat.com/2019/09/how-china-challenges-the-eu-in-the-western-balkans.

[56] Aleksandar Vasovic, 'Serbia wants billions in foreign loans to invest in infrastructure', *Reuters* (12 July 2019), www.reuters.com/article/us-serbia-investment-china/serbia-wants-billions-in-foreign-loans-to-invest-in-infrastructure-minister-idUSKCN1U71VG.

[57] Noah Buyon and others, 'Nations in Transit 2020' (*Freedom House*, 2020), https://freedomhouse.org/sites/default/files/2020-05/NIT_2020_FINAL_05062020.pdf.

[58] Brahma Chellaney, 'China's Debt-Trap Diplomacy', *Project Syndicate* (23 January 2017).

[59] 'Montenegro Fears China-backed Highway Will Put it on Road to Ruin' *Financial Times* (10 April 2019), www.ft.com/content/d3d56d20-5a8d-11e9-9dde-7aedca0a081a.

[60] More on this issue in: Boris Vukicevic, 'Foreign Relations of Post-Independence Montenegro: A Change of Direction' (2017) 26 *Lithuanian Foreign Policy Review* 107.

[61] Doehler (n 55).

coal power units. One example is the coal power plant in Tuzla, Bosnia and Herzegovina with a Chinese investment that is supposed to replace the older plant and cause less pollution.[62] However, building a coal power plant does not contribute towards the EU and ECT principles for sustainable development and climate change action. This move is damaging to Bosnia's already unsteady EU aspirations. It is becoming obvious that in the past, the EU might have overestimated Russian influence in the region, while it has clearly underestimated China's. There needs to be a clear action from the EU which will ensure more coherent external action and to show through the example of sincere cooperation how the future member states need to act on the international arena.

V. Analysis: The BRI and the EU Member States – Breach of Sincere Cooperation?

Given the vast number of EU Member States involved in the BRI in various ways and the EU's intensifying relations with China, the involvement of the EU with the BRI appears more essential than ever, perhaps as a form of constrained mixity. There are those who contend that the EU itself should join the BRI.[63] Others go further and argue that the EU should create its own rival BRI initiative.[64] Whatever the view taken, it is an extraordinary state of affairs that the scope of Member State non-binding initiatives and EU actions traverses so many comparable crossing points. It appears that a highly artificial view of sincere cooperation and the common commercial policy prevails despite an ever-increasing span of case law to the contrary. 'Does Europe matter?' is now a common refrain on EU-China BRI relations where the EU has been unable to halt the 'divide and rule' approach of China ongoing with Europe for some time.[65] This Chinese approach has challenged the EU's role on the international scene. The EU has been promoting its strategic interests, standards, values, as well as development objectives by negotiating trade agreements with a wide range of partners and by profoundly supporting the multilateral trade cooperation. Nowadays, with BRI being a megaregional arrangement[66] that strongly affects the world in the twenty-first century, the EU role in connection to the BRI needs to be reassessed. Having a unified EU position towards BRI is especially important in the context of the autonomous EU Member States actions that have been damaging to EU unity, competence and foreign policy goals. After the agreement in principle we contend that little will change in the short-term. Several more immediate and likely points of concern and breach of sincere cooperation by the independent EU Member State actions are assessed here.

[62] Mladen Lakic, 'Bosnia's China-Funded Power Plant Gets Green Light' (*Balkan Insight*, 7 March 2019), https://balkaninsight.com/2019/03/07/bosnias-china-funded-power-plant-gets-green-light/.

[63] Eg Ken Moak, 'Why the EU should join the BRI' (10 April 2019), https://news.cgtn.com/news/3d3d414f324d544f33457a6333566d54/index.html.

[64] 'Europe needs its own Belt and Road Initiative' *Financial Times* (28 November 2019), www.ft.com/content/a282e618-1120-11ea-a7e6-62bf4f9e548a.

[65] Jinghan Zeng, 'Does Europe Matter? The Role of Europe in Chinese Narratives of "One Belt One Road" and "New Type of Great Power Relations"' (2017) 55 *Journal of Common Market Studies* 1162; Kingsbury (n 5).

[66] According to Wang, 'The Belt and Road Initiative Agreements: Characteristics, Rationale and Challenges' (n 33).

At present, over 15 and likely under 22 EU Member States have signed MoUs or other types of cooperation agreements with China within the BRI.[67] In the process of negotiating and signing these agreements, the Member States have been systematically ignoring the EU rules, mainly by bypassing the European Commission before entering into trade deals with China. The Commission does not appear to have contemplated actions against the Member States, arguably being careful not to take action with respect to China in any form that might jeopardise its broader engagements on the CAI. Member States are obliged in the area of trade and energy to inform the Commission and other Member States about opening negotiations and to submit for scrutiny the negotiated agreements or MoUs. In all cases and to the best of our knowledge, the EU executive has not been consulted prior to any of the agreements being made.[68] Moreover, there is a deficit of publicly available information and data on Chinese investments into the EU, since there is no publicly available inventory of official BRI projects, nor is there an inventory of Member States' contributions to financial institutions involved in the BRI. Notably, the EU has been developing a subsidies Regulation to be used against state-supported foreign companies operating in the EU bringing competition tools to bear on international trade where foreign hand-outs distort the European market – to be applied to market competition, mergers and acquisitions, and public procurement – arguably with China as its key subject and object.[69] Some suggest the number of EU actions against China in the form of legal tools continues to grow as a lengthy list.[70] Additionally, these MOUs have had a significant political impact, especially because of how they diverge from the EU-China 2020 Strategic Agenda for Cooperation. The Strategic Agenda defines conditions and guarantees that should be expected from China, such as rule of law, fair trade and investments. However, the MOUs prioritises bilateral strategic and economic cooperation, with little attention to the rule of law and fair economic competition.

The main concern about Member States' MoUs with China is located in the Chinese lack of transparency in international trade, which favours unfair economic competition. The Chinese companies which are controlled by the government and benefit from the state's financial backing are playing a different game in the international trade arena. Also, as Andersen observes, a problem for European businesses arises from the fact that there will not be an even playing field if they compete with businesses along the Belt and

[67] For a detailed typology of the BRI Agreements see: Wang, 'The Belt and Road Initiative Agreements: Characteristics, Rationale and Challenges' (n 33).

[68] More on this issue can be found in the Report of the European Court of Auditors, 'The EU's response to China's state-driven investment strategy' (2020), www.eca.europa.eu/Lists/ECADocuments/RW20_03/RW_EU_response_to_China_EN.pdf.

[69] European Commission, 'Commission proposes new Regulation to address distortions caused by foreign subsidies in the Single Market' (5 May 2021), https://ec.europa.eu/commission/presscorner/detail/en/ip_21_1982.

[70] Eg evolving trade defence instruments (anti-dumping and anti-subsidy duties); allowing those duties to be used against companies subsidised by the Chinese government but exporting from another country; tightening up screening of inward foreign direct investment (FDI) for national security reasons; developing an anti-coercion tool to use against foreign governments acting illegally; producing a toolbox for member states to manage risky entities (Huawei) from 5G networks; banning imports made with forced labour; and requiring European companies to exercise 'due diligence' in eliminating labour and environmental abuses from their supply chains Alan Beattie, 'The EU is trailing China's trade distortions all round the world' *Financial Times* (10 May 2021), www.ft.com/content/0e94cd4e-16f9-4bfc-8bba-333027fb95ed.

Road, if they do not meet and guarantee the same levels of human rights protection.[71] It might also lead to an indirect penetration of lower human rights and labour standards into the European markets.

Reciprocity when it comes to the market access is another important issue concerning the EU in its relations with China.[72] When it comes to the EU position towards China, the EU has to consider the balance between the protection of values and human rights with ensuring strategic interests, especially in the field of investments and trade relations. The EU went a step further by adopting a mechanism to screen foreign investment at EU level, clearing the path for closer monitoring of third country companies willing to invest in the EU's critical sectors.[73] This will allow the EU for the first time to collectively address investments that represent potential risks to the bloc's security or public order. This does not mean that existing national screening mechanisms will be harmonised or national powers to approve foreign investment operations will be removed, but instead, it will boost cooperation in this field among EU partners.

EU Member State engagement with the BRI appear contrary to the EU commitments to good global governance and commitments to upholding international law in Article 21 TEU. The underlying idea of Article 21 – to have the EU as a responsible actor in international relations – is therefore undermined. According to Article 21, the fundamental principles of the European Union shall be exported to the outside world, but at the same time the Union will conduct its external actions in accordance with the fundamental principles underlying international law in general, and the UN Charter in particular. The EU external action rests on values and principles that are oriented towards peaceful coexistence, respect of international law and promotion of human rights and democracy, all of which seem to be weakened by individual Member States' involvement with the BRI. It appears also increasingly obvious that the Member state actions thwart EU global action, impinging upon unity and espouse non-European values or weaken the protection of rights, standards and values indirectly through Chinese financial supports and investments.

VI. Conclusions

This chapter has considered how the social and legal relevance of sincere cooperation is put in doubt every time the Member States impeded EU action in connection to the BRI, done mainly because of the lack of legal infrastructure, increasing breadth of EU negotiations, or the murky legal contours of the sincere cooperation. The subject of EU international relations continues to witness a chronic informalisation, with the rise in the use of soft law instruments. These developments are significant in connection

[71] Henrik Andersen, 'Rule of Law Gaps and the Chinese Belt and Road Initiative: Legal Certainty for International Businesses?' in Martinico and Wu (n 26).

[72] Alexandra Brzozowski and Jorge Valero, 'Don't be naive with China', EU leaders tell Italy' (*Euractiv*, 22 March 2019), www.euractiv.com/section/economy-jobs/news/dont-be-naive-with-china-eu-leaders-tell-italy/> accessed 15 January 2021.

[73] Regulation (EU) 2019/452 establishing a framework for the screening of foreign direct investments into the Union [2019] OJ L79I/1, which is effective starting 11 October 2020.

with the EU's most complex international opponent and potential partner – China and its Belt and Road Initiative. China is acknowledged to be seeking regional influence through mechanisms other than formal international law, principally BRI, as a set of domestic policies and economic instruments which are seemingly contrary to the key EU principles of external action. EU Member State engagement with the BRI is contrary to EU commitments to good global governance and commitments to upholding international law. With BRI building its strong foothold in Europe, China has managed to divide the EU bilaterally and carve up the Member States in ways in which no other global power has so managed. The EU Member States increasingly disrespect the duty of sincere cooperation as to the BRI or show its irrelevance by hindering EU action. The role of the EU as a long-standing proponent of multilateralism is to provide leadership to strengthening the existing alliances and building new ones which will contribute to defending the rules-based trading system. There needs to be a clear action from the EU which will ensure more coherent external action and to show through the example of sincere cooperation how the future member states need to act on the international arena.

The chapter has critically explored the gaps in the reality of joint participation and its excessive formalism which is argued to be mismatched with practice in regards to the BRI. The chapter considered how sincere cooperation is chronically under- and over-enforced, creates unnecessary power imbalances, with minimalist case law which favours larger states. It is bound up with an extraordinary array of principles from effectiveness, coherence and consistency. The absence of treaty rules on the seemingly grey areas surrounding the boundaries of EU action appears readily deployed by the EU itself. Joint participation state of the art is argued not to capture contemporary practice, especially it does not capture how trade is increasingly embedded in subjects such as security where significant national competences exist, and therefore warrant more critical reflection as a future research agenda.

14

The Status of the United Kingdom Regarding EU Mixed Agreements after Brexit

CHRISTINE KADDOUS AND HABIB BADJINRI TOURÉ

The European Union may conclude international agreements jointly with its Member States. As is well known, these agreements derive their mixed nature from the fact that they are not concluded solely by the European Union in situations in which its competences do not entirely cover the envisaged agreement.[1] Member States therefore participate in these agreements as contracting parties alongside the Union. Participation in mixed agreements is a consequence of the legal situation regarding the division of competences between the Union and the Member States. Whereas the issue of 'facultative mixity' and the related one of 'obligatory mixity' are largely debated in doctrine with regard to choices the Council may have to decide on mixity,[2] they are not specifically dealt with in this contribution, which focuses on Brexit and the legal and practical challenges surrounding mixity in this specific context.

Mixed agreements may be bilateral or multilateral;[3] each of these categories entails different challenges and considerations. Trade and cooperation agreements as well as association agreements are concluded by the EU and its Member States on the one side, and a particular state (or group of states), on the other side. Such agreements are considered *bilateral* in nature. The Economic Partnership Agreement between the EU and the SADC EPA states (EU-SADC EPA)[4] and the Stepping Stone Economic

[1] Ch Kaddous, 'Les accords mixtes', in N Aloupi, C Flaesch-Mougin, Ch Kaddous, C Rapoport, *Les accords internationaux de l'Union européenne (Commentaire J. Mégret, 3e éd.)*, (Bruxelles, Éditions de l'Université de Bruxelles, 2019) 301. On mixity, see also Ch Hillion/P Koutrakos (ed), *Mixed agreements revisited*, (Oxford, Hart Publishing 2010) 396; E Neframi, *Les accords mixtes de la Communauté européenne: aspects communautaires et internationaux*, (Bruxelles, Bruylant, 2007) 711.

[2] Recently in M Chamon and I Govaere (eds) *The Law and Practice of Facultative Mixity* (Brill, Leiden, 2020) 447.

[3] Ch Kaddous, 'Les accords mixtes', in *Les accords internationaux de l'Union européenne (Commentaire J. Mégret, 3e éd.)*, (n 1) 307.

[4] Economic Partnership Agreement between the European Union and its Member States, of the one part, and the Southern African Development Community (SADC) EPA States, of the other part [2016] OJ L 250/3.

Partnership Agreement between the EU and Ghana (EU-Ghana EPA)[5] are examples illustrating this category of bilateral mixed agreements. Other mixed agreements are conventions or agreements open to three or more contracting parties, where the EU is only one of various parties. Such agreements are *multilateral* in nature and the Marrakech Agreement establishing the WTO (WTO Agreement) is one of these. We will use these agreements to examine the legal status of the UK towards EU bilateral and multilateral mixed agreements. Both the UK and the EU are designated as contracting parties to these agreements. Since the UK is no longer an EU Member State, the question arises about the status of that country with regard to these mixed agreements concluded prior to its withdrawal. As the practice of concluding mixed agreements is a feature specific to the EU, the withdrawal of the UK from the EU brings its share of new legal challenges.

According to Article 50(3) TEU, 'the European Treaties shall cease to apply to the UK from the date of entry into force of the Withdrawal Agreement'. The question arises whether the international agreements concluded by the EU and its Member States also cease to be applicable to the UK from that same date. The answer to this question is negative. The Withdrawal Agreement, in force since 1 February 2020, provides that the UK remains bound by its obligations under these international agreements during the transition period provided for in the agreement.[6] This period expired on 31 December 2020 and no indication is given as to what would be supposed to happen then.

The issue of the status of the UK towards these pre-Brexit mixed agreements is complex in terms of both international and EU law. It also brings into discussion the notions of autonomy and sovereignty dear to all Member States. When a state decides to conclude (or not to conclude) an international agreement, it exercises its sovereign rights in taking the decision to participate (or not) in a specific agreement. However, once the international agreement has entered into force, that state is bound by that agreement jointly with the other contracting parties to the same agreement.[7] In the situation of mixed agreements, the question brings to the fore the issues related to the status of EU Member States as autonomous subjects of international law but acting in a complementary way to the EU. It will also shed the light on the content and scope of Member States' sovereignty during their EU membership.

This contribution, which is not an exhaustive examination of the subject, attempts to clarify the status of the UK in relation to specific mixed agreements. The first part examines the status of the UK as a contracting party to the above-mentioned bilateral and multilateral mixed agreements. As we will see, the UK's status as a 'contracting party' to these two categories of agreements has different meanings (section I). Second II analyses the impact of the UK's withdrawal from the EU on its participation to the same mixed agreements.

[5] Stepping Stone Economic Partnership Agreement between Ghana, of the one part, and the European Community and its Member States, of the other part [2016] OJ L 287.

[6] Art 129 § 1 of the Agreement on Withdrawal between the European Union and the United Kingdom Agreement on the withdrawal of the United Kingdom of Great Britain and Northern Ireland from the European Union and the European Atomic Energy Community, (2019/C 384 I/01), 12 November 2019.

[7] Art 24 of the Vienna Convention on the Law of Treaties of 1969.

I. The Determination of the UK's Status as a Party to EU Mixed Agreements

This section aims to examine the status of the UK in relation to the mixed agreements concluded before Brexit in more detail. Two situations are to be distinguished: agreements in which the UK participated as an EU Member State as well as in its own right (section I.A) and those in which it participated as an EU Member State only (section I.B).

A. Mixed Agreements Concluded by the UK as an EU Member State as Well as in its Own Right

According to Article 2 of the Vienna Convention on the Law of Treaties of 1969 (VCLT), a party to an international agreement 'means a State which has consented to be bound by the treaty and for which the treaty is in force'.[8] Consent is expressed by means of an act of ratification which each state sends to the depositary of a given treaty.[9] A joint reading of Article 2(1)(b) and (g) of the VCLT can lead to the conclusion that the EU and its Member States have separate party status. For example, Article XI of the WTO Agreement considers as original members of the Organisation, the 'Contracting Parties to GATT 1947 at the date of entry into force of this Agreement, and the European Communities'. In accordance with this provision, the EU Member States are also 'full members of the WTO with all the rights and obligations that this entails'[10] in the same way as the EU is. The EU's accession to the WTO, alongside the accession of its Member States to the same organisation, has not formally altered the rights and obligations of individual EU members, including the UK, which are members of the WTO despite their EU membership.[11] Thus, also before Brexit, the UK enjoyed a separate WTO membership status along with that of the EU.[12]

Since the entry into force of the EEC Treaty and more particularly since the setting up of the common external tariff, the transfer of powers which has occurred in the relations between the Member States and the Community has been put into concrete form in different ways.[13] Accordingly, the Community assumed the powers previously exercised by Member States in the area of trade. Today, the EU has 'in practice' superseded its Member States, including the UK, in the WTO matters covered by the common commercial policy. The UK was part of the package of 'European Union' arrangements

[8] Art 2 § 1, g) VCLT.

[9] Art 2 § 1, b) VCLT.

[10] *EC and Certain Member States – Large Civil Aircraft (Airbus)*, Panel Report (adopted 1 June 2011), WT/DS316/R, para 7.174.

[11] ibid.

[12] L Bartels, 'The UK's status in the WTO after Brexit', (2016), https://papers.ssrn.com/sol3/papers.cfm?abstract_id=2841747. This has also been stated in the WTO case law, *EC and Certain Member States – Large Civil Aircraft (Airbus)*, paras 7.174–7.175.

[13] Joined Cases 21 to 24/72, *International Fruit Company NV and others v Produktschap voor groenten en fruit*, EU:C:1972:115, paras 16–18.

in the WTO trade negotiations.[14] The UK's membership and participation in the WTO has evolved in line with the evolution of the distribution of competences between the European Union and its Member States in the area of trade. This leads to the distinction to be made between the participation in the WTO, on the one hand, and the exercise of the rights and obligations attached to the WTO membership, on the other hand.

The fact that the areas governed by the WTO fall within the scope of the EU Common commercial policy, belonging today to the exclusive competence of the Union,[15] allows the EU to speak with one voice at the WTO. It is almost always the representative of the European Commission who speaks on behalf of all EU Member States at WTO meetings.[16] Nowadays the EU is representing its members in all the functioning organs of the WTO.[17] It exercises competences that were previously in the hands of the Member States in the field of application of the GATT and the WTO. Nevertheless, during the period of EU membership, the UK was also a WTO member in its own rights, next to the EU.

EU Member States, as sovereign states under international law, have ratified the WTO Agreement and are bound by that agreement, which continues to be in force for them as long as they do not denounce or terminate it. A distinction must therefore be made between the 'genuine' participation to the WTO and the exercise of the rights and obligations attached to WTO membership in the management of the existing WTO agreements and in the negotiation of future agreements. As long as the UK was part of the EU, it was bound by the internal rules of division of competences within the EU legal order. It did fully participate in the formulation of the EU common commercial policy and took part in the decision-making process within the EU Council, but it had had limited representative tasks as an EU Member State within the WTO system.[18]

Overall, despite these aspects linked to the division of competences between the EU and its Member States, the UK has enjoyed a full and complete status in the WTO as an EU Member State but also in its own right[19] and will continue to possess all of these rights and obligations once it leaves the EU.[20]

[14] S Meunier, 'L'Union européenne et l'OMC : la 'mondialisation maîtrisée' à l'épreuve', in G Boismenu, I Petit (eds), *L'Europe qui se fait*, (Paris, Les presses de l'Université de Montréal, 2013) 218–21.

[15] O Blin, 'OMC et imputabilité : le cas de l'Union européenne': 'Since the entry into force of the Treaty of Lisbon and the application of Article 207 of the TFEU, the Union's exclusive competence has been substantially extended to cover not only goods but also all services, the commercial aspects of intellectual property and even direct investment' (own translation), in V Tomckievicz, (ed) *Organisation mondiale du commerce et responsabilité*, (Paris, Pedone 2014) 189; F-X Priollaud, D Siritzky, *Le traité de Lisbonne. Texte et commentaire article par article des nouveaux traités européens (TUE-TFUE)*, (Paris, La documentation française 2008) 304; W Igler, 'L'Union européenne et l'Organisation mondiale du Commerce', (*Fiche technique sur l'Union européenne 2020*, novembre 2019) 4.

[16] www.wto.org/english/thewto_e/countries_e/european_communities_e.htm.

[17] D Braun, T Baert, 'The European Union in the World Trade Organization Post-Lisbon: No single Change to the Single Voice? in Ch Kaddous (ed), *The European Union in International Organisations and Global Governance* (Hart Publishing, 2015) 109–15; F Hoffmeister 'The European Union in the World Trade Organisation – A Model for the EU's Status in International Organisations?, in Ch Kaddous (ed), *The European Union in International Organisations and Global Governance* (Hart Publishing, 2015) 121–41; T Perišin, 'The EU's influential role in global trade policy' in RA Wessel and J Odermatt (eds), *Research Handbook on the European Union and International Organisations*, (Edward Elgar Publishing, 2019) 256–74.

[18] ibid.

[19] G Van Der Loo, S Blockmans, 'The Impact of Brexit on EU's International Agreements', (2016) *CEPS* https://www.ceps.eu/ceps-publications/impact-brexit-eus-international-agreements/.

[20] See section II of this contribution.

B. Mixed Agreements Concluded by the UK as an EU Member State Only

The agreements under consideration in the present section are the bilateral mixed agreements referred to in the introduction, the EU-SADC EPA and the EU-Ghana EPA. The status of the UK, and more generally the status of any EU Member State, as contracting parties to these agreements, relies on the existence of fields of cooperation that go beyond the exclusive competences of the EU.[21] The Member States should not be considered as having an independent and autonomous status as states parties to these mixed agreements.[22]

In the case of the EU-SADC EPA and the EU-Ghana EPA, the UK is identified as a contracting state to the agreements. However, it is not considered as an autonomous contracting party. It participates in the agreements only as an EU Member State. This is a prerequisite for being part of 'the EC party' or 'the EU party'. The EU is identified in these agreements as 'the EC party' or 'the EU party'.[23] Basically, the UK and the other EU Member States will act, in these agreements, for their implementation and management according to the division of competences between the EU and the Member States. These agreements contain clauses which limit the territorial scope of application on the European side to the territory of the EU Member States. Consequently, in order to be part of the 'EU party' bloc, a state must belong to the EU. Although the Member State must individually fulfil the treaty formalities related to the signature and ratification of international agreements, membership of the EU is a prerequisite for the participation in the mixed agreements.

The EU-SADC and EU-Ghana EPAs are also international agreements.[24] Under international law and pursuant to Article 2(1)(g) VCLT, the UK as well as the other Member States are contracting parties to these agreements. During the ratification process, each of the Member States and the EU itself have deposited, in accordance with the letter and spirit of the VCLT, a different instrument of ratification by which it consented to be bound by the Treaty.[25] These very facts imply that where an international agreement is signed by the EU and its Member States, each Member State remains free under international law to terminate that agreement in accordance with the termination procedure under that agreement. It participates in the agreement 'as a sovereign State, not as a mere appendage of the European Union'.[26] However, as already mentioned, all mixed agreements form also an integral part of EU law[27] and 'are closely connected to other EU legislation and policies'.[28] Under EU law, the UK has participated in the agreements in its capacity as an EU Member state.

[21] Ibid.

[22] I Bosse-Platiere, C Flaesch-Mougin, C Billet, C Delcourt, A Hamonic, A Hervé et C Rapoport, 'Brexit et action extérieure de l'Union européenne', (2016) 4 *RTD Eur* 759, 765.

[23] Art 72 EU-Ghana EPA; Art 104 EU-SADC EPA.

[24] Ch Kaddous, 'L'arrêt France c. Commission de 1994 (accord concurrence) et le contrôle de la "légalité" des accords externes en vertu de l'art. 173 CE : la difficile réconciliation de l'orthodoxie communautaire avec l'orthodoxie internationale', (1996) 32 *Cahiers de droit européen* 613, 622–23.

[25] E. Neframi, 'Brexit et les accords mixtes de l'Union européenne', (2017) 63 *AFDI* 360, 365.

[26] See the opinions of Sharpston AG in Opinion 2/15, EU:C:2016:992, para 77.

[27] Case 181/73, *R. & V. Haegeman v Belgian State*, EU:C:1974:41, para 5.

[28] RA Wessel, 'Consequences of Brexit for International Agreements Concluded by the EU and its Member States', (2018) 55 *CML Rev* 101, 120.

It is worth noting that the partners of the EU, ie, Ghana and the SADC in our examples, intended to conclude the agreements with the EU, and not with the Member States independently of their EU membership. The contracting party 'the Union and its Member States' has a composite character that implies prior membership to the EU and application of the agreement on the territory of the EU. The Member States constitute the elements of a whole participating in the mixed agreements in a complementary manner.[29] In the light of these considerations, a Member State cannot be considered as constituting an autonomous and independent contracting party to these mixed agreements. According to this line of reasoning, the non-ratification of a mixed agreement by a Member State could also be considered as a breach of the sincere cooperation principle enshrined in Article 4(3) TEU.[30] The respect of this principle exits form the process of negotiation till the ratification (and even beyond).[31] However, the European Union has no enforcement power on the Member States to oblige them to ratify a mixed agreement.[32] The issue has to do with the autonomy of the Member States to conclude or not a mixed agreement.

The nature and the specificity of EU law brings an approach different from the one of classical international law. From an international law perspective, the UK is an independent and autonomous contracting party to the above-mentioned EPAs. From an EU law perspective, the autonomy enjoyed by the Member States at the time of the ratification of the agreements disappears during the period of EU membership. It is regained after the withdrawal from the EU. However, the continuation of the participation to these agreements for the State leaving the EU does not make sense as the obligations and rights resulting out of these agreements are dependent on and linked to EU membership. This reasoning is fully in line with the mechanism established in the EU legal order, according to which the state acceding to the EU accepts a limitation of its sovereignty and a transfer of its powers or some of them to the EU.[33] The Member State will regain its full rights and competences once it leaves the EU. However, throughout the period of membership, the EU Member State has to act in accordance with the transfer of competences it has agreed upon through its accession to the EU.

Overall, although formally a party to these mixed agreements on an individual basis, the Member State is bound by its EU membership and does not enjoy the autonomy that is attached to this status under international law.[34] Since the meaning of the status

[29] Ch Kaddous, 'De quelques défis liés à la conclusion des accords mixtes', in Liber amicorum Antonio Tizzano, *De la Cour CECA à la Cour de l'Union : le long parcours de la justice européenne*, (Torino, G. Giappichelli, 2018) 448; E Neframi, 'Brexit et les accords mixtes de l'Union européenne', (n 25) 363–64.

[30] E Neframi, 'Brexit et les accords mixtes de l'Union européenne', (n 25) 365. On the sincere cooperation principle and mixed agreements, see Ch Kaddous, 'Les accords mixtes', in *Les accords internationaux de l'Union européenne (Commentaire J. Mégret, 3e éd.)*, (n 1) 308; Ch Hillion, 'Mixity and coherence in EU external relations : the significance of the duty of cooperation', in *Mixed Agreements Revisited*, op cit 87–116.

[31] Ch Kaddous, 'Les accords mixtes', in *Les accords internationaux de l'Union européenne (Commentaire J. Mégret, 3e éd.)*, (n 1) 308.

[32] See the examples of the Agreement with South Africa of 1999 and the Association Agreement with Ukraine commented by Ch Kaddous, 'Les accords mixtes', in *Les accords internationaux de l'Union européenne (Commentaire J. Mégret, 3e éd.)*, (n 1) 316–17.

[33] Case 6/64, *Costa v ENEL*, EU:C:1964:66, para 1141.

[34] On the respective powers of the contracting parties, see Court of Justice's judgment in Case C-28/12 *Commission v Council*, EU:C:2015:282, para 47, according to which: the contracting parties to a mixed agreement concluded with third countries are, on the one hand, the Union and, on the other, the Member States.

of 'contracting party' to these two categories of mixed agreements is now clarified, let's turn now to the analysis of the impact of the UK withdrawal from the EU on its participation to these mixed agreements after the end of the transition period.

II. The Impact of Withdrawal on the UK's Participation in EU Mixed Agreements

The Withdrawal Agreement came into force on 1 February 2020. The transition period that began on that date expired on 31 December 2020. During this period, the UK remained bound by its obligations under the international agreements concluded by the EU, by Member States acting on its behalf or by the EU and its Member States acting jointly.[35] Article 129(2) of the Withdrawal Agreement also states that representatives of the UK shall not participate 'in the work of anybody set up by international agreements concluded by the Union, or by Member States acting on its behalf, or by the Union and its Member States acting jointly', unless exceptional invitation from the Union. The EU was also responsible for notifying the other parties to those agreements that, during the transition period, the UK was to be treated as a Member State for the purposes of those agreements.[36] However, given the absence of indications as to the post-transition period, it is important to determine more closely the UK's participation in both the WTO (section II.A) and the specific bilateral mixed agreements under scrutiny in this contribution (section II.B).

A. Continued UK Participation in the WTO with Adaptations

In accordance with Article 129 of the Withdrawal Agreement, throughout the transition period, the international agreements to which the EU and the UK were parties continue to apply to that state. After 31 December 2020, the situation is different. The UK is no longer an EU Member State but remains a member of the WTO in its own capacity. Indeed, the withdrawal from the EU did not automatically lead to termination of the UK membership to the WTO, for the reasons explained in section I.

From an international law perspective, the termination of EU membership has no impact on the WTO membership. One of the effects of the withdrawal from the EU is to allow the withdrawing state to regain the full extent of its sovereign powers and rights. While EU membership has contributed to modify the exercise of the rights associated to WTO membership, the withdrawal from the EU allows the UK to resume its place in the WTO in a fully autonomous and independent manner. Furthermore, the WTO Agreement does not provide for a clause that would preclude the UK from continuing

When negotiating and concluding such an agreement, each of those parties must act within the framework of the powers available to it and with respect for the powers of any other contracting party.

[35] Art 129(1) of the Agreement on Withdrawal between the European Union and the United Kingdom.

[36] Infra-paginal note to Art 129.

to apply the WTO agreements.[37] Hence the UK remains a party to the WTO,[38] but adaptations are still required. A notification as to the changing of the situation as well as to adjustments of some of the commitments are considered necessary to reshape the participation of the UK in the diverse WTO agreements.

On the one hand, the EU has, in accordance with Article 129 of the Withdrawal Agreement,[39] informed the other parties and the organisation of the termination of the UK's membership.[40] On the other hand, the UK has sent a communication stating that it is and will continue to be a member of the WTO and will represent its interests in the WTO by ensuring compliance with its obligations.[41] On 31 December 2020, at the end of the transition period, a new communication was sent by the UK confirming its continued membership despite its withdrawal from the EU and above all its commitment to assume its obligations under the WTO Agreement.[42] Thus, for example with regard to goods, since the end of the transition period, the UK has been 'fully respecting all the concessions and commitments in Schedule XIX. This includes, in accordance with Article XXVIII: 3 and Article 5 of the GATT 1994, the modification of its commitments'.[43] This full resumption of its commitments is made necessary and unavoidable by the end of its participation in the EU and will obviously require certain adjustments and corrections appropriate to its new situation. The same applies to services.[44] Even though the UK is a founding member of the GATT and an original member of the WTO, its concessions and commitments on goods and services were contained in the EU's schedules of concessions and commitments.[45] This implies that at the end of the transition period during which the UK was considered an EU Member State, there is a need to adapt the commitments and concessions to the new situation of that state. It therefore required a substantial reassessment of the terms of its participation in the WTO since it was no longer part of the customs union established as part of its EU membership.

The UK now resumes its commercial obligations, which have been separated from the EU's list of concessions. In this sense, it has undertaken five rounds of negotiations between September 2019 and December 2020 with several WTO Member States under Article XXVIII of GATT 1994. It has also taken a similar step in relation to services and has committed itself to 'update Members following the conclusion of these procedures'.[46]

[37] L Robert, 'Le Brexit et les accords mixtes : un exemple d'imbroglio juridique analysé', (2017) *Observatoire du Brexit*, https://brexit.hypotheses.org/1000.

[38] General Council, 'End of the UK-EU Transition Period – Communication from the United Kingdom', WT/GC/226, 4 January 2021, p 1.

[39] Infra-paginal note to Art 129.

[40] Communication from the European Union to the Director-General concerning the Agreement on the withdrawal of the United Kingdom of Great Britain and Northern Ireland from the European Union and the European Atomic Energy Community, WT/LET/1462, dated 27 January 2020; L Robert, 'Le Brexit et les accords mixtes : un exemple d'imbroglio juridique analysé', op cit.

[41] General Council, '*The United Kingdom's Withdrawal from The European Union – Communication from the United Kingdom*', WT/GC/206, 1 February 2021.

[42] General Council, 'End of the UK-EU Transition Period – Communication from the United Kingdom', WT/GC/226, 4 January 2021.

[43] Ibid, p 2.

[44] Ibid, pp 2–3.

[45] Ibid, p 1.

[46] Ibid, p 2.

In its communication to the WTO Member States, the UK states that for all trade agreements concluded since the establishment of the WTO to which the UK is not a full party because it participated as an EU Member State, the UK assures it has taken the appropriate steps to accede to these agreements or confirm its continued acceptance and implementation of them after the end of the transition period.[47] In the same line, the UK deposited its instrument of accession, on an individual basis, to the Agreement on Government Procurement (GPA),[48] ensuring that from 1 January 2021, the GPA will enter into force for the UK as such.[49] It has also notified its acceptance and continued full participation in many other agreements including the Protocol amending the TRIPs Agreement, the Protocol amending the WTO Agreement (the Trade Facilitation Agreement) and the 2015 Protocol to the Agreement on Trade in Civil Aircraft.[50]

As will be analysed hereafter, the impact of the UK withdrawal from the EU on its participation to bilateral mixed agreements is different from the one exercised on its participation to the WTO and to the WTO Agreements due to the specific status encountered by the UK in these agreements. While it is possible that in theory the UK may continue to enjoy the status of party to these agreements, in practice it will be difficult for it to apply them in particular because of their scope of application limited to the EU Member States territories.

B. Renegotiation by the UK with the Partner Third Countries

The bilateral mixed agreements under scrutiny are those based on the UK participation as an EU Member State. Different issues need to be addressed. The first and main one is whether the UK shall be considered as continuing its participation to these agreements after its withdrawal from the EU. If this is legally the case, one has to examine the steps to be taken if the termination of the agreements by the UK is to be pursued or if the continuation of the relationship between the UK and the partner third countries is favoured.

The Withdrawal Agreement only settles the issue as to the participation of the UK to these agreements during the transition period without considering what happens afterwards. The Trade and Cooperation Agreement, signed on 30 December 2020, does not consider the issue either.[51] To address the main issue, we will first assess whether the participation of the UK to these mixed agreements is continued (section II.B.i), and examine afterwards the impact of application of Article 50 TEU and of the territorial

[47] General Council, 'End of the UK-EU Transition Period – Communication from the United Kingdom', WT/GC/226, 4 January 2021, p 2.

[48] United Kingdom Notification of Deposit of an instrument of accession, in its own right, to the Agreement on Government Procurement, WT/LET/1498, 2 December 2020.

[49] United Kingdom Notification of Accession to the Agreement on Government Procurement, WT/LET/1503, 4 January 2021.

[50] See the various communications from the UK, available on the WTO website : WT/Let/1500, WT/Let/1501, WT/Let/1502.

[51] Trade and Cooperation Agreement between the European Union and the European Atomic Energy Community, of the one Part, and the United Kingdom of Great Britain and Northern Ireland, of the other Part, L 444/14, 31 December 2020.

clauses included in the mixed agreements (section II.B.ii). Finally, we will present the solutions to be envisaged in the cases of termination or continuation of the relationship between the UK and the partner(s) and focus on the latter situation (section II.B.iii).

i. Continued UK Participation in EU Bilateral Mixed Agreements

As already stated, the participation of the UK in the bilateral mixed EU-SADC EPA and EU-Ghana EPA presupposes EU membership. Since its withdrawal from the EU, the UK has not met this condition.

From an international law perspective, if the UK does not denounce the mixed agreements, it would continue to be a party to them. By virtue of Article 42 VCLT, the termination of a State's party status to a treaty can only take place in accordance with the provisions of that treaty or of the VCLT itself. Where the treaty has a denunciation clause, the situation is governed by Article 54 VCLT. Where it does not provide for such a clause, Article 56(1) VCLT establishes the principle of presumption of non-denunciation. In the mixed agreements under scrutiny, each of them has a denunciation clause by the activation of which a state may terminate its participation.[52] These agreements do not however provide any indication as to the situation where a state withdraws from the EU. What could then be inferred from this?

At the time the 1969 Vienna Convention was concluded, the European practice of mixed agreements was quite new. It started in the beginning of the 1960s with the conclusion of the Association agreement with Greece (1961) and with Turkey (1963). The VCLT does not contain therefore any rule addressing specifically this category of international agreements. However, in international law the principles of the relative effect of treaties, predictability and security and presumption of non-denunciation of treaties prevail. No one source has more or less value than another. Accordingly, a state is a party to two different treaties, the denunciation of one of them does not, unless otherwise specified, entail the termination of its status as a party to the other treaty. By virtue of Article 70 VCLT, the withdrawal of a state from a treaty extinguishes the treaty relationship that existed only between that state and each of the other parties to that treaty as from the date on which such denunciation or withdrawal takes effect.[53] This means that the termination of these treaty relations does not affect the relations of the withdrawing state with states parties to another international agreement. In other words, in application of Article 70 VCLT, the termination of treaty relations resulting from mixed agreements is not automatic under international law.[54] This logic applies especially when the treaties in question have been the subject of separate ratification by the state concerned.[55] The withdrawing state remains bound by the treaty relationship under international law until it denounces the treaty relationship.[56] Similarly, under

[52] Art 75(7) EU-Ghana EPA; Art 114(2) EU-SADC EPA.

[53] Art 70(2) VCLT.

[54] In the same way, see UG Schroeter and H Nemeczek, 'The (Uncertain) Impact of Brexit on the United Kingdom's Membership in the European Economic Area' (2016) 27 *EBL Rev* 927, 930.

[55] IACtHR, *The Denunciation of the American Convention on Human Rights and the Charter of the Organization of American States and their Consequences on the Obligations of States in the Field of Human Rights*, Advisory Opinion OC – 26/20, November 9, 2020, Series A n° 26, pp 34–52, paras 87–154.

[56] In the same sense, E Neframi, 'Brexit et les accords mixtes de l'Union européenne', (n 25) 370.

the presumption of non-denunciation, where the treaty has not provided for denunciation, no state has the possibility to do so, unless the exceptions provided for in letters a) and b) of Article 56(1) VCLT relating to parties' intention and nature of the treaty are met. An interpretation a fortiori would lead to the conclusion that since mixed agreements have not provided for the termination of a member's membership on the basis of its withdrawal from the EU, they therefore theoretically and formally maintain its participation to the said agreements. From an international law perspective, the idea of termination cannot apply in this case, unless one considers, which is not our view, that the withdrawal constitutes a fundamental change of circumstances according to Article 62 VCLT.[57]

It is worth noting that the two EPAs with Ghana and SADC contain a provision on the accession of new members to the EU. The interpretation of this provision is of interest as to the issue under examination. Indeed, according to this provision, from the date of its accession to the EU, any new Member State shall, by means of a clause to that effect in the Act of Accession, become a party to the agreements. If the Act of Accession to the EU does not provide for such automatic accession of the Member State to the agreements, the EU Member State concerned shall accede by depositing an Act of Accession to the agreements with the General Secretariat of the Council of the EU, which shall transmit a certified copy[58] to the EPA states.

Given the absence in the mixed agreements of any provision regarding the withdrawal from the EU, an analogous analysis could be proposed. It would lead to the conclusion that when a state withdraws from the EU, it may lose its participation to the mixed agreements if the Withdrawal Agreement provides for an automatic termination of the participation of that state to the mixed agreements. In the absence of such a provision in the Withdrawal Agreement, the withdrawing EU Member State will only lose its contracting party status by sending a notification of denunciation. In other words, the UK stays a party to these agreements as long as it has not terminated them in conformity with their own terms or with the VCLT. Consequently, until the UK submits such notification of denunciation in accordance with the provisions of the said mixed agreements, it remains 'formally' a party to these agreements although substantial difficulties prevent it from exercising its rights. In practice, these agreements de facto do not apply anymore to the UK as it ceased to be part of the EU territory since its withdrawal. This is also recalled by the UK government, which recognises that 'the Stepping Stone Economic Partnership Agreement between Ghana, of the one part, and the European Community and its Member States, of the other part … ceased to apply to the United Kingdom on 1st January 2021.'[59] Consequently, the UK Government 'has developed

[57] For a discussion of the clausula rebus sic stantibus, see notably Ramses A Wessel, 'Consequences of Brexit for International Agreements Concluded by the EU and its Member States', op cit, 122; Y Kaspiarovich and N Levrat, 'The UK and EU mixed agreements after Brexit: the case of the EEA', (2018) *European Futures*, www.europeanfutures.ed.ac.uk/the-uk-and-eu-mixed-agreements-after-brexit-the-case-of-the-eea/; L Robert, 'Le Brexit et les accords mixtes: un exemple d'imbroglio juridique analysé', op cit.

[58] Art 77 para 2 EU-Ghana EPA; Art 118 para 2 EU-SADC EPA.

[59] Department for International Trade, Continuing the UK's trade relationship with Ghana (Interim Trade Partnership Agreement between the United Kingdom of Great Britain and Northern Ireland, of the one part, and the Republic of Ghana, of the other part, Presented to Parliament by the Secretary of State for International Trade by Command of Her Majesty), Policy Paper, April 2021, www.gov.uk/government/publications/continuing-the-uks-trade-relationship-with-ghana-parliamentary-report/continuing-the-uks-trade-relationship-with-ghana-web-version.

new agreements that replicate, as far as possible, the effects of the EU's trade arrangements with partner countries, as they applied to the United Kingdom prior to the end of the transition period'.[60]

ii. *Application of Article 50 TEU and of the Territorial Clauses in the EU Mixed Agreements*

In accordance with Article 50(3) TEU, the European Treaties shall cease to apply to the withdrawing state from the date of entry into force of the Withdrawal Agreement. As international agreements concluded by the EU alone or jointly with the Member States form an integral part of EU law,[61] they do not apply to the UK after its withdrawal. As early as 2017, the European Council has specified that 'the United Kingdom will no longer be covered by mixed agreements'[62] as soon as the withdrawal is effective. According to Article 216(2) TFEU, 'agreements concluded by the Union shall be binding on the institutions of the Union and on Member States'. A combined reading of Articles 50 TEU and 216 TFEU implies that the withdrawal from the EU affects the status of the withdrawing state as contracting party to international agreements concluded jointly with the EU.

Some authors believe that it would be possible to envisage an automatic termination of the UK's participation in the mixed agreements 'because mixed EU FTAs are essentially "bilateral" in nature, and the UK will no longer qualify as a formal "party" to these FTAs particularly under EU law'.[63] However, as mixed agreements are concluded in compliance with the division of competences between the EU and its members, a twofold result can be envisaged. On the one hand, the provisions falling under EU competence will no longer be applicable to the withdrawing state even without denunciation on its part. On the other hand, as to the provisions falling under the competence of the Member States, the UK could formally, as a state, continue to apply them, since from an international law point of view it had the necessary standing to be bound by them even before its withdrawal.[64] Notwithstanding the fact that it is not easy to distinguish between the provisions which fall under the EU exclusive competence and the ones they do not, there is little point considering the UK bound by only parts of the agreements if the mixed agreements have been concluded by the Member States in a complementary approach to the EU participation to the same agreements.

Moreover, according to the territorial clauses included in the mixed agreements, these apply to the territories to which the European Treaties are applicable, ie, the territories of the EU Member States. Since the end of the transition period, the Treaties no longer apply to the UK territory. In these circumstances, if the UK were formally and

[60] Ibid.

[61] Case 181/73, *R. & V. Haegeman v Belgian State*, EU:C:1974:41, para 5.

[62] European Council (Art 50) guidelines for Brexit negotiations, 29 April 2017, para 13, www.consilium.europa.eu/fr/press/press-releases/2017/04/29/euco-brexit-guidelines/.

[63] RG Volterra, 'Brexit Negotiations Series: The Impact of Brexit on the UK's Trade with Non-EU Member States Under the EU's Mixed Free Trade Agreements', (2017), *OBLB*, www.law.ox.ac.uk/business-law-blog/blog/2017/05/brexit-negotiations-series-impact-brexit-uk's-trade-non-eu-member.

[64] G Van Der Loo, S Blockmans, 'The Impact of Brexit on EU's International Agreements', (n 19).

theoretically to retain its status as a party to these agreements from a 'formal' point of view of international law, it is substantially losing the possibility of enjoying the rights associated with that status because of the territorial application clauses. Additionally, territorial clauses are not alien to international law since treaties are applicable only in the territory of the states parties.[65] With the withdrawal from the EU, the mixed agreements at stake will no longer apply to the UK as their scope of application is limited to EU Member States territories, or to the territories where the EU treaties apply.[66]

Consequently, two main solutions can be envisaged depending on whether the UK aims at terminating or not the relationship that exist with the partner third states. If the termination is pursued by the UK, this would imply a classical termination of the mixed agreements according to their respective denunciation clauses. On the contrary, if the UK wishes to maintain the relationship with the partner third states, it may either renegotiate its participation to the same mixed agreements (under other conditions) or negotiate new agreements with the third states to replace the previous relationship that existed before its withdrawal from the EU. The following subsection will focus on the solutions that allow the maintaining of the relationship with the partner third states.

iii. Possible Solutions to Ensure the 'Continuity' of the Relationship between the UK and the Partner Third Countries

This section aims to examine the possible solutions from a theoretical point of view before analysing the practice developed by the UK with its partners. The first solution that may envisaged is the continuation of the participation of the UK in the existing mixed agreements. The agreements with Ghana and the SADC states do not contain lists for the division of competences between the EU and its Member States. Therefore, if the UK wants to continue to apply these agreements, negotiations are needed to adapt them to the new situation. This means that the continued participation of the UK will be subject to the willingness of the partner third states, the EU and its Member States. This corresponds to what has been proposed by the European Council in April 2017: the idea of a constructive dialogue under a possible common approach towards partner third states, relevant international organisations and the EU.[67] These negotiations might also bring a change in the nature of these mixed agreements, moving them from bilateral to multilateral context. In this respect, the continuation of the UK's participation would require 'a legal instrument (for instance a protocol) stating that the UK takes over the rights and obligations it previously had under the agreement as an EU Member State and that it joins the agreement as a third party'.[68] However, the renegotiation of the same mixed agreement would require the consent of all previous contracting parties and may render the exercise very unlikely. This solution of renegotiation and adaptation to the

[65] Art 29 VCLT.

[66] See in the same sense, RG Volterra, 'Brexit Negotiations Series: The Impact of Brexit on the UK's Trade with Non-EU Member States Under the EU's Mixed Free Trade Agreements', op cit.

[67] European Council (Art 50) guidelines for Brexit negotiations, 29 April 2017, (n 62); J Odermatt, 'Brexit and International Law : Disentangling Legal Orders', (2017) 31 *EIL Rev* 1051, 1061.

[68] G Van Der Loo, S Blockmans, 'The Impact of Brexit on EU's International Agreements', (n 19).

new legal situation of the UK after Brexit has been applied for the participation to the WTO Agreement, but this agreement is from its origin a multilateral mixed agreement.

As to mixed agreements of a bilateral nature, the most effective solution to ensure the continuation of the legal relationship between the UK and the partner third states would be the negotiation of new agreements. This would in principle require from an international law perspective but also from an EU law perspective, as already mentioned, a formal termination of the existing mixed agreements by the UK.[69] The denunciation should be undertaken by the UK according to the procedures foreseen in the respective mixed agreements, even if the EU notified the third parties the change in the composition of its membership and in its territory.[70] From an international law perspective, such notifications by the EU cannot be considered as implicit denunciations on behalf of the UK. Only the UK is able to take such action.

In practice, the UK did apply a pragmatic and effective approach. It took advantage of its withdrawal from the EU to 'renegotiate' the existing mixed agreements and forge new bilateral links with states with which conventional links existed under the aegis of its EU membership. In this perspective, the UK has concluded for example a post-Brexit agreement with Iceland and Norway with a view to continuing trade relations with these two countries. This agreement ensures that companies will be able to access the UK market and vice versa under the same conditions since the end of the transition period.[71] Similarly, the UK has sought to replicate, as far as and as soon as possible, the relationship it had with Switzerland before its withdrawal from the EU and concluded many international agreements with that country.[72] Ghana and the UK announced that they had reached a consensus on the main elements of a trade agreement that would replicate the effects of the trade relationship between Ghana and the UK prior to the end of the transition period following the withdrawal of the UK from the EU.[73] These new agreements ensure the 'principle of continuity' with the partner third countries and aim at avoiding a disruption in legal relationships. These agreements refer to the EU mixed agreements to which the UK and the third countries were parties and acknowledge the end of their application between them due to the UK withdrawal from the EU.[74] This type of provisions, that is included in many of the new agreements concluded by the UK with its partners, can be considered as mutual recognitions of the end of the EU mixed agreements' application in the relations between the UK and the partner third countries.

[69] Ibid.

[70] E Neframi, 'Brexit et les accords mixtes de l'Union européenne', (n 25) 370.

[71] Department for International Trade and Ranil Jayawardena MP, 'United Kingdom, Norway and Iceland sign trade continuity agreement', Press release, 8 December 2020.

[72] www.gov.uk/government/collections/eu-exit-transition-switzerland.

[73] www.gov.uk/government/news/ghana-uk-joint-statement-ghana-uk-trade-partnership-agreement.

[74] For example, in the agreement between the UK and Switzerland on the rights of citizens, Art 1 of the agreement refers to the mixed agreement on free movement of persons of 1999 that ceases to apply between Switzerland and the UK as a consequence of the UK withdrawal from the EU, https://assets.publishing.service.gov.uk/government/uploads/system/uploads/attachment_data/file/767003/Agreement_between_the_United_Kingdom_of_Great_Britain_and_Northern_Ireland_and_the_Swiss_Confederation_on_citizens__rights_following_the_withdrawal_of_the_United_Kingdom_from_the_European_Union_and_the_Free_Movement_of_Persons_Agreement.pdf.

III. Conclusion

According to international law, each EU Member State has a status as a contracting party to the mixed agreements concluded by the EU. However, that status differs on the basis of the nature of the mixed agreement at stake. In multilateral mixed agreements such as the WTO Agreements, Member States are contracting parties as EU members in their own right, even though in practice the rights and obligations are exercised by the EU. In the case of the bilateral mixed agreements examined in this contribution, the EU Member States only participate in these agreements because of their EU membership. The territorial scope of application of the said agreements is also limited, on the EU side, to the territories of EU Member States. Hence, when a Member State withdraws from the EU, it finds itself in a situation where it is still formally a party to mixed agreements that no longer apply to it. Under these circumstances, two main solutions may be envisaged. In order to maintain the relationship with the partner third countries, the first solution would be to renegotiate the agreements to adapt them to the situation post-Brexit. This solution was applied in a multilateral context for the UK's continued participation to the WTO Agreements. However, it proves to be unlikely in view of the bilateral mixed agreements, where the renegotiation of fully new agreements between the UK and the partner third countries were favoured. In this latter situation, the two steps of ending the application of the EU mixed agreement and the conclusion of a new agreement may take place simultaneously in the same text.

The UK's situation as to EU mixed agreements requires to be assessed both from an international and EU law perspectives, in order to avoid inadequate outcomes that result from analyses that take into consideration only one of these perspectives. The specificity of EU law and the competences' transfer within the context of EU membership cannot be ignored. However, after its withdrawal from the EU, the withdrawing state gains back control and recovers its full competences to conclude autonomously new agreements with the partner third countries in the respect of public international law.

15

Unmixing Mixed Agreements

Challenges and Solutions for Separating the EU and its Member States in Existing International Agreements

YULIYA KASPIAROVICH AND RAMSES A WESSEL

I. Introduction

The practice of concluding mixed agreements – agreements to which both the European Union (EU) and its Member States are parties – is one of the hallmarks of the Union's external activities.[1] No other international organisation has a division of competences with its Member States that is so complex as to lead to this type of international agreements. In classical international law parlance, we would call such agreements 'multilateral' as they comprise more than two contracting parties. Yet, it is a truism that within the EU, the practice is much more complex. The main reason for the EU and its Member States to resort to mixed agreements is that in many areas the EU still lacks the competence to sign and conclude the more comprehensive international agreements without the participation of its Member States. As for the EU Member States, they would not be competent to conclude such agreements on their own whenever the related competences have been transferred to the Union. Concluding these agreements would lead to a breach of the obligations under the EU treaties.

From an EU law perspective, mixed agreements are usually analysed through the prism of their negotiation and ratification by the Union and its Member States, with a

[1] As a lot has been written on this topic, we refer to some key publications only: Henry G Schermers, 'A Typology of Mixed Agreements', *Mixed Agreements* (Kluwer Law and Taxation 1983); Joni Heliskoski, *Mixed Agreements as a Technique for Organizing the International Relations of the European Community and Its Member States* (Kluwer Law International 2001); see also contributions in this edited book: Christophe Hillion and Panos Koutrakos (eds), *Mixed Agreements Revisited: The EU and Its Member States in the World* (Hart Publishing, 2010); Merijn Chamon and Inge Govaere (eds), *EU External Relations Post-Lisbon: The Law and Practice of Facultative Mixity*, (Brill|Nijhoff, 2020); Eleftheria Neframi, *Les accords mixtes de la Communauté européenne : aspects communautaires et internationaux* (Bruylant 2007); Christine Kaddous 'Les accords mixtes', Niki Aloupi, Catherine Flaesch-Mougin et al (eds), *Les accords internationaux de l'Union européenne* (Éditions de l'Université de Bruxelles, 2019) 301–43.

clear focus on the division of competences. Thus, the participation of EU Member States in different types of mixed agreements has inspired a legal classification in terms of 'obligatory', 'facultative', and even 'false' mixity.[2] As also further analysed below, in principle, the type of mixity depends on the *nature* of competence of the EU in relation to the conclusion of an international agreement.[3] In other words, the competence division and the nature of the Union's competence[4] are the key elements in determining whether Member States' participation is necessary (obligatory) or just possible (facultative). This issue is usually analysed in both a pre-[5] and post-negotiation context.[6]

The question of the 'degree' of participation of the EU and its Member States in a mixed agreement dates back to the early years of the EU's external activities. The practice of annexing declarations of competence was sometimes required by EU treaty partners in order to determine the respondent party in case of a dispute,[7] and eventually a responsible party.[8] Although, declarations of competence were considered by the CJEU as being 'a useful reference base',[9] this practice did not flourish, simply because it was very difficult to update the declarations with regard to the evolving nature of EU external competences. Moreover, it has always been quite difficult to draw a clear dividing line between EU and Member States competences in the agreements. This brings us to the

[2] See the chapter by Gesa Kübek and Joni Heliskoski in the volume.

[3] See in general, Allan Rosas, 'Mixity Past, Present and Future: Some Observations', Merijn Chamon and Inge Govaere (eds), *EU External Relations Post-Lisbon: The Law and Practice of Facultative Mixity* (Brill Nijhoff, 2020) 8–18; On the debate about 'obligatory' vs 'facultative' mixity after Opinion 2/15, see among others: Marise Cremona, 'Shaping EU Trade Policy Post-Lisbon: Opinion 2/15 of 16 May 2017: ECJ, 16 May 2017, Opinion 2/15 Free Trade Agreement with Singapore' (2018) 14 *European Constitutional Law Review* 231; David Kleimann and Gesa Kübek, 'The Signing, Provisional Application, and Conclusion of Trade and Investment Agreements in the EU. The Case of CETA and Opinion 2/15', https://papers.ssrn.com/abstract=2869873; Gesa Kübek and David Kleimann, 'The Singapore Opinion or the End of Mixity as We Know It' (*Verfassungsblog: On Matters Constitutional*, 23 May 2017); Daniel Thym, 'Mixity after Opinion 2/15: Judicial Confusion over Shared Competences' (*Verfassungsblog: On Matters Constitutional*, 31 May 2017); Hannes Lenk, 'Mixity in EU Foreign Trade Policy Is Here to Stay: Advocate General Sharpston on the Allocation of Competence for the Conclusion of the EU-Singapore Free Trade Agreement' (2017) 2 *European Papers* No 1; European Forum; Insight of 26 March 2017; www.europeanpapers.eu; page 357; Laurens Ankersmit, 'Opinion 2/15 and the Future of Mixity and ISDS' (*European Law Blog*, 18 May 2017); David Kleimann, 'Reading Opinion 2/15 Standards of Analysis, the Court's Discretion, and the Legal View of the Advocate General' [2017] EUI Working Papers.

[4] For political considerations regarding the choice for mixity, see among others: Sophie Meunier and Kalypso Nicolaïdis, 'EU Trade Policy: The Exclusive versus Shared' Competence Debate' in Maria Green Cowles and Michael Smith (eds), *Risks, Reform, Resistance, and Revival* (Oxford University Press, 2000); on 'EU External Competence', see Andrea Ott in: Ramses A Wessel and Joris Larik, *EU External Relations Law: Text, Cases and Materials* (Bloomsbury Publishing 2020).

[5] Cremona, 'Shaping EU Trade Policy Post-Lisbon' (n 3).

[6] Guillaume Van der Loo and Ramses A Wessel, 'The Non-Ratification of Mixed Agreements: Legal Consequences and Solutions' (2017) 54 *Common Market Law Review* 735; Kleimann and Kübek (n 3); Marise Cremona, 'The Withdrawal Agreement and the EU's International Agreements' (2020) *European Law Review* 237.

[7] Andrés Delgado Casteleiro, 'EU Declarations of Competence to Multilateral Agreements: A Useful Reference Base?' (2012) 17 *European Foreign Affairs Review* 491.

[8] The international responsibility of the EU is an uneasy issue per se, for a detailed analysis see: Andrés Delgado Casteleiro, *The International Responsibility of the European Union: From Competence to Normative Control* (Cambridge University Press 2016); also the chapter by Andrés Delgado Casteleiro and Cristina Contartese in this volume.

[9] Case C-459/03, *Commission v Ireland*, EU:C:2006:345, para 109.

core of the present contribution: the difficulty of 'unmixing' a mixed agreement with a view to the distribution of competences. Strangely enough, this difficult task has not been extensively addressed earlier and became of particular importance in the context of Brexit and the legal debate on the UK's participation in EU international agreements as a third state.[10]

Among other things, Brexit provides the legal community with a very concrete instance of the unpacking of mixed agreements. Rather than discussing whether mixity is needed in a certain situation, Brexit forces us to approach the issue from the opposite perspective and to witness the dissolution of mixity. 'Taking back control' implies the reclaiming of competences by the UK that were previously exercised by the EU, and an 'unmixing' exercise seems necessary to better assess the division of competences between the EU and its Member States, as it reveals how a former EU Member State can actually leave/denounce/not apply an agreement to which it became a party as an EU Member State.[11] This process also helps to better understand the nature of mixed agreements under both EU and international law.

In this chapter, we try to answer the classic but still complex question of how to differentiate between EU and Member States' competences and responsibilities under mixed agreements. In order to address this question and try to disentangle mixed agreements, we will structure our chapter as follows. In section II, we will address possible reasons to 'unmix' existing agreements. In section III, we will analyse legal tools that might be used to separate EU and Member States' competences under a mixed agreement. Finally, in section IV, we will see how this plays out in a concrete situation by using the CETA agreement in the Brexit context as an example. More specifically, we will analyse the UK's participation in CETA beyond the transition period in order to draw lessons about the possibility to disentangle EU and Member States' competences in mixed situations.

II. Reasons to 'Unmix' Mixed Agreements

Having recourse to mixed agreements is a very 'convenient' way to evade difficult questions concerning the exact delimitation of competences. After all, in these situations,

[10] Ramses A Wessel, 'Consequences of Brexit for International Agreements Concluded by the EU and Its Member States' (2018) 55 *Common Market Law Review* 101; Joris Larik, 'Brexit, the Withdrawal Agreement, and Global Treaty (Re-)Negotiations' (2020), 3 *American Journal of International Law* 443; Jed Odermatt, 'Brexit and International Law: Disentagling Legal Orders' 31 *Emory International Law Review* 24; Cremona, 'The Withdrawal Agreement and the EU's International Agreements' (n 6); the same debate regarding UK's participation in the EEA agreement: Ulrich G Schroeter and Heinrich Nemeczek, 'The (Uncertain) Impact of Brexit on the United Kingdom's Membership in the European Economic Area' (2016) 27 *European Business Law Review* 921; Christophe Hillion, 'Brexit Means Br(EEA)Xit: The UK Withdrawal from the EU and Its Implications for the EEA' (2018) 55 *Common Market Law Review* 135; also the chapter by Christine Kaddous and Habib Badjinri Touré in this volume.

[11] On Brexit and EU external relations law, see especially: Ramses A Wessel, 'You Can Check out Any Time You like, but Can You Really Leave?: On "Brexit" and Leaving International Organizations' (2016) 13 *International Organizations Law Review* 197; Joris Larik, 'Brexit, the Withdrawal Agreement, and Global Treaty (Re-)Negotiations' (n 10); Joris Larik, 'EU External Relations Law and Brexit: "When Pluto Was a Planet"' (2020) 1 *Europe and the World: A Law Review*; Jed Odermatt (n 10).

to the outside world, the EU and its Member States are often presented as a single party.[12] As Chamon argues: 'In terms of competences, mixity is convenient because it allows the precise division of competences between the EU and the member states to be held in abeyance. By concluding the agreement as one meta-party, all matters under the agreement are by definition covered in terms of competences.'[13] As the decision to opt for mixity is exclusively based on EU law (and perhaps on national democratic considerations), reasons to 'unmix' international agreements should perhaps first of all be found in that legal order. At the same time, there can also be international (treaty) law reasons to disentangle EU and Member State competences.

A. The Respondent Party Status

In fact, a first reason to disentangle EU mixed agreements finds its basis in international law and flows from a third party's needs to determine the respondent party from the EU side in the case of a dispute arisen under a mixed agreement. In this case the 'unmixing' is related to establishing the correct respondent. This is particularly important in case of the need to attribute a wrongful act to a particular party and trigger international responsibility.[14] As we have seen, declarations of competence have not proved to be particularly useful, due to the dynamic nature of the competence division.

B. A Member State Leaving the EU

A very concrete reason to 'unmix' certain agreements is provided when a Member State is leaving the EU. With regard to the distribution of competences between the EU and its Member States, the question arises to what extent the withdrawing state would or could continue to remain a party to EU mixed agreements after it has left the EU. Considering that an EU Member State concludes mixed agreements in two capacities – as a state party on the basis of its own international capacity and as an EU Member State by virtue of Article 218 TFEU[15] – it may also need to negotiate its withdrawal from mixed agreements. Reasons to reconsider the status of the withdrawing state as a party to existing mixed agreements may flow from both EU and international (treaty) law as well as from the provisions of a specific mixed agreement.

[12] See on the complexities related to this 'EU party', Sabrina Schaefer and Jed Odermatt in this volume.

[13] Merijn Chamon, 'Provisional Application of Treaties: The EU's Contribution to the Development of International Law' (2020) 3 *European Journal of International Law* 883; Guillaume Van der Loo and Ramses A Wessel (n 6) 738.

[14] See further the contribution by Andrés Delgado Casteleiro and Cristina Contartese in this volume.

[15] Especially through the participation of Member States' governments during the whole procedure enshrined in Art 218(2) TFEU, Consolidated version of the Treaty on the Functioning of the European Union [2016] OJ C 202: 'The Council shall authorize the opening of negotiations, adopt negotiating directives, authorise the signing of agreements and conclude them'.

C. A Member State Denouncing a Mixed Agreement while Remaining an EU Member State

The question of the distribution of competences between the EU and its Member States may also come up if a Member State decides to denounce a mixed agreement to which it is a party, while remaining an EU Member State. While the situation may be more difficult to imagine in the case of bilateral agreements, withdrawing from larger (global) multilateral agreements is perhaps easier to envisage. In the case of its intention to withdraw from an existing mixed agreement, the Member State would first of all need to find a solution under EU law in order to identify provisions of the agreement it would continue to be bound by as an EU Member State by virtue of Article 216(2) TFEU.[16] At the same time, under international treaty law, third parties will most probably have to be informed, and even renegotiations may be in order.[17] After all, in this situation, the Member State would become fully accountable not only for those areas for which it co-signed the agreement in the first place, but also for (even) less well-defined parts of the agreement falling under shared competences.

An example of this uneasy situation can be found in Italy's withdrawal from the Energy Charter Treaty (ECT),[18] despite the fact that this case is quite specific. The ECT was signed in 1994 by the EU, Euratom and 51 states and entered into force in 1998.[19] Under EU law it is a mixed agreement, as both the EU and its Member States are parties to it. In 2009, with the entry into force of the Lisbon Treaty, the EU gained an exclusive competence in the field of foreign direct investments (FDI).[20] In terms of the distribution of competences under EU law, the ECT could nowadays have been easily concluded as an EU-only agreement. Furthermore, after the transfer to the EU of the competence over FDI, the debate with regard to incompatibility of intra-EU investment dispute settlement systems with EU law arose.[21] According to Article 26(4) of the ECT, an investor can bring a dispute against a contracting party before an arbitral tribunal. Such a dispute can also arise in an intra-EU setting. It is worth reminding that the ECT did not

[16] For this issue, refer the opinion of Sharpston AG in Opinion 2/15, EU:C:2016:992, fn 29.

[17] Cf Art 54 VCLT. Art 55 VCLT becomes relevant when the withdrawal of an EU Member State results in the number of the parties falling below the number necessary for the entry into force of the agreement.

[18] For this particular case, see: Gaetano Iorio Fiorelli, 'Italy Withdraws from Energy Charter Treaty' (*Global Arbitration News*, 6 May 2015). Authors are perfectly aware of the very complex situation of the ECT under the EU law and refer to the following literature for a more detailed analysis: Graham Coop, 'Energy Charter Treaty and the European Union: Is Conflict Inevitable?' (2009) 27 *Journal of Energy & Natural Resources Law* 404; Matthew Happold and Thomas Roe (eds), 'European Union Law and the Energy Charter Treaty', *Settlement of Investment Disputes under the Energy Charter Treaty* (Cambridge University Press, 2011); Jan Kleinheisterkamp, 'Investment Protection and EU Law: The Intra- and Extra-EU Dimension of the Energy Charter Treaty' (2012) 15 *Journal of International Economic Law* 85; Angelos Dimopoulos, 'The Validity and Applicability of International Investment Agreements between EU Member States under EU and International Law' (2011) 48 *Common Market Law Review* 31.

[19] Rafael Leal-Arcas, *Commentary on the Energy Charter Treaty* (Edward Elgar Pub 2018).

[20] Meunier Sophie, 'Integration by Stealth: How the European Union Gained Competence over Foreign Direct Investment' (2017) 55 *Journal of Common Market Studies* 593.

[21] Kleinheisterkamp (n 18).

include a disconnection clause with regard to the relationship between the EU and its Member States. In 2014, Italy decided, in accordance with Articles 47 and 49 of the ECT, to withdraw from this treaty. Of course, such a decision can be considered as being fully respectful of EU law, especially today with regard to the recent *Achmea* judgment.[22] Probably for this reason the Italian decision was not opposed by the EU in terms of the distribution of competences between the EU and Italy as the Commission did not initiate an infringement procedure against Italy for the violation of Article 216(2) TFEU. However, it also reveals the nature of the ECT as either an 'incomplete' mixed agreement, or as a multilateral agreement. As Rao argues, following the *Achmea* judgment, even if Italy is no longer a contracting party to the ECT, a foreign investor (also an EU investor in theory) can still bring a claim against the EU in case of a wrongful act committed by Italy.[23] Of course, such a scenario might lead to an infringement procedure under Article 259 TFEU to transfer responsibility back to Italy. This example shows that today almost the entire scope of the ECT is covered by EU exclusive competences, and that Italy thus remains bound by this agreement on the basis of Article 216(2) TFEU as an EU Member State.

D. A Member State is Unwilling or Unable to Ratify

Comparable, but nevertheless different, is the situation where a Member State is unable or unwilling to ratify an agreement. The situation of an *unwilling* Member State is less obvious, but might occur when a Member State had voted against the decision to conclude the agreement in the Council, and subsequently refuses to ratify the agreement. A similar situation may occur after a change of government in a Member State, where the new government sees it as its democratic duty to no longer live up to the obligation to try and ratify the agreement as soon as possible. Both situations would result in a violation of a number of EU (and possibly also international[24]) rules and principles,[25] but the Council in the end may be faced with a situation that would be difficult to resolve politically.

A situation in which a Member States is *unable* to ratify is more familiar and may occur on the basis of a negative referendum or a national parliament refraining from providing the necessary approval. The situation occurred, for instance, when the Belgian parliament did not immediately approve CETA,[26] or when the Netherlands government was faced with parliamentary objections based on referendum results with regard to the EU-Ukraine Association Agreement.[27]

[22] Case C-284/16, *Slovak Republic v Achmea BV*, EU:C:2018:158.

[23] Giammarco Rao, 'The Withdrawal of a European State from the ECT in Light of the Achmea Case' (2018) 3 *European Investment Law and Arbitration Review Online* 154.

[24] While there is no obligation to ratify, Art 18 of the VCLT does contain the obligation for a state 'to refrain from acts which would defeat the object and purpose of a treaty' after its signature.

[25] Guillaume Van der Loo and Ramses A Wessel (n 6).

[26] See the chapter by Manon Damestoy and Nicolas Levrat in this volume.

[27] As it was the case with the referendum in Netherlands regarding EU-Ukraine DCFTA: Ramses A Wessel, 'The EU Solution to Deal with the Dutch Referendum Result on the EU-Ukraine Association Agreement' (2016) 1 *European Papers – A Journal on Law and Integration*; Guillaume Van der Loo, 'The Dutch Referendum

In these situations, an 'unmixing' exercise may be necessary to, for instance, allow for a split of the original agreement into an EU-only and a mixed agreement, as was done in the case of the EU-Singapore agreement after *Opinion 2/15* and may still be necessary for CETA in case of domestic ratification problems.

E. Deciding on the Scope of Provisional Application

Another situation in which an 'unmixing' exercise – or at least a concrete mapping of the various competences – may be helpful concerns the provisional application of mixed agreements. Usually, the Council's decision regarding the conclusion and provisional application of an international agreement list the provisions of the agreement to be applied provisionally.[28] This list helps to determine the distribution of competences between the EU and its Member States under an international mixed agreement, and not only reveals which parts of the agreements are already functional in practical terms, but may also help national parliaments to understand which provisions of the agreement form part of a national approval procedure as part of the ratification by Member States.[29]

In these situations, the distribution of competences under EU law is crucial. In all four mentioned cases, it is important to determine the provisions of a mixed agreement covered by EU exclusive and shared competences, and provisions covered by EU Member States' exclusive competences, if of course such a thing still exists.[30]

III. How to 'Unmix' a Mixed Agreement?

While the reasons to analyse a delimitation of competences may be clear, the question of how to proceed in doing that remains a difficult one. As mixed agreements are products of EU law, legal solutions should primarily be found there. Thus, following the lifetime of an agreement and the procedure enshrined in Article 218 TFEU, we can identify four legal instruments relevant for our 'unmixing' exercise. First, the legal bases for the conclusion of a mixed agreement should be considered as a useful tool to determine the nature of competences the agreement is based on within the EU legal order. However, negotiation mandates are usually secret or outdated. In the case of CETA, for instance, the Council's decision allowing the Commission to start negotiating CETA was issued in April 2009. When in 2016 the agreement was ready to be signed, the distribution of competences within the EU had changed dramatically with the entry

on the EU-Ukraine Association Agreement: Legal Options for Navigating a Tricky and Awkward Situation' (*CEPS*, 8 April 2016); Reuters, 'Dutch Referendum Voters Overwhelmingly Reject Closer EU Links to Ukraine' *The Guardian* (7 April 2016); Kaddous (n 1).

[28] Merijn Chamon, 'Provisional Application of Treaties' (n 13).

[29] See also the chapter by Sabrina Schaefer and Jed Odermatt in this volume.

[30] Bruno De Witte, 'Exclusive Member State Competences: Is There Such a Thing?' in Sacha Garben and Inge Govaere in *The Division of Competences between the EU and the Member States: Reflections on the Past, the Present and the Future* (Hart Publishing 2017).

into force of the Lisbon treaty. Second, the CJEU's case law, especially under the opinion procedure of Article 218(11) TFEU, is particularly helpful to shed some light on the division of competences.[31] Third, Council decisions on the provisional application of a mixed agreement usually provide a clear list of competences and their scope within the agreement. Finally, the declarations of competence, briefly discussed above, might still be a useful legal tool. We will turn to each of these tools in more detail.

A. The EU Legal Basis for and the Classification of Mixed Agreements

The most sensible way to disentangle a mixed agreement would be to look at the legal basis of the negotiation directives adopted by the Council. The main problem here, however, is the evolutionary nature of EU external competences as the competence division may have changed after the period of negotiation and conclusion. Another clue could be found in the nature of mixity, whether it is 'obligatory' or 'facultative'. Yet, despite multiple efforts to classify mixed agreements, in terms of internal distribution of competences, and legally justify their necessity, it appears that sometimes political considerations take over and it is not always clear why the Council in the end opted for mixity.[32] Thus, the choice for a mixed agreement may not always reflect legal reality, making the disentangling exercise even more difficult.

For some time now, the notion of 'facultative mixity' has been helpful to make sense of the situations in which the Council actually has a choice to opt for mixity.[33] While the absence of any Member States' competences (eg a pure trade agreement) would lead to an 'EU-only' agreement, and a shared 'coexistent' competence (eg development cooperation) would lead to an obligatory mixed agreement, a choice for mixity does exist in situations of shared 'concurrent' competences (eg environmental policy) or parallel competences (eg CFSP).[34] The decision for mixity or EU-only is usually taken within the Council following the procedure enshrined in Article 218 TFEU; more precisely, when it adopts 'a decision authorising the opening of negotiations'[35] (although CETA

[31] Opinion 1/94, *WTO Agreement*, EU:C:1994:384; Opinion 2/15, *Free Trade Agreement between the EU and Republic of Singapore*, EU:C:2017:376.

[32] Cremona, 'Shaping EU Trade Policy Post-Lisbon' (n 3); see also: Meunier and Nicolaïdis (n 4); Meunier Sophie (n 20); Christine Kaddous, 'De quelques défis liés à la conclusions des accords mixtes', *Liber Amicorum Antonio Tizzano – De la Cour CECA à la Cour de l'Union: le long parcours de la justice européenne* (G. Giappichelli 2018) 448–59; or, it might also function the other way around when an agreement is designed to be signed as a mixed one but it is signed by the EU only, see the example of the association agreement with Kosovo given in: Wessel (n 10), fn 11.

[33] Schermers (n 1); also contributions by Marc Maresceau, 'A Typology of Mixed Bilateral Agreements', as well as by Ramses A Wessel, 'Cross-pillar Mixity: Combining Competences in the Conclusion of EU International Agreements', in: Hillion and Koutrakos (n 1); and for a more detailed analysis: Chamon and Govaere (n 3); Allan Rosas (n 3).

[34] Rosas (n 3).

[35] Art 218(3) TFEU, Consolidated version of the Treaty on the Functioning of the European Union [2016] OJ C 202.

shows that this decision may also be taken at a later stage). Even the CJEU, the ultimate instance to 'insure that in the interpretation and application of the Treaties the law is observed',[36] for a moment lost the logical path of reasoning why an international EU agreement must be mixed.[37] The Court later corrected what seemed to have been an interpretative mistake in *Opinion 2/15* on the direct relationship between shared competences and mixity[38] in its *Germany v Council* (OTIF) judgment:

> Admittedly, the Court found, in paragraph 244 of that Opinion, that the relevant provisions of the agreement concerned, relating to non-direct foreign investment, which fall within the shared competence of the European Union and its Member States, could not be approved by the Union alone. However, in making that finding, the Court did no more than acknowledge the fact that, as stated by the Council in the course of the proceedings relating to that Opinion, there was no possibility of the required majority being obtained within the Council for the Union to be able to exercise alone the external competence that it shares with the Member States in this area.[39]

It follows from the reading of this paragraph, that despite the fact that the EU could have concluded the international agreement on the basis of a combination of exclusive and shared competences, it had to conclude it in a mixed form to get the required majority within the Council. The degree to which the EU external relations law community reacted to the neglect of the facultative mixity option in Opinion *2/15*[40] clearly revealed the importance of the issue in the debates.

Political consideration aside, a clear legal justification for an agreement to be mixed is needed to avoid the legal conundrum that facultative mixed agreements might lead to. Especially, when the only way to control the exercise and the division of competences between the EU and its Member States in a mixed agreement is through the Article 218(11) TFEU Opinion procedure before the CJEU. The usefulness of this procedure was already clear from earlier cases such as Opinions 1/94[41] and 2/15,[42] in which the Court extensively analysed the distribution of competences under, respectively, WTO agreements and the 'new generation' free trade agreement between the

[36] Art 19 TEU, Consolidated version of the Treaty on European Union [2016] OJ C 202.

[37] See the debate following the Opinion 2/15, *Free Trade Agreement between the EU and Republic of Singapore*, EU:C:2017:376 on facultative and mandatory mixity; Kleimann and Kübek (n 3); Guillaume Van der Loo, 'The Court's Opinion on the EU-Singapore FTA: Throwing off the Shackles of Mixity?' (2017) *CEPS Policy Insights*; Lenk (n 3); also in numerous blogposts: Kübek and Kleimann (n 3); Ankersmit (n 3).

[38] Opinion 2/15, *Free Trade Agreement between the EU and Republic of Singapore*, EU:C:2017:376, para 244; at para 243 the Court states that investments, other than FDI, are not part of the CCP and thus fall within shared competences. Following, it concludes that 'the envisaged agreement (with Singapore) cannot be approved by the European Union alone'.

[39] Case C-600/14, *Germany v Council*, EU:C:2017:935, para 68: see on this also the chapter by Merijn Chamon and Marise Cremona in this volume.

[40] See this recent study: Chamon and Govaere (n 3); also: Merijn Chamon, 'Provisional Application of Treaties' (n 13); see also contributions by Eleftheria Neframi, 'The Dynamic of the EU Objectives in the Analysis of the External Competence', and by Merijn Chamon, 'Constitutional Limits to the Political Choice for Mixity' in: Eleftheria Neframi and Mauro Gatti (eds), *Constitutional Issues of EU External Relations Law* (Nomos, 2018).

[41] Opinion 1/94, *WTO Agreement*, EU:C:1994:384.

[42] Opinion 2/15, *Free Trade Agreement between the EU and Republic of Singapore*, EU:C:2017:376.

EU and Singapore. For the purpose of the present contribution, however, it is not at all helpful that the choice for mixity is sometimes based on purely political considerations, rather than on agreed legal classifications. This renders a disentanglement on the basis of legal arguments more difficult. As Chamon argues:

> The traditional and among practitioners still prevailing view is that the choice for mixity (in so far as mixity is not legally required) is a purely political one: Member States may and will insist on being involved as parties to the agreement whenever the agreement is not wholly covered by EU exclusive competences. That approach significantly hampers the EU in its external action, which begs the question whether the political choice for (facultative) mixity should not somehow be legally qualified and, if so, how this could be done, without imposing EU exclusivity.[43]

While a thorough analysis of competences and of the 'type of mixity' may indeed be helpful in delineating the respective competences, the fact remains that the very nature of mixed agreements is that EU Member States sign and conclude these agreements alongside the EU as *proper* contracting parties. As we have seen, this implies that they must ratify (the complete) mixed agreement according to their internal constitutional requirements, despite the fact that some parts of the agreement are not covered by Member State competences. 'Unmixing' exercises may be helpful to indicate to national parliaments where the national competences lie. At the same time, they may limit the arguments to be used by national parliaments and exclude areas that are clearly (and exclusively) covered by EU competences.[44] The classic problem with mixed agreements is that the non-acceptance by one single Member State of a mixed agreement can block its entry into force for all other Member States and external treaty partners. Of course, such a situation creates legal uncertainty, not just for the parties, but also for other stakeholders (such as, for instance, investors). After many years of intense negotiations and the eventual official signing of the treaty, a non-ratification leads to obvious frustration. On the one hand, one may perhaps not blame national parliaments (or voters in a referendum) for using this last resort approach when there has been a lack of transparency and democratic consultation during the negotiation procedure. On the other hand, it is clearly problematic (and perhaps not even democratic) when one (small) Member State representing just a fraction of the population in all parties can block the entire ratification process,[45] and in particular when this is done with reference to a part of the agreement that falls under EU exclusive competence.

[43] Merijn Chamon, 'Constitutional Limits' (n 40) 165.

[44] A case in point was the above-mentioned refusal by the Cypriot parliament to approve CETA. Merijn Chamon and Thomas Verellen, 'Whittling Down the Collective Interest' (*Verfassungsblog Staging*, 7 August 2020); 'Halloumi Cheese Puts EU's Canada Trade Deal to the Test' *POLITICO* (4 August 2020).

[45] Merijn Chamon and Thomas Verellen (n 44), as well as the discussion following this blog post with comments by Ramses A Wessel and Wolfgang Weiss. Interestingly enough, Chamon and Verellen argue that: 'the Cypriot parliament rejected the agreement over the issue of the protection of Halloumi cheese. If this is indeed the case, the Cypriot representatives acted ultra vires. Appellations of origin come under the exclusive competence of the EU in the framework of the Common Commercial Policy'. It suggests that Cypriot MPs cannot refuse the ratification of the CETA on the substantial ground falling under EU exclusive competences. It seems to suggest that it would be possible to divide a bilateral facultative mixed agreement in terms of EU and Member States' competences and participation as separate contracting parties.

B. The Council's Decision on Provisional Application

A tool that, at least prima facie, seems more accurate is the decision by the Council on the provisional application of an agreement as it provides a solid reference for a division of competences between the EU and its Member States under a mixed agreement. After all, only those provisions covered by EU competences can provisionally be applied. As held by Chamon: 'Provisional application allows federal polities such as the EU, where both levels of government are constitutionally competent to act (independently) on the international plane, to pursue effective external action, minimizing the cumbersome effects of the polity's complex internal division of competences.'[46] Sometimes, however, provisional application of an EU agreement might last for years without the agreement ever being ratified by all EU Member States ('incomplete mixity').[47] Over time, the division of competences may have changed, for instance in the basis of new interpretations by the Court. But more importantly, the Council decision was not adopted with the idea of 'unmixing' in mind. Its objective was to allow for certain parts of the agreement to become functional prior to a full entry into force of the agreement. Admittedly, here as well, political arguments may have played a role on deciding on what could provisionally be applied and this could affect the practical value of this tool to 'unmix' international agreements. At the same time, in terms of legitimacy, the decision taken by the Council on the provisional application of an agreement is approved at least by the majority of Member States and not by a single state, as in the case of ratification.

C. Declarations of Competence

To what extent can so-called declarations of competence be helpful for an 'unmixing' exercise? From an international (treaty) law perspective, it is difficult to attribute a *sui generis* nature to an EU mixed agreement, thus regular rules need to be followed. The division of competences between the EU and its Member States is part of the internal law of a contracting party.[48] As long as an agreement is concluded by more than two parties, it is usually classified as a multilateral agreement. However, the notion of 'contracting party' in an EU mixed agreement is blurred and EU legal doctrine seems to agree on the bilateral nature of EU mixed agreements which are concluded with one third party only.[49] For example, in the CETA agreement contracting parties are identified as follows: 'Canada, of the one part, and the EU and its Member States, of the other part, hereafter jointly referred to as the "Parties"'.[50]

[46] Chamon, 'Provisional Application of Treaties' (n 13) 31–32.

[47] Guillaume Van der Loo and Ramses A Wessel (n 6).

[48] See more extensively on this issue also the chapter by Sabrina Schaefer and Jed Odermatt in this volume.

[49] See the contribution by Panos Koutrakos, 'Managing Brexit: Trade agreements binding on the UK pursuant to its EU membership', in Juan Santos Vara and Ramses A Wessel (eds), *The Routledge Handbook on the International Dimension of Brexit* (Routledge, 2020).

[50] Comprehensive Economic and Trade Agreement (CETA) between Canada, of the one part, and the European Union and its Member States, of the other part [2017] OJ L 11/1057. See more extensively on the notion of 'EU party' the chapter by Sabrina Schaefer and Jed Odermatt in this volume.

According to international treaty law, the status of the 'contracting party' to an international agreement implies that a state ratifying an agreement participates in it in its full capacity.[51] AG Sharpston defends the same position in her opinion regarding the distribution of competences in the EU-Singapore FTA:

> If an international agreement is signed by both the European Union and its constituent Member States, both the European Union and the Member States are, as a matter of international law, parties to that agreement. That will have consequences, in particular in terms of liability for a breach of the agreement and the right of action in respect of such a breach. For the sake of transparency within the European Union and in the interests of the third country (or countries) with which that international agreement is being concluded, it would therefore seem desirable for such decisions to indicate very clearly the precise aspects of shared competence which the Member States (acting in their capacity as members of the Council) have agreed shall be exercised by the European Union, on the one hand, and which are (still) being exercised by the Member States, on the other hand. A declaration of competences annexed to the agreement in question would, it seems to me, also not come amiss.[52]

AG Sharpston advocated a more transparent approach regarding the distribution of competences between the EU and its Member States under a mixed agreement for the sake of legal certainly with regard to third states. A declaration of competence annexed to EU mixed agreements would not 'come amiss' as it would allow third states to correctly address the responsibility for a breach of the agreement.[53] In practice, the issue of international responsibility of the EU and its Member States under a mixed agreement would not appear to cause problems in terms of attribution of a wrongful act[54] as the EU would usually claim responsibility in different international fora even in 'mixed' situations.[55]

The classic problem with declarations of competence, however, is that they have hardly been helpful in practice. They are often attached to international agreements at the request of third state parties who are (understandably) confused by the division of competences in the EU. At the same time, the question remains to what extent these declarations provide a fully correct picture of the division of competences, also given the fact that they are hardly ever updated.[56] Any future role for this type of declarations should thus imply a more precise and dynamic description of the division of competences, based on legal criteria.

[51] Art 14 'Consent to be bound by a treaty expressed by ratification, acceptance or approval', Vienna Convention on the Law of Treaties (1969) 1969 (1155 UNTS 331 ('VCLT')).

[52] Sharpston AG in Opinion 2/15, EU:C:2016:992, para 76.

[53] Casteleiro (n 8); also: Emilija Leinarte, 'The Principle of Independent Responsibility of the European Union and Its Member States in the International Economic Context' (2018) *Journal of International Economic Law* 171.

[54] See the chapter by Andrès Delgado Casteleiro and Cristine Contartese in this volume.

[55] Gracia Marín Durán, 'Untangling the International Responsibility of the European Union and Its Member States in the World Trade Organization Post-Lisbon: A Competence/Remedy Model' (2017) 28 *European Journal of International Law* 697; Plarent Ruka, *The International Legal Responsibility of the European Union in the Context of the World Trade Organization in Areas of Non-Conferred Competences* (Springer International Publishing 2017); Angelos Dimopoulos, 'The Involvement of the EU in Investor-State Dispute Settlement: A Question of Responsibilities' (2014) 51 *Common Market Law Review* 1671; Jan Kleinheisterkamp, 'Financial Responsibility in European International Investment Policy' (2014) 63 *International and Comparative Law Quarterly* 449.

[56] Ramses A Wessel, 'Consequences of Brexit for International Agreements Concluded by the EU and Its Member States' (n 10).

The above short analysis shows once more that numerous legal practices of the EU as a polity are problematic from an international law perspective.[57] From that perspective, EU mixed agreements are perhaps the most problematic case, as they aggregate all possible inconsistencies with international treaty law.[58] While the focus of the present chapter is on EU law, an international law perspective should always be part of any 'unmixing' exercise, as the concrete example below will also testify.

IV. The Practice of 'Unmixing' a Mixed Agreement

The Brexit context is highly relevant for the topic of this chapter as it provides us with a very concrete and practical reason to come up with answer to what may have struck some as largely theoretical. The question came up whether the UK can remain bound by EU mixed agreements, or at least by those parts which are not covered by EU exclusive competence.[59] Is it possible for the UK to 'take back control', meaning taking back competences that were once conferred to the EU, and remain fully bound by EU mixed agreements as a third party (turning the bilateral mixed agreements into trilateral agreements)? EU Member States are bound by mixed agreements both as a matter of EU law (Article 216(2) TFEU) and as matter of international law (Article 26 VCLT and customary international law). Furthermore, they are also bound by possible specific provisions on withdrawal in the respective mixed agreement. AG Sharpston argues that:

> Finally, where an international agreement is signed by both the European Union and its Member States, each Member State remains free under international law to terminate that agreement in accordance with whatever is the appropriate termination procedure under the agreement. Its participation in the agreement is, after all, as a sovereign State Party, not as a mere appendage of the European Union (and the fact that the European Union may have played the leading role in negotiating the agreement is, for these purposes, irrelevant). If the Member State were to do so, however, the effect of Article 216(2) TFEU will be that – *as a matter of EU law* – it continues to be bound by the areas of the agreement concluded under EU competence (because it is an EU Member State) unless and until the European Union terminates the agreement. The ability to act independently as an actor under international law reflects the continuing international competence of the Member State; the fact that the Member State remains partially bound by the agreement even if, acting under international law, it terminates it reflects not international law but EU law.[60]

[57] Casteleiro (n 8); also: M Lickova, 'European Exceptionalism in International Law' (2008) 19 *European Journal of International Law* 463; Paz Andrés Sáenz De Santa María, 'The European Union and the Law of Treaties: A Fruitful Relationship' (2019) 30 *European Journal of International Law* 721.

[58] Schroeter and Nemeczek (n 10); also: Nicolas Levrat and Yuliya Kaspiarovich, 'Are EU Member States Still States According to International Law?' (2019) GSI Working Papers Prof. PhDc LAW 2019/02.

[59] See also the chapter by Christine Kaddous and Habib Badjinri Touré in this volume.

[60] Sharpston AG in Opinion 2/15, ECLI:EU:C:2016:992, para 77, fn 29 to this paragraph states: 'I leave to one side the question whether, if a Member State were unilaterally to withdraw from an agreement concluded by both the Member States and the European Union without first engaging in dialogue with the EU institutions (in particular, with the Commission and the Council), that might be considered contravene the duty of sincere cooperation under Article 4(3) TEU'.

Consequently, since the end of the transition period, as a matter of principle, the UK is no longer bound by EU-only agreements as it was only bound by these as a matter of EU law.[61] The situation may be different with regard to mixed agreements, as in that case the UK is bound by virtue of both EU and international law due to its individual ratification.[62] In order to address this issue, we will need to identify relevant law applicable to the UK post-Brexit, aiming to analyse its participation in existing EU mixed agreements. Clearly identifying the law governing different types of relations under a mixed agreement, would allow us to 'unmix' it and to see to what extent the UK might remain a contracting party. However, this issue cannot be discussed in a legal vacuum. For this reason, political considerations and the will of all contracting parties should be taken into account. In general, if a former EU Member State is no longer willing to be considered as a contracting party to EU mixed agreements, even if theoretically it could do so, and prefers to conclude 'roll-over' agreements with the rest of the world, it can perfectly do so. As trade is one of the major concerns of the UK's post-Brexit agenda, we chose to look at mixed (comprehensive) trade agreements, and more precisely at CETA.

A. The UK's Participation in EU Mixed Trade Agreements

The Withdrawal Agreement (WA) between the UK and the EU was signed on 17 October 2019 and entered into force on 1 February 2020.[63] As is well-known, Article 126 WA[64] envisaged a transition period for the UK until the end of 2020.[65] The WA also included provisions regarding the application of international agreements to which the UK is a party (as a former EU Member State) ensuring continuous participation of the UK in EU international agreements during the transition period.[66] The UK thus remained bound by all EU international agreements during the transition period by virtue of EU law (Article 216(2) TFEU) as enshrined in the WA, on the one hand, and by virtue of international law, on the other hand.[67] However, only substantive EU law was

[61] This was mentioned on numerous occasions: Ramses A Wessel, 'Consequences of Brexit for International Agreements Concluded by the EU and Its Member States' (n 10); Jed Odermatt (n 10); Joris Larik, 'Brexit, the Withdrawal Agreement, and Global Treaty (Re-)Negotiations' (n 10).

[62] See also: Marise Cremona, 'Making Treaties and Other International Agreements: The European Union' in Curtis A Bradley, Marise Cremona (eds), *The Oxford Handbook of Comparative Foreign Relations Law* (Oxford University Press, 2019).

[63] Agreement on the withdrawal of the United Kingdom of Great Britain and Northern Ireland from the European Union and the European Atomic Energy Community [2020] OJ L 29 ('WA').

[64] Art 126 ibid.

[65] Art 132 ibid.

[66] Art 129(1) ibid: 'Without prejudice to Article 127(2), during the transition period, the United Kingdom shall be bound by the obligations stemming from the international agreements concluded by the Union, by Member States acting on its behalf, or by the Union and its Member States acting jointly, as referred to in point (a)(iv) of Article 2'.

[67] Cremona, 'The Withdrawal Agreement and the EU's International Agreements' (n 6).

applicable to the UK during the transition period, also with regard to its participation in EU international agreements.[68] The UK was not allowed to participate in international institutional settings resulting from EU international agreements.[69] Whether this was in conformity or not with international treaty law remains doubtful. Article 129 WA included a very interesting footnote which stated: 'The Union will notify the other parties to these agreements that during the transition period the United Kingdom is to be treated as a Member State for the purposes of these agreements'.[70] As Koutrakos argues: 'From a policy point of view, given the scope and depth of the WA, it may be difficult to envisage third states raising obstacles to this course of action'.[71] Practically, we would agree. However, from the perspective of international law, it is problematic. The fact that the UK was not supposed to participate in the institutions of EU international agreements might be a reason for EU treaty partners to invoke a fundamental change of circumstances under international treaty law[72] or to initiate the negotiation of more favourable conditions under the agreement (something which, however, has not yet occurred in practice with a view to the EU agreements).

At the same time, one may argue that the notification proposed in the footnote to Article 129(1) WA was not really relevant for external treaty partners. After all, the WA is concluded between the EU and the UK and is not supposed to have any effect on third parties.[73] If EU external treaty partners to mixed agreements wish to raise objections, they may claim a proper denunciation of the agreement by the UK according to agreement's provisions (again, something that has not occurred).[74]

All in all, the UK enjoyed relative legal security with regard to its participation in EU international agreements until the end of the transition period. Furthermore, the UK was allowed to negotiate its own trade agreements with the rest of the world without breaching the principle of sincere cooperation.[75] Article 129(4) WA provided the UK

[68] Art 129(2) Agreement on the withdrawal of the United Kingdom of Great Britain and Northern Ireland from the European Union and the European Atomic Energy Community [2020] OJ L 29: 'During the transition period, representatives of the United Kingdom shall not participate in the work of any bodies set up by international agreements concluded by the Union, or by Member States acting on its behalf, or by the Union and its Member States acting jointly'.

[69] For a detailed analysis of the withdrawal agreement, see: Steve Peers, 'EU Law Analysis: Analysis 1 of the Revised Brexit Withdrawal Agreement: Overview' (*EU Law Analysis*, 18 October 2019); Steve Peers, 'EU Law Analysis: Analysis 2 of the Revised Brexit Withdrawal Agreement: Transition Period' (*EU Law Analysis*, 18 October 2019); Steve Peers, 'EU Law Analysis: Analysis 3 of the Revised Brexit Withdrawal Agreement: Dispute Settlement' (*EU Law Analysis*, 18 October 2019); Steve Peers, 'EU Law Analysis: Analysis 4 of the Revised Brexit Withdrawal Agreement: Citizens' Rights' (*EU Law Analysis*, 19 October 2019).

[70] Footnote to Art 129(1) Agreement on the withdrawal of the United Kingdom of Great Britain and Northern Ireland from the European Union and the European Atomic Energy Community [2020] OJ L 29.

[71] Panos Koutrakos, 'Managing Brexit: Trade agreements binding on the UK pursuant to its EU membership', in: Juan Santos Vara and Ramses A Wessel (eds), *The Routledge Handbook on the International Dimension of Brexit* (Routledge, 2020) 79.

[72] Art 62 'Fundamental change of circumstances', Vienna Convention on the Law of Treaties (1969). Yet, as also indicated by the ICJ in the 1997 *Gabcikovo-Nagymaros* case, the conditions for invoking 62 VCLT are very restrictive.

[73] Art 34 'General rule regarding third States', ibid: 'A treaty does not create either obligations or rights for a third State without its consent'.

[74] Larik, 'EU External Relations Law and Brexit: "When Pluto Was a Planet"' (n 11) 458.

[75] Art 4(3) TEU, Consolidated version of the Treaty on European Union [2016] OJ C 202.

with a 'flexible reading of the duty of sincere cooperation'.[76] The trade and cooperation agreement (TCA) concluded between the EU and the UK to govern their relationship beyond Brexit does not address this specific issue.[77]

Thus, in the field of EU exclusive competence, the UK has 'taken back control' and has been and is negotiating agreements with third countries. This can be seen as forming part of the 'Global Britain' post-Brexit trade strategy.[78] To a large extent, the UK has been copy-pasting existing EU trade deals with third countries as part of its 'roll-over' strategy.[79] On the basis of Article 129(4) WA, these new agreements could enter into force only after the transition period.

The remaining question is whether former EU Member States could remain a party to EU bilateral mixed agreements as a third state. Again, Brexit may offer some insights. After the entry into force of the TCA, the loyal cooperation duties between the UK and the EU no longer apply and a simple protocol or declaration to each agreement suffices to disentangle EU and UK competences under mixed agreements. In this scenario, the UK would remain bound by the same EU mixed agreements but only as matter of international and UK law.[80] While theoretically possible, this option no longer seems to be on the table, given the UK's activities to replace ('roll-over') existing EU agreements by UK agreements with third states. At the same time, as one of the present authors has argued elsewhere, a situation like this could perhaps be possible in the case of large multilateral agreements, but is less well understandable in the case of bilateral agreements to which the UK was merely a party on the basis of its EU membership.[81]

The main challenge for the UK, as also pointed out by Larik, is to settle the post-Brexit relationship with the EU under mixed agreements.[82] It is also what seems to be explicitly requested by the Canadian government before settling any trade agreement with a post-Brexit UK.

[76] Art 129(4) WA states that the UK 'may negotiate, sign and ratify international agreements entered into in its own capacity in the areas of exclusive competence of the Union, provided those agreements do not enter into force or apply during the transition period, unless so authorised by the Union'; see also Panos Koutrakos, 'Managing Brexit: Trade agreements binding on the UK pursuant to its EU membership', in: Vara and Wessel (n 71) 82.

[77] Trade and cooperation agreement between the European Union and the European Atomic Energy Community, of the one part, and the United Kingdom of Great Britain and Northern Ireland, of the other part (TCA) [2020] OJ L 444.

[78] Tim Robinson and Jon Lunn, 'Brexit Reading List: Global Britain' (2020) House of Commons Library Briefing Paper 8338; also: Pauline Zittel, 'Brexit and a "Global Britain": International Trade Agreements and the Ambitious Exit Strategy of the United Kingdom' (2020).

[79] See Adam Lazowski, 'Copy-pasting or negotiating? Post-Brexit trade agreements between the UK and non-EU countries' and Panos Koutrakos, 'Managing Brexit: Trade agreements binding on the UK pursuant to its EU membership', especially the list of already "copy-pasted" agreements', p 81, in: Juan Santos Vara and Ramses A Wessel (n 71).

[80] Panos Koutrakos, 'Managing Brexit: Trade agreements binding on the UK pursuant to its EU membership', in: Vara and Wessel (n 71) 77.

[81] Ramses A Wessel, 'Consequences of Brexit for International Agreements Concluded by the EU and Its Member States' (n. 10).

[82] Joris Larik, 'Brexit, the Withdrawal Agreement, and Global Treaty (Re-)Negotiations' (n 10) 458: 'In any event, for external trade partners with which the UK intends to negotiate new agreements, the challenge remains that the UK is yet to clarify its future relationship with the EU, which will commence at the end of the transition period'.

B. The UK's Participation in CETA and the Challenge of 'Unmixing' it

The UK's post-Brexit international trade policy was to negotiate roll-over agreements with the rest of the world in order to secure continuous trade on agreed terms and not fall back on WTO conditions. This 'Global Britain' strategy implies (re)negotiations with external treaty partners. Some treaty partners are more willing to negotiate than others. As regards Canada, its position is very clear:

> When the transition period ends on December 31, 2020, the UK will no longer be bound by the EU's treaties with third countries, including CETA. Canada-UK bilateral trade would no longer benefit from any CETA preferences and would be based on WTO rules, including most-favoured nation (MFN) tariffs on goods.
>
> Now that the UK has left the EU, it will have the jurisdiction to negotiate trade agreements. And once there is more clarity on the UK's trade relationship with the EU, Canada intends to re-engage with the UK to discuss how our bilateral trade relationship can be strengthened. Any future trade agreement between Canada and the UK would be influenced by the UK-EU trade negotiations, as well as any unilateral UK approaches.
>
> Whatever the outcome of the UK-EU trade negotiation, Canada's trade with the EU will continue to be governed by the terms of CETA.[83]

It thus appears that the Canadian government did not consider any possibility of the UK's continued participation in CETA after the transition period. This may first of all be read as a confirmation of the bilateral nature of CETA. But it can also be perceived as a negotiation strategy, as the UK seeks to propose more advantageous trade conditions to Canada without CETA.[84] Another important element with regard to Canada's position vis-à-vis CETA is that even without the UK's participation, the agreement will continue to govern trade relations between Canada, the EU and its remaining 27 Member States. Furthermore, CETA is currently provisionally implemented,[85] and it is interesting to note that it was ratified by the UK as early as 17 May 2017.[86]

All in all, the question remains whether we can apply the legal tools that were presented above to this situation. This would call for a short assessment of CETA's legal basis under the EU law, the CJEU case law, the Councils' decision on provisional application and the existence of a declaration of competence.[87] It seems that the most

[83] 'Brexit and United Kingdom-European Union Trade Negotiations: Summary Information for Canadian Companies' (Government of Canada, Trade Commissioner Service, 18 November 2019).

[84] Panos Koutrakos, 'Managing Brexit: Trade agreements binding on the UK pursuant to its EU membership', in: Vara and Wessel (n 71) 82. The author argues: 'Another example of how the policy of rollover agreements did not take sufficient account of the broader trade policy reality is illustrated by the absence of an agreement with Canada. The publication by the British Government on the 13 March 2019 of its temporary tariff rates policy, according to which 87 per cent of imports by value would be eligible for tariff free treatment, removed any incentive for Canada to extend automatically the post-Brexit application of the CETA to the UK.'

[85] Comprehensive Economic and Trade Agreement (CETA) between Canada, of the one part, and the European Union and its Member States, of the other part (Art 30.7) OJ L 11.

[86] Dominic Webb, 'CETA: the EU-Canada free trade agreement', House of Commons Briefing Paper No 7492, 7 May 2019.

[87] No declaration of competence was annexed to CETA.

useful tool to 'unmix' CETA has been the Councils' decision concerning the provisional application of the agreement. According to this decision 'parts of the Agreement falling within the competence of the Union may be applied on a provisional basis, pending the completion of the procedures for its conclusion'.[88] Article 1 of the decision lists the exceptions and limitations to the provisional application, meaning provisions of CETA not falling within the EU exclusive competences. In practice, this decision indeed allows for a certain degree of disentangling of EU and Member States competences in the agreement.

V. Conclusion: One Cannot Unscramble Scrambled Eggs

This chapter has sought to turn a classic problem in EU external relations law upside down by not looking at reasons for mixity, but for tools to 'unmix' existing international agreements concluded by the EU and its Member States. We have analysed several reasons why disentangling EU and Member States competences would be necessary and we assessed the various tools to be able to do that.

While a combination of these tools can indeed provide quite an accurate line of demarcation between the competences, there is no perfect solution and this exercise may remain somewhat messy. Indeed, it proves quite difficult to unscramble scrambled eggs. This should not come as a surprise, as mixed agreements have the advantage that there is no need to be that precise on the division of competences, at least not towards third parties. These agreements sometimes deliberately allow the EU and the Member States to simply leave some issues open, knowing that under international law they are all bound and will be able to solve potential disputes internally on the basis of EU law.

The, perhaps somewhat disappointing, conclusion would be that there does not seem to be a hundred percent watertight way to 'unmix' mixed agreements. Despite the existence of legal tools, the division of competences is dynamic and changes over time. Furthermore, as mixity is not just a legal exercise, 'unmixing' may also be influenced by political considerations. Nevertheless, both the recent withdrawal of a Member States and the increasingly active role of national parliaments, reveal the need for the EU institutions to become more precise on the division of competences at the time of the conclusion of mixed agreements.

[88] Council Decision (EU) 2017/38 of 28 October 2016 on the provisional application of the Comprehensive Economic and Trade Agreement (CETA) between Canada, of the one part, and the European Union and its Member States, of the other part, OJ L 11, (4).

INDEX

Introductory Note

References such as '178–79' indicate (not necessarily continuous) discussion of a topic across a range of pages. Wherever possible in the case of topics with many references, these have either been divided into sub-topics or only the most significant discussions of the topic are listed. Because the entire work is about 'joint participation in international agreements', the use of this term (and certain others which occur constantly throughout the book) as entry points has been restricted. Information will be found under the corresponding detailed topics.

www.ingramcontent.com/pod-product-compliance
Ingram Content Group UK Ltd.
Pitfield, Milton Keynes, MK11 3LW, UK
UKHW020239290926
15470UKWH00002B/635

9 781509 945870